CU00631530

ALESSSANDRO and DOMENICO
SCARLATTI
Two Lives in One

ROBERTO PAGANO

ALESSANDRO and DOMENICO SCARLATTI
Two Lives in One

Translated by Frederick Hammond

LIVES IN MUSIC Series No. 6

PENDRAGON PRESS
Hillsdale, N.Y.

TITLES IN THE SERIES: LIVES IN MUSIC

No.1   *HUGUES CUENOD—WITH A NIMBLE VOICE*
        Conversations with François Hudry
        Translated by Albert Fuller
No.2   *NICOLAE BRETAN—HIS LIFE—HIS MUSIC*
        By Harmut Gagelmann
        Translated by Beaumont Glass
No.3   *ENTRANCING MUSE*
        A DOCUMENTED BIOGRAPHY OF FRANCIS POULENC
        By Carl B. Schmidt
No. 4   *PIED PIPER: THE MANY LIVES OF NOAH GREENBERG*
        By James Gollin
No.5   *PEGGY GLANVILLE-HICKS: A TRANSPOSED LIFE*
        By James Murdoch
No.6   *ALESSANDRO AND DOMENICO SCARLATTI:*
        TWO LIVES IN ONE
        By Roberto Pagano
        Translated by Frederick Hammond
No.7   *THE CHEVALIER DE SAINT-GEORGES*
        VIRTUOSO OF THE SWORD AND THE BOW
        By Gabriel Banat
No. 8   *IRVING FINE*
        AN AMERICAN COMPOSER IN HIS TIME
        By Phillip Ramey

Library of Congress Cataloging-in-Publication Data

Pagano, Roberto.
  [Scarlatti. English]
  Alessandro and Domenico Scarlatti : two lives in one / by Roberto Pagano ;
translated by Frederick Hammond.
     p. cm. -- (Lives in music series ; no. 6)
  Includes bibliographical references (p.   ) and index.
  ISBN 978-1-57647-108-1
  1. Scarlatti, Alessandro, 1660-1725. 2. Composers--Italy--Biography. 3. Scarlatti,
Domenico, 1685-1757. 4. Composers--Biography. I. Title.
  ML410.S22P313 2006
  780.92'2--dc22
  [B]
                              2006031934

Copyright 2006 Pendragon Press

CONTENTS

List of Illustrations   *viii*

Translator's Preface   *ix*

Author's Preface   *xi*

Prologue   *xxi*

I. *the Scarlattino, alias the Sicilian*   *1*

II. The Genius of Parthenope, the Glory of the Sebeto,
   the Delight of Mergellina   *14*

    La Scarlati, her brother, the viceroy   *22*

    Baptism at the sign of the heraldic riddle   *26*

III. Maecenas atavis edite regibus...   *35*

    The Orpheus of the Princes   *46*

IV. *... a falling virtù*   *57*

V. *... in Palermo, with the universal indulgence of all
   the Virtuosi and Composers of Music ... "*   *71*

    ...the prodigious harmony of Don Emanuello
    Rincon de Astorga   *80*

VI. *... an Eagle, whose Wings are grown*   *89*

VII. Fugue for two voices, with some liberties   *108*

VIII. Polish Intermezzi - 1:

    *I was born of a Gallic cock a simple hen, /Lived
    among the Pole-try and then a queen ...*   *124*

IX.   Polish Intermezzi - 2:

    To Rome I came, Christian and not Christine   *133*

X. A time of penitence and of darkness   *145*

    Nostalgia for Christina   *158*

    escorted only by his ability (which is greatly
    advanced ...)   *161*

    Et in Arcadia ego ...   *165*

XI. Fugue in two voices with many artifices   *169*
     ... in Venice, where virtù finds every esteem and
       favor   *178*

XII. Roseingrave, Handel, and the devil   *192*
     ... on the occasions of greatest need ...   *199*
     ... made to return here to the service of this
       royal Chapel by His Eminence ...   *208*
     ... a graceful and most pleasing comedy
       in music ...   *214*
XIII. Bloodless disputes of courteous patrons, against
     the background of a war which only indirectly
     besieges Rome   *217*
     A barony that kills music   *221*
     Aurea mediocritas romana   *225*

XIV. *... et petisse, ut vellet, ipsum emancipare et a*
     Patria potestate, et paternis nexibus liberare ...   *232*
     Portuguese glories of a delayed Ulysses   *246*
     The two Domenicos?   *252*
     Heic situs est eques Alexander Scarlactus ...
     musices instaurator maximus   *260*

XV. *Music, the solace of illustrious Souls ...*   *273*
     Ma in Ispagna...   *282*
     ... filium bonae memoriae equitis Alexandri   *298*

XVI. *I believe that the waters of the Manzanares*
     must be the waves of Lethe ...   *312*
     Compositions *born ... in the service of the*
     deservedly most fortunate ... PRINCESS OF
     THE ASTURIAS   *322*
     Salve Regina   *342*
     Last Sonatas for Harpsichord of D. Domenico
     Scarlatti, composed in the Years 1756 and 1757,
     in which he died   *346*

Appendix: Scarlatti's Emancipation   *350*

Bibliography   *352*

Index   *364*

LIST OF ILLUSTRATIONS

Fig. 1   G.M.Testana: Portrait of Christina of Sweden   6
          (Stockholm, National Museum)

Fig. 2   Nicola Vaccaro: Portrait of Alessandro Scarlatti   26
          (Naples: Biblioteca del Conservatorio S. Pietro a Majella)

Fig. 3   Francesco Solimena: Portrait of Alessandro Scarlatti 1692   27
          (Madrid: Duchess of Alba)

Fig. 4   Cardinalium S. E. R. Imagines: Portrait of Cardinal Pamphilj   44
          (Biblioteca Apostolica Vaticana)

Fig. 5   Cardinalium S. E. R. Imagines: Portrait of Cardinal Ottoboni   45
          (Biblioteca Apostolica Vaticana)

Fig. 6   G.D. Capiglia, M. Pitteri: Portrait of the Grand Prince   49
          Ferdinando de'Medici ("Serie Allegrini," Florence,
          Biblioteca Marucelliana, XVIIbis, n. 36)

Fig. 7   Filippo Juvarra: Set for Alessandro Scarlatti's Ciro   219
          (Turin, Biblioteca nazionale.)

Fig. 8   After Jacopo Amigone: Titlepage of Domenico Scarlatti,   280
          Essercizi (Washington, Library of Congress)

Fig. 9   Nicolaus Valleta: Maria Barbara de Braganza   288
          (from G.B. Marini, Storia della Musica,
          Biblioteca Apostolica Vaticana)

Fig. 10   Pier Leone Ghezzi: Farinelli in a Female Role   291
          (New York, The Pierpont Morgan Library)

Fig. 11   Domenco Scarlatti: Autograph letter to the Duke of Huescar   317
          (Madrid, Museo Alba)

Fig. 12   Binding of the Venice manuscripts   325

Fig.13   Antonio de Velasco: Portrait of Domenco Scarlatti   *334*
        (Istituiçao José Relvas, Alpiarça, Portugal)

Fig. 14   Spanish harpsichord ca. 1720   *338*
        (Collection of Rafael Puyana, Paris)

Fig. 15   Domenico Scarlatti, Sonata K. 521, Parma manuscript   *347*

TRANSLATOR'S PREFACE

On October 26, 1953, the 268th anniversary of its subject's birth, the Princeton University Press published Ralph Kirkpatrick's *Domenico Scarlatti*. It was a revelation for its scholarly rigor and colorful writing, its wealth of new documentation, its recovery of the primary printed and manuscript sources of the sonatas, and for the musical insights of the greatest Scarlatti performer of the time. Kirkpatrick's book, together with his edition, performances, and recordings of sixty of the sonatas, became the primary agent in transforming the perception of its subject from Schumann's contemptuous "dwarf among giants" into the creator of one of the greatest surviving bodies of keyboard music.

A half-century later, the publication of the present revised version of Roberto Pagano's *Scarlatti: Alessandro e Domenico: due vite in una* (1985) in an English translation represents another quantum leap in Scarlatti studies. The fifty years following Kirkpatrick's pioneering work have produced extensive researches, especially into Portuguese and Spanish sources such as archival documents and musical manuscripts, which have transformed our knowledge of Domenico's biography, sometimes in surprising ways. His life had seemed to move from the relative obscurity of his operatic career in Italy to an equal obscurity as private musician to the Portuguese Infanta Maria Barbara, whom he followed to Spain when she married the heir to the Spanish throne.

We now see Domenico Scarlatti as a leading musical figure at the Portuguese court and a cosmopolitan traveler, whose fame in France was such as to induce the Portuguese ambassador to pay off his gambling debts to save his king's reputation. This weakness for gambling, proposed by Burney as the reason for the final assembling of the corpus of sonatas, was questioned by Kirkpatrick but is thus now fully confirmed. Kirkpatrick spent several years directing a concert series for Colonial Williamsburg, in the course of which he acquired a somewhat unreasonable dislike of the English eighteenth century. He therefore subjected the accounts of Burney, Hawkins, Mainwaring, and Roseingrave concerning Domenico to especially skeptical scrutiny; Pagano usually accepts their credibility.

In another case, a garbled reference to a secret marriage in a document preserved in the Scarlatti family, whom Kirkpatrick located by thumbing through the Madrid telephone directory, turns out on further research to concern not Alessandro but Domenico in his old age, treating his son Alexandro with all the repressive hauteur of his own father.

Not only does the present study summarize the results of this half-century of research, it is equally valuable for scraping off certain barnacles that have clung tenaciously to the history of the two Scarlattis, notably the forgeries of the Florentine scholar Mario Fabbri of documents from the court of Ferdinando de' Medici.

As its sub-title "two lives in one" suggests, however, this state-of-the-art biography of Alessandro and Domenico Scarlatti is presented in a particular context. First, since Domenico's legal emancipation from his father has always seemed to lie at the heart of his biographical mystery, Pagano examines the histories of father and son as a symbiotic relationship in which a corrected text and a new reading of the legal document of emancipation becomes central. Second, he locates their relationship in the cultural context of seventeenth-century Sicily and southern Italy. Palermitan by birth and profoundly Sicilian, Pagano rightly observes that even today the traditions which formed the lives of the two Scarlattis are still active in Sicily. It cannot be sufficiently emphasized nonetheless that this is not a "fictionalized" biography, but a study in cultural anthropology: Margaret Mead, not Truman Capote.

Pagano writes a rich and varied Italian and draws on a tremendous repertory of historical and literary sources. His book is not a streamlined dictionary item (although he is the author of the entries on the two Scarlattis in the 2000 New Grove Dictionary), but rather a panorama of place and period. Both Sterne and Stendhal (a particular Sicilian favorite) come to mind in the way in which the author himself becomes a personality in the story he is recounting, permits himself digressions, doubts, second thoughts, and even recantations.

As Domenico himself addressed his readers, "Show yourself then more human than critical, and thereby increase your own Delight."

Frederick Hammond
Bard College
Annandale-on-Hudson,
New York, 2005

AUTHOR'S PREFACE

The scarce biographical material securely related to Domenico Scarlatti has been exploited in various ways by those who have preceded me in writing about this extraordinary man and his brilliant music. Several decades ago Massimo Bontempelli could affirm that all poets should envy Scarlatti

> the good fortune of having almost obliterated the traces of his daily life, of having left biographers little or nothing to dig up, to inflate, to disseminate.[1]

Today such reasons for envy are fewer, insofar as the researches that Ralph Kirkpatrick pursued for almost twenty years have produced results throwing light on many biographical episodes previously unknown or often mythified by oral tradition or written legends.

Even more than twenty years after Kirkpatrick's death anyone who wishes to approach Domenico Scarlatti cannot ignore the critical biography in which a half-century ago the great American harpsichordist brought together all his experience as a leading performer, his scholarly passion, his discipline as a writer of history. Only after the publication of his book[2] which the Edizioni RAI have finally made available to readers of Italian have I agreed to write on Domenico Scarlatti; and I have done so not claiming to add much to the biographical data furnished by Kirkpatrick but with the conviction that I can read the human experience of the musician in a new key, one dictated by my intimate knowledge of his father's life and of a southern mentality that may have controlled—and in any case conditioned—the behavior of the Sicilian clan into which Domenico Scarlatti was born.

I certainly did not wish to write a fictionalized or "invented" biography. My analysis of events and facts relates the little that we

---

[1] Massimo Bontempelli, *Passione incompiuta. Scritti sulla musica 1910-1950* (Milan: Mondadori, 1958).

[2] Ralph Kirkpatrick, *Domenico Scarlatti* (Princeton, N.J.: Princeton University Press, 1953 [hereafter Kirkpatrick, *Scarlatti*]); Italian translation by Mariacarla Martino, (Turin: ERI, 1984).

know about Domenico Scarlatti to the influence exercised on him by a father who must have behaved in a manner absolutely consistent with traditions that have been changed in Sicily only in the smallest degree by the three centuries that have passed. Let no one think that I wish to claim Domenico Scarlatti's glory for my own island; indeed, I have sought the roots of certain of his sufferings in the Sicily that is familiar to me. I well know that the corpus of his sonatas—the part of his output that has left its mark on the history of Western music—shows that he is perhaps more significantly linked to the Iberian peninsula than to Italy.

Logically, a consideration of the apotheosis that took place in Spain concludes the human parable I have attempted to reconstruct: it is in the relation between Spain and Sicily that we must seek the distant origins of a conditioned mentality to which I shall refer constantly. In this sense, my book may be considered a southern "reply" to the positivistic rigor of the biography masterfully worked out by Kirkpatrick and to which, in all humility, I refer the reader who desires a more "correct" approach to the data.

I do not claim that my interpretation is the only one possible, but in the years that have witnessed the dispersion into vast areas of the civilized world of a leprosy that began in my own country and that is tied to delusive forms of blind group obedience and to obscure yet unmistakable principles of authority, it seemed to me stimulating to reread the complementary unfolding of two unusual biographies in the light of conditions with which a Sicilian would be perfectly familiar.

Thirty years ago, in writing the biography of Alessandro Scarlatti[3] I found myself bringing out certain characteristics of its protagonist that tarnished the halo of the plaster saint dominating the gallery of myths forming the so-called Neapolitan School. It is always dangerous to swim against the current of tradition. The few criticisms made of my work by generous and illustrious reviewers mostly concerned my suggested revaluation of the image of a "capo" whom everyone would clearly prefer to identify with a sort of bearded God the Father, ever intent on radiating a beneficent influence on his family and disciples.

The late Malcolm Boyd[4] declared himself astonished by the fact that I had given credence to a whole string of disappointments leading

---

[3] Roberto Pagano and Lino Bianchi, *Alessandro Scarlatti*, with a General Catalogue of his works edited by Giancarlo Rostirolla (Turin: ERI, 1972 [hereafter *Scarlatti ERI*]).

[4] Review of the book cited in n. 3, *Music & Letters* IV (1983), 474-5.

me to conclude that papà Alessandro desired "at the age of forty eight .
. . only a tranquil and respected old age." Boyd further claimed that my
judgment on the disparity between Alessandro's artistic worth and his
human weaknesses of was based only on Dotti's notorious satire (forgetting, by the way, that I said that I had read it with bitter amazement)
and that, in fact, it contradicted everything I had written about the musician. I maintain that I had the right to be astonished in turn, insofar as I
continue to believe—as this book should make clear—that all the elements of Alessandro's biography contribute to throwing light on the fragility of the man, a fragility rooted in the Sicily that I have reason to
know better than many others. But perhaps the arguments were not
sufficiently explicit. This is suggested to me by the fact that in spite of
the flattering reviews which greeted the first biography of Alessandro in
the seventy years since the classic one by Dent, no one thought that its
author might have some useful contribution to make to the Colloquium Alessandro Scarlatti held at Würzburg in 1975. Only four
years later did the publication of the congress report[5] allow me to
learn that in his opening address Prof. Osthoff had rejoiced to see
"the unavoidable Italian element happily replaced" by the participation of a Fellow of the Center of German Studies in Venice, Lorenzo
Bianconi.[6]

    Am I over-reacting? Perhaps, but when an obvious misreading
induces an *Herausgeber* clearly unacquainted with Arcadian poetry to
disfigure one of the rare and always welcome foreign editions of
Scarlatti's vocal music[7] by writing "Curilla" instead of the obvious
"Eurilla" (and then to tie himself in knots, given the evident mismatch
of the syllables, by suggesting that the performer sing "Ah, Curilla"[8]), I
tell myself that the Italian element is not *abdingbar*, negotiable, but
unersetzlich, irreplaceable.

    Having said that, I do not wish to make a mountain out of a
molehill. An indiscriminate attack on the German mentality would be
unjust, especially since a real lighthouse of civility has shone on Italian
music of the past from the German Historical Institute of Rome, mainly
through the merit of Friedrich Lippmann. In any case, gall gives place

---

[5] *Colloquium Alessandro Scarlatti.* Würzburg 1975, ed. Wolfgang Osthoff and Jutta
Ruile-Dronke (*Würzburger Musikhistorische Beiträge* 7) (Tutzing: Hans Schneider,
1979).

[6] *Colloquium Alessandro Scarlatti,* 2

[7] Alessandro Scarlatti, *Correa nel seno amato,* Cantata for soprano, two violins, and
continuo, ed. Otto Drechsler (Kassel: Bärenreiter, 1974).

[8] *Correa nel seno amato,* 19n.

to honey in recognizing in foreign scholars such as Edwin Hanley, Malcolm Boyd, Donald Jay Grout, Frank D'Accone, William C. Holmes, and Thomas Griffin (and the participants at Würzburg, of course) the merit of having advanced decisively our knowledge of Alessandro Scarlatti, of his music, and of his time. On the "Dominican" side, having given the honor due—and deeply felt by me—to the memory of Ralph Kirkpatrick, I continue with Kenneth Gilbert, to whom I owe valuable information and particularly generous assistance; with Joel Leonard Sheveloff, whose weighty *Revaluation*[9] was continued in the critical survey for the 1985 anniversary celebrations, the contents of which contradicted its title, "Tercentenary Frustrations;"[10] with Malcolm Boyd, whose contribution[11] achieved a balanced account of the material available at the time of its publication (1986). This is combined with his important original contributions as the scholar to whom goes credit for having given a decisive impulse to the researches in Spanish archives and libraries. These investigations have fostered the discovery of important manuscript sources that provide a more adequate evaluation of Domenico Scarlatti's fortunes on the Iberian peninsula, with which the most important part of his musical activity is linked. Then follows Eva Badura-Skoda, who having discovered the important Viennese manuscript collection which had belonged to the Archduke Rudolph directed Seunghyun Choi's researches on it. Two outstanding scholar-interpreters do honor to Italy: Emilia Fadini (to whose meticulous care we owe the critical edition of the Sonate published by Ricordi) and the late Laura Alvini (who undertook for the Società per Edizioni Scelte the publication in facsimile of the Venice manuscripts); the premature and tragic death of Scott Ross transfers to the cold immutability of recordings—all too reductive—the evidence of a Scarlattian flair that brought us memorable interpretations in live performances. Frederick Hammond distilled in a lively and valuable summary[12] his experience as a performer and scholar, ripened in his long association with Kirkpatrick; he has honored me by placing me in the company of extraordinary Master.

[9] Joel Leonard Sheveloff, "The Keyboard Music of Domenico Scarlatti: A Re-Evaluation of the Present State of Knowledge in the Light of the Sources," Ph. D. diss., Brandeis, 1970 [hereafter Sheveloff].

[10] Sheveloff, "Domenico Scarlatti: Tercentenary Frustrations," The Musical Quarterly 71 (1985), 399-436; 72 (1986), 90-118.

[11] Malcolm Boyd, Domenico Scarlatti: Master of Music (London, 1986). 12 Frederick Hammond, "Domenico Scarlatti," in Eighteenth-Century Keyboard Music, ed. Robert L. Marshall (New York: Schirmer Books, 1994) 154-190.

[12] Frederick Hammond. "Domenico Scarlatti," in *Eighteenth-Century Keyboard Music*, ed. Robert L. Marshall (New York: Schirmer Books, 1994) 154-190.

To Paolo Isotta, who originally reviewed my biography of Alessandro Scarlatti in enthusiastically favorable terms, I owe much gratitude for having welcomed the first edition of this volume in the series "Musica e Storia" directed by him and Pietro Buscaroli for Mondadori. In the course of the volume I have paid my most important debts to Italian colleagues and friends, happy to testify my appreciation for the rigor that characterizes the work of the youngest of these and proud to quote the comment of an illustrious American scholar at the end of the international conference on seventeenth-century Naples in 1985: "If these young people work this well, soon there won't be anything for us foreigners to do in Italian libraries and archives."

I was right to direct my appreciation to the young: the disastrous fantastications of a contemporary of mine, now deceased, have damaged the reconstruction of a milieu as it emerged with convincing seductiveness from "documents," which there is every reason to suspect are in fact non-existent. The revelation of the imposture[13] has come precisely from the "youthful" sector, and the fact that two Italian scholars, together with two German ones, completed the painstaking investigations, that resulted in unmasking these falsifications, shows that the Couperinian *réunion des goûts*, which I hoped would be transferred to the field of musicology, is happily in progress; it also shows that I was not wrong to affirm that "many things have changed since Goethe judged that the inhabitants of the South were too happy to tread the right path in their search for wisdom."

In June 1985 I concluded the Foreword to this book by recognizing that it remains "far more debatable, by comparison with its predecessor" but declaring that I had plunged with resolution "into my *Scarlatti Soliloquium,* certainly as displeasing to the worshippers of sacred images as to the promotors of a musical historiography fundamentally opposed to the attempt to seek life within the dusty piles of documents which are—and remain—the delight and despair of every researcher." The employment of these expressions, insidiously similar to those employed by Mario Fabbri in singing the praises of his resurrection of the *costume* and *sensibilità* of distant times, which his mystifications ought to have assisted, now dictates a thoughtful clarification: working on the materials collected here—whose checking is facilitated by the archival or bibliographic references offered to the reader—has induced and con-

---

[13] Juliane Riepe, Carlo Vitali, Antonello Furnari, *"Il Pianto di Maria* (HWV 234): Rezeption, Ueberlieferung und musikwissenschaftliche Fiktion. Mit einen Anhang von Benedikt Poensgen," *Goettinger Haendel-Beitraege* V (1993), 270-307.

tinues to induce me to formulate biographical hypotheses that may not be shared by the reader, or may even be belied by new evidence. However, I hope that I have offered sufficiently clear indications so that the established data remain clearly distinct from my interpretations of the whole context, which are guided by the direct knowledge of the conditioned mentality to which I believe that both the deeply Sicilian Alessandro and his son Domenico—as well as the picturesque "Barone d'Astorga" and so many of the other characters who crowd this book—conformed.

In 1985 I announced that a technical *pendant* dedicated to the keyboard production of Domenico Scarlatti would form a sequel to the present "novel": "In that same spirit which induced certain Almighties of Claviermusik to purge the excesses of temperament displayed in an initial *fantasia* by the severity of the concluding *fuga*." Such a *pendant* still has not taken final form because the immense quantity of musical material to control has discouraged any hasty operations of synthesis.

Although I maintain that the approach that I have chosen for biographical treatment remains valid, experiences that have ripened through research and teaching continue to impress themselves on my understanding of the keyboard music of the greatest harpsichordist of all time. The deeper I penetrate into the corpus of the Scarlatti sonatas, the more I realize how inappropriate are certain forms of radical revaluation. Having allowed myself a certain flexibility concerning performance on the fortepiano, which I continue to consider interesting and permissible, I am frankly astonished to witness the overturning of a factual reality that I continue to believe is linked in its essential character to the harpsichord, and I find absurd the process that for more than a decade has tended to remove the *Sonate* from the instrument for which all too much evidence tells us they were conceived. The connection between Domenico Scarlatti and the "Arpicembali" of Cristofori and Ferrini is undeniable and should be carefully considered, but it seems to me ill-advised to transform the prince of harpsichordists into nothing less than *"the first great advocate of the Florentine cembalo col'pian' e forte."*[14] I hope the revision of this text will clarify my position on this matter.

Gerhard Doederer has established with absolute certainty the date of Domenico Scarlatti's arrival in Lisbon, 29 November 1719, cast-

---

[14] David Sutherland, "Domenico Scarlatti and the Florentine piano," *Early Music* XXIII (1995), 243-256, 244. In my entry on Domenico Scarlatti in the 2000 New Grove I quoted the final sentence of the article inaccurately. The author had reason to complain of this, insofar as his essay recognized that Scarlatti had a priority but not an

ing some doubt on the biographical hypotheses that I had previously formulated. It does not seem to me that the important discoveries of the Portuguese musicologist greatly change—except in specific data—the outlines of Domenico Scarlatti's biography as I have reconstructed it. I can understand a certain reluctance to attribute to a man of the eighteenth century the casual mobility which characterizes our jet-set era, but by 1985 Jane Clark had already inferred from Frank Walker the "suspicion that Scarlatti was constantly in motion" between 1719 and 1728. The recent discovery of letters from the Portuguese ambassador at the French court, Luis de Cunha, reveals that Domenico was present in Paris in May of 1724 and August of 1725. An old tradition has him at Naples in 1725 to take leave of his dying father. In any case, the unequivocal evidence of Quantz informs us that Domenico left the Iberian peninsula at least once after his transfer to Lisbon. The documents published by Prof. Doederer establish new points of certainty in Scarlatti's biography and definitively disprove the hypothesis of a long stay in Sicily, which had been suggested to me by notarial documents certifying the presence in Palermo on April 16, 1720 and December 9, 1722 of a "Dominicus Scarlatti," certainly a musician, since he was a member of the Unione di Santa Cecilia.

I find a characteristic reflection of the special connection between Domenico Scarlatti and the Baron d'Astorga that apparently goes back to the youthful days of the two composers but which was consolidated in Palermo (to which I suppose that the baron attracted his friend, before the latter had him invited to Lisbon) in the persistent contiguity of their works in the library of Farinelli, whose precious inventory has recently been published by Sandro Cappelletto.[15]

Benedikt Poensgen politely reproached me for not having checked the "memoria" of Giovanni Maria Casini, which Mario Fabbri claimed to have transcribed "in its entirety" from the Archive of the Basilica of San Lorenzo in Florence.[16] Since a scholar should publish the documents that he has discovered with the aim of facilitating the work of other colleagues and not in order to oblige them to a continual

---

exclusive advocacy that would overlook the decisive value of the contributions of Liszt, Chopin, Rachmaninoff and Bartók. Apologies to Mr. Sutherland do not change my aversion toward the withdrawal of the Scarlatti repertory from its essential area of harpsichord music.

[15] Sandro Cappelletto, *La voce perduta —Vita di Farinelli evirato cantore* (Turin: 1995) 211-23.

[16] Benedikt Poensgen, *Die monodischen Lamentationen Alessandro Scarlattis—* Magister Artium der Universität Hamburg (Hamburg: 1994), 37.

and laborious verification of his findings, I was simpleminded enough to believe that every mystification had been banished from the field of studies which, like the *carmina* of the ancients, do not render much *panem* to those who dedicate themselves to them. In the presence of a proven act of bad faith, the Cartesian *Dubito, ergo sum* imposes itself, but it becomes all to facile an attitude.

We now know that at least a pair of documents which Fabbri declared that he had rescued from the oblivion and disorder of the Florentine archives were the distilled products of their "discoverer's" disastrous imagination. The pitiless and impeccable researches of Juliane Riepe, Carlo Vitali, and Antonello Furnari have literally destroyed the "memoria" of Francesco Maria Mannucci, which the Florentine musicologist claimed that he had been lucky enough to copy in the Archivio Capitolare of the Basilica of San Lorenzo. It was the memoria's categorical attribution to Handel of the *Pianto della Madonna*— in the meantime identified as a work of Giovanni Ferrandini—that alerted the trio of young musicological detectives. In 1993 their fully-documented unmasking of Fabbri's imposture was published in the *Göttinger Händel-Beiträge*, with an appendix by Poengsen, dedicated to the parallel demolition of the "memoria Casini" and wittily titled "Once is happenstance, twice is coincidence, three times is a bad habit."

At the risk of offending the sensibilities of so many of my Tuscan friends (to whose facile partisan retorts I expose myself willingly, reminding them that not only Sciascia's abate Vella but also Cagliostro were my own countrymen), I enjoy imagining that the origin of the imposture lay in that Tuscan quick-wittedness displayed in the hoax of the false Modiglianis in Leghorn and which in the past gave Florence the deceptions of Gianni Schicchi, the pranks of the priest Arlotto—and the harpsichords of Franciolini. May we consider Fabbri a "singular Florentine spirit" (*fiorentino spirito bizzarro*)? Since Dante's phrase refers to the pride of Filippo Argenti, I maintain that in the misdeeds of the pioneer of postwar Italian musicology there also contended a "bizzaria" in the more modern sense of "eccentricity," in addition to the proud certainty of "hoodwinking everybody" (*tutti gabbati*). It is distressing that the *scelerum inventor*—or, if you prefer, the Fabbri-cator of these deceptions—depended on the difficulty of access to his archival sources, on those "shadows" of ours that his researches should have contributed to dispersing.

The results of the researches of João Pedro d'Alvarenga offer the biographer new material of great interest, which he does not succeed in damaging by his tendency to condemn the researches of others in order to transform mere hypotheses into undoubtable conclusions: some of his suppositions contradict much more solid biographical data. Even his most detailed research appears guided by a tendency that shows up in many studies by illustrious pioneers of Portuguese musicology in which a kind of parthenogenesis saves the genius of Portugal from embarassing foreign dependences. For example, despite the unequivocal nature of much evidence and the value that João V wished to give to engaging Domenico Scarlatti, since Alvarenga judges very reductively the traces left by the Italian in the musical life of Lisbon, he concludes that the composer's transference to Lisbon did not produce the effect desired by the king. From this, it would seem almost as if João V had decapitated the Cappella Giulia only to insure a good teacher for his brother, Don Antonio. The limit seems to be reached when Alvarenga considers a possibility that is simply ridiculous: that Domenico's fruitful relationship with Maria Barbara dated only from the Infanta's move to Spain.

D'Alvarenga is right, instead, when he stresses the lack of evidence that Domenico Scarlatti was present at the performance of his *Festeggio armonico* (Lisbon, 11 January 1728) or at the complicated nuptial ceremony which took place in January of 1729 in the pavilion set up on the border between Spain and Portugal. Nothing, however, except for the marriage that Domenico contracted on 15 May 1728 in Rome, informs us that he spent the entire period there, between his departure from Lisbon and his return, documented by the entry of an anonymous diarist.

The Portuguese scholar is in excellent company when he attacks my discoveries in Palermo. He is unaware, however, that by the time I read my paper at the Scarlatti Conference held at Boston University in February 1998—and more recently in my biographical entry for the new edition of the *New Grove Dictionary*— I had laid out the problems posed by the identification of my "Dominicus Scarlatti," which are appropriately developed here. The supposition that I had resolved an imaginary abbreviation of "Dominus" as the "Dominicus" which appears—clearly written out in full—in two notarial acts would be childishly offensive, if D'Alvarenga were not the promoter of an hypothesis that Domenico was absent from Lisbon for two years. This excludes the more reasonable possibility of seasonal leaves such as those in 1708 that had been explicitly provided for Alessandro Scarlatti in the decree of the Viceroy Grimani, restoring him to his position at the head of the Royal Chapel of Naples. The London hypothesis has considerable interest since it would completely justify Domenico's passages through Paris, now certain, but without other documentation. I cannot fail to hope for a deepening of specific researches in those two capitals, although it is not difficult to foresee that only a stroke of good fortune could reward the bold spirits who undertake them.

The two decades since the publication of the *Due vite* have seen the text of the volume considerably enlarged. The new version is born of an exchange that seals my thirty years' friendship with that lovable fount of knowledge, Frederick Hammond: his fine translation of my text is his response to the same labor that I dedicated to his fundamental *Frescobaldi*, finally available to Italian readers after nineteen years of well-merited fame.

There is a considerable difference between our two tasks: both arise from sincere enthusiasm. But Fred's long discipleship with Ralph Kirkpatrick made him a competent Scarlattian; I could only contribute to *Frescobaldi* as a translator not unaquainted with the appropriate terminology and as an ex-harpsichordist fascinated by the music of the great Ferrarese.

The close attention my friend gave to every detail of my Scarlattian labors has made it possible to check the text in ways my diverse occupations would have rendered impossible in the past. Details that were simply unavailable in 1985 have, in recent years, enriched a great tapestry that still retains some areas of shadow. Fred Hammond's support and sponsorship have persuaded Pendragon Press to welcome this compendium of fifty years of study to its prestigious catalogue.

It is my pleasure, as well as my duty, to share the merit of this result with the person who made it possible.

R. P.

Palermo, 2005

PROLOGUE

Certain books which we have read as adolescents leave with us a few clear memories, surrounded by a haze of accompanying circumstances. In my memory as an adult, books that ended up in the cellar, such as The *Three Musketeers* of Dumas or the first of its sequels, remain above all centered on the deeds of the four heroes, loyal to the point of absurdity. In *Twenty Years After,* the loves of Anne of Austria and Mazarin remain in the background, mixed up with the tumults, the intrigues, and the contradictions of the Fronde. This does not prevent a reference to those bedside books of long ago from springing up automatically when, with the interests and information of adults, we concern ourselves with the historical period to which they refer. Today, I am no longer capable of remembering—and I lack the time to check it—whether Dumas noted so striking a phenomenon as the systematic importation of Italian art and artists, willed by Cardinal Mazarin more for inflicting a solemn mortification on the nationalistic pride of his enemies, the Frondeurs, than for pleasing the tastes of his lover, the queen.

In 1646 the disgrace and exile of the Barberini cardinals, whom Mazarin welcomed to France, allowed him to profit by the unemployment of the musicians who were threatened by the closing of the great theater that the nephews of Urban VIII had opened in Rome. Mazarin attracted the best of them to Paris, combining them with other singers from various Italian cities to form a truly exceptional vocal bouquet and offering it to the widow of Louis XIII and her court. It was a political operation clearly thought out and rendered possible by the contributions of various Italian princes desirous of ingratiating themselves with France. Prominent among them was the Duke of Modena, who appointed the contralto Venanzio Leopardi to accompany two fine boy castrati, hired for the occasion, to Florence, the rendezvous of the troupe headed for France. Some months earlier another correspondent had sent to the duke from Rome detailed information concerning one of these young nightingales:

> Marc'Antonio called the Bolognese, is at present at the [Jesuit college of St.] Apollinare, 13-14 years of age, sings well and [is] of a good school with suave manners, has a large voice for being young, he will have a great success since he is very alert and intelligent.[1]

[1] *I-MOs, Relazoni d'alcuni musici*, quoted by Henry Prunières, *L'opéra italien en France avant Lulli* (Paris: Champion, 1913/1975), 377.

A happy prediction, when we remember that the Queen of France appreciated the little castrato so much that she kept him with her at the dissolution of the troupe.

At this point the reader will ask why I am disinterring muske-teers, queens, and cardinals in order to recount the lives of musicians who had little indeed to do with France. But the story that I wish to tell begins far away, in both time and space, and acquires meaning only when it expands over all of non-German Europe (including a more or less imaginary England, as we shall see). Victims as we are today of the mania for travel (and I include in this category quick round-trips dic-tated by reasons of work, as well as the astonishing escapes to remote paradises that the consumer society slaps under the noses of bored rich women and more modest workers in search of unusual vacations), we can no longer appreciate how important and how exceptional travel was in past centuries. I am old enough to have heard accounts of people whose grandparents made their wills before facing a journey that today involves only an hour by autostrada; perhaps for this reason I attribute great importance to the movements of the protagonists in my story, to their opportunities for confronting the most diverse experiences that such displacements offered to travellers and to the people who came in con-tact with them.

Only in constant motion and through a variety of relations with people of different cultural and artistic formation could Domenico Scarlatti develop an accumulated potential which, not in the seeming success of the first phase of his career but in the blessedly static oasis of his extraordinary old age, would permit him to distill for us the bitter-sweet and perfumed honey of a sonata-production that all too many con-siderations force us to consider unique of its kind.

I have already stated in the first part of this text that Palermo and Sicily would be the needle of my compass; the continuation of the text would also be inconceivable without constant reference to this premise, which serves to connect with Sicily even a detail which has no relation to our story. A few decades before the events in France already mentioned there had departed from Palermo two Mazarins destined, like so many Sicilians, to find their fortunes far from their native land: the Jesuit Giulio (sent around Italy by the powerful and efficient Company to which he belonged to pour out the streams of his eloquence as a preacher and the treasures of his erudition) and his nephew Pietro, trans-planted to Rome as a young man with an administrative post in the ser-vice of Prince Colonna and remembered today for having fathered an-other and more famous Giulio: the lovelorn cardinal who responded with

important artistic revolutions (and not only artistic ones: Jean François-Paul de Gondi, Cardinal de Retz, another French cardinal of Italian origin, tells us something of them) to the confused attempts at political revolution set in motion by his enemies.

The momentary supremacy of the Frondeurs had brought discomfort and persecution to the Italian singers transplanted to Paris; only the final consolidation of Mazarin's power could have assured a winning game, as it were, for Italian opera. The Pyrrhic victory that Manfred Bukofzer assigned to a single episode covers instead the final results of the entire transplant operation, which was poisoned by an intriguer of genius: the Florentine Giambattista Lulli, more than willing to transform himself—in fact as well as in name—into Jean-Baptiste Lully. In the meantime some of our musicians had judged it prudent to return to Italy; among these was Marc'Antonio Sportonio, the young singer whom Anne of Austria had retained in her service.

In 1653 we find him in Palermo, employed to perform four roles in the prologue and in an "attione tragica" staged by the Jesuits to celebrate the taking of Barcelona. Even before Lorenzo Bianconi kindly pointed out to me in the researches of Thomas Culley[2] a definitive confirmation of the links between Sportonio and Carissimi's famous singing-school at the German-Hungarian College of Sant'Apollinare, I had supposed that the Jesuits deserved the credit for summoning to Palermo this strong support for their artistic initiatives. In the years following his debut, Sportonio became a real protagonist of the musical life of Palermo, enriching by the variety of his experiences in Rome and in France the resources of a milieu otherwise tied to local traditions.

It is particularly significant to find him employed in two roles in the *Giasone* of Cavalli, whose performance in 1655 apparently began the transplanting of opera to Palermo and to Sicily, the work of "Musicians of the Accademia of the Sconcertati" not further identified.[3] The *Ceremoniale of the Viceroys* preserved in the Archivio di Stato of Palermo relates that four years later during a celebration organized for the birth of the Infante, there entered the salone of the Royal Palace— transformed into a garden for the occasion—a chariot on which was enthroned:

[2] Thomas D. Culley, *The Jesuits and Music* (Rome/St.Lois: Jesuit Historical Institute, 1970), vol.I, 219-220, 226-227, 272.

[3] See *Contezza del Giasone . . . da Rappresentarsi nel Teatro di questa Città di Palermo, dà Musici Accademici Sconcertati* (Palermo: Nicolò Bua, 1655) the only known copy (*I-Rc:* Rome, Biblioteca Casantense) bears handwritten annotations concerning the interpreters of certain roles, kindly pointed out to me by Lorenzo Bianconi.

the famous singer called Marc'Antonio, and he began to rise very slowly upwards where there was placed a kind of heaven, singing, and while he was in the air they brought down four dancers fallen from four comets, and they did a most beautiful dance.[4]

From 1661, on at least three occasions Sportonio offered the Palermitans a new aspect of his talent. In the preface to the libretto of *Elena* we read:

Whether you are a Practitioner, or a Listener, I beg you not to marvel at seeing me appear not in the mantle of the Musician, but in that of a Composer [...] up to this point I have lived as a singer (whatever it appeared to you, I am satisfied). It is true: from now on [I live both] as a Singer, and Practitioner, since this possibility cannot be denied me [...].[5]

Sportonio was thus a famous singer in 1658 when he acted as best man at the marriage that founded an important family of musicians. On that day, 5 May, Pietro Scarlata of Trapani was united in matrimony with Eleonora d'Amato, a relative of Vincenzo and Paolo Amato, two famous priest-artists of seventeenth-century Palermo.

Vincenzo Amato was a figure of note in the musical life of the city: in 1656 the publication of two collections of sacred music had consolidated his prestige, smoothing the way for his subsequent appointment as maestro di cappella of the Palermo cathedral (1665). His two Passions in recitative style (*secondum Johannem* and *secondum Mattheum*) met with particular favor, remaining in the repertory of Palermitan churches for a good two centuries after the death of their composer.

Five years younger than his brother, Paolo Amato dedicated himself with passion and profit to the studies of jurisprudence, mathematics, architecture, geometry, and optics. The longevity that did not bless Vincenzo allowed his younger brother to enjoy his well-earned success at length, confirmed by a prestigious appointment. As architect of the Senate of Palermo, Paolo supervised the planning and construction of some of the most important monuments of the Sicilian Baroque: for decades he designed most of the triumphal displays and floats, altars, and Easter sepulchers destined to enrich the spectacular component of the sumptuous Palermitan festivities.

The baptismal acts of the children—or rather the daughters—of the Scarlatas suggested to me the idea of a kinship between Eleonora

---

[4] *I-PLa, Ceremoniale de' Signori Viceré*, Palermo, Archivio di Stato (Pronotaro del Regno, vols. 1060-1067); double listing: I, 496; col. II, 252.

[5] Libretto printed in Palermo, P. dell'Isola, 1661; copy in I-PLcom (CXXXVI D 33).

and the famous Amato brothers: every time the sacrament was administered to a child of the female sex born to Pietro and Eleonora Scarlata,
the parish priest of Sant'Antonio Abate gave permission to Don Vincenzo
Amato to officiate in his place. To Vincenzo, note, and not to Paolo. If
we remember that in one of the baptismal acts we find Antonio Valenti,
another musician active in Palermo, as godfather, and that Sportonio
had been a witness at the wedding of the Scarlatas, the circumstance that
Don Vincenzo regularly substituted for the parish priest on these occasions not only confirms the couple's link with the musical life of the
city, but does so by a hierarchy of participation which I maintain was
dictated by the same courtesies that still today in Sicily a young mother
would consider were owed to an important relative who was also priest.[6]

Vincenzo Amato officiated at three baptisms: in 1659 that of
Anna Maria Antonia Diana, the firstborn of Pietro and Eleonora (she
died barely eight months later); in 1661 that of a new Anna Maria (the
source of the Roman scandal of 1679); in 1663 that of Melchiorra Brigida
(according to Frank Walker, the source of the Neapolitan scandal of 1684).
We must admit that Don Vincenzo was not a good omen for his
baptizands: the first did not live to be a year old, and the others were not
what you would call the consolation of the family.

Immediately after Anna Maria Antonia Diana, Pietro Alessandro
Gaspare came into the world. Remove his first name (which repeats
that of his father) and his last (the patron saint of Trapani), and you have
the Alessandro destined to become famous in the history of European
music. Before he died, Pietro Scarlata continued to honor the Mediterranean tradition of proliferation to which so many of his descendants
also conformed. Between 1665 and 1669 the parish priest of
Sant'Antonio baptized another three males (Vincenzo Placido, Francesco
Antonio Nicola, Antonio Giuseppe), while for a fourth—Tommaso, by
his own declaration a native of Palermo—the baptismal record has never
been found.

Thirty years ago, when I wrote the first biography of Alessandro
Scarlatti to appear after Dent's fundamental study, the hypothesis that
Pietro Scarlata was a musician seemed to me supported by the relation-
ships which linked Alessandro's father to a certain number of protago-

---

6 The custom—quintessentially Sicilian—of improperly calling "uncles" (*zii*) older
persons wo are not closely related to us, led me to use, clearly unfortunately, an expression that misled the author of the entry on Vincenzo Amato in *The New Grove* I.
Vincenzo and Paolo Amato had no siblings. I had supposed they were the relatives,
not the brothers, of Alessandro Scarlatti's mother.

nists in the musical life of the city.[7] The misreading of a family name, "Spatonio" instead of "Sportonio" had led Dotto[8] to let pass unobserved the presence of an important "compare d'anello" or best man. My hypothesis has since been confirmed by two important notary documents, discovered and published by D'Arpa, which assign a definite musical identity to Pietro Scarlata.[9] The first of these[10] contributes to setting the founder of that dynasty of artists firmly in perspective within the Sicilian scenario to which my interpretation of the facts is tied.

On 14 August 1652 Andrea Scarlata contracted with P. Cesare del Bosco, superior of the Jesuits, to have his son Pietro—"a cleric"— participate for a year in the services celebrated with music every Friday and Saturday in Palermo at Casa Professa and the Collegio del Cassaro. The pay was fixed at five *onze* a year for the Fridays and the same for the Saturdays, as well as six *tarì* for each extra service. Two elements that emerge from the text of the document anticipate exactly details that will recur in the biography of the most famous of Andrea's many grandsons: the exercise of the *patria potestas* (which Alessandro will reluctantly renounce after repeated requests from the already famous Domenico) and Pietro's casual departure from his clerical status, one evidently little tied to mystical necessities, in order to contract marriage. In full observance of the *patria potestas,* it was Andrea Scarlata who obligated himself for the *"servitia personalia [...] ut dicitur per canto"* of his son Pietro, who is declared to be a "clerico" but is not a member of the Society of Jesus, which the stipulation of an otherwise unnecessary contract makes clear. If the young man was still a churchman when there appeared on the horizon the possibility of concluding the advantageous marriage from which our musical dynasty would originate, tonsure and cassock must have been laid aside with a lack of scruple comparable to the one that, some seventy years later, would transform the

---

[7] Pagano 1972, 9-10 and 20.

[8] Paolo Dotto, "Dov'è nato Alessandro Scarlatti" in *Il Giornale di Sicilia,* 3-4 September 1926. The real discoverer of Alessandro's birthplace was Ulisse Prota Giurleo, who had announced it in his essay *Alessandro Scarlatti "il Palermitano"* (La Patria & la Famiglia), based on Neapolitan documents and published in Naples a few months earlier. Later researches, carried out in Rome by Pasquale Fienga and in Palermo by Ottavio Tiby and myself, have allowed the correction of erroneous data and a more consistent reconstruction of the biographical facts about Alessandro Scarlatti and his relations.

[9] Umberto D'Arpa, "La famiglia Scarlatti: nuovi documenti biografici," in *Recercare* II (1990), 243-247.

[10] *I-PLa, Notai defunti:* notaio Crisostomo Barresi, vol. 1565, cc. 1367-8.

severe "abate Scarlatti" into the bubbly Domenico, prolific in other things as well as in composing sonatas.

To complete the integration of the information published by D'Arpa, another notary act finds Pietro Scarlata engaged by the impresario Pietro Rodino, together with Antonio Valenti and Antonio Licari, to "represent two operas in music, one called l'Elena and the other la Didone" in the Carnival of 1664.[11]

---

[11] "[R]appresentare due opere in musica una nominata l'Elena et l'haltra la Didone:" *I-PLa, Notai defunti:* notaio Giovanni Luigi Panitteri, vol. 2780, cc. 293-4.

I

The Scarlattino, alias the Sicilian

In 1672, facing the threat of a terrible famine, the Senate of Palermo was constrained to banish "foreigners" from the city. Given the harshness of the time, Pietro Scarlata and Sportonio himself could be considered such, notwithstanding their long stay in the Sicilian capital; in any case we know that in the same year the twelve-year-old Alessandro and his lively little sisters set out for Rome. If Sportonio himself, certainly placed in jeopardy by the famine, did not accompany the young Scarlatas to Rome, I maintain that the former student of Sant'Apollinare furnished the emigrants with efficacious letters of recommendation. I assume that musicians of the experience of the late Vincenzo Amato and Sportonio had already discovered in Alessandro an uncommon talent: it is impossible for me to believe, in fact, that the boy left his native land deprived of music as well as of bread. I think that six years of study in Rome could strengthen an apprentice who had already begun, but certainly they would not have been sufficient for an immigrant "outsider" to reach the privileged position in the starry musical heaven of the papal city that Alessandro Scarlatti enjoyed at less than twenty. If we bear in mind that the young Sicilian was backed by Sportonio, even the legend that Alessandro was a puilof Carissimi in the last year of tha venerable musician's life might regain a certain credibility. I have written *Scarlatti* in place of the preceding *Scarlata,* always employed in Palermitan archival documents, on purpose: in their Roman "upward mobility" the Sicilian Scarlatas believed it advantageous to cultivate by means of a closer homonymy the hint of a relationship with a family of Tuscan Scarlattis prominent not only in Rome but in many other European capitals.

    The comparatively recent ascent of these Tuscan Scarlattis was due to the political talent of an abate Pompeo Scarlatti, agent of the Duke of Bavaria in Rome, whom the chronicler Valesio almost never mentioned without calling him "most fortunate." This he could not do, naturally, on 12 September 1703, when an apoplectic stroke sent the abate off to the other world, and this time Valesio's comment tells us that the departed, "born in a low condition, with his industry and activity had attained the management of serious affairs in this court and had raised his family to a place of respect."

1

Alessandro must have had some contact with abbé Pompeo and his close relatives; we will discuss this later, in the context of the Arcadia or of Maria Casimira of Poland. An examination of the census of the Roman parish of Sant'Andrea delle Fratte[1] reveals, however, that another "Florentine Scarlatti" might have served as a humble link between Alessandro and the highest Roman artistic circles. By 1660 we find Cosimo Scarlatti in the house of Cavalier Bernini; in 1678 the same census reports that in "his own palace, and inhabited by the Sig. Cavalier Gio. Lorenzo Bernini" there lives "his son, the Most Illustrious Monsignor Pietro Filippo Bernini canon of Santa Maria Maggiore" together with other members of his household and "Cosimo Scarlati," who this time is called "Monsignor's Chamberlain," aged "an[ni] 69."

How does this concern Alessandro, you will ask? Lodged in the same palace we find: "Sig.ra Madalena widow an. 68 / Sig.ra Antonia Anzalone niece an. 19 / Sig.ra Anna Niece an. 24 / Antonio Magistri an. 15 nephew / Carlo Carrese ser.e an. 30" with a note that adds alongside Antonia Anzalone, "Alessandro Scarlatti her husband anni 19."

Arnaldo Morelli informs me that such information was collected after Easter; I have reason to believe, however, that it refers to the beginning of the year, and we shall presently see why.

In any case, it shows that Alessandro was precocious, and not only in music. Another book from the same parish, the marriage register, shows him before the altar of Sant'Andrea delle Fratte, intent on binding himself forever to Antonia Maria Anzalone. The document refers to her as "Puella Romana" and mentions that both the young spouses had lost their fathers. If the death of Pietro Scarlata had laid prematurely the responsibilities of a *paterfamilias* on the shoulders of his firstborn, only an unpardonable optimism could have induced Alessandro to add to the worries his brothers (and his sisters!) caused him, worries that thirty years later he would be obliged to describe as "the heavy weight of a numerous family."[2] A strong odor of fish arises from the registers

---

[1] Documents preserved in the Archive of the Vicariato of Rome; Parish of Sant'Andrea delle Fratte. The matrimonial act, II, 1647-1675, c. 171v published by Pasquale Fienga ("La véritable patrie et la famille d'Alessandro Scarlatti," *Revue Musicale* 10, n. 3., 227ff. and reproduced in *Scarlatti* ERI, between 48-49. Cosimo Scarlatti, as "maestro di casa," also formed a part of Bernini's small entourage (together with his pupils Mattia de Rossi and Giulio Cartari and three unspecified "members of his household") when the great architect went to Paris between 29 April and 15 October of 1665, at the invitation of Louis XIV to whom he proposed projects for the reconstruction of the Louvre (cf. Valerio Mariani, *Gian Lorenzo Bernini* [Naples: Società Editrice Napoletana, 1974], 81).

[2] Letter of 18 April 1707 to Ferdinando de' Medici; in Mario Fabbri, *Alessandro*

of Sant'Andrea dolle Fratte, but if there had been a lapse it was paid for on the barrelhead: the birthdate of their first child precedes by only a week the completion of the ninth month of their marriage. As at the wedding of his parents, Alessandro had a singer as his best man: Carlo Antonio Ferri, a tenor whom the documents of San Gerolamo della Carità describe as active in their choir, which Alessandro directed. The other witnesses are Carlo Carrese, whom we have already encountered in the house of Maddalena Magistri (the last place in the entry, reserved for him by the scribe after a boy of fifteen, suggests that the abbreviation "ser.e" should be read as "servitore," but this would conflict with his role as a witness, unless he worked for a third party) and a Giuseppe Fortuna. If it is true that the couple both came from the same parish, they did not remain for long in Antonia's aunt's house: the parish census for the following year reveals that a new nuclear family had formed in the "Block of the Cavalier Bernini": "Sig. Alessandro Scarlatti M[aestro] di Musica [anni] 19 / Sig.a Antonia his wife 20 / Leonora Scarlati widow 50 / Anna Maria sister 16."

The absence of little Pietro, born January 5, suggests that at least in this case the information refers to the beginning of the year. Since biographers of Scarlatti have ridiculed Anna Maria's tendency to rejuvenate herself, let us note that already here the foresighted young lady has declared herself a year younger.Lodged in the immediate vicinity, in a "private house of Sig. Gregorio Falchetti," we find Maddalena Magistri with Francesco Carrese, a widower (probably a relative of Carlo), and Antonio Boni, a clergyman nephew.

In the following years the births of the little Scarlattis necessitated several moves. In 1681, still in the "Block of Bernini" "facing the [College of the] Propaganda [Fide]," we find Leonora Scarlatti with her children Anna Maria, Melchiora, Giuseppe, and Tomaso, while our musician had moved to the "Strada Felice," into the house of Sig. Mattia di Rossi (another architect, a pupil of Bernini). That the gathering of this information was made with a certain laxity is suggested by the presence of Giuseppe Scarlatti both in Alessandro's house ("brother") and with his mother, where he figures duly as "son." In addition to this peripatetic guest, Alessandro lodged under his own roof his wife, his two sons Pietro and Benedetto, his sister-in-law Anna, and "Camilla Zoccarelli wet-nurse." Giuseppe Scarlatti maintained his curious ubiquity the following year as well. We find him "facing the Propaganda," where a mysterious "Placido Crimaldi" has inserted himself into the house of

Scarlatti e il Principe Ferdinando de' Medici (Florence: Olschki, 1961), 85 [hereafter cited as Fabbri, *Scarlatti*].

mamma Eleonora. His name heads the list and he seems to function as the head of the family in an atmosphere of relative well-being, which allowed the widow to house her two daughters, her sons Giuseppe and Tomaso, and even an "Angela Firruni servant." Giuseppe also appears in the "Palace of sig. Mattia di Rossi," where in addition to the couple Alessandro and Antonia there are also their children Pietro, Benedetto, and Raimondo, and a new "Dionisia wet-nurse." All these details show that the prolific Antonia Anzalone was not able to nurse her own children and that the expenses of the young "Maestro di Musica" were mounting.

The baptismal acts of Alessandro's children reflect the stages of his success. We start from the relative obscurity of his wedding witnesses, but already his firstborn son is held at the baptismal font by a son of the great Bernini, and for the remaining children born in Rome we shall see filing into Sant'Andrea delle Fratte Don Benedetto Pamphilj (represented by a secretary), Cardinal Maidalchini, and Donna Flaminia Pamphilj Pallavicini; and finally the *Majestas Reginae Sueviae,* the priceless Christina, represented by her factotum, the Conte d'Alibert. The ascending curve revealed by the baptismal acts has its precise correlative in the area of aristocratic patronage: Scarlatti began with the Duke of Paganica, courageously disposed to commission from "the Scarlattino, alias the Sicilian" the composition of one of the oratorios to be sung on Fridays in Lent at the Oratorio del Santissimo Crocifisso; he rose to the favor of the Pamphilj, and finally achieved the protection of Christina of Sweden.

The accounts of the period tell us that Alessandro's promising beginnings were threatened by a scandal. Referring to the performances of *Gli equivoci nel sembiante* given at the Collegio Clementino, the *Avvisi di Roma* say: "And the news is that a Sicilian, the composer of the music of the said *commedia,* is in notable disfavor with the Court of the Vicar [of Rome] for an illicit marriage made by his sister with a cleric. But the Queen sent one of her carriages to pick him up, so that he could play with the orchestra, when the Cardinal Vicar was also himself waiting on Her Majesty."[3]

The Roman sojourn of Christina of Sweden (see Fig. 1 on page 6) was a succession of attempts and achievements, both equally sensational. In writing the biography of Alessandro Scarlatti I have narrated in great detail the guerilla war between the Queen, whom her contempo-

---

3 Quoted in Alessandro Ademollo, *I teatri di Roma nel secolo decimosettimo* (Rome: L. Pasqualucci, 1888 [hereafter Ademollo, *Teatri*], 157). This earliest phase of Alessandro's activity has been meticulously reconstructed, with rich documentary quotations, by Frank A. D'Accone in *The History of a Baroque Opera: Alessandro Scarlatti's* Gli equivoci nel sembiante (New York: Pendragon, 1985).

raries felt justified in calling "the Pallas of the North," and Innocent XI Odescalchi, in turn nicknamed "Papa-minga" (in his native Milanese dialect, "the pope who says 'no'")—a double allusion to his Lombard origins and to his denials of protests against the often ridiculous austerity of his papacy. Here I must emphasize that this relationship with his first protectress planted in Alessandro Scarlatti the seeds of two absurd hopes. First, that of living forever in the splendors of a success capable of placing him beyond financial need, and the even more utopian hope, that made his Sicilian pride wish to batter down the class barriers that separated him from his rich and aristocratic patrons, to see such barriers abolished in the name of a higher refinement of taste realizable only in the domain of the most profound artistic competence.

A notable influence was exercised on the young musician by the woman who had killed Descartes with pneumonia by summoning him to Sweden to impart to her a learning that fell mostly on an inadequate cultural foundation. As we have seen, the salvation of Alessandro prefigures the plot of the first act of *Magic Flute:* there is a young man in danger, a high priest who threatens him, and a queen who functions as *deus ex machina,* furnished with the obligatory chariot. Alessandro/ Tamino remained too fascinated by his *sternflammende Königin* to discover the negative side of that unpredictable personage. But the high officials of the Church who had flung open the gates of Rome to the illustrious pilgrim—thinking only of the publicity connected with the spectacular conversion of a Lutheran queen—paid dearly for their excessive optimism. Certainly Christina's strong personality, the perpetual contrasts between her outbursts of anger, her constant display of the most varied cultural interests, and the real infallibility of her artistic taste left lasting memories in her young protégé. A quarter-century after the "Basilissa's" death Scarlatti was still remasticating Cartesian commonplaces going back to Pythagoras that he had assimilated through her, declaring weightily for the benefit of Ferdinando de' Medici—the other sensitive patron with whom Alessandro attempted to revive the dialogue too soon interrupted by his own departure for Naples and by the subsequent death of the Queen of Sweden—that music was the daughter of mathematics.[4]

Jean Lionnet advanced the hypothesis that Alessandro was already the composer of a little opera which was to have been presented at the beginning of 1678 in the Bernini palace, but which was cancelled

---

4 "...this science—for such is the Art of musical composition, as the daughter of Metamatics [sic]": letter of 1 May 1706 to Ferdinando de' Medici, Fabbri, *Scarlatti,* 70.

Plate 1
G.M.Testana: Portrait of Christina of Sweden
(Stockholm, National Museum)

owing to the increased severity of the pope's prohibitions.[5] The musical text has survived in a manuscript, now in the Vatican Library, which is anonymous owing to the loss of its titlepage. Pietro Filippo Bernini, the supposed author of the libretto and future godfather to Alessandro's first son, could allow himself to joke about the character and adventures of his young protégé: the subject of the opera concerns the vicissitudes and the loves of a brother and sister, obliged by hardships to leave their native Sicily to make a new life in Cicero's Tusculum. The attribution was contested by D'Accone,[6] but the later teasing of Alessandro that we find in the libretto of *L'Onestà negli amori* strengthens the hypothesis proposed by the late French scholar.

Certainly the earliest stages of Alessandro's career justified his optimistic additions to the population. But along with faith in the importance of his own role within the family clan the intrepid youth brought from his native Sicily a proud certainly of his own merits, which perhaps betrayed itself in displays of arrogance not always appropriate to the circumstances. We find evidence of this in the comic scene inserted into act two of the second Scarlatti opera known to us, *L'onestà negli amori.* [7] It seems that the librettist of this new musico-dramatic effort, by which the young musician could now vaunt the title of *Maestro di Cappella* to the Queen of Sweden, was again the young Bernini. In the third act of the opera the dialogue between two comic characters contains an explicit reference to the "Sicilian youth" whose preceding opera (i.e., *Gli equivoci nel sembiante)* had achieved such success that it was repeated many times in different places; the composer, the libretto tells us, must have "brought from the farthest reaches of the Christian world a bag full of arias," and was perhaps influenced by Arabic music. I have noted elsewhere that Alessandro lacked the sense of humor to laugh at the double-entendre that praised the fertility of his melodic invention; but "the far reaches of Christianity" and "Arabia" are subjects that still today send many Sicilians into a rage. The fact remains that Alessandro reacted irritably by refusing to set to music the verses which poked gentle fun at him.

Was Alessandro really so touchily Sicilian? I believe so, and before going further I will seek to explain in what sense he had been

---

[5] Jean Lionnet, "A Newly Found Opera by Alessandro Scarlatti," *Musical Times* CXXVIII (1987), 80-81.

[6] Frank A. D'Accone, "Confronting a Problem of Attribution *ossia* Which of the two is Scarlatti's first opera," in *The Journal of Musicology* XXVII (1999), 168-192.

[7] See [Accademia Musicale Chigiana],"Curiosità Scarlattiane. Le prime opere di Scarlatti," in *Gli Scarlatti (Alessandro-Francesco-Pietro-Domenico-Giuseppe). Note e documenti sulla vita e sulle opere,* Siena: Ticci [hereafter *Gli Scarlatti],* Siena, 1940, 43.

unable to emancipate himself from the Sicilian mentality, even if life
had detached him physically so soon from the island of his birth.

Many and powerful are the consequences of a formation that
Sicilians breathe in with the air, assimilate along with their first food,
which coincides with a world-view based on the contrast between the
most extreme individualism and the innate fragility of the single person.
From that arises a permanent condition of isolation, a reaction to a morality founded more on appearances and conventions than on personal
certainties. Worried by his own weakness, the individual seeks support
in traditions that offer possible elements of security: an absolute awareness of his place in the social context and his consequent right to claim
from the weaker what the stronger demand from him. I leave it to historians and sociologists to determine how much Sicily's long subjection
to geographically remote governments contributed to the formation of
such a mentality, but even before socio-psychological research and studies
of the Mafia phenomenon identified the determining force of authoritarian behavior in Sicilian social life, a southern literary tradition had indicated in the overbearing influence of too many bosses ("mamma-
santissima")—here the neologism is applied as much to simple fathers
of families as to the holders of Mafia power—a constant factor capable
of strongly influencing the formation of characters subject to systematic
disturbances of psychological equilibrium. If even today the collective
behavior of Sicilian society is still based on the unquestioned authority
of whoever holds power in each single cell of the great pyramidal bee-
hive that forms the complete complex, in past centuries the weight of
that despot on his subordinates could be crushing.

Only a few decades have passed since the time when a similar
description was applicable to all of Sicilian society, and a comparison
with the past reveals that the anarchy of the young has been able to
defeat despotism in what was the most typical—and weakest—of its
strongholds: the family microcosm. Here the father lorded it over everyone, and too often the behavior of this miniature "boss" was dictated
by a blind desire for revenge, by the will to make those who were subject to him pay for the bitter humiliations that other and more powerful
rulers inflicted on him outside the sanctuary of his own home. The present
reversal of the situation, disproportionate like every reaction too long
delayed, might make an epoch in which the abusive will of a father
weighed heavily on all the members of the family seem remote. In reality, the motorcycles or the drugs *à gogo* now easily available reveal how
slender was the authority of the man whose bluster only masked his own
weakness.

Motorcycles and drugs were still to come in the seventeenth century, but other types of disorder could infiltrate family stability. I believe that at least a part of Alessandro's later behavior as father/master, the jealous guardian of his children's "mantle of virtue," can be attributed to the bitterness he accumulated in his own youth, when he attempted to impose himself as *paterfamilias* on the brothers and sisters whom the death of Pietro Scarlata had made his responsibility.

In that phase Alessandro must have attempted damage control, and when he became aware that he did not have sufficient force to impose his own will successfully, at least he acted to preserve certain appearances. If he tried to take a high hand with his sister Anna Maria for her intrigue with a cleric, all he could manage was to resolve the miserable intrigue by the doubtful and scandalous respectability of a sacrilegious marriage. Above all, these marriages contracted at such early ages tell us that brother and sister had in common certain physical needs related to their nature as children of the South. They also shared the music profession, a profession that gave luster to Alessandro but for Anna Maria brought only troubles in the Rome of Papa-minga.

Despite the euphemism that called female singers "virtuose," in the social conventions of the period the public exercise of their profession was the confession of a disposition to debauchery, and this rendered their life particularly problematic in the Rome of a pope who proclaimed himself the enemy of scandal. Innocent XI's election to the papacy had provoked a metamorphosis that made him deny the fanatical love for the theater he had professed as a cardinal; this must have provoked absolute fits of rage in Christina of Sweden. If we believe the author of an *Istoria secreta* of Christina's Roman years, Cardinal Benedetto Odescalchi did not hesitate one evening to join the select group of cardinals who were guests of the Queen in her box at the theater. When he had become pope, "he undertook to destroy the theater in which he had customarily taken so much pleasure." To accomplish this more easily, he issued a rigorous edict "[...] by which he prohibited women from performing in the theater, preferring that young *musici* [castrato singers] perform their parts dressed in female clothes, against the express prohibition of Holy Scripture."[8]

Wishing to destroy the evil growth at its roots, Papa-minga took care to accompany the "fierce edict" of 4 May 1686 with serious penalties for teachers who dared concern themselves with the singing talents

---

[8] See *Istoria degli Intrighi galanti della regina Cristina di Svezia e della sua corte durante il di lei soggiorno a Roma,* ed. Jeanne Bignami Odier and Giorgio Morelli (Rome: Palombi, n.d. [1979] [hereafter *Istoria secreta*], 62-63).

of aspiring *virtuose*. We know that the Church limits the dogma of papal infallibility to matters of faith and morals, and it is well that this should be so since it would be sufficient to think of the number of "romanine" who flourished in the later history of opera to realize that the fulminations of Innocent XI did not accomplish the final solution of the problem.

This furor of intolerance exploded when the Duke of Mantua— a worthy predecessor of the imaginary personage behind whose identity the prudence of the Verdi's librettist Piave would conceal François I in *Rigoletto*— replied to the pope's question about what had impressed him most at Rome: that natural or artificial beauties and archaeological monuments were poor things in comparison with the singing of an incredibly beautiful girl whom the Duke had the good fortune to discover in the Eternal City. That was all it took to unleash a new massacre of the innocents, and female singers were immediately given a harsh choice, exactly as we shall see happening in Naples: exile or entry into a convent. The new Herod also followed his historical model by missing the main object of his persecution: but to reach safety Angela Voglia, called Giorgina, did not have to face a long journey on a donkey. The girl so imprudently admired by the Duke of Mantua had only to reach the Lungara, the area within which an imprudent predecessor of Papa-minga had guaranteed absolute autonomy to Christina of Sweden.[9]

Once again Pallas/Queen of the Night rose up against the Curia in defence of an unjustly threatened artist. One cannot say, however, that all her interventions had happy results, at least for herself. In this case, two years later a serious outrage suffered by the same girl under the hospitable roof of the Queen would provoke in her overly generous protectress an attack of rage that suddenly degenerated into a fatal apoplexy. In summarizing the travails of the singer (which in the past had already aroused the interest of Ademollo and more recently have been re-examined by Giorgio Morelli[10]), I wrote that she was worthy of the pen of Voltaire or of Sade. Giorgina/Justine was unlucky as long as she remained faithful to the poor French sculptor whom she loved, but when

---

[9] Benedetto Croce, *I Teatri di Napoli. Secolo XV-XVIII* (Naples: Arturo Berisio, 1968 [hereafter Croce, *Teatri*], I, 172-173) (which in turn quotes A. Ademollo, "Le avventure di una cantante al tempo d'Innocenzo XI, *L'Opinione* XXXIII (1880), no. 206, and A. Ademollo, "La Giorgina," *Fanfulla della Domenica* III (1881), no. 49.) Croce assigns the Roman sojourn of the Duke of Mantua to 1679, which instead should be predated by a year (see A. Gabrielli, "Un duca di Mantova a Roma," *Archivio Storico Lombardo,* 1889, 25-41.)

[10] Giorgio Morelli, "Una celebre 'canterina' romana del Seicento: la Giorgina," *Studi Secenteschi* XV (1975), 157-180.

she became the favorite of an important Spanish personage her fortunes changed radically.[11] This was her "façade;" Morelli rightly reminds us that Giorgina was not different from the other "virtuose." We shall rediscover this heroine of an immoral fable in favor in Naples.

With a prudence that her scandalous marriage belied, Anna Maria did not expose herself to the persecuting fury of Innocent XI by exercising her profession as a singer in Rome. Her only documented appearance in a public theater occured in Venice in 1680, in a minor role in *Il ratto delle Sabine*,[12] an opera of Pier Simone Agostini performed by a company of "virtuosi" that included the great Siface as well as Cecchino de Castris, the corrupt busybody destined to become the evil genius of Alessandro's future protector, Ferdinando de' Medici. The activity of the young Anna Maria Scarlatti, however, must have been more intense and lucrative than the theatrical documents reveal: this will be confirmed by the contract of her second marriage.

Before following the Scarlatti family as it insinuated itself into the musical milieu of the city where Domenico was to be born, let us return for a moment to Rome, where we encounter Don Gasparo de Haro y Gusman, Marchese del Carpio, the ambassador of the Catholic King who was about to move to Naples as Viceroy. Remember his name. For the moment he is an important personage in the Rome of Innocent XI and Christina of Sweden. He had made a reputation for himself by organizing rich open-air entertainments to celebrate the name-day of the Queen of Spain and in January 1682 by inventing a spirited conjuring-trick to combat the increasing harshness of the papal prohibitions. "The Spanish Ambassador is performing in his palace comedies in Spanish, saying that the Pope does not wish to have ones in Italian performed, and thus he does not contravene his orders."[13]

Don Gasparo de Haro had other things to be forgiven. The manuscript chronicle already quoted says that at the beginning of 1683, when he had left for Naples the pope "sent all his soldiers to take possession of his neighborhood, Piazza di Spagna, and cleaned out the malefactors who had taken refuge there."[14] The Lungara of Christina of Sweden was not the only place to offer a well-patronized *refugium* to the Roman

---

[11] Pagano, *Scarlatti* ERI, 142.

[12] Libretto in *I-Bc*. See Alfred Wotquenne, *Catalogue de la Bibliothèque du Conservatoire Royal de Musique de Bruxelles ... Annexe I. Libretti d'opéras et d'oratorios italiens du XVIIe siècle* (Brussels: Schepens and Katto, 1901 [hereafter Wotquenne], 113).

[13] Letter of the secretary Paolo Negri to the minister San Tommaso, quoted by Ademollo, *Teatri,* 166.

[14] *Istoria secreta,* 142.

peccatores; nonetheless, it makes a certain effect to read in a Neapolitan diary of the same period that before officially taking up his duties the new Viceroy had "terrorized the evil-doers"[15] sufficiently to encourage the populace to go about at night with greater safety. "Scrusciu di scupa nova!"—"The clatter of a new broom!" we would say in Sicily.

Since the news of his new post had already spread in Naples, well before his departure from Rome the Marchese del Carpio had received an important and significant homage: a visit from the Duke and Duchess of Maddaloni, Neapolitan aristocrats of the very first rank who had come to Rome in full dress "to enjoy the holy devotions,"[16] to attend some splendid spectacles in defiance of Papa-minga, and to leave their "large and beautiful galley of eighteen banks [of oars]"[17] at the disposal of the new Viceroy for his use on his journey. The date of this visit—which was not the only one, as we shall see, that the Maddaloni made to Rome— coincides with the first rising of Scarlatti's star. Prota Giurleo wrote that precisely "in the house of the Ambassador"[18] the Duke of Maddaloni had been present at a performance of *Gli equivoci nel sembiante.* As Thomas Griffin noted, "No documentary proof is adduced to support such a claim,"[19] but the specification that the young maestro "had not yet entered the service of Christina of Sweden, contenting himself with the modest title of Maestro di Cappella of San Geronimo della Carità,"[20] makes me think that Prota Giurleo, the ever-deserving pioneer of Scarlatti studies, was referring to a libretto of the *Equivoci* printed for the occasion and not known to us.

That the Maddaloni were more than favorably impressed with the little opera and its young composer is confirmed by the fact that, on their return to Naples, they immediately did everything necessary to

13 Letter of the secretary Paolo Negri to the minister San Tommaso, quoted by Ademollo, *Teatri,* 166.

14 *Istoria secreta,* 142.

15 Domenico Confuorto, *Giornali di Napoli dal MDCLXXIX al MDCIC,* ed. Nicola Nicolini (Naples: Lubrano, 1930 [hereafter Confuorto], I, 95).

16 Innocenzo Fuidoro, *Giornali di Napoli dal MDCLX al MDCLXXX,* ed. Vittoria Omodeo (Naples, 1943, IV, 264).

17 Confuorto, I, 14.

18 Ulisse Prota Giurleo, "Breve Storia del Teatro di Corte e della Musica a Napoli nei sec. XVII-XVIII," *Il Teatro di Corte nel Palazzo Reale di Napoli (* Naples, 1952 [hereafter Prota Giurleo, "Breve Storia"], 33).

19 Thomas Griffin, "Nuove fonti per la storia della musica a Napoli durante il regno del Marchese del Carpio (1683-1687)," *Rivista Italiana di Musicologia* XVI (1981), 207-228 [hereafter Griffin, "Nuove fonti"], 209.

20 Prota Giurleo, "Breve Storia," n. 33.

launch Alessandro by organizing in their magnificent palace "a lovely comedy in music, with a truly royal staging, called *L'Equivoci nel sembiante*, with the Viceroy and the Vicereine and a great number of ladies and cavaliers present, served a great quantity of sweets and flavored waters."[21] Since the performance took place on 2 March 1680, the Viceroy was still the Marqués de los Velez, and the little opera must have left a more than favorable memory with del Carpio's predecessor since he arranged a repeat performance in the Royal Palace on December 21 to celebrate the birthday of the Queen Mother. If the dedication of the libretto printed for this new occasion[22] had not been signed by "The Musicians of the Royal Chapel," one might imagine a spoken performance of the text, given the statement that "the present Drama" appeared in the "World Theater" "stripped of that lovely melody, with which so gracefully adorned when it traveled recently through the Roman theaters." These are obscure secrets of the hyperbolic prose of the seventeenth century (unless one of Scarlatti's future colleagues/rivals had inflicted on the *Equivoci* one of those drastic reworkings that in the coming years would furnish Alessandro's daily bread).

Even if the whole affair must not had been too pleasing to the ancient musical luminaries of the city, the Maddaloni had done things on a grand scale in order to attract attention to their new musical celebrity. In the meantime, pressing financial difficulties had constrained Christina of Sweden to reduce her expenses and consequently to dismiss the Conte d'Alibert and who knows how many musicians. It was probably the support of the Maddaloni (but perhaps also a more or less direct entreaty from the Marchese del Carpio) that tipped the scales in favor of Naples, encouraging Alessandro Scarlatti and his family to depart from a city in which the operatic theater had a hard and ever more uncertain life, toward the city destined, because of that move, to wrest from glorious Venice the scepter of "Capital of Italian Opera."

Christina of Sweden could not lament too much the departure of her little Scarlatti. After all, Alessandro had chosen to move to the city in which the Basilissa had dreamed, in her political machinations, of a second abortive attempt at sovereignty.

---

[21] Confuorto, I, 34.

[22] *Gli equivoci nel sembiante. Drama per musica rappresentato nel Real Palazzo a 21 decembre 1681 giorno del Compleaños della Regina Madre nostra Signora* (Naples: C. Porsile, 1681). Libretto in I-Bu.

II

The Genius of Parthenope, the Glory of the Sebeto, the Delight of Mergellina

In his new city Alessandro Scarlatti must have believed he had recovered the self-confidence that the flickering star of Christina of Sweden and his other Roman troubles had jeopardized. If it is true, as seems possible, that he had already come to Naples previously to supervise, personally, the production of *Gli equivoci* for the Maddaloni, Scarlatti must have felt, at least initially, that he had come home: for many centuries Sicily and southern Italy, together or apart, had shared a common history.

Obedient to what has been defined as a "continental ambition," the Angevins had transferred the capital of their kingdom from Palermo to Naples, sowing in Sicily the seeds of a discontent that would bear bloody fruit in the Sicilian Vespers of 1282. On the other hand, the island's later separation from southern Italy would serve only to prepare it for its transformation into a Spanish province —a perfect analogy with Naples two centuries later. The conquest of Naples by Alfonso V was a decisive step in this reunion. When I note that Diomede Carafa, an ancestor of the Duke of Maddaloni, commanded the three hundred soldiers who in 1442 used its aqueduct to penetrate into the besieged city, you will understand why Alessandro Scarlatti had good reason to hope that, with the patronage of Maddaloni, Naples would promise him a tranquillity not offered by the Rome of Papa-minga.

The Duke and Duchess of Maddaloni lived on a grand scale. The chronicles of the period often contain news about them and allow us to point out, among other things, that the habit of travel for pleasure—so infrequent at this period—also distinguished them clearly from their contemporaries. It is unnecessary to state that the style of their journeys was appropriate to the scale of living of this powerful family. When they had left their "adorned galley" at the disposal of the Marchese del Carpio the Maddaloni certainly were not obliged to walk: in order to reach Rome they had employed a fleet of five vessels. But periodic journeys to the papal city were customary for the Maddaloni, who at various times had set up housekeeping in Rome or Frascati, in the course

of their laborious but finally unsuccessful attempts to marry their eldest
son to the sister of Cardinal Pamphilj, another powerful Roman protector of Scarlatti. On more special occasions the Maddaloni also betook
themselves to other "principal cities of Italy," alternating exercises of
devotion (we will see how appropriate these were for expiatory purposes) with more worldly pilgrimages. If jets and sleeping-cars had not
still been *in mente Dei* at the time of the Maddaloni, a visit to Venice
might be considered the equivalent of those which today send so many
opera fans to Salzburg, Bayreuth, Glyndebourne, and Aix-en-Provence.

But luxury and journeys make only a partial contribution to a knowledge of the temperament of Alessandro's Neapolitan patrons. Even if
the relations between the couple were correct on the surface, Confuorto as
usual does not stint on juicy details capable of marring our illusion of harmony between these protagonists of a life-style that today is unimaginable.

The duke loved the more traditional forms of libertinage: we see
him threatening "boffettoni" (slaps)[1] to a female singer guilty of having
refused to attend—but only because of a previous engagement—the gallant gathering (read: crush) to which the arrogant nobleman had invited
her on behalf of a group of gentlemen including the viceroy's nephew.
The duke's anger also fell on the other party of nobles (and they say that
southern Italians are individualists!) whom the loyal Giulietta—the stage
and "professional" name of the diva—had not wished to disappoint.
Although the viceroy prevented the duels that would have resulted,
Maddaloni demonstrated the degree to which his rival had incurred his contempt by sending a Carafa bastard to the party as a provocation.

The reports do not tell us how the duchess reacted to such excesses.
In compensation, they hint that she arranged the murder of her husband's
attorney [*procuratore*] "because she was ill-disposed to him for often
taking her husband away from her and bringing him to whores and for
other fundamental causes."[2] I do not know how "fundamental" these
other causes could be, but I would not say that her resentment against
the unfortunate man (guilty of having taken too literally his functions as
"procurer") was that of a loving wife, all the more so since the Neapolitans maligned her excessive affection for Don Marino Carafa, her
husband's brother. It is worth noting that several years later a chronicler
saw the sad deaths of Don Marino and of the duchess' firstborn son as
divine punishments for "the licentious example [...] given to all these
women of Naples."[3]

1 Confuorto, I, 47.
2 Confuorto, I, 26.
3 Confuorto, II, 292.

Like so many other amorous ladies of high social position, Emilia Carafa knew all to well that the worldly prestige which had made her the "leader of all the noble women"[4] depended on her association with her husband; from that came the violence of her reactions to anyone who threatened in any way the stability of her position at the pinnacle of society. The same source recounts that at least one other human life weighed on the conscience of the duchess: that of a poor lackey, who in Rome had dared to ridicule a Maddaloni servant because the legitimate protests of the ladies of the papal court had forced the proud Emilia to renounce a privilege that she had usurped for herself.[5] On other occasions new crimes resulted from the touchiness of those who felt themselves even indirectly offended. There was an immense scandal, for example, when in the absence of the duke (who was late in returning from Spain, where he had gone to receive the Order of the Golden Fleece that the court had awarded him), Prince Ottaiano disfigured Donna Emilia's secretary with two knife-slashes and a sword-whipping, shouting for all to hear: "I'm not doing this to you, but to the duchess!"[6] It seems that, with the consent of that fearsome noblewoman, an attempt was made to murder a man under the prince's protection, the sworn enemy of a ne'er-do-well to whom the Maddaloni had offered sanctuary in one of their fiefs. No matter how excellent the relations that linked them with the perpetrators of such serious crimes, the viceroys could not just stand by and wring their hands, even if after much fuss everything vanished like a soap bubble: in the South more than elsewhere the ancient saying held that "the gallows is only for the poor." For the rich, after their excesses there remained the annoyance of making themselves scarce for a while, followed by house arrest (in this case for two months since the viceroy had demanded a reconciliation enforced by the "royal oath not to offend")[7] and by a fine of six thousand ducats, paid by the mother-in-law of the violent prince, instead of the thirty thousand initially claimed by the Royal Court.[8]

But not everything was luxury, love, or crime in Spanish Naples: neither the viceroy nor the noble class dominated it by themselves. We also have to take into account religion (or rather a numerically constant clerical class, which was called on to enforce the ostentatious religiosity

[4] "Mastressa": Confuorto, II, 5.
[5] Confuorto, II, 157.
[6] Confuorto, I, 97-98.
[7] Confuorto, I, 104.
[8] Confuorto, I, 102.

that was an essential component of the Baroque *Lebensanschauung* and to maintain a certain state of dependence on Rome sufficient to justify the fears of the Neapolitan king who later described southern Italy as being bounded on the north by holy water and on every other side by salt water. We also have to take into account the arts, wonderfully located in a country where the plants flower twice a year, but often called on only to provide a smiling façade for the darkness behind. Religion and art did not always proceed in harmony, especially when events occurred that disturbed the established equilibrium; and they were in harmony even less when female singers were involved.

This Alessandro Scarlatti must have discovered immediately.

Having evoked the powerful supporters who welcomed the young musician in Naples, I must now introduce his principal opponent.

One of the first items in the *Giornali delle cose successe in Napoli* from which I have extracted most of the preceding facts concerns an undertaking which allows Confuorto to present us with a three-dimensional picture of Don Geronimo della Marra, Grand Chaplain of the Royal Palace. A rigid moralist, this priest took perhaps too seriously his role as chief enemy of evil in the milieu I have described. Concerned with keeping up appearances, the viceroys could not ignore his scandalized protests, but things went on as usual; the stubborn chaplain learned no life-lessons from the virtually incontrovertible fact that the improprieties he pointed out succeeded, in southern fashion, in resisting every attack.

At the beginning of March 1679 (just when Christina of Sweden was defending Alessandro from the thunderbolts of the Roman Curia) the Viceroy Los Velez consented, under pressure from the Grand Chaplain who in turn had been entreated by "many ladies," to banish from Naples "certain courtesans of the first rank;" these were guilty of having passed themselves off as ladies (without troubling to respect certain distinctions, "they went out in gay carriages with pages and footmen, and to church with velvet cushions") and of having impoverished many noble houses "with their whorish customs." The diarist Confuorto furnishes a list of the courtesans exposed to persecution (for once, I could not locate one singer!) but he adds: "some of them set off at once for Rome" (falling from the frying pan into the fire), while others, trusting more to the efficacy of the protection that they had enjoyed, took refuge on the outskirts of the city persuaded that "once things had cooled down they would not have to leave." A footnote to the diary— "as, in fact, they remained"—tells us that their trust was rewarded.[9]

[9] Confuorto, I, 4-5.

Prota Giurleo notes that all the musicians of the Palace were under the jurisdiction of Don Geronimo, "a prelate of severe and upright habits, with great understanding of musical matters, friend and admirer of the composers Coppola and Provenzale." (If Marra preferred these local celebrities to musicians like Ziani and Scarlatti, who had come to disturb his earthly paradise, his "great understanding" seems doubtful.) From the documents concerning the chaplain, Prota Giurleo learned about his initiative against "the incipient corruption of sacred music" and against "that mixture of ecclesiastical and theatrical style which is beginning to be deplored in the Royal Chapel." (This suggests that, in the clutches of the Grand Chaplain, Pergolesi would have had a hard time writing his *Stabat mater*). Prota Giurleo could even follow this defender of the oppressed in his maneuvers on behalf of musicians, never named but clearly recognizable, who were threatened by foreigners "protected by powerful support,"[10] and in his reasonable requests for recompense sufficient to permit the musicians of the Royal Chapel to attend to the musical services required of them in tranquility, without the need to find additional employment that would lead them to neglect their duties. Concerning the last request, if the viceroy had for once paid attention to the suggestions of Don Geronimo, one of the principal causes of friction between him and Alessandro Scarlatti might have been removed. The problem of the multiple occupations of musicians arose even in that society, so different from ours. Obtuse and sectarian as he was, the Grand Chaplain understood (better than those who today legislate in matters of performance and public instruction) that the problems of clandestine employment will be solved appropriately only when we decide to recompense those who deserve it adequately (and *only* those who deserve it).

A certain amount of time would pass, in any case, before the blind hostility of the Grand Chaplain would be unleashed against Alessandro Scarlatti.

We have considered probable but not definite an earlier visit of Scarlatti to Naples for the production of his successful *Equivoci.* It is certain that in the summer of 1683 the impresarios of the Teatro San Bartolomeo turned to Alessandro to assemble for them a good opera troupe and its orchestra (five dependable players: the overcrowded anthill of the orchestra pit was yet to be invented) for the winter season, which they wanted to be brilliant in contrast with the previous seasons, presented with difficulty by the aged and financially harassed Gennaro Delle Chiavi.

---

[10] See Prota Giurleo, "Breve Storia," 32.

At the beginning of the year the Marchese del Carpio had finally succeeded Los Velez as viceroy; to him poor Delle Chiavi had dedicated *La Fiordispina,* which was produced for his arrival. "Text and music certainly by Neapolitans,"[11] Prota Giurleo gives as his verdict, unaware of the existence of a libretto with the same name by the Palermitan poet Antonio Salamone, set to music by none other than Sportonio and printed twice, in 1678 and 1680, in Palermo. If I consider that the *Orfeo* of Aurelio Aureli was performed at Naples in the same season, and that Mongitore ends his list of the works of Salamone with a "Dramatico operi inscripto, l'Orfeo nonnulla addidit,"[12] it seems to me that a connection with Palermo exists. That all of this should lead to Scarlatti is not inevitable, even if Prota Giurleo asserts that the company employed that season came from Rome.[13] The connection with Alessandro could emerge from the choice of an opera by Sportonio, even if the Teatro San Bartolomeo did not need Scarlatti in order to maintain contact with his native city: the poet of the theater (and therefore the reworker of others' texts) was Andrea Perucci, another Palermitan who had left Sicily in his youth.

Was Alessandro already in Naples in 1682? We might infer this from the deposition given by his sister Melchiorra in 1688, prior to her marriage: "Although I am a native of the said City of Palermo, nonetheless I left my said Country in the year 1672, at about nine years of age, since I was not of age to be married, and I went to live in the City of Rome, where I remained continuously for a period of ten years, until the year 1682, at which time I left the said City of Rome and came to live in this City of Naples, where I have lived continuously since then..."[14]

If Alessandro had indeed been involved in that obscure Neapolitan season, the thesis that Melchiorra was a singer would acquire more credibility; but it is difficult to imagine an earlier move, insofar as the researches of Arnaldo Morelli[15] show that Scarlatti was busily occupied in Rome for all of 1682. The Roman scholar's patient archival exploration has revealed to historians the exact terms of the official debut of the

---

[11] Prota Giurleo, "Breve Storia," 36.

[12] Antonio Mongitore, *Biblioteca Sicula,* ... (Palermo: Diego Bua, 1708/Felicella, 1714 [hereafter Mongitore, *Biblioteca*], I, 51.

[13] Prota Giurleo, "Breve Storia," 36.

[14] Ulisse Prota Giuleo, *Alessandro Scarlatti "Il Palermitano," La patria e la famiglia* (Naples, 1926), 18.

[15] Arnaldo Morelli, "Alessandro Scarlatti maestro di Capella in Roma ed alcuni suoi oratori," *Note d'Archivio per la storia musicale—nuova serie II* (1984)[hereafter A. Morelli, "Scarlatti"], 117-144.

eighteen-year-old musician, hired as *maestro di cappella* at San Giacomo degli Incurabili from 16 December 1678 and active at the church until the end of 1682. The document in which a substitute for Alessandro is approved and refers to a "permission for the Scarlatti" dates from the beginning of 1683: to replace Scarlatti, a certain Belardino De Santis is named *pro interim;* this would leave time for the Neapolitan hypothesis if Morelli had not also established that Scarlatti was active as maestro di cappella for the Christmas eve ceremonies at San Gerolamo della Carità, and that he had already taken over that post from Antonio Foggia (as would occur at Santa Maria Maggiore two decades later).[16] To preclude any idea of an extended stay in Naples, I add that the *status animarum* records of Sant'Andrea delle Fratte show that Alessandro and his immediate family continued to reside in Rome. Beyond that, we have surveyed the activities of the maestro di cappella of two churches without taking into account another extremely important undertaking by the young Scarlatti, that of completing and staging—in Rome and in defiance of Papa-minga—a new opera destined to repeat the success and the wide diffusion of the *Equvoci: Il Pompeo.*

And here we are at last in 1683, the year of Alessandro's documented entry into the musical life of Naples. At the beginning it must have been smooth sailing: the season opened with great success, since the impresarios had spared no expense to obtain fashionable singers. Paoluccio (the soprano Paolo Pompeo Besci, formerly in the service of Christina of Sweden), Brunswick (the contralto Giuseppe Costantino), and the Bolognese Laura Rossi supported a pair of stars of the first magnitude: the great Siface (who apparently was loaned by the Duke of Modena at the request of the viceroy) and Giulietta Zuffi (whose vocal merits could not rival those of Siface, but who was a sure draw in Naples: evidently she had returned to the favor of the Duke of Maddaloni, and perhaps the threatened slaps had turned into languid caresses.)

As long as it was a matter of gaining applause for *Il Lisimaco, L'Aldimiro, La Psiche,* and finally *Il Pompeo,* Alessandro Scarlatti continued to display on his libretti the title of *Maestro di Cappella of the Queen of Sweden,* and everything went well. The problems began at the height of Carnival: the ancient Pier Andrea Ziani whom Ciulla De Caro, another influential singer-impresaria, had imported from Venice and who had been named Maestro of the Royal Chapel, was dying, and what Prota Giurleo has called "the Scarlattian party"[17] (an anything but ho-

---

[16] Church composer (ca. 1650-1707), son of the more famous Francesco, whom he succeeded as *maestro di capella* at Santa Maria Maggiore.

[17] Prota Giurleo, "Breve Storia," 38.

mogeneous coalition in which male and female aristocrats rubbed elbows with singer-prostitutes) began to move its pawns to have the young Sicilian named to the post upon the imminent death of the old maestro. Considering the esteem that Alessandro must have enjoyed with a viceroy who had witnessed his dazzling Roman ascent, I have the impression that the nobles and singers were expending a great deal of effort in battering down an open door. However, there was the prestige of certain local virtuosi to defend, and as usual Don Geronimo della Marra set off, lance at the ready, by writing to the viceroy—in florid Castilian, but without mincing words— that certain past unfortunate experiences ought at least to serve to indicate the grounds for avoiding a scandal. Therefore it was appropriate to remember that the moribund Ziani, a man "of habits that were not a credit to his previous life," had obtained his post "not by the path of merit, but by that of favoritism," disappointing His Majesty's faithful vassals in spite of their "wide and experienced services." The chaplain went so far as to declare that on the basis of that precedent other persons in the same condition would be able to advance similar claims, and that His Excellency, "pondering the past absurdity" ["ponderando el absurdo passado"][18] would do well to give preference to vassals of His Majesty, who above all were born with the obligation of serving their king. Don Geronimo was forgetting that Alessandro was also born with the same obligation; whether or not the viceroy told Marra so to his face, it is certain that the date of Scarlatti's appointment follows the death of Ziani by five days but is only a week after the viceroy could have read the advice of his zealous but arrogant chaplain.

In addition, the solemn ceremonies of Holy Week were approaching, and the Marchese del Carpio had no intention of respecting the ancient tradition—worthy of Papa-minga—that would have obliged him to do not only liturgical but musical penance as well by listening to four old castrati sing pieces in outmoded style, as long as Scarlatti, Siface, Paoluccio, and Brunswick, who were waiting to appear triumphantly on the stage, banished the yawns aroused by all that antiquated rubbish. The appointment of Scarlatti and the still wiser decision also to employ "mercenary" musicians (this is what the theatrical performers were called disdainfully by their unqualified but haughty colleagues) aroused a veritable pandemonium. The most important singers of the Royal Chapel actually mounted a strike; Francesco Provenzale,[19] the unnamed candi-

---

18 Prota Giurleo, "Francesco Provenzale," *Archivi* XXV (1958), fasc. 1, 53ff. [hereafter Prota Giurleo, "Provenzale"], document VIII.
19 Ca. 1626-1704: "the first prominent Neapolitan musician to compose opera." (Grove 1980).

date of the chaplain, handed in his resignation from the post of honorary maestro di cappella. Don Geronimo was acting as puppeteer, but the viceroy cut the strings of his marionettes by accepting coldly the resignation of the offended "patriot" and replacing all the striking singers with the hated mercenaries. Among the newly enrolled members of the Royal Chapel we find Francesco Scarlatti as second violin; at least with his brothers, Alessandro succeeded in exercising the role of imposing and beneficent patriarch. It is perhaps appropriate to note here that Francesco had arrived in Naples from his native Palermo as a "small child, who was not marriagiable, since he could not be more than six or seven years old" (from the customary prematrimonial declarations collected by the diligent Prota Giurleo).[20] Francesco's further, more precise information is important: he never left Naples after that move (and before the successive departures with which we will be concerned): there is where at least some of the Scarlatas ended up who did not follow the Roman trio in 1672.

La Scarlati, her brother, the viceroy

In the face of so serious a defeat, Don Geronimo did not relax his grip. Since open battle would be unfavorable to him, he had to resort to more subtle means, perhaps anticipating the techniques of Don Basilio or those which have rendered the anonymous exposé so frequent in the political behavior of our own time. At any rate, less than a year after the debacle of the Royal Chapel, Confuorto (uninterested when it was a question of appointments or dismissals) makes room in his *Giornali* for a new and memorable scandal:

> At the beginning of November the Secretary of Justice, named Don Giovanni di Leone, Don Emanuele * * *, majordomo, who was also Governor of Pozzuoli, and a favorite page were stripped of their offices and disgraced by the signor Viceroy, because they maintained close and illicit relations with certain actresses, one of whom was called la Scarlati, whose brother was made *maestro di cappella* of the Palace by the said Viceroy in competition with other patriotic virtuosi. Because they had set up a triumvirate, disposing at their will of the appointments and offices customarily awarded, giving them to those who offered and paid them the highest price and committing other illegal acts to make money and to please their whore-actresses; and they did that without the knowledge of the signor Viceroy, who, when he had been advised of everything, de-

prived them of their offices, as I said, and disgraced them; and he
ordered the Scarlati and her female companions either to leave this
city or to shut themselves up in a convent, and in conformity with
this order, they placed themselves in the monastery of Santo
Antoniello near the Vicaria.[21]

All of Scarlatti's biographers have censured the hypocrisy of a viceroy who was capable of punishing male and female favorites as an example while leaving Alessandro and Francesco Scarlatti, the beneficia-
ries of such corruption, in their places. I believe that I have thrown some
light on the backstage life of the court, but I must admit that I have
always wondered about a possibility overlooked by everyone: as long as
the only source of the scandalous news was Confuorto's diary, the "whore
actresses" were not necessarily identified as singers, and this would have
allowed us to consider a Scarlatti sister (Melchiorra?) who was a prose
actress. However, the documents discovered in Munich and published
by Griffin confirm that "la Scarlati" belonged to the world of music, and
they also show that the scandal was such as to rebound from Naples to
Rome and from there to Germany. The first of the two "avvisi politici"
speaks of the exemplary nature of the dismissals, which were intended
to show all the household of the Viceroy "how to live in the right way,"
and of "certain Actresses confined to a convent by reason of impropri-
ety." The second "avviso" establishes firmly that the "Actresses" are
"singers" and reveals the identity of the not-unforeseen *dea ex machina*
who was able to soften the wrath of the credulous viceroy, and finally to
resolve after two months the crisis created in the theater by an opera
company shorn of its female component:

> From Naples we hear that the signor Viceroy at the Inst*igation*
> [Griffin's reading, but without having seen the document I imagine
> that the abbreviated word was "Inst*ance,"*] of the Duchess of
> Matalona has freed two singing Actresses from the Conservatorio.

If, as is probable, the other singer freed was Giulietta, Emilia Carafa
showed herself as generous toward the distressed musician whom she
protected as she was toward a husband given to more doubtful forms of
patronage.

This new contretemps, however, revealed to Alessandro how mistaken had been his first impression of Naples as the symbol of an achieved
security. To be successful in his career—and his was already a triumph—
was not necessarily the same thing as being successful in his life: music
was a great deal, but it was not everything if a maestro of his worth

[21] Confuorto I, 119.

could be subjected to such severe constraints. If Christina had still been the powerful queen of Sweden with a royal throne and riches sufficient to permit her the most refined intellectual or artistic caprices, probably the young maestro di cappella could still have hoped to save himself by returning to the favor of a patroness so well disposed toward him. In Naples, despite the powerful support of the Maddaloni, a viceroy who was perfectly aware of the merits of his preferred musician could not ignore completely the protests of a bureaucrat who dared to spread the rumor that the appointment of the new maestro di cappella was the re- sult of the whoring intrigues of his sister.

The whoredom of his sister: even to be suspected of acquiescence in the busy affairs of his lively little sisters was an outrage for the proud Sicilian ; imagine what Alessandro must have suffered when it was thrown in his teeth, more or less openly, that his appoinment was owing to this type of *fabor* and not to the *merito* that all Italy recognized in him! When the Marchese del Carpio acted out his farce of reprimands and pardons, Scarlatti must have swallowed his bile, reproaching his weakness, his betrayal of the role of harsh *paterfamilias,* for the conduct of sisters who should never have left the straight and narrow path.

Just at this time one of the three associates in the venture that had engaged Scarlatti at the Teatro San Bartolomeo who was a painter, pro- duced a portrait in which I find, in the sense of Wilde's Dorian Gray, the shadow of the disillusion which was beginning to weigh on the physical appearance of an ornately dressed young man, pathetically assuming an attitude of intimate severity. Permit me a short digression on the painter, before you read of my reactions to that picture: the detour will not break the thread of our discourse.

In the century with which we are concerned, a characteristic inter- connection governed the relations between the arts in the largest cen- ters. In Alessandro's Roman experiences we have seen Bernini junior appear as a man of the theater but with all the prestige of his glorious name; now we must remember that the associates in the venture that had contracted Scarlatti and the other musicians for the Teatro San Bartolomeo included the Roman scene designer Filippo Schor and two Neapolitan paint- ers: Francesco della Torre, a pupil of Luca Giordano in glass-painting, and Nicola Vaccaro, the son of the considerably more famous Andrea.

Prota Giurleo[22] has revealed the double activity of Vaccaro senior in two fields which might appear distant and irreconcilable to anyone

---

[22] Prota Giurleo, *Pittori napoletani del Seicento,* Naples: Fiorentino, n. d. [1953], 163.

who considered the life of a painter with regard only to his apparent success as an artist. From this point of view, it is astonishing to learn that even at the height of his fame Andrea Vaccaro was never willing to give up his hereditary post of scribe of the Great Court of the Vicaria because that humble position assured him a foothold in the legal class, which was much more firmly placed on the social pyramid of the seventeenth century than a single artist could ever be, subject as he always was to the caprices of the powerful. Much less wise than his father, Nicola Vaccaro never even considered claiming his inheritance of the post of scribe; instead he hurriedly put aside brushes, paints, and canvas and threw himself into squandering his father's considerable substance in the managerial venture which at the end of three years had forced him to return to his first profession, ruined and disgraced. *Cherchez la femme:* Vaccaro was impelled to so senseless an undertaking by his love for a singer—it goes without saying, the ubiquitous Giulietta. In the course of the history of the Scarlatti family we shall find Alessandro, finally settled in the uneasy decorum of his maturity, in a friendly relationship with a painter considerably better-balanced and more famous than Vaccaro: Francesco Solimena,[23] who painted at least one portrait of the aged Scarlatti now in the private collection of the Dukes of Alba in Madrid (Fig. 3, see page 27). Contrary to what I had previously supposed, there is no relation between this impressive portrait and the picturesque but somewhat crustacean picture commissioned by Padre Martini. Impelled by his business relations with Scarlatti, Nicola took up the neglected tools of his former trade in order to transmit the "unequivoco sembiante" of the celebrated *maestro di cappella* (see Fig. 2 on page 26).

Now that we know more about Vaccaro, the predecessor of Wilde's Basil Hallward, let us return to his Dorian Gray. You will recall that Wilde's hero discovers with horror a cruel smile that has marred the expression of his mouth in the splendid image painted by his friend, and he immediately attributes the change as the moral response to his cynical abandonment of a young actress. I relate Vaccaro's portrait to a similar early manifestation of a first stage of interior decadence. If however Scarlatti's image seems to reflect evil deeds, they are those of others; added to the wounds of his outraged pride they transform his face into a mask of severe composure from which, however, the expression of the eyes transmits the collapse of so many glorious certainties. I admit that my analysis does not conform to Wilde's story: the fervent Christian faith that Alessandro professed prohibited him from swearing

---

[23] 1657-1747: a Neapolitan artist described in 1733 as "the greatest painter in the world."

*Fig.2 Nicola Vaccaro (1655-1706): Portrait of Alessandro Scarlatti
(Naples: Biblioteca del Conservatorio S. Pietro a Majella)*

*Fig.3 Francesco Solimena (1651-1747): Portrait of Alesssandro Scarlatti 1692
(Madrid, Duchess of Alba.)*

the mad oath of Dorian Gray (one far indeed from the ideas of a Sicilian, accustomed to regard the veil that separates death from life as thin). Least of all would the young musician have desired to drag along with him forever the image of his first two human defeats in the form of a portrait that to me appears bereft of any magic powers.

It is worth remembering that the Baroque conception transmitted to us by the seventeenth-century biographer Carlo Cesare Malvasia required that the model be presented "adopting that movement and gesture, which were characteristic and frequent in the nature and the character of that subject; and not depicting them motionless and insensible, but in action and motion."[24]

In portraying Alessandro, Vaccaro heeded these precepts only in part: his model was "motionless" if not "insensible," but he was so because this was the way Alessandro Scarlatti wished to appear to others, with a determination quite consistent with his own "nature and character." Although Vaccaro made a great fuss over the flourishes of the jabot to swell the importance of his subject, attempting to conceal his dry lankiness, the lack of proportion between the various details of the picture is its real defect, and the roll of music that the young maestro di cappella carries under his arm is an insult to the rules of perspective and appears unrelated to the painted figure. Only my decision to concede to Vaccaro the merit of having transmitted to us a psychological portrait of Alessandro Scarlatti in a delicate moment of his human experience could induce me to read in that roll of paper the support that the musician, shaken by the unsteadiness of human certainties, sought more and more in his own career as an artist. The rest of Alessandro's story will show us that glory and honors would arrive abundantly, but if we look at the portrait once again, the face resembles that of a Cherubino who had grown up with the nightmares resulting from the punctual fulfillment of Figaro's farewell: "Not much cash!"

And his family kept on growing.

Baptism at the sign of the heraldic riddle

A bit more than a year after the scandal that had both pleased and cheated the Grand Chaplain and his patriotic virtuosi, Alessandro (now established in Naples with his whole family) had the sixth of his children baptized, the first of the five to be born at the foot of Vesuvius. Giuseppe

---

[24] Carlo Cesaro Malvasia, *Felsina pittrice. Vite de pittori bolognesi*. Bologna, 1678, II, 129.

Domenico—subsequently always called Domenico, even in official documents, when the tone of the discussion did not justify the use of characteristically southern diminutives such as "Mimo" or "Minichino"[25]—
was born on 26 October 1685. Considering the rank of the personages
who on the following November 1 held the child at the baptismal font,
Kirkpatrick correctly observed that such important names prophesied
that the newborn boy would lead his life under royal patronage; but he
erred in identifying as the vicereine of Naples the mysterious and genea-
logically improbable "Eleanora del Carpio Princess of Colobrano" who,
according to the parish records, served as godmother to the newborn
child alongside the Duke of Maddaloni, the inevitable godfather.

In those years the Princess of Colobrano was Eleanora Cardines,
heiress of the title and wife of another Domenico Carafa, a close relation
of the Maddaloni and "called by reason of his wife Prince of Colubrano,"
according to our diarist.[26] By birth, the noble lady had nothing to do
with the Carpio; even less would aristocratic protocol have allowed her
to use their name, which in any case no scribe would ever have dared to
attach, except by a mortal blunder, to anyone who did not have a close
and recognized blood-relationship with the viceroy. I confess that I have
always suspected that the "del Carpio" was a misreading of "Cardines,"
before the direct consultation of the clearly-written document categorically refuted such an hypothesis, while suggesting another one that is
justified by the rigidity of etiquette. Contrary to other baptismal records,
the name of the godmother precedes that of the godfather; from what I
know of the Duke of Maddaloni, I could never imagine that all the gallantry in the world could induce him to concede to another—lord or lady
makes no difference in this case—a precedence hallowed by current usage. The "del Carpio" (which in any case would have been improperly
used as a family name, since it is followed by the title which in fact the
noblewoman bore) then re-emerges to suggest the hypothesis that the
princess found herself serving as the proxy of the vicereine or of her
daughter, Donna Caterina de Haro y Gusman, Marchesina del Carpio.
In this case the precedence would be justified by protocol, and the omission of a few words could be explained by the anxiety of a writer intimidated by the unaccustomed presence of such important personages, intent on stating their high-sounding personal particulars. But the presence of such favored godparents was not alone sufficient to guarantee a

---

[25] So I wrote, before discovering that Domenico is nicknamed "Minichino" only in
the Fabbrian *imbroglio*.
[26] Confuorto, I, 363.

brilliant future for the newborn boy: in that case, a *commater* of the rank of Christina of Sweden would have assured for Alessandro's two Roman sons a fate quite different from the obscurity that was to be theirs.

To complete for the moment the examination of the relations between Alessandro Scarlatti and the Neapolitan aristocracy—or at least those that emerge from reading the baptismal records of his four subsequent children—let us note that *Giuseppe Nicola Roberto Domenico Antonio* had as godparents the Prince of Colobrano and the Princess of Tarsia; *Caterina Eleonora Emilia Margherita,* the Prince of Avellino and again the Princess of Colobrano (evidently doomed to the role of proxy, since this time she participated on behalf of the Duchess of Maddaloni); *Carlo Francesco Giacomo,* the eldest son of the Duke of Laurenzana (Don Carlo Gaetano, but as proxy for Carlo Caracciolo Duke of Ajrola), and Donna Aurora Sanseverino ("a very beautiful, kind, and lively lady," the diarist says,[27] who was the daughter of the Prince of Bisignano and, widowed by the Count of Conversano, had married Don Carlo Gaetano). The ample list of children is completed by *Giovanni Francesco Diodato,* who must have been born unexpectedly since his baptism involved only the midwife, so that he was considered a "democratic child" by Prota Giurleo.[28]

To the bitter discovery of the unforeseen disappointments of Naples was now added the "heavy weight" of a family that continued to become ever more "numerous."[29] We certainly cannot lament Alessandro's southern acquiescence in the decrees of Providence that filled his house with babies, since greater prudence on his part would have left in limbo Domenico, the sixth child of a father so doggedly employed in exercising the conjugal duty/pleasure which is still called in Sicily "u spassu d'u puvireddu" ("the poor man's amusement"), especially when it leads to such striking effects on the birth-rate. In the face of his increasing need to earn money, Scarlatti must have realized bitterly an unfortunate fact: his Neapolitan patrons were much freer with encouragement than with contributions; the documents show that not even the administrators of the Royal Chapel were punctual in their payments, since on 27 February 1699 Alessandro had to petition the viceroy like a beggar, asking the Spanish administration to pay him his back salary.[30] The unhappy man

---

[27] Confuorto I, 148.

[28] "Palermitano," 37.

[29] Letter to Ferdinando de' Medici, 18 April 1707, in Fabbri, *Scarlatti*, 85-86.

[30] Prota Giurleo, "Breve Storia,"61. The petition bears the date 27 February 1699.

could not foresee the still more tragic situation in which, through similar delays on the part of the Austrian administration, he would die in poverty twenty-six years later.[31]

It was natural that in these conditions his interest in Rome should revive, but Christina—always short of cash and in any case near death—could not help him. Other generous patrons were not lacking, however, and there were always churches and congregations disposed to pay well for music that Alessandro would have had to compose without recompense in Naples, at least for the Royal Chapel. Thus there began one of those painful situations in which an employee forgets his own duties, and ends by feeling for them a distaste destined to break out in ill-timed displays of impatience. Even when Alessandro and his musicians succeeded in finding other opportunities of earning money in Naples, their behavior remained disgraceful. One of the Grand Chaplain's customary reports exposes disconcerting instances of absenteeism and insubordination that could not be justified even by the inadequacy of their earnings. Always in Spanish—and therefore in a language that the viceroy certainly could not pretend not to understand— Don Geronimo decrees that some errors would deserve clemency if real amendment followed, but perseverance in the same errors merits severe punishment. We thus discover that the viceroy ordered that a month's salary be withheld from the musicians who were absent without excuse from the celebration of the Immaculate Conception; but just when the chaplain thought that this harsh lesson would bear the desired fruit, Alessandro and other musicians dared to desert the preparation of the *villancicos* scheduled for Christmas Eve. Scarlatti had arrogantly alleged that he did not possess the music, but when "Francisco Provenzal, segundo Maestre" of the Royal Chapel attempted to repair the damage, he had been sabotaged by "the Maestre della Capilla Alexandro Escarlate," who had carried off "las mejores vozes," in order to perform in other churches in payment for the duties that he would have been obliged to perform gratis by the job that he had deftly stolen from the zealous Provenzale.[32]

Let us quickly close this dark page (but only waiting to re-open it on the occasion of similar Roman episodes) by observing that Alessandro must indeed have been infuriated to behave in a manner so far from the professional demeanor he displayed on other occasions. It would be

---

[31] Franceso Corticelli and Paologiovanni Maione, *Musica e Istituzioni musicali a Napoli durante il viceregno austriaco (1701-1734)* (Naples: Luciani, 1993), 21-22.

[32] Prota Giurleo, *Provenzale,* doc. XIV, 78.

simplistic to consider his behavior ill-bred contempt: it seems evident to me that his lack of punctuality and persistent absenteeism are to be viewed as angry reactions to the inadequancy of his compensation. We should add that a certain type of musical *routine* (in the French sense of "business as usual"), creates situations of stagnation, and the desire to escape coincides with the need for supplementary earnings. History tells us often enough of musicians who, having reached coveted goals, soon realized the disproportion between their earnings and their artistic satisfactions, between their earnings and the obligations connected with them. All too often the formerly desired prize turned into discomfort, impatience, into the need to find *something else* to do, to discover further sources of income, perhaps masking an inadequate sense of duty under the pretext of irrepressible artistic needs.

In the case of certain paradises of absenteeism petulantly invoked by Mozart when his native Salzburg gave him claustrophobia, an impartial historian cannot but be shaken by the violent brutality of the majordomo's famous reply in the form of a kick; but the historian must side with the employer, that Archbishop Colloredo whom traditional music history presents as a pitiless oppressor of genius and who is summarily exposed to the scorn of music lovers only because he claimed that the necessary work should be produced in return for the fees that had been promised and that were regularly paid. Having attempted to rehabilitate the ill-famed archbishop, I must report that other sources unrelated to music describe him as a congenial prelate of the Enlightenment.

Let no one accuse me of thinking like a reactionary: I have already written that when remunerations are inadequate they must be rendered fully satisfactory, but only for those who do indeed deserve them. If today a mindless politics has succeeded—with unhappy consequences, to say the least—in the most inhumane levelling-out of compensation, I must necessarily look with regret on past epochs in which public and private patronage could stimulate and reward more reasonably the participation of workmen who were called on to furnish distinctly individual products.

I have cited the cases of Scarlatti and Mozart (but I could also mention Handel, Porpora, Piccini, Cimarosa, and Paisiello, avoiding the pitfalls of nineteenth-century victimization), omitting the singers. Then as now, the "star system" spared the male and female divas the worries that assailed the poor devils called on the draw the carts, or rather the triumphal chariots, on which the singers swaggered while enjoying their tributes of idolatry.

Among the many causes of the strain to which Alessandro's pride was daily subjected was the contrast between the fate of the envied but penniless maestro di cappella and the good fortune of so many other personages whose dishonest behavior was far from that incumbent on the austere father of a large family. Alessandro's profession obliged him to deal with female singers every day of his life. But only if we believe a poisonous satire concerning a Scarlatti aged almost fifty can we imagine the rigid mannequin depicted by Vaccaro dispensing with his armor of jabot and tailcoat to practice extramurally and with the "virtuose"—those emporia of lewdness—the sport to which he gave himself with such diligence in the privacy of his own bridal chamber. No: Giulietta and her companions (and here Alessandro had to repress a blush of shame, thinking of *la Scarlati)* were for him necessary evils, the risky ingredients of a culinary art which gave good results only if practised by a subtle cook. Let Vaccaro ruin himself for the lovely eyes of Giulietta: Alessandro instead was sworn to economic ruin by the most rigid observance of his own virtue!

And then there were the castrati, capable of capricious behavior sufficient to put even the vagaries of the women singers in the shade. Perhaps it was the pleasant memory of Sportonio (a paradoxical father-figure deprived of the indispensable accessories for that role)that assuaged Alessandro; perhaps it was the fascination with the "singing elephants" bestowed by a maestro who better than any other knew how to compose music suited to exalt the specific vocal qualities of each one of them; the fact remains that the relationship must not have been problematic, since we do not know of a single episode (and the stories about the caprices of the "evirati" are numerous) that goes beyond the limits of a courteous and correct professional behavior. We should add that for a southern ultra-macho male such as Scarlatti showed himself to be in every sense, his compassion for their losses must have created a cushion of permanent indulgence, sufficient to eliminate every possibility of friction.

Let us remember that when financial need did not compel him to absenteeism and to the other derelictions that enraged Don Geronimo, Alessandro could be a real model of professionalism. We can be sure of this from his full availability with regard to certain requests from singers (Mozart will maintain exactly the same attitude, boasting that he could cut his arias to measure, exactly like a good tailor), even if pride then impelled him to declare that his hand had been forced by commands from higher up. To understand this attitude, let us re-read the preface printed in the libretto of Legrenzi's *Odoacre* on the occasion of the Neapolitan repeat of the opera:

This Drama which on other occasions has appeared in the most famous theaters of Italy, illuminated by the harmonious notes of that Giovanni Legrenzi, who while he lived appeared to be an intelligence descended to earth from the spheres of melody; having now reached our stage in Naples, it too experiences the universal fate of Dramas; which, whether in Poetry or in Music, never appear in a new theater without taking on new forms, and likenesses; therefore, since Sig. Alessandro Scarlatti, *maestro* of the Royal Chapel here, has had to reform it as to the music, in order to adapt it to the skills of the Musicians who must perform it, he has adapted it, impelled by the Command, and by the obligation that he has incurred; whence his modesty has decreed, that the Ariettas recomposed by him have been countersigned [to mark them] from those originally prepared, so that (as he said) the glory of the aforesaid Legrenzi, to whose immortal memory he forever professes eternal respect, should not be prejudiced by his weaknesses.[33]

Even discounting this profession of humility which only Alessandro's correspondence with Ferdinando de' Medici would rival, it should be repeated that Scarlatti was always able to appreciate the true value of those of his colleagues who merited so high a recognition. And we may be sure that he did not trouble himself too much about the higher salaries often linked with some fashionable female singer or with the castrati who were *à la mode* in the theaters and who appeared on the same payment-sheets as Alessandro; but when it was a question of male attributes, try to find a better-paid tenor or bass! It seems to me amusing to stress this, even though I well know that it reflects the market created by the fashions of the time: a market and a fashion that the poor and very aware Scarlatti was forced to endure.

The preface to the libretto I have quoted throws a certain light on the activities—secondary in appearance only—which a maestro di cappella was supposed to pursue. But that was not a purely Neapolitan failing. Elsewhere as well "Dramas" were reworked (sad fate: today fashionable musicology seeks to respect the slightest detail of the original texts, it is the directors who make the unfortunate operas which fall into their clutches assume "new forms and appearances") and Alessandro Scarlatti, perfectly integrated into the *routine* of his time, declared with an excess of modesty that he had been "impelled by the Command, and by the obligation that he had incurred" to rework an old score. He was then free to rush off to increase by an entry of doubtful validity the Leporellian catalogue which by the end of his life would reach the truly "incredible" number of one hundred fourteen works for the stage.

---

[33] Quoted in Piero Fogaccia, *Giovanni Legrenzi* (Bergamo, n.d., [1954]), 95-196.

III

Maecenas atavis edite regibus
o et præsidium et dulce decus meum!

. . .

Quodsi me lyricis vatibus inseres
sublimi feriam sidera vertice

In recalling the initial phases of Alessandro Scarlatti's career I have already noted the negative effect his relations with various powerful personages had on him. These personages had inherited—with varying qualifications and in unequal measures—the role of patron that the Basilissa had so effectively sustained in her declining years. For Scarlatti, only Christina, a mother-refuge disguised as a man, would remain his *"præsidium et dulce decus"* (protection and sweet grace). To continue the outline of the Horatian ode, "to raise his head proudly to the stars thanks to the recognition and the support of the powerful" was one of the most fatal human blunders of our deluded musician, who continued to hope for the impossible even when harsh reality should have taught him that a sort of sadistic cruelty can induce a powerful "protector" to play cat and mouse with his "protégé." Seen in this light, the career of Alessandro is a series of great hopes disappointed, nourished by a proud assurance of his own worth and by the pathetic hope of seeing it recognized by someone who would have the resources to sustain the artist whom he appreciated and preferred above any other.

Since I must not rewrite Alessandro's biography but rather draw from it elements useful for explaining the frustrating consequences of human relations and artistic experiences that were gratifying in appearance only, I will proceed to a kind of catalogue of those in whose service—either as superiors or as paying patrons—Alessandro found himself working until another Scarlatti emerged from the clan to divide the patronage of some of them with his father, before finding his own more pleasing and finally more satisfactory protection.

One of the principal promoters of Alessandro's early successes merits a special place among his supporters. You will recall that one of the musician's Roman sons had been held at the baptismal font by a proxy for Don Benedetto Pamphilj, the future abortive brother-in-law of the Maddalonis' eldest son. The researches of Lina Montalto highlighted the decisive role that Pamphilj played in the Roman launching of "Scarlattino" even before Benedetto received the cardinal's hat that his mother, whether through naiveté or imprudence, requested from Papaminga through the unlikely support of Christina of Sweden. Pamphilj was not what we would call an ascetic: he loved life, art, and even gambling, but as a cardinal he was only moderately worldly by comparison with some other wearers of the purple whom we will soon encounter. A man of his time, he left a favorable impression on his contemporaries by his urbane and gentlemanly manners; at the same time he was perfectly adequate to the important roles assigned to him by the various popes who succeeded each other in the course of his long and happy life. In his Neapolitan isolation Alessandro must have discovered with real joy that he had not been forgotten by the patron of his earliest years. From a Rome that itself could offer a notable choice of opportunities to so important a patron, Benedetto Pamphilj continued to send Alessandro literary texts to set to music, and rivals of the stature of Pasquini, Corelli, Lulier, and Gasparini did nothing to hinder the continuation of a relationship that favored their distant colleague. The esteem Alessandro enjoyed with these illustrious musicians (and which he reciprocated, almost always sincerely, as I have already noted) was such, indeed, that they often willingly collaborated in the performance of the music that arrived from Naples by participating in the concerts or spectacles organized by the cardinal. If he compared this spirit of "fair play" on the part of musicians of great ability with all the intrigues of Naples, Alessandro must have felt that Cardinal Pamphilj's requests emanated from Paradise, from an Eden that our musician hurried to regain physically every time the cardinal's most pleasing "high commands" succeeded in forcing open the links of his Neapolitan chain.

We shall see that in certain cases only deference to the reigning hypocrisy made the viceroy conceal his own role of accomplice, when he was not himself the moving power behind those flights. In practice, the relationship of the viceroys with Scarlatti was fairly consistent and followed the forms of behavior already described in the case of the Marchese del Carpio. We should remember that only at the end of the Spanish period did the royal court appear in Naples; and it did so— paradoxically—with a brief sojourn of the "French" Philip V. Previously, obvious considerations of political expediency had made the selection of the viceroys, the living emanations of an invisible and distant power, favor aristocrats of high lineage endowed with a notable knowledge of the political problems of Italy. These problems ranged from the governance of distant "kingdoms" and "duchies" to uneasy relations with the pope in a Rome which was the scene of perpetual clashes between a "Catholic" king and a king who declared himself "Most Christian," but who was not sufficiently so to give up the possibility of an alliance with the Grand Turk.

In this situation the passage of the same person from one to another of these offices, according to a typical itinerary, was quite natural. We have already seen the Marchese del Carpio move from Rome to Naples. The same journey would be reserved for another marchese, Luigi de la Cerda di Cogolludo, who, however, managed to inherit the title of Duke of Medina Coeli from his father before becoming viceroy of Naples. We have already encountered this gentleman: he was the *deus ex machina* who, at the death of Christina of Sweden, saved Giorgina from being put in a convent by making her his own favorite (even if his desire to save appearances dictated the rather cruelly paradoxical description of the singer as the "first lady" of his duchess's suite), disappointing the admiring and panting Duke of Mantua and more than one Roman cardinal. Cogolludo always loved to display a clamorous splendor, and his enterprises at the summit of Baroque society had positive consequences for art but not always for artists, in Naples as well as in Rome. In his former office of General of the Galleys of Naples he had actually wished to outshine the viceroy himself, entertaining the great names of the Neapolitan aristocracy on one of his "most gallant feluccas." The Marchese del Carpio was not the man to put up with such a challenge and forced the boat of the enraged duke to return to port before embarking to disport himself on his own craft. If we can believe it, Cogolludo was brought to his senses by none other than the Duke of Maddaloni, a member of the party.[1] With all his arrogance, Domenico Marzio Carafa was still perfectly aware of the symbolic value that the hierarchical ranking of every single personage assumed in the permanent pageant of society as a spectacle for the edification of the masses.

The heir of a noble house which Saint-Simon enjoyed tracing in a multi-century genealogy (even to the point of discovering a bastard, although an illustrious one),[2] Don Luigi de la Cerda had eight sisters, all duly married to grandees of Spain. The sixth of them was wedded to Filippo Colonna, Duke of Tagliacozzo and Prince of Palliano, whose

[1] Confuorto I, 128-129.
[2] Louis de Rouvroy de Saint-Simon, *Mémoires* (Paris: Editions Ramsay, n.d. [1977-79] [hereafter Saint-Simon, *Mémoires*]), XVI, 351-357.

father Lorenzo Onofrio, the Constable of the Kingdom of Naples, was an important personage with all the qualifications for inclusion in our gallery of patrons. In 1682, on the arrival of his daughter-in-law from Spain, the Constable organized a whole cycle of operatic performances in his Roman palace. Innocent XI "took umbrage," Ademollo tells us, even though "they calmed him by saying that it was a bagatelle for the amusement of the bride."[3] A bagatelle worthy of the grandeur of the family that she had joined, since at the beginning of 1683 Donna Laurentia de la Cerda Colonna found herself the dedicatee of an important novelty that her father-in-law and her husband wished to secure for their private theater: the *Pompeo* of our own Scarlatti.

But the protagonists of this part of our story are so entangled in a web of mutual relations that I can equally well continue the discussion by focusing my attention on Don Filippo Colonna or on his brother-in-law. The father of the former ruled the interim government of Naples between the death of the Viceroy del Carpio and the arrival of his successor, Francesco Benavides Conte di Santo Stefano. The latter first got himself into trouble with the Spanish court by directing at his own whim the votes of a group of cardinals faithful to Spain in the conclave that followed the death of Innocent XI. The scandalous result was the election of Cardinal Ottoboni, to the displeasure of Charles II of Spain. (Exactly twenty years later the jealous intrigues of Mme. des Ursins would crown the woes of Medina Coeli, then prime minister of Spain, with an accusation of high treason and an imprisonment pathetically consoled by the loyalty of the unsinkable Giorgina.) The gossip columns report that the Marchese of Cogolludo had allowed himself to be corrupted by Ottoboni's partisans in return for "many thousands of scudi received for the said purpose, and by the promise of a cardinal's hat of his choice, and both were carried out, since he received the promised *dobles* and the hat, which he bestowed on Monsignor Giudice, who was then made a cardinal."[4] Cardinal Giudice was another fervent admirer of Scarlatti in our spiderweb, but we shall speak of him later when, as viceroy of Sicily, he became the promoter of a notable relaunching of Alessandro's operas in his native city. For the moment, since I have mentioned the Colonnas first, let us penetrate the Janus-like mysteries of their relations with Alessandro Scarlatti in Naples and in Rome.

On his arrival in Naples, "the Constable [Colonna] appeared quite dedicated to the affairs of government and equally dedicated to relax-

---

[3] Ademollo, *Teatri,* 166.
[4] Confuorto I, 293.

ation and enjoymento, not omitting to entertain himoelf with the card-
game of *ombra* in the evening."[5]

But there were other games that interested the Constable. In seeking to escape the snares of female singers, Lorenzo Onofrio Colonna
gave the gossipy Confuorto the opportunity of transmitting a splendid
snapshot of seventeenth-century life:

> There has arrived, speeding by post horses, a lady, the love of
> the Constable, as it is said, and I saw her pass wearing a short and
> outlandish riding habit, on horseback with a mask, following the
> postillion, and with others of her suite at hand.[6]

Unaware of an incongruity to which the experiences of his daily
life had inured him, the diarist continues his chronicle by informing us
that immediately afterward the Constable had betaken himself to worship the Holy Sacrament (in thanksgiving for favors received?) at the
Quarant'Ore of the Spirito Santo. But a true protagonist in the field of
religion (in the negative, for the purposes of our gallery) was about to
arrive in Naples: after years of vacancy of the archiepiscopal see, the
Neapolitan Cardinal Antonio Pignatelli came to take possession of it,
welcomed emotionally by his fellow-citizens (first of all—need we
say?—the Duke of Maddaloni, who hastened to send a "sumptuous re-
past" to the cardinal on the evening of his arrival). Ten years later, at
least the many devotés of opera and of female singers would wish to
retract their homages when their cardinal, having succeeded pope
Ottoboni, validated his choice of the menacing name of Innocent XII by
renewing still more ridiculous persecutions, culminating in the destruction of the Roman opera theater of Tor di Nona. In the face of this
display of new outbursts of intolerance, we see that Rome was not the
promised land that it might seem for a composer of the level of Alessandro
Scarlatti: operatic activity would always remain exposed to an uncertain
fate, and although church music prospered widely it offered no prospect
of earnings in any way comparable with those offered by the theaters.

For the moment, however, the situation remained generally favorable: it is precisely the strange maneuvers in Naples between the Constable and Alessandro that confirm this.

In writing about Alessandro I have pointed out that there is a certain contrast between the favorable attitude of patronage that the Colonna
adopted in Rome and the fact that the Constable had immediately ac-

[5] Confuorto, I, 195.
[6] Confuorto, I, 195.

cepted Scarlatti's resignation from the post of Master of the Royal Chapel, only too obviously occasioned by one of his encounters with the unavoidable Don Geronimo della Marra. Alessandro had excellent reasons to absent himself from Naples in January of 1688. In Rome, although the French controversies embittered the attitude of Innocent XI, Cardinal Pamphilj was promoting an interesting revival of *Rosmene* enriched by the participation of Arcangelo Corelli in the orchestra (the celebrated violinist, who had permanently entered the cardinal's service, had even gone to live in an apartment in his palace), while the Constable Colonna and another aristocrats were given permission to organize opera performances in their palaces.

When Don Onofrio Colonna accepted Alessandro's resignation in Naples, the musician did not risk much: a royal decree of 1679 declared null and void "all the permissions and offices"[7] bestowed by a viceroy in the period after which he had been notified of the arrival of his successor. By naming Tommaso Pagano to the vacant post only five days before leaving for Rome, perhaps Don Onofrio had secured for himself, without arousing the suspicion of personal interests, Scarlatti's participation in the performance which he planned for his own *rentrée*.

The joy of the chaplain and his new protégé who shared my name was short-lived, however. On March 11—when the move to Rome had produced the desired results—the new viceroy, the Count of Santo Stefano, restored to Alessandro Scarlatti "the post of Maestro of the Royal Chapel, in the place of the one who serves there now."[8] What an eventful life! It must have seemed wise to Alessandro's protectors, however, to procure him a post and its accompanying earnings that would keep him more firmly anchored in Naples. On 1 March 1689 Scarlatti took up service at the Conservatory of Santa Maria di Loreto as maestro di cappella, with the duty of "giving lessons in playing and singing" every morning to the students assigned to him by the Governors of the Conservatory.[9] After barely two months, Alessandro had the audacity to request a month's leave "so that he could go to Rome for certain matters of his." But this was only the beginning: when two-and-a-half months had passed without his taking the trouble to give any news of himself, the administrators were convinced that he would not return in the foreseeable future, "since the hot weather was well advanced." We can only

---

[7] Quoted in Prota Giurleo, "Breve Storia," 48.

[8] Prota Giurleo, "Breve Storia," 48.

[9] Employment contract in Salvatore Di Giacomo, *Il Conservatorio dei Poveri di Gesù Cristo e quello di S. Maria di Loreto* (Palermo: Remo Sandron, 1928 [hereafter Di Giacomo, *Poveri*]), 202-203.

share their decision to dismiss the renegade "and to choose someone else in his place who can attend and be responsible with that punctuality which the post and its duties require."[10]

We have arrived at the destruction of another myth: the claim that Alessandro was a good teacher. At the risk of again offending the sensibilities of my censors, I shall repeat that it was Alessandro's works and not the man himself who instructed the young. Moreover, he himself clearly recognized that he was so little endowed with the patience indispensable to every good teacher that he confided to a worthy colleague the task of perfecting the talents of the musical genius whom he soon discovered in his own family.

Let us attempt to follow the deserter in his Roman escape, which is particularly mysterious since it coincides with a period that was unpromising for the earnings that Alessandro sought. Christina of Sweden had died on April 19, and on August 12 Innocent XI had followed her. Who could have attracted Scarlatti to a city disposed only to sumptuous funerals? A recent hypothesis suggests the possibility that by July of 1687 Cogolludo had already employed Alessandro and other Neapolitan musicians (at liberty for the occasion owing to the serious illness of the Viceroy del Carpio) to reinforce the Roman legions whom he employed in a splendid serenade for the Queen's name-day. In supposing this possibility Griffin[11] sets up a connection with the ex-General of the Galleys, who had profited by his experiences in Naples when the ships which he commanded found a brilliant (and uncompetitive) employment in the splendid maritime serenades the Marchese del Carpio organized on the seashore to celebrate royal birthdays and name-days.

The fact that Prota Giurleo did not report any reaction on the part of the Grand Chaplain during Alessandro's long absence from Naples might suggest that the new viceroy's acquiescent attitude was dictated by an explicit request from the ambassador, who wished to entrust to Scarlatti the composition and performance of one of his serenades. But in this case as well Alessandro would have given himself a great deal of work without any real certainty of compensation. Pasquino, the Roman statue on whom satirical poems were displayed, had commented sharply on the splendid festivities organized the previous year: "The Marchese of Coccogliudo does everything he ought and owes for everything he does."[12]

---

[10] Di Giacomo, *Poveri,* 204.

[11] Griffin, "Nuove fonti," 227.

[12] Quoted by Ademollo, *Teatri,* 192. After the marchese was transferred to Naples as viceroy, Valesio noted that he had "left an undying memory of himself in Rome with

Straining at the bit while holding his feet in two uncomfortable stirrups, as it were, Scarlatti began to look across the Tiber in his dreams of escape/establishment. He had already formed a new relationship with the patron in whom he would place his greatest illusions, but in the meantime the intrigues of the corrupt Spanish ambassador had given Rome a new pope who, as a good Venetian, could never have opposed the theaters. In addition, the reappearance of the most shameless nepotism on the part of Alexander VIII Ottoboni offered Scarlatti a new mirage of patronage, destined to nourish the daydreams of his mature years.

Given his venerable age, the new pontiff well knew that he did not have much time to carry out his own projects. It was no surprise, then, that Alexander VIII began his pontificate by naming as "General of Holy Church" Prince Antonio Ottoboni, the head of his family. The accumulation of benefices at the pope's disposal then rained down on a greatnephew (another Pietro), barely twenty-two, who from one day to the next found himself cardinal, Vice-Chancellor of the Church, Legate of Avignon, and fabulously rich. So much of God's bounty—never was the expression closer to the reality—did not fall into a void. Even if another fierce pasquinade immediately declared that Peter (the pope) had robbed Peter (the Church) to adorn Peter (the nephew), for his entire life the powerful cardinal was such a spendthrift as to defeat, at least in part, the intentions of his great-uncle. The acute Président de Brosses, who knew Pietro Ottoboni almost fifty years later, described him as "dissolute, discredited, debauched, ruined, a lover of the arts, great musician."[13] In the course of a half century of gilded debauchery, Ottoboni was able to demonstrate to an astonished Europe that there did not exist financial resources sufficient to satisfy a thirst for luxury that found its greatest satisfactions in art. His was the production of the painters whom he valued (often with the right of first refusal); his were the most beautiful women (employed, it seems, by the painters in the cardinal's service as models for the portraits of madonnas and saints that adorned the walls of his splendid bedchamber); his was the inspired choice of musicians of great worth, whom he encouraged with ever-flattering commissions and collaborations. (Like Pamphilj, Ottoboni was a poet; but if it is

---

debts amounting to hundreds of thousands of *scudi*, never paid more than in part" (21 November 1701); but he added later (7 January 1702) that there had arrived news from Naples that the ex-ambassador had "taken 200,000 *pezze* with interest from the Marchese of Sesto Spinola to pay in part his debts, which amounted to more than 350,000, and had pledged his dukedom of Cordova."

13 Charles de Brosses, *Lettres familières écrites d'Italie en 1739 et 1740* (Paris: Didier, 1931), I, 489.

true that he was also a composer, certain contemporary accounts speak badly of an interminable opera attributed to him). It is possible, however, that the term "grand musicien" (which Brosses, a most refined connoisseur of the subject, applied to Ottoboni half a century later) referred to the entertainments which the cardinal put on in the Palazzo della Cancelleria beginning on Monday, 11 July 1689, in the form of a "literary academy." Valesio tells us that "the accompaniment of music and sinfonie" was entrusted, it goes without saying, to the most acclaimed musicians of Rome.

For all practical purposes, Ottoboni replaced Pamphilj in his role of patron when Don Benedetto moved to Bologna as Cardinal Legate. When that employment ceased, Pamphilj reinserted himself into Roman artistic life in a more discreet manner, not deeming it prudent to measure himself too openly against a new papal nephew by a direct confrontation that could only have wasted his notable fortune; it was a wise choice, worthy of the personage whom I have attempted to describe. Even the comparison of portraits of the two cardinals justifies, in terms of personal good looks, the greater success of the younger one (see Figs. 4 and 5 on pages 44 and 45); but a thousand nuances tell us that despite the fineness of his features, Ottoboni lacked the delicate discretion of Pamphilj, who always knew how to avoid the complex political intrigues of the period. Ottoboni, on the other hand, wallowed in them, always in search of personal advantage. In 1710, for example, when Ottoboni succeeded in being named Cardinal Protector of France by pretending to be indifferent to this new and profitable post, Saint-Simon expressed his own unfavorable opinion on the choice of a Venetian (whose country "jealously impedes its own subjects from attaching themselves to rulers or princes of any importance"), by describing Ottoboni as a "broken basket, who, with great resources, great benefices, and the highest offices of the Roman court, was despised for the disorder of his expenses, of his affairs, of his conduct, and of his morals, although with much wit, and even capable of business, and pleasant in commerce."[14]

When we have clarified that "business" is employed in the sense of diplomacy and that by "commerce" the duke means social relations, we may consider that the presentation of this important figure in our gallery of patrons is complete. You have already understood that Alessandro Scarlatti was greatly mistaken in thinking that he could rely on this "broken basket" to resolve the problems of putting his own finances in order. Meanwhile, there would have been Corelli to displace:

---

[14] Saint-Simon, *Mémoires,* VII, 444.

Fig.4 Cardinalium S. E. R. Imagines:
Portrait of Cardinal Benedetto Pamphilj
(Biblioteca Apostolca Vaticana)

Fig. 5. Cardinalium S. E. R. Imagines:
Portrait of Cardinal Pietro Ottoboni
(Biblioteca Apostolica Vaticana)

the rich, unproblematic Corelli (who possessed a magnificent picture collection—twenty-two Poussins, as against Ottoboni's one hundred—and who at his death would allow the cardinal to choose one of them in his memory). When Corelli's former patron had moved to Bologna, Ottoboni had peacefully detached Arcangelo from Pamphilj by offering him the use of an apartment in his own palace. But there was no need to put the musical skills of the two in confrontation: by comparison with Corelli, the impoverished Scarlatti was the distressing picture of the *homo sine pecunia,* the last thing that someone of Ottoboni's character would have wanted to see about him all the time.

"The Orpheus of the Princes"

But perhaps we err in identifying the Spanish ambassador to justify Alessandro's protracted absences from Naples. As I have already written, the beginning of relations with a new patron had opened a definitive page in the human and artistic experience of Scarlatti.

Ferdinando de'Medici's extraordinary qualities nourished Alessandro's hope of seeing a rebirth of the age of Christina of Sweden. To understand the degree to which such a hope could be deceptive, it is necessary to reflect on how much Scarlatti himself had changed in the few years that had passed. He was much more mature in his art, but he was worn out by life, by compromises, by mortifications. If it had been Basil Hallward in place of the obtuse Vaccaro who painted the famous portrait, who knows what transformations would have been reflected on the magic canvas!

Alessandro was no longer the headstrong young man who had sought in a relationship with the fascinating virago come to rescue him from his troubles a compensation for his need to confront a paternal authority that had failed him too soon. For him Christina had been a "father" when, dressed inelegantly but always as a queen, she punctuated even the most elevated discourses with gruff scolding and with the foul language of a common soldier; she had been a "mother" because she was a woman and in addition his female rescuer. This was the human relevance of the encounter, which significantly took place in Rome, between the young man "from the borders of Christianity" and the queen who had descended from other borders, from the cold mists of Lutheran Sweden. It is not at all surprising that in idealizing her memory the man who had already been sorely tried by life had believed that he had preserved her image intact in order to confide it to a new predestined protector (in Alessandro's utopian hopes) who would free him from the assaults of everyday life in exchange for the elevated artistic communion of which he showed himself the worthy recipient.

On 19 October 1688, the Grand Prince Ferdinando (the unusual title borne by the heir to the Grand Duchy of Tuscany) applied through his secretary to Don Sebastiano de Villa Real y Gamboa, Grand Chamberlain of the Viceroy Santo Stefano, to ask "Sig. Alessandro Scarlatti, celebrated Composer and Master of Music" to serve his Serene Highness "promptly [...] in the composition of an opera for which the first act is now being sent," with the idea of following up with the second and then the third, and so on, until the assurance that all the texts had been set to music had arrived from Naples.[15] Villa Real's response must have been particularly rapid since on November 2 a missive from Florence thanked him for having convinced Scarlatti to accept the commission, despite the fact that the composer was "involved in the obligation of three other Comedies" in preparation for the Neapolitan opera season.

Ferdinando de' Medici had an excellent reason for asking Scarlatti to serve him "promptly." He wanted a new opera by the "celebrated composer and master of music" to enrich the festivities which, at the beginning of 1689 (exactly a century after the memorable celebrations that framed the marriage of Ferdinando I and Christine of Lorraine), were to assure a splendor and solemnity appropriate to the marriage the Grand Prince had allowed to be forced on him, *obtorto collo,* for reasons of state. I have noted on another occasion the youthful excesses of Ferdinando, a refined patron of the arts and a thorn in the heart of an hypocritical father who, at the price of a moralism which he imposed harshly on himself and on his subjects, had hoped to exorcise the dissoluteness that all too clearly foretold the imminent collapse of the Medici.

Harold Acton has devoted a fine book[16] to the tragic twilight of this great family, to which I have confessed my past indebtedness. Now, however, I can draw directly on two of his manuscript sources in examining more closely that part of their tragicomic epic that concerns our subject.

In the early years of Cosimo III's reign it still seemed that the destiny of depraved ruin could be averted. The "handsome Prince," future father of our Ferdinando, traveled about the courts of Europe making "many French princesses" fall in love with him and receiving as a gift from the Sun King a splendid jewelled sword as well as an important promise of political support. Unfortunately, Cosimo chose the most shrewish of the princesses who sighed for him: Marguérite Louise, daugh-

---

[15] Quoted in Fabbri, "Scarlatti," 35.

[16] Harold Acton, *The Last Medici,* (London, 1932 [hereafter Acton, *Last Medici*]).

ter of Gaston d'Orléans and therefore a niece of Louis XIV. From the inferno that was the married life of these ill-assorted spouses were born the last three Medici: Ferdinando, Gian Gastone, and Anna Maria Luisa. The manuscript I employed[17] indicates as the principal source of discord between the couple the severely Spanish life-style of the dowager Grand Duchess (who had a strong influence over her son) against the liberal French style of her capricious daughter-in-law. Our anonymous pamphleteer is on the side of the ill-tempered Marguérite Louise, since he takes the trouble to enumerate circumstances that offer ample justification for the resentment of the young Grand Duchess and her subsequent escape to refuge in France: the doubtful influence exercised on her husband by a certain "Cosimino of his Chamber," a handsome Turkish convert to Christianity who had become "the favorite and confidant" of the Grand Duke; the usual love-affairs that produced Cosimo's low-born illegitimate daughter (prudently concealed and later forced to take religious vows); and Cosimo's indecorous sharing of the favors of a certain aristocratic bedchamber, which he finally succeded in reserving to himself by imprisoning his rival under the pretext—all too clearly symbolic—of having caught him poaching game.

The prejudice of the pamphlet's author is obvious, since he deliberately ignores the Grand Duke's attempts to avoid the scandal of a separation and indeed depicts him as happy to have gotten rid of a mad wife at the price of 40,000 *scudi* a year, an exorbitant sum for a miser. Left with such a father, the three children certainly suffered from the loss of maternal affection.

The manuscript tells us that Ferdinando was also a Prince Charming (Bernini described him as well-formed), dedicated to the sciences and the chivalrous arts. "Cheerful and always gracious in his glance and his appearance," he offered a pleasing contrast to the dark severity of the Grand Duke. Cosimo III was disliked by his subjects, who were exorbitantly taxed and were rightly concerned about the influence that the duke's increasing bigotry assured for certain of his directors of conscience.

In addition to architecture and drawing, the Grand Prince cultivated the mathematical sciences passionately and was a great sports enthusiast and participant, a generous patron of the games then in fashion (*pallacorda, pillotta,* and *pallone grosso*—the ancestors of lawn tennis—

---

[17] *Storia della nobile e reale Casa dei Medici,* doubtfully attributed to Avv. Luca Ombrosi, ms. in *I-Fr* [hereafter cited as Ombrosi (?), *Storia*], published as Luca Ombrosi, *Vita dei Medici sodomiti* (Rome: Canesi, n.d. [1965], [hereafter Ombrosi (?), *Vita*]).

Fig.6 G.D.Campiglia, M. Pitteri: Portrait of the Grand Prince Ferdinando de' Medici
("Serie Allegrini," Florence, Biblioteca Marucelliana, XVIIbis, n.36.)

soccer, and football) as well as of the "most famous players" who practiced them. Collecting pictures and other works of art did not distinguish him from the other Medici, but it was in music that Ferdinando's
talents were truly exceptional: "he played various instruments to perfection, but [he played] the harpsichord as a great master, he delighted greatly
in music and also sang with grace," the manuscript informs us, and on
another page redoubles the praise:

> This Prince possessed musical counterpoint in such a fashion
> that when he was at Venice and there had been set before him a
> most difficult harpsichord piece, he not only played it easily at sight,
> but then, without looking at it again, to the amazement of all those
> nobles, he repeated it wondrously.[18]

Trusting in the beneficent influence that a learned man of letters
and scientist could exercise on his versatile but eccentric son, Cosimo
III had the habit of avoiding direct contact with the Grand Prince by
employing Francesco Redi to communicate his directions about conduct or expenses. To the fussy habits of this exceptional intermediary
we owe the detailed transcription of these third-party conversations which
throw a ray of light on the relations between father and son. Perhaps the
Grand Duke would have had nothing to reproach in his son's love for
music if certain intemperances had not led to real scandals. Let us return for a moment to our anonymous source, which will make us understand better the contents of Redi's notes:

> Even during the minority of His Highness it had happened that,
> since as I have said above, he delighted in music, a certain Petrillo,
> a famous singer of handsome aspect and gentility, had occupied the
> first place in His Highness's favor to the shame and envy of the
> courtiers, and he enjoyed it for a long time. It happened one day
> that when [Ferdinando] was at the harpsichord he made [Petrillo]
> sing a beautiful aria, which he performed with so much grace and
> fantasy that out of pleasure His Highness embraced him, saying:
> Bravo, bravo. Petrillo, overcome and surprised by such an action
> on the part of the Prince, paying no attention to the fact that His
> Highness's tutor, the Marchese Albizi, was present, hugged the
> Prince tightly and kissed him on the face: at which the Prince, sur-
> prised, seeing the threatening Albizi, said to him: Marchese Albizi,
> what do you think? Albizi answered: He merits severe and exem-
> plary punishment. Petrillo, who was terrified, and who had found
> himself in greater intimacy with the Prince, not knowing what to

18 Ombrosi (?), *Storia,* c. 139.

do at such an unexpected occurrence, left quickly and fled from the palace and from the country [...]."[19]

Our chronicler asserts that Petrillo would certainly have obtained pardon for his imprudence by following the hypocrite Ferdinando in the comedy and throwing himself at his feet to beg for clemency. If I recall the heads cut off and displayed at the Bargello for homosexuality, the threatened "exemplary punishment," and the aggravating circumstances of *lèse majesté,* I can only express all my solidarity as a Sicilian who is never sure of his own rights in the face of authority, and who is therefore psychologically disposed to an unreasonable but unconquerable fear merely if a man who differs from him only in wearing a uniform accuses him of the most trifling traffic violation.

From time to time Redi transmitted requests from the Grand Prince; on at least two occasions these regarded the journey to Venice that in discussing the Maddaloni I have compared to today's more frequent operatic pilgrimages. By comparison with the evidence accepted by earlier scholars, Reinhard Strohm attributes greater scope to Ferdinando's travels. He suggests that it was the Grand Prince and not his brother Gian Gastone who invited Handel to Italy when they met in Hamburg. Strohm's arguments have their strongest point in a more logical reading of Mainwaring but remain literally built on air when they seek support from the "researches of Fabbri."[20] The passage Strohm cites does not establish any relation between the "journeys outside the Grand Duchy" and the engagement of "some singers, from afar off, for the service of the Comedia at Pratolino," except to clarify the fact that none of these enterprises could have been undertaken by the Grand Prince without the consent of his father.

I am agreeable to the idea that an invitation so weighted with musical consequences had been formulated by Ferdinando and not by his pathetically colorless brother, but so unaccustomed a journey throws other shadows on a picture that is already unclear. To betake oneself far from Italy—even to a city marked by unusual operatic activity—in order to hire singers destined for Italian operatic performances would have been an undertaking completely worthy of certain eccentricities of

---

[19] Ombrosi (?), *Storia,* c. 135v.

[20] The reference to Fabbri, "Scarlatti," 60, which speaks of two journeys of the Grand Prince to Venice and refers to the request for an authorization from Cosimo III to summon some singers "from afar, for the service of the Comedia in Pratolino," is inappropriate since the source does not state that Ferdinando ever left to carry out these hirings in person.

Ferdinando (and of many other Medici, with the possible exception of Cosimo III) but the unhappy situation of a child separated from his mother suggests to me that this brief visit to the north might in some way have been combined with secret opportunities of meeting Marguérite d'Orléans. Secret, insofar as I cannot think that the Grand Duke, generous only with the spies who furnished him regular and detailed accounts of the less than edifying behavior of his shrewish wife, would have furnished his rebellious son with the means for so dangerous a meeting. That some subterfuge was possible, I argue from the new material that has come to light concerning Marchese Albizzi, whom the researches of Gino Corti[21] have removed from the role of *L'ajo nell'imbarazzo* (Donizetti's "Embarassed Tutor") to transform him into the companion at the orgies of the intemperate Ferdinando, who had been incautiously entrusted to his care. In publishing certain letters (to Porpora and to Vivaldi) written by the tutor, now the impresario of the Teatro La Pergola, Corti noted that Luigi Passerini had given an "anything but flattering portrait" of Luca Casimiro degli Albizzi (1664-1745), describing him "in his youth" as "nothing other than the inseparable companion of the misdeeds and the vices of the Grand Prince Ferdinando de' Medici until the latter's death." If the dates furnished by Corti are exact, our Mentor/Minerva was in fact born a year after his Telemachus, thus exploding the harsh image depicted in the pamphlet. That Albizzi was indeed a debauché is confirmed by the following: at an advanced age, loving "passionately the lovely sex," he convinced the Accademici Immobili to name him steward of their theater in order "to have the opportunity of being constantly in the midst of female singers and dancers."[22]

To this picturesque but not completely edifying portrait the late William C. Holmes added decisive new brush-strokes with his exploration of the *mare magnum* of Albizzi's letters, now preserved in a private archive.[23] On behalf of Ferdinando De' Medici, Luca Casimiro corresponded with the Florentine resident in Naples, obtaining from him confidential information that creates a forceful counterpoint to the official

---

[21] Gino Corti, "Il Teatro La Pergola di Firenze e la stagione d'opera per il carnevale 1726-1727, *Rivista Italiana di Musicologia* XV (1980), 82-188, 182 (Hereafter Corti, "Pergola").

[22] Corti, "Pergola"; quoted by Pompeo Litta, *Famiglie celebri italiane, 1819-1883,* series II, vol. I, "Albizzi da Firenze," xxi.

[23] William C. Holmes, "Lettere inedite su Alessandro Scarlatti," in *La musica a Napoli durante il Seicento: Atti del Convegno Internazionale di Studi —Napoli, 11-14 aprile 1985* (Rome: Torre d'Orfeo, 1987 [hereafter Holmes, "Lettere"], 369-378).

correspondence of the Grand Prince, which had already been employed by Mario Fabbri. Thus we learn that Albizzi was a "confidant" of Ferdinando de' Medici, and we shall no longer be surprised that he raised no objection when Redi reported to him that Cosimo III was giving permission for Ferdinando to betake himself to Venice, on the condition that "his tutor and guardian Marchese Luca Casimiro degli Albizzi" form part of the "splendid court" that was to accompany him. We read this detail in the same anonymous manuscript, which also gives us other information on the Venetian pilgrimages of our pleasure-loving melomane:

> Great honors were given [to Ferdinando de' Medici] by the Republic, which conferred Venetian nobility on him and had him sit in the Council, and by all the nobility, who vied in public and private celebrations. Here he took into his service a handsome singer called Cecchino de' Massimi, because he had been brought up by that family, but his own family was de Castris, according to others Don Checco, and he occupied the place of Petrillo, who had been chased off, and he so insinuated himself into His Highness's soul that he became the arbiter of his court, and the Prince decided upon nothing unless it had first been approved by Checco, and in those things that His Highness resolved upon without his opinion, [Checco] became haughty and tried to outdo the Prince himself in the choice of the rarest things, as in the brilliance of the choice of pastimes such as *pillotta, pallacorda,* and *pallone,* in which he imported from afar better players to oppose the ones chosen by His Highness, and His Highness was pleased by that and vied with them at their practice-sessions.

> This familiarity gave such power to Checco that he became the arbiter of the Prince's spirit and the despot of his Court, and the first gentlemen, not only of the court, but also of the city fawned on him outwardly, but within themselves they hated him to death, while he acted the part of the superior and the great man with them, and treated his equals the same way; by which they were offended beyond measure, and not only these but also the father, the Grand Duke, knew the most secret matters that had passed between the Prince his son and his favorite, but more than any other the Princess Violante his wife complained [...]. She saw that she was little loved by her husband, and discovered the reason, so that when a great lady who found herself ill-treated by her husband came to her, she said: Madam, I sympathize with you, but you must know that under these sleeves I bear open wounds which are deeper than yours [...].[24]

[24] Ombrosi (?), *Vita,* 110-111.

The beginning of the passage that I have quoted refers to the journey which Ferdinando succeeded in extorting from his father in return for his promise to bid farewell to the unwedded state. Venice was the most appropriate place for that kind of farewell, but all the same the hypocrite Cosimo III instructed Redi to convey to the Grand Prince his paternal and unbelievable counsels: Ferdinando was to stay far away from the Carnival celebrations because these were harbingers of eternal damnation; to avoid his customary inappropriate familiarities with singers; to abstain from participating in courtly *conversazioni* and diversions; and—the best for last—to promise not to frequent the Duke of Mantua, who was completely discredited by the illicit relationships he had contracted in Venice. (Perhaps Cosimo III did not know that the circle of the duke's illicit relationships extended to all the principal cities of Italy: in Naples, Confuorto noted that "since this prince was very libidinous and intemperate," he "had brought for his sensual appetites the singer Nina Scarano, with whom he slept that night, having done the same the previous night with Giulietta, another singer."[25] As you see, the duke knew exactly where go in order to contract his liasons). One might ask if the Grand Duke had understood that his son did not want to make a pilgrimage to the shrine of St. Francis at La Verna or to the Holy House of Loreto. To warn children against certain kinds of gluttony is almost the same as forcing them to indigestion, but Cosimo III was certainly not an intelligent educator. Redi tells us clearly that the Grand Duke had sent his son these counsels because his conscience demanded the assurance that the prince attend to his own conscience, in Venice and especially during Carnival. Any comment is superfluous, but that such a sermon should come from a descendant of Lorenzo the Magnificent can only demonstrate how much the Medici had changed for the worse before their inglorious sunset.

As if the results of the first voyage had not been sufficient, there would be another. Let us re-open the chronicle:

> His Highness wished to make another trip to Venice, one that was indeed fatal for him, since he was in love with a beautiful and noble Lady, who was loved as well by the Duke of Mantua; because the latter was also in Venice, there arose extraordinary anger and jealousy, and enormous disturbances were about to follow under other pretexts; but since His Highness had brought valorous men with him, and in addition [there were] countless of his subjects who lived in that city, as well as the entourages of the most notable person-

25 Confuorto I, 149.

ages who comprised that Most Serene Republic, it suited Gonzaga to clear out of Venice and return to Mantua so as not to fall into some uncommon misfortune.

His Highness, who remained winner and master of the field, redoubled his efforts with the said lady, who showed herself averse to any intimacy with the prince, and one evening His Highness asked her how much longer she wished to make the heir of Tuscany suffer: to which she replied: Signor Prince, my family recognizes endless obligations to the house of Medici, nor will I permit a Prince of your rank to be betrayed by me; know then that I am in such a state that satisfying you will be condemning you to suffer forever. Do not let appearances deceive you; believe one who loves you as much and more than herself.

The Prince thought it was a crafty ploy, and [not] the result of sincerity, as in fact it was, therefore he answered: I know where this argument comes from; I am not as deformed as Gonzaga, and I have riches equal and superior to his, and such a false answer depends on the fact that Gonzaga is the favored one, and Medici the scorned one. She answered: Signor Prince, since you have believed that my sincere expressions are false, take from me what pleases you, but do not then complain of me because I have spoken to you with such affection and sincerity. Behold the rash prince in Pandora's box: he slaked his thirst on this poison, which led him to his tomb, as I shall recount. He left to return to Florence and brought with him together with his misfortunes a pretty singer called la Bambagia [...].[26]

If I have invoked the name of Sade in discussing Giorgina, for Ferdinando's unfortunate sexual conversion, I should refer to Thomas Mann's celebrated reworking of Nietzsche's adventure in the bordello at Cologne "Death in Venice."

The material regarding Ferdinando de' Medici's character and his reactions to his father's repression have given his portrait dimensions that unbalance the equilibrium I had hoped to maintain for this gallery of patrons. However, his character deserved to be presented without leniency and in all the complexity that emerges from the documents I have quoted. My readers can evaluate the enormity of the blunder that induced Alessandro Scarlatti to give a blind and sometimes indiscreet trust to the generosity of the Grand Prince, turning to him with the absurd certainty of seeing all the problems that assailed him "on his occa-

[26] Ombrosi (?), *Vita,* 112-113.

sions of greatest need" magically resolved. Ottoboni and Ferdinando will give the *coup de grâce* to Alessandro's last illusions and make him feel, at the age of forty-eight, that "desire for a tranquil and respected old age," which Malcolm Boyd could not accept. Alesssandro's mature industry in Naples and his final move to Rome have little in common with the feverish activity that characterized his youthful years. The unequivocal testimonies to the exceptional character of Alessandro's reputation fostered the rosy hypothesis of his final deliverance from that "heavy weight of a numerous family," which had so heavily conditioned the freedom of his human choices, if not his artistic ones.

But the discussion of our patrons has led me too far; I turn back, again directing my interest to our hero's difficulties in coming to grips with his not-always-commendable relatives.

IV

...a falling virtù

I have already had occasion to declare that the identification of *la Scarlati* (Anna Maria, who we know was a singer, or Melchiorra, as Walker would have it)[1] is not worth all the ink it has caused to flow,[2] since placing the cross of a bad reputation on the shoulders of the older sister would not make the younger one a saint. Too many indications identify Anna Maria with the Roman scandal; it is the Neapolitan outrage that leaves a small margin of doubt, but even after accepting the possibility that Melchiorra sang in the opera season preceding the scandal-laden one, I find it hard to believe that she was *la Scarlati.* Let us see why.

The cast printed on the libretti of the operas performed in 1684 does not include any singer of this name, nor does a *Scarlati* figure among the lists of musicians and singers from the documents discovered and published by Prota Giurleo. In these we find instead a *Catherina Scarano* and an *Agata Carano*, family names which might sound similar to that of Alessandro, who was the general director of these engagements. *Agata Carano* (sic), "called La Reginella," continued to sing in Palermo between 1696 and 1702[3] in operas by Gasparini and Alessandro Scarlatti. This excludes the possibility of identifying Carano with Anna Maria, who married the rich Nicola Barbapiccola in 1699 and no longer trod the boards. Catherina Scarano, instead, was the eager "Nina Scarano" whom Confuorto shows us as intent on satiating the "sensual appetites" of the Duke of Mantua, fresh from a happy night with Giulietta.[4] Can we suppose that she was *la Scarlati?* In this case, prostitution for money would be more than proven. This is only a new hypothesis, which finds documentary confirmation, however, when we apply the inductive methods recently instituted in government inquiries into illegal profits

.

[1] Frank Walker, "A Libel on Anna Maria. Additional Notes," in Edward J. Dent, *Alessandro Scarlatti* (London: Arnold, 1960 [hereafter Dent, *Scarlatti,* and Walker,Additional"]), 239-241.

[2] *Scarlatti*, ERI, 78.

[3] Information from my compilation of musical activities in Palermo.

[4] Confuorto, I, 149.

On the basis of Anna Maria's single documented appearence onstage in public (the second female lead in the *Ratto delle Sabine* of Pier Simone Agostini, Venice, 1680[5]), the dimensions of her official career would certainly not justify the accumulation of the considerable fortune that our singer was not loath to detail in the documents of a second marriage which, by uniting her to a well-off ship-owner (like a mini-Onassis), signalled for her the achievement of respectability. It is the more than suspect accumulation of cash, works of art, furniture, and jewels, which the singer declares to be "her own goods and money [...] acquired by her own *virtù*"[6] that identifies Anna Maria as *la Scarlati.* The squalid Melchiorra and her scoundrel of a husband (a certain Nicola Pagano—the name still offends me—a double bass player, an impresario almost certainly acting as a front man, and a genuine Valzacchi out of *Rosenkavalier)* never resorted to legal or notarial documents except to immortalize their image as unscrupulous starving jackals. We have already mentioned the marriage of this enterprising couple: it was celebrated 5 May 1688 in the same Neapolitan parish church in which three years earlier the importance of the personages participating in Domenico Scarlatti's baptism had flustered the scribe. This time his pen ran easily since no one could be intimidated by the names of the three poor plebeians who served as witnesses: first among these, in every sense, was Alessandro Scarlatti.

Quite a different picture emerges from the documentation concerning the second marriage of Anna Maria. On 9 February 1699—and therefore at a good thirty-eight years of age—the ex-singer and rich widow joined her fate to that of a widower: Nicola Barbapiccola, owner of one of the galleys of the Royal Neapolitan Squadron, the *San Giuseppe.* In the prematrimonial contract discovered by Prota Giurleo, Anna Maria was coyly evasive, guided by the double desire of taking ten years off her age and of erasing a part of her own life, making only unavoidable references to her past. Certain facts must have been altered in order to make the time-sequence add up: even the upright Alessandro had to confirm that her preceding marriage with Paolo Massonio Astrolusco had been celebrated fourteen years before in the Roman church of Sant'Andrea delle Fratte. If Massonio was the clergyman (and this I would deduce from the lawsuit pending in the Camera Apostolica for

---

[5] Wotquenne, 113.

[6] *Capitoli matrimoniali tra Anna Maria Scarlatti e Nicola Barbapiccola* (doc. I) in Ulisse Prota Giurleo, "Notizie intorno ad Anna Maria Scarlatti (1661-1703)," *Archivi* XXVII (1960), nn. 3-4 ([hereafter Prota Giurleo, "Anna Maria"]).

the thousand *scudi* set up as a dowry but never paid), the marriage had been celebrated exactly twenty years before. Since there were the unfortunate anagraphical falsehoods to cover up, Anna Maria's poor brother also had to confirm the false wedding date: no one would have believed that the widow about to remarry had contracted her first marriage at the age of nine! The reader of these documents must therefore navigate this stormy sea of declarations in such a manner as to distinguish useful information from that which is less reliable. For the purposes of our story it is not worth much to know that Don Paolo Massonio was "tall, slender, of red and white complexion, red hair, black eyes"[7] and that he went off to die "in Hungary, in the place called the Danube,"[8] especially since the dates of his departure to follow the Imperial army and of his later death remain doubtful because they are calculated with reference to the uncertain date of his marriage. It is rather the marriage-articles drawn up with Barbapiccola that are important, inasmuch as they facilitate researches into Anna Maria's fortune, showing that she was a kind of goose with the golden eggs, which the Scarlattis could not easily give up.

> The said Signora Anna Maria, providing her own dowry, promises to give and assign as dowry to the said Signor Nicola ten thousand ducats in this manner, that is, two thousand ducats in cash free and clear, which the said Sig. Nicola declares and acknowledges that he has received and holds in so many silver pieces, another four thousand ducats as the price and value of so many goods, furniture, and household furnishings, gold, worked silver, and jewels, which the said Sig. Nicola also declares and acknowledges to have received and to hold from the said Signora Anna Maria. For the remaining four thousand ducats, to complete the said dowry, when the said marriage will be contracted, the Signora Anna Maria cedes and assigns to him a like sum owed to the said Signora Anna Maria by the magnifico Cristoforo Schor, architect of the Royal Palace, for an equal sum lent to him by this Signora Anna Maria in the month of August of the past year 1698, which four thousand ducats the said magnifico Cristoforo promised and bound himself to pay and restore to her within a year with an interest of 240 ducats, at the rate of six per cent, in conformity with a certified loan document drawn up by the notary Pietro Angelo Volpe of Naples. And the Signora Anna Maria, to augment her said dowry, also cedes and assigns to the said Sig. Nicola, her future husband, the thousand scudi of capital in Roman coinage together with several annuities

---

[7] Prota Giurleo, "Anna Maria," 355.
[8] Prota Giurleo, "Palermitano," 9.

of due four-monthly installments depending on the inheritance of
the late Paolo Massonio, the same thousand scudi that the said late
Paolo Massonio endowed this said Signora Anna Maria with as
appears from legal documents promulgated in the sublime city of
Rome, for which there is a lawsuit pending in the Reverenda Camera Apostolica. When Sig. Nicola will have received the dowry-
goods in the manner *ut supra,* he promises to hold, guard, and preserve them well and diligently and to safeguard them above all and
any of his goods and lands present and future, and to restore them
and to pay to the said Signora Anna Maria and to the children to be
born of the present marriage, in case of the dissolution of the present
marriage through the death (which God forbid) of either of these
future spouses and in any other case, place, and event of the restitution and assurance of the said dowry *juxta* the use and custom of
this City of Naples, commonly called 'in the old-fashioned way.'
With the exception however and expressly reserved to the said Signora Anna Maria the power and faculty to will and dispose of all
her dowry, the custom of the said City of Naples notwithstanding,
since these are her own goods and the money of this Signora Anna
Maria acquired by her own *virtù,* etc."[9]

If you have had the patience to read it attentively, the document that I have just quoted offers keys that open closets crammed
with skeletons.

Above all, in exactly twenty years of "virtù" Anna Maria had
been able to put together a fortune equivalent to what her famous brother
could have accumulated only by setting aside the entire earnings of an
equal number of his seasonal engagements,[10] without touching them even
to alleviate "the heavy weight of a numerous family."[11] Only a year
earlier, Anna Maria had at her disposal a good six thousand *scudi* in
cash; that she had lent four thousand to a stage designer only confirms
the proverb that the devil's wheat turns into chaff. There emerges clearly,
however, from this detail a sort of moral obligation committing the singer
to support with her own "ill-gotten gains" the ruinous speculations of
someone who was endeavoring to maintain a "façade" of theatrical activities. But this financing of activities in which Alessandro and Francesco
were already involved and which would soon provide bread for other
members of the "numerous family" offers a new justification for the

---

[9] *Capitoli matrimoniali* (cf. n. 6).

[10] Prota Giurleo, "Breve Storia," 37. He received a payment of five hundred *scudi* on
the occasion of his first documented Neapolitan engagement.

[11] Prota Giurleo, "Breve Storia," 42. Later accounts of his enterprises assign to him
three hundred ducats.

humiliating acquiescence of the penniless patriarch in such legal false-hoods. Perhaps he was persuaded that he had finally eliminated the cause of these scandals by a respectable marriage that miraculously erased the stains cast on the family honor by the "virtù" of Anna Maria.

The poor singer—we will soon see why I refer to a woman whose riches have shocked me as "poor"—showed good taste in painting. The list of her "furnishings" includes some pictures which, if they were au-thentic, must have been worth a good deal more than the few hundred ducats awarded them in an estimate that lumps them together with other "household furniture" and with "gold, worked silver, and jewels," for a total value of four thousand ducats.[12] This dry enumeration is trans-formed into the catalogue of a miniature museum in which we find, with justifiable surprise, a *Saint John* of Caravaggio, a *Saint Catherine* of Sassoferrato, two Salvator Rosas, an *Erminia and Tancred* by an uni-dentified painter, a Madonna of Carlo Maratta, and—a striking excep-tion in the midst of so many sacred subjects—the portrait of a noble-woman considered a real model of non-conformism: "la Mazzarini":[13] Maria Mancini, the niece of Cardinal Mazarin, whose pitiless uncle had married her off, almost by force, to the Constable Colonna to prevent her from crowning a sensational flirtation with the young Louis XIV by matrimony. I was not mistaken in speaking of a veritable spiderweb of relationships, capable of linking characters of our story who are only seemingly distant from each other in time and space. Maria Mancini Colonna's behavior anticipates that of Marguérite Louise d'Orléans by a flight from the conjugal roof for fear of being poisoned. Her frighten-ing husband is the lively Constable whom we have seen intent on pro-tecting Alessandro and offering expensive operatic trifles to his Spanish daughter-in-law after he had imported his masked lover to Naples and had soothed his conscience by prostrating himself before the altar of a sumptuous church.

We have already commented on the paradoxical fate of a Giorgina who was rewarded by fortune only at the height of her notoriety. In the same years that saw Anna Maria Scarlatti enter the respectability of her second marriage, Giorgina found herself thrust to the pinnacle of Nea-politan society by her position as the favorite of a viceroy—Medina Coeli—who was capable of exiling an aristocrat guilty only of having looked too attentively at the "the vicereine's lady of honor," and who was jealous of the his lover's vocal talents.

---

[12] *Capitoli matrimoniali.*
[13] Prota Giurleo, "Anna Maria," 355.

Anna Maria's fate is similar to that of the heroine of a moralizing fable: rich and happy in her libertinage, she did not taste for long the joys of domestic life that she had acquired too late. When she had given birth to two children she began to waste away:

> Being seriously ill with a sickness that had continued for many months, from which she later died, Signora Anna Maria Scarlatti, at the instigation of Nicola Pagano and his wife Melchiorra Scarlatti, under the pretext of giving her a change of air, was induced to transfer herself to the house of the said couple at the Largo del Castello, bringing with her much furniture and jewels of notable value, belonging to the magnifico Don Nicola Barbapiccola, where she dwelt about three months, supported, her expenses paid, and looked after by her husband, and, despite many suggestions made to her both by the said couple and by other Relatives of hers, that she should dispose insofar as she could of her dowry to their benefit, but also of many goods of her husband, as 'extra-dowry' goods, it was not possible for them to achieve that aim, for which she had been taken away from her husband's house, whence, after the said Pagano had consumed and sold whatever she brought from her own house, finally he brought her back to her husband's house, where on 13 October 1703 of her own free will she made her testament, in which, after her death, she named Nicola Barbapiccola as having the usufruct of all the goods of her dowry (except for some legacies of furniture and sacred objects), with the obligation, however, of nourishing and supporting those children of hers in his guardianship, and she named as her general and particular heirs her children Carlo and Giuseppina, and if both of them died, their Father would inherit, and if he predeceased them, the collateral Relatives of her husband would inherit half of the said inheritance, and the brothers and sister of their mother and their heirs and successors the rest; whence since the relatives of Anna Maria saw that their scheme had failed, after a few days they induced the said Anna Maria, who was almost dying, to move to the house of Orsola Breglia, a midwife, in the street of the Calzettari, behind the church of San Giuseppe, with the excuse of better treatment and greater care of her person, where, twenty-three days after the first will, while Anna Maria was in continual pain, bereft of all human help and attended only by Religious, out of her senses, these same relatives of hers had her make another will with a notary brought there by night, in which she named her children as her heirs in all her dower goods, except for many obligations, restrictions, entails, and legacies to the benefit of her Relatives, both in goods and in money, which absorbed much more than the tenth part of the said dowry along with many other irregularities, disproportionalities, and outrages

which one reads there, to the point of leaving her brother Alessandro
as co-guardian, which by law cannot be done by a mother. By
virtue of which, with neither the participation nor the consent of
her wards, on their behalf the preliminary summons of the Great
Court of the Vicariate was sent off, which is very unfavorable and
damaging to the said wards, since no account can be taken of it, all
the more since previously another testament much more favorable
to them had been made. For this reason they request the Holy Royal
Council to defer to them the inheritance of their mother by preserving the form of the previous testament, and to that end not only remove the inhibition made by the Vicariate at the request of Alessandro
Scarlatti who claims to be co-guardian, but also of the personal
good of their Father, by order of the same Holy Royal Council."[14]

What a set! And yet the document is silent about the most dis-
gusting circumstance: these parasites were robbing the poor dying woman
just at the time when a generous undertaking by Nicola Barbapiccola
had made it possible to present an opera season in which the talents of at
least three Scarlattis found employment: Domenico (his debut as an opera composer), Tommaso (tenor), and Giuseppe (scene designer). If you
cast your pearls before swine ...

In confirmation of what I have already said about his role, in
this case most unpleasant, of *paterfamilias,* Alessandro (who was employed elsewhere) was chosen to represent the interests of this Neapolitan rabble. The directives which he sent to an attorney more than once
afflicted the unfortunate Barbapiccola, who suffered the sequestration
not only of his dead wife's fortune but of his own as well. The negotiations dragged on, but finally the hungry beasts had to content themselves with the offal that their rich victim threw them in order to shut
them up. Although Anna Maria had written clearly in her dower-acts
that she remained free to dispose of her own goods, "the custom of the
City of Naples notwithstanding," the ruling prevailed that allowed a testatrix the freedom to dispose of no more than a tenth of her fortune that
was set up as a dowry. By a grotesquely comic formula— "with the
opinion of their common Lawyers, and to avoid the hatreds and rancors
that lawsuits customarily bring, especially between relatives"—the parties reached an agreement whereby Barbapiccola made a pretense of
acceding to the substance of the testament that had been extorted, but
succeeded in obtaining an extremely low estimate for the furniture and
furnishings (the Caravaggio was valued at barely 20 ducats, and a lot

---

[14] Appeal presented by Nicola Barbapiccola to the S. R. Consiglio, quoted in Prota
Giurleo, "Anna Maria," 356-357.

comprising the Sassoferrato, a harpsichord, and a harp had a similar valuation). He did not mention the 2000 *scudi* he had received in silver, and he calmly deducted from the available sum the 50 ducats due for the five hundred masses that the dead woman had wished to be celebrated for her soul. The tenth part was calculated at 443 ducats (4000 owed by Schor, plus 437/1/10, "the price of the dower furniture") from which the previous 50 were deducted. Thus there remained 393 ducats and some small change, for which the clever Barbapiccola offered an absolute pre-emption of the Schor debt, which in the meantime had been reduced "with great effort" by a thousand *scudi*. Other controversies were smoothed out by leaving to Barbapiccola the dower jewels, valued at barely 172 ducats. The expenses for medical care were considered excessive (they were claimed by Pagano, although Anna Maria's husband had provided amply for his wife's care), and Barbapiccola even refused to pay for the funeral of the poor woman dragged "extra domum," while he consigned to the crowd of beggars twelve ducats, but only to reimburse their friend Andrea Binda for the "expenses spent in the said lawsuit."

I have called Barbapiccola clever, but in truth he was not sufficiently so. After a year and a half the Scarlatti gang, not trusting Schor's solvency "since he was not only a foreigner but because he possessed no property of any sort in this city," petitioned the viceroy (and he agreed, alas) that both the architect and Barbapiccola should be constrained to pay off the balance under threat of prison. Naturally, it was Barbapiccola who paid. Eleven years later he was still waiting to be repaid, and thus Prota Giurleo had every reason to suppose that the Roman architect had carried his debt to the grave.

The presence of a mysterious legacy, apparently annulled by the final settlement, throws a pathetic shadow on both of Anna Maria's testaments: "Item she leaves to the Rev. Father Fra Vincenzo Salvador of the Order of Preachers [Dominicans], resident in the Convent of the Rosary of the Palace, two hundred ducats once and for all, so that he may carry out what she has communicated to him verbally for the easing of her conscience, without the said Father Fra Vincenzo being held to give account of it at any future time either to her said heirs, or to the Tribunal of the Fabbrica or any other Tribunal, which aforesaid two hundred ducats her said heirs may give him in four payments, or at the most in six, so that the said Father Fra Vincenzo may distribute them to the persons entrusted to him verbally, provided that it not exceed the limit of a year and a half ..."[15]

---

[15] First testament (document II) in Prota Giurleo, "Anna Maria," Appendix, 363.

And in the other legacy extorted from her. "Item the magnifica Anna Maria testatrix wills, orders and expressly commands that immediately following her death, there must be paid to the very Rev. Fra Vincenzo [...] of the Dominican Order, her confessor in the venerable church of the Most Holy Rosary of the Palace, one hundred eighty-nine ducats in cash one time only, for the said Father Confessor to give them to the person who was spoken of and named *ad aures* by the said testatrix to the said Father Confessor for fulfilling certain scruples that she had, and for the quiet of her soul [...]."[16]

The attempt to reduce the "weights" in the second testament is evident; this is repeated in the drastic reduction of the masses for her soul, provided for to the number of a thousand in the first testament. The mysterious legacy indicates but does not clarify further misfortunes in the singer's life: an illegitimate child, a ruined family, a victim of an abuse of power from higher up? Another provision of the second will shows another weakness, this time entirely feminine, on the part of the dying woman. Anna Maria declares that she "owns as extra-dotal possessions" certain objects—"a little cross of diamonds, a wedding dress of cloth of silver, a diamond jewel, a pair of diamond tassels and two bunches of chains of massy gold and another dress of green brocade, that is, petticoat and manteau"—and she "orders and commands that immediately after her death all the aforesaid jewels, chains, and garments must be sold [...] and the price of them must be [...] deposited in a public bank, here in Naples, from which it cannot be removed in any manner and for any reason whatever, but [...] employed for the purchase of an equal number of annuities intested to the said Carlo and Giuseppa Barbapiccola her blessed minor children [...].[17]

It is this detail that seems to show a functioning ability to understand and to will legally that is omitted from Barbapiccola's account. Here it is not the Paganos or the Scarlattis who advance their own interests; it is the dying woman herself who demands that certain of her feminine ornaments should not pass on to embellish a future Signora Barbapiccola. Anna Maria knew her husband well: he had married her only seven months after he had been widowed, and in fact he did contract a third marriage in 1705.

However, the comparison between the two testaments offers us an opportunity for investigation, since the distribution of the legacies in the extorted will reflects an hierarchic order accepted by Anna Maria's family.

---

[16] Second testament (document III) in Prota Giurleo, "Anna Maria," 365-366.
[17] Prota Giurleo, "Anna Maria," 367.

In the first testament monetary legacies to Anna Maria's relatives are excluded; her sister Melchiorra inherits only a "Persiana in
Prince-colored brocade as a memento," while the nieces, mother, and
sister of Barbapiccola are significantly favored. The second testament
emphasizes the removal of "many things" from the fortune set up as a
dowry, even if it returns to employing the formula "acquired by her own
virtù" which is particularly grating given the circumstances and the previous use made of it. There is however a contrast between recourse to
the right of transgressing Neapolitan custom and the declared intention
to conform to it, and in that I read a further demonstration of a capacity
to understand and to will: perhaps Anna Maria realized the breach of trust
that was taking place and wished to leave her husband and her children the
possibility of vindicating their rights in full.

Let us now seek to describe the booty that the Scarlatti clan, led
by that terrible namesake of mine, sought to extract from the tragedy which
deprived them of an economic support that they had enjoyed for too long.

Alessandro had the lion's share, in implicit recognition of his
supremacy: eighty ducats in cash and "a silver table-service of many
pieces with its case 'alla forestiera.'" Francesco also received preferen-
tial treatment: 50 ducats in cash. Melchiorra, Tommaso, and Giuseppe
were to receive 25 ducats each, and the same went to Andrea Binda (the
violinist who, as a friend of the Scarlattis, assumed the prepayment of
the expenses of the lawsuit with Barbapiccola). Other smaller legacies
went to Anna de Santis (9 ducats) and to "Mattia her Comare [godmother
or crony], daughter of Comare Tedesca" (6 ducats). There is a notable
legacy of 40 ducats to the "magnifica Ursola Breglia," the midwife who,
in collusion with the Paganos, had opened her house to the dying woman.

As regards the other legacies, the "table service" destined for
Alessandro (which was to have gone to Anna Maria's mother-in-law) is
listed together with the legacies in cash, while the objects follow separately.

We find assigned again to Melchiorra "a brocade dress in Per-
sian style" and to a certain Angela Senato the same "black dress of dam-
ask with silver" intended for her in the first testament, here accompanied by "a mattress stuffed with wool, in sign of gratitude." For Christina Scarlatti, Alessandro's daughter, there is "a fine sheet with lace and
a Flemish missal as a token of gratitude"; for Antonia Carbone (wife of
Tommaso) "a chamber robe of *canna secca* brocade"; for Francesco "a
bedcover embroidered with silk and a mattress stuffed with wool."

Since the legacies in cash amount to 285 ducats, it is credible
that they were respected when Barbapiccola, blackmailed by the threat
of imprisonment, paid off the debt that had not been honored by Schor;

there were thus another 108 ducats to divide, in compensation for the non-consignment of the intended objects. I would not like to have been present at the division, all the more so since at the end of the second testament there were other dispositions regarding further destinations of objects. One of Nicola Barbapiccola's nieces re-emerges to be assigned the "dress of green cloth adorned with white taffeta" formerly reserved for her sister, who was now left high and dry; there is a "bonnet with silver and gold ribbon" for Flaminia and Cristina Scarlatti (Alessandro's daughters) as well as for Melchiorra; finally there is "a fan with two sticks of silver ribbon" for Donna Giuseppa Ferrera, wife of a certain Filippo Ferrera. What induced Anna Maria to direct Binda to sell her "Giamberlucco di Scarlatto" ("scarlet hooded Turkish coat"), assigning the proceeds to pay as many masses as could be celebrated at ten *grana* apiece: was the coat perhaps a trophy of prostitution, or a shameful homage to "virtù" from a fortunate admirer, or did the dying woman feel the same anxiety that she expressed about her other "galanteries"?

In any case, we now know a good deal more about this charming family.

The force of habit induced by those same worshipful accounts of Alessandro that I am attempting to combat has led me to describe him as a man of great integrity, but it seems to me that the facts I have just recounted compromise at least the adjective. Playing at being the "capo," he found himself involved in pitiless machinations, based on endless contradictions. The passive Arabo-Sicilian component of his background did the rest: faced with the choice between breaking every tie with unworthy relatives or pretending ignorance in order to salvage the prestige that had made him the unquestioned leader of his family circle, the Dorian-Scarlattino of the rough exterior but essentially fragile character collapsed into the easier alternative.

Opportunism? Perhaps, but not only that: if we consider the overall image of the clan that the documents transmit, the internal distribution of the specific importance of the individuals is above criticism. Even the Paganos, who had stirred up the whole mess, limited themselves to depriving the dying woman only of what she had brought to their house; in the division of the official proceeds of their despicable behavior they remained within the hierarchy that the sums of the bequests scrupulously respected. In the testament arising from the lies of the two Paganos, Nicola was not even named; nor were the nephews of Anna Maria, including Pietro and Domenico, who were already visible on the miniature stage of the artistic affairs of the family workshop.

A workshop that was sometimes obscure, but one in a constant cycle of production: this is what his family had become for Alessandro, an individual betrayed by his own inclination to the rectitude of a suffering (here employed also in the sense of "putting up with") but unrenouncible vocation to command.

In life, as in the everyday business of music, this concealment behind the outward appearances of a façade conformed to the times. Without the weight of his family, perhaps Alessandro Scarlatti would have lived very differently, far from everything that could influence his choices as an artist of the most refined elitism. His experiences in Rome had shown him the musician that he might have been: if in truth he was in contact with the aged Carissimi, that simple man revered by everyone must have suggested to him a goal to reach, in artistic success if not in life (Carissimi's life was too austere for a fiery Sicilian in full adolescent development). But it was Corelli above all who incarnated, in his leisurely independence, in the thrifty administration of his own artistic talents, in the ease of his relations with patrons from whom he obtained everything without asking for anything, the type of musician which Alessandro would have liked to be. Without the probity of artistic judgement that, despite the poison spread by Dotti in the satire of which we will speak, remains the happiest aspect of Scarlatti, envy would have ruined his relationship with Corelli beyond repair.

I do not believe that Alessandro was untruthful when he declared to Geminiani that he found nothing really exceptional in the compositions of Corelli. In any case, it was a question of instrumental music, which Scarlatti always seemed to consider a minor genre, and the sonorous perfection of Corelli's concerti and sonatas rested more on the successful employment of the strings than on that elegance of harmonic invention that Scarlatti put at the summit of his own artistic interests. Alessandro never concealed the profound impression he had received from hearing the effects that Corelli could obtain from instrumentalists who were extraordinarily disciplined and trained to work together in the execution of his concerti. Even in Naples, on an occasion when Alessandro could have inflicted a solemn mortification on his rival, his behavior towards his admired and beloved colleague was affectionately deferential. We shall soon have occasion to take up again the question of Alessandro's relationships with the best musicians of his time; for the moment, let us return to the family, or more exactly, the workshop.

The sensationalism that had marked the first stages of Alessandro's career, the protection of Christina of Sweden, of Benedetto Pamphilj and of the Maddaloni, had aroused an interest in him that soon extended far enough to make Scarlatti regret that he could not execute better the desires of distant patrons. His correspondence with Ferdinando de' Medici shows us in detail the means by which he delivered the operas that had been commissioned by a patron whose own level of specific competence guaranteed Alessandro's absolute respect for Ferdinando's intentions. In sending the Grand Prince the third act of *Arminio,* the composer got off on the right foot by having "the boldness to commend to the special high Protection and most proficient understanding" of his patron "the customary diligence of his Virtuosi," so that they should respect the indications of the composer and should conform "their performance of the Arias" to the "idea" that had given birth to them," "blindly and with all resignation, to the pure taste"[18] of the commissioner. In such conditions it is significant that Scarlatti declared that he knew that the greatest glory that he could ever hope for was that of conforming to the preferences of a patron who was endowed with such exceptional capacities of judgment and detailed advice:

> Your Royal Highness who, as you are capable, also knows how to fix beforehand most appropriate rules for a better result than I know how to do myself, since I can be deceived by a passion for my own creation and by the weak perception of what works better for the ear and the understanding.[19]

If this was Scarlatti's behavior under the best possible conditions, imagine what aesthetic compromises he must have been disposed to when requests for his music came to him from peripheral places that the speech of the time would have called, "not the most principal." Above all, the problems connected with the maintenance of a family whose members were predominantly active in the musical or theatrical fields must have suggested to Alessandro that he profit from that circumstance by assuming a tacit sponsorship of enterprises linked with his family and covered by a prudent anonymity: enterprises acceptable to—and on at least two occasions certainly accepted by—theatrical ventures and audiences who were resigned almost in advance to doing without the effective, personal, and exclusive contribution of the fashionable musician whom all Italy was celebrating.

We have said that the diffusion in every geographical direction of operas originally composed for Rome or Naples should be related to the notoriety of the "Scarlattino," to his "bag full of arias" and—there is

---

[18] Letter of Alessandro Scarlatti to Ferdinando de' Medici, Rome, 28 July: in Fabbri, "Scarlatti," 51-52.

[19] Fabbri, "Scarlatti," 52.

nothing new under the sun—to the halo of scandal that had surrounded
the first stages of his career. If in Munich people could be interested in
learning that in far-off Naples a powerful noblewoman had obtained the
liberation of two prostitutes from the Spanish viceroy, it shows that
modern glossy magazines did not invent anything. Opera did not arouse
curiosity only because of its artistic merits, but also for the unmistakably ambiguous fascination which in the mentality of the period was
tied to an anticipation of "la dolce vita," of a Baroque demi-monde.
While awaiting a direct experience of opera (not always likely), the plea-
sure-lovers of the provinces—and Munich was a province by comparison with Naples or Venice, especially in their roles as capitals of opera—fantasized salaciously, hoping that some fine day complacent impresarios and open-minded singers would arrive in flesh and blood.

But perhaps the curiosity of the Bavarians was more justifiably
aroused: I am thinking of a visit of the twenty-one-year old Alessandro
to Munich and Vienna which Eva Badura-Skoda considers highly probable.[20] In any case, what I have written about the German cities is not
valid for Vienna. Specific political reasons impelled an emperor who
called himself "Roman" to patronize the theatrical genre that fashionable educated tradition continued to consider derived from classsical
tragedy. In the striking spread of Italian opera throughout Europe the
gilded emigration of poets and musicians toward Vienna is a special
case, and it is indeed strange that Alessandro's success did not result in a
permanent transfer to the Habsburg capital. His relations with Vienna
must truly have been born under an evil star: proof of this is the failed
performance of *Giunio Bruto o vero la Caduta dei Tarquini,* the splendid opera that Cardinal Albani had ordered on behalf of Joseph I from
Carlo Francesco Cesarini, Antonio Caldara, and Alessandro Scarlatti for
the music (an act apiece); and Filippo Juvarra for the sets. The recipient
of this artistic effort by a real consortium of talents was unable to enjoy
its results, inasmuch as, "unable to control his zeal, given over to pleasure," he died of smallpox (this was the official version: "but it was
believed, that the strain brought on his health by his excesses greatly
assisted this illness in taking away his life").[21] We shall find other members of the Scarlatti clan in Vienna, but before following their adventurous pilgrimages let us return to Sicily for a moment.

---

[20] Eva Badura-Skoda, "Ein Aufenthalt Alessandro Scarlattis in Wien im Oktober
1681," *Die Musikforschung* XXVII, 1974, 204.

[21] Ludovico Antonio Muratori, *Annali d'Italia dal principio dell'Era volgare sino
all'anno MDCCLXIX* (Naples: Alfano, 1758 [hereafter Muratori, *Annali])* XVI, 120.

V

"... in Palermo, with the universal indulgence of all the Virtuosi and Composers of Music..."

According to the documents known to me, Alessandro Scarlatti never set foot in Sicily after his youthful exodus: all those who have indulged their imaginations by stating that he was present at performances of his operas or at one of the first oratorios he composed[1] have been fantasizing.

As had previously occurred in Naples, in Sicily it was a nobleman who introduced the music of the deserter, and certain coincidences are striking: once again the opera chosen is *Gli equivoci nel sembiante,* and the nobleman is a relative of the Maddaloni who had come to settle in the Sicilian fiefs that he had inherited from the Branciforte. (Almost all of them had belonged to Francesco Branciforte e Barresi, the husband of Donna Giovanna d'Austria, of whom we shall speak presently.)

It is symptomatic that the music of Alessandro Scarlatti reached his native land under the banner of decentralization, of bringing art out of political capitals into the hinterland. This was not the savage decentralization to which certain demagogues of our own day have entrusted the destruction of serious initiation into the music of the "poor blacks" to whom certain politicians make great efforts to sell trinkets. On the contrary, Don Carlo Carafa, Prince of Butera, was an unusual feudal aristocrat, balanced, so to speak, between past and future. His decision to withdraw from the general urbanization of the aristocracy in Palermo or in the second capital at Messina, and to install himself in one of his several baronial palaces (at Mazzarino) belongs to traditions that could be considered remote by the end of the seventeenth century. The addition of a theater to his chosen palace conforms to his desire for a daily existence made comfortable by luxuries worthy of a great city. His decision to endow his small palace with a printing press (or two, the historians disagree), destined to print the prince's *operette morali* although

---

[1] *Agar et Ismaele esiliati* (with a new title, *L'Abramo);* the music might have been unchanged, unless the singers employed in the performance demanded some modifications.

aimed toward the future is rooted in a particular tradition of the house of Branciforte: we shall speak of it again.

We know of the performance of the *Equivoci* at Mazzarino by means of a single libretto, naturally printed on the spot (but by the same Giuseppe La Barbera who three years earlier had published "In Venice & in Trapani" *L'Ulisse in Feacia).* The earlier libretto of this music drama with such assorted topographical indications tells us it was "performed in the theater of the City of Trapani." The Mazzarino libretto mentions "Carnival of the year 1688," but a correction of the date in ink, which could only be deciphered through a photographic reproduction, suggests the possibility of a delayed performance (or a repeat) assignable to 1692. (Carafa died on 1 June 1695.) If we remember that Carlo Carafa had also inherited the title of "head of the nobility," it might sadden us to know that he was intent on celebrating Carnival mewed up in an insignificant little town, surrounded by only a few courtiers, although by doing so he affirmed his right to live in a feudal dimension. This decentalization of operatic activity does not prevent me from discerning the fine hand of this sensitive aristocrat, certainly proud of having made himself the promotor of so important an artistic *rentrée,* in the succeeding openings of contacts between the Scarlattis and Sicily.[2]

Abramo was sung in Palermo in 1691[3] on the initiative of one of the Companies of the Most Holy Rosary—the one that had its headquarters in Santa Cita (or Zita, according to the libretto), the beautiful oratorio that Giacomo Serpotta had begun to decorate with his extraordinary stucco-work five years earlier. It is significant that the music of Alessandro Scarlatti found a picturesque placement in the sculptural decoration entrusted to the greatest Palermitan artist of the moment. However, since it is my intention to emphasize the relation with Don Carlo Carafa, I note that the church of Santa Cita lies in the immediate vicinity of Palazzo Butera (later Palazzo Monte di Santa Rosalia), which belonged to our Neapolitan noble who had now emigrated to Sicily.

If the performance at Mazzarino in 1688 and the execution of *Abramo* can plausibly be ascribed to the initiative of the Prince of Butera, his role as a supporter of Scarlatti's music is less apparent in the first documented performance of an opera by Alessandro in Palermo. In the course of the 1689-1690 operatic season we find the best-known singers in the most important musical chapels of Palermo and Monreale joining together to perform *Il Pompeo* appropriately. The sequence *Equivoci-*

2 Pagano, *Vita,* 456-457.
3 Ibid., 458.

Pompeo repeats in Sicily the successful precedent of Naples, and if there were ever a favorable occasion for Alessandro to return in person, this would have been the moment. At that period Palermo was experiencing the brilliant inauguration of a new viceroy— Giovan Francesco Pacheco, Duke of Uzeda—a great lover of the arts and sciences who had encouraged the recently-founded Union of Musicians to build one of the best theaters of the period.

The viceroy's role as patron and the weight of the aristocracy's financial support had been considered decisive for the construction of the Santa Cecilia, but this hypothesis must be considerably revised since the researches of Anna Tedesco have shown that the theater was able to open (28 October 1693) thanks to the economic sacrifices of Baldassare Gonzales, a poor musician who was ruined by this undertaking.[4] It has not been possible to distinguish in which of the two small pre-existing theaters *Il Pompeo* was performed. The performance of this opera— which precedes the opening of the theater of the Union of Musicians by three years—inaugurated the presence of female singers on the stages of Palermo, a practice destined to nourish the interests of aristocrats more disposed to the private frequentation of "virtuose" than to the enjoyment of their talents on the stage.

The importance of the responsibilities that he had exercised elsewhere would have left Alessandro cold to any nomination as head of one of the musical chapels active in Palermo. However, the prospects of this relaunching of operatic activity made it advantageous for him to set up a long-term operation for useful contacts between the great opera composer and his native city: a local branch of the Scarlatti musical workshop, by means of which Alessandro found at least a partial solution to the problems of employment and earnings for many members of his family.

We have seen that Francesco Scarlatti was recruited as a violinist and was subsequently attached to the Royal Chapel of Naples in 1684, at the time of Alessandro's installation as head of the same institution. If we are to trust what Dent[5] wrote after having consulted the relevant documents, the two brothers received their pay for just a year; but we know that Alessandro lost his post only much later, and the length of the connection is confirmed by his collisions with the Grand Chaplain.

With regard to Francesco as well, the information furnished by the English scholar contradicts a request from the musician, who in Feb-

---

[4] Anna Tedesco, *Il Teatro Santa Cecilia e il Seicento musicale palermitano* (Palermo: Flaccovio, 1992), 74-75 and 161-164.

[5] Dent, *Scarlatti,* 34; 1960 reprint with Walker, "Notes," 238.

ruary 1691 must have been still a dependent of the viceroy since he asked for permission to betake himself to Palermo "to attend to certain special interests of his."[6] In Naples, Francesco had already contracted a marriage (18 March 1690) with a certain Rosalina Albano who on December 23 of 1690 had presented him with his first son.[7] A comparison of the payments found in the documents of the theatrical enterprise of 1684 reveals that Francesco was paid 80 ducats as against the 90 of Petrillo (the violinist who would later get Corelli into trouble), the 45 ducats of the poet Andrea Perrucci, the 300 ducats of Alessandro Scarlatti, and the 520 of Giulietta.[8] Alessandro must have decided that at Naples the "patriotic virtuosi" would never leave greater scope for Francesco. It is possible, instead, that the signals coming from Palermo at the beginning of Uzeda's reign allowed him to hope for a more advantageous development of Francesco's career. If we look at the official documents, however, the traces of Francesco's passage through the musical life of Palermo are less than substantial (a performance of the dialogue *La profetessa guerriera* in 1703, as against the two performed in Rome in 1699 and 1710), especially if compared with the records of the birthdates of his other children and the death of Rosalina Scarlatti (29 June 1706). These detail the composition of the family that weighed on the widower: his children Matteo, Antonio, Eleonora, Giovanni, and Dorotea, plus an otherwise unidentified Anna Castelli, who Tiby supposes dealt with domestic matters.[9]

In reality, the role of Francesco Scarlatti in Palermo must have been that of a semiclandestine surrogate for his brother, perhaps assigned to some church as composer (a *Mass* and a *Dixit* dated Palermo 1702 and 1703 are today preserved in an English library)[10] and almost certainly employed to adapt scores by Alessandro to local necessities. Francesco succeeded in winning himself a tiny place in the more extensive musical encyclopedias as a third-class musician, leaving negligible traces on the history of music; who knows if he in fact deserved the unenviable fate that was already reserved for him during his lifetime?

---

[6] Prota Giurleo, "Palermitano," 21, quotes a petition to the viceroy preserved in the Archivio di Stato, Naples, *Mandatorum,* 298, 61.

[7] Prota Giurleo, "Palermitano," 20-21.

[8] Prota Giurleo, "Breve Storia," 42.

[9] Ottavio Tiby, "La famiglia Scarlatti: Nuove Ricerche e Documenti," in *Journal of Renaissance and Baroque Music* I, 1947, 275-290 [hereafter Tiby, "Scarlatti"], 12.

[10] *New Grove Dictionary,* s.v.

A handwritten annotation on the copy of an oratorio libretto by
Francesco performed in 1710 in Rome gives the judgment: "music not
considered good."[11] In Vienna in 1715, in a vain attempt to extort from
the Emperor the appointment of vice maestro, Francesco claimed to have
"exercised the Post of Maestro di Cappella in Palermo, with the universal indulgence of all the Virtuosi and Composers of Music." It might
seem strange that he cites (and almost certainly increases in length) his
service rendered "for the course of 26 years" in Palermo, without mentioning his activity in Rome and Naples. But, as I had suspected, there
were political merits to be added to the evidence. The documents discovered and published by Andrea Sommer-Mathis[12] confirm the declaration of Johann Joseph Fux (who expressed an opinion in favor of the
appointment) that Francesco had been driven from Palermo "by the enemies of the house of Austria."[13] Another petition addressed to the
Emperor reveals a greater misfortune, much greater. Expelled from Sicily under sentence of death, Francesco nearly lost his life during a sea
storm near the island of Lipari and did lose all his goods (and who knows
how many manuscript pieces by his brother, if Francesco's role of
Alessandro's proconsul in Sicily is true). The petition contains other
important biographical details: Francesco "was expelled ignominiously
with his entire Family under punishment of death if he returned to that
Country" for the "affection" shown by him for the Most August Imperial House. After disembarking in Naples, he betook himself to Barcelona
(and here the coincidence with the career of Emanuello Rincon d'Astorga
confirms the close relationship between the two fugitives) and from there,
not having had "the good fortune that her Majesty the Empress was
pleased with him," he moved on to Vienna. Here another petition informs us that Francesco's five children remained in Naples in conditions of poverty which could only aggravate their uncle Alessandro's
financial situation.

Further information concerning Francesco says that he was striv-
ing busily in England (this is why his Palermitan manuscripts have come
down to us: in his native city they would have been lost) after having

---

[11] See Domenico Alaleona, *Storia dell'Oratorio musicale in Italia* (Turin: Bocca,
1908), 419, 430.

[12] Andrea Sommer-Mathis, "Nuevos documentos sobre la circulación de músicos a
principios del siglo XVIII" in *ARTIGRAMA, Revista del Departemento de Historia
del Arte de la Universidad de Zaragoza, Monografico dedicado a la MUSICA,* no. 12,
Zaragoza, 1996-1997, 45-77.

[13] Cf. La Mara (Marie Lipsius), "Briefe alter wiener Hofmeister," *Musikbuch aus
Österreich* VII (1910), 5.

profited in Naples (February 1719) from the pro-Austrian sentiments that had not been sufficient to insure him the appointment in Vienna. Walker takes from Dent the notice of Francesco's presence in the Chapel Royal at the date given, but then tracks him down in London, where he appeared in concerts at the Hickford Room (1 May 1719, 1 September 1720, 16 March 1724), resigned to his role as "brother to the famous Allesandro Scarlatti," but sufficiently courageous to present music "the greatest part of his own composition."[14]   Walker also quotes a letter from the Duke of Chandos to Doctor Arbuthnot in which he speaks of the possible engagement of *Scarlatti's Brother;* Walker notes that the absence of Francesco's name from the lists of the Chandos concerts at Cannons indicates that the possibility came to nothing.[15]   The names of the two correspondents show clearly that in London Francesco Scarlatti moved in the circle of George Frideric Handel, whose relationships in Italy with Alessandro and Domenico deserved to leave more lasting traces than those preserved in the surviving documentation. The marriage contract between Alessandro Binda (godson of his great Scarlatti namesake and younger brother of the Andrea Binda whom we have encountered in the Barbapiccola-Scarlatti-Pagano mess) and Eleonora Scarlatti, a daughter of Francesco born in Palermo, would have it that he died before 12 June 1726.[16] However, Christopher Hair[17] concludes that the declaration given by the family members on this occasion was false and accepts the musician's removal to Dublin, where in August 1733 a Francesco Scarlatti declared in the *Faulkner Dublin Journal* that he was not responsible for the debts of Jane Scarlatti, "eloped from her said husband." At the beginning of January 1741 the same newspaper announced a "Concert of Vocal and Instrumental Musick, for the Benefit of Signior Scarlotti, who, thro' a long Confinement by Sickness, is reduced to very distressful circumstances."

We have said that in the last decade of the seventeenth century there existed in Palermo conditions favorable to Francesco Scarlatti's return, conditions determined by the activity of the Union of Musicians, which was patronized by the Viceroy Uzeda and by the aristocracy.

The Duke of Uzeda was a great lover of the arts and sciences: so much so as to devastate the Sicilian cultural patrimony, despoiling it "of the rarest books, and of the most remarkable manuscripts, which he

14 Dent, *Scarlatti,* 35.
15 Walker, "Additional," 239 [219?].
16 Prota Giurleo, "Anna Maria," 371 n.
17"Scarlatti, Francesco, Antonio Nicola,"*The New Grove Dictionary of Music 2,* XXII, 397.

bought or wanted to be given to him," the Abate Di Blasi informs us. Di Blasi adds that whoever wanted favors or government jobs set to work searching for those "precious monuments,"[18] certain of being able to trade them off against their own claims. Official accounts attribute to Uzeda the merit of financing the Union of Musicians for the construction of the Santa Cecilia theater, but the astute nobleman limited himself to directing the income from certain taxes toward the theater; for the rest, he willingly permitted the incidental expenditures to come from the usual aristocrats on the trail of "virtuose" but did nothing to prevent the enterprise from ruining poor Gonzales.[19]

It is worth the effort to retell the history of this enterprise, which was typical of the relaunching of musical initiatives connected with the renewal of contacts between the Scarlattis and their native city. In a manuscript dedicated to *Churches and Unions of Confraternities* [20] Canon Mongitore complains that the Union of Musicians is "the most unsettled profession in providing itself with a private church." In 1691 (when the relaunching was in progress, after the season which had presented *Il Pompeo*) the Union had decided to build itself a small church "with the intention of making it with the passage of time into a large one in the same place, with the small church then as a sacristy," and these laudable proposals were promptly carried out. On July 7 of the same year a vicar of the archbishop could solemnly bless the little church and open it for worship; but then the Musici "thinking worse, built the Theater to perform staged operas with music in it [...] in the place where they had planned to build the church. The little church, however, has remained almost abandoned, since they are thinking of building another church elsewhere." In a passage of his *Diario* the same Mongitore specifies that "from last year, 1692, they began in Palermo the new theater of the Union of Musicians, for the purpose of performing their operas in music [...] they began it near the old Fair, of noble architecture and excellent capacity, since not only the musicians themselves but also many gentlemen and the Viceroy Uzeda contributed to the expenses necessary for the building. Begun therefore last year 1692, this year 1693 it was per-

---

[18] See Giovanni Evangelista Di Blasi, *Storia civile del regno di Sicilia* (Palermo, 1818) XIV, 381.

[19] Anna Tedesco, *Il teatro Santa Cecilia,* passim.

[20] Manuscript in the Biblioteca Comunale of Palermo, Qq. E. 9. The excerpt relating to the Church of the Union of Musicians (p. 417 of the manuscript) is reproduced in the Appendix to Roberto Pagano, "Le Origini ed il primo statuto dell'Unione dei Musici intitolata a Santa Cecilia in Palermo" [hereafter Pagano, "Origini"], *Rivista Italiana di Musicologia* X (1975), 526-563.

fected; and on this day 28 October was performed there the first opera, which was the tragedy of S. Rosolia [sic], composed by Dottor D. Vincenzo Giattini of Palermo, with the title *L'Innocenza penitente,* which appeared in print in Palermo in the same year."[21]

I have already suggested elsewhere[22] that the "tragedy" of Santa Rosalia, set to music by the Palermitan Ignazio Pùlici, was a sort of dialogue performed with scenery but not a real opera. I find indirect confirmation of this in the libretto of *Penelope la casta,* dedicated by the Musici to the Duchess of Uzeda, at whose "mighty gesture" the "harmonious fabric" of the new theater had risen, renewing the feat of Amphion. In the dedication we also read that the famous Matteo Noris "has with the oracle of his mouth authenticated this [opera] of Penelope as the most inspired one of all those that have ever issued from his pen" and that the Musici, desirous of honoring their theater "with so famous a Drama," obtained it for their "first effort" from "the one who has enriched it with notes as noble as they are inspired." The preface to the libretto then informs us that in Palermo they eliminated the "ideal visual effects" which in Venice, where *Penelope* was staged in 1685 with music by the leading Venetian opera composer, Carlo Pallavicini, demonstrated the "charm of the stage-machines" customary in "those famous Theaters"; it also informs us that in Palermo, as usual, there were added "some very few scenes & arias suited to the taste of the country & to the special talent of our protagonists," without, however, changing the plot.[23]

Following my previous suppositions, I confirm my idea that *Penelope* was "the first product of the activity carried out in the operatic sector of Palermo by the Scarlatti workshop, which had its headquarters in Alessandro's Neapolitan dwelling and its Sicilian branch office in Francesco's."[24] Bianconi's objection about the existence of certain textual variants in the librettos of Venice, Palermo, and Naples (in 1696 Alessandro, short of time, would present a new reworking of *Penelope,* miraculously carried out "in the short space of a few hours")[25] only confirms what the already-cited libretto of *Odoacre* has told us concerning "the universal influence" that imposed on "Drami" an unfaithfulness to their original texts.

---

21 Gioacchino Di Marzo, *Biblioteca Storica e letteraria di Sicilia* (Palermo, 1871)VII, 117.

22 Pagano, *Vita,* 462.

23 Ibid.

24 Ibid., 463.

25 Lorenzo Bianconi, "Funktionen des Operntheaters in Neapel bis 1700 und die Rolle Alessandro Scarlattis," Würzburg, 1975, I, 34 n.

To realize the importance of the relaunching that coincided with the opening of Santa Cecilia, it is sufficient to recall the three years of routine administration that preceded the *Penelope,* which was immediately followed by a *Theodora Augusta* that I consider decidedly a workshop product, and a *Gerusalemme liberata* of Venetian derivation (1695).

I maintained that the mention of Francesco Gasparini's presence in Palermo, drawn from the libretto of his *Alarico overo l'ingratitudine gastigata,* performed at the Teatro S. Cecilia in 1706, referred to the production of *Totila in Roma* (1696), in whose libretto Maria Rosa Borrini appears among the singers as Maria Rosa Gasparini: she had been married to the musician since 1685. A fortunate discovery by Anna Tedesco has clarified that for the season 1699-1700 husband and wife obligated themselves to

> Domenico Di Dominici, tenant [*gabellotto*] of the Teatro Santa Cecilia, the one to compose two operas, all the prologues and intermezzi, play the harpsichord and direct, the other to sing in the four operas which will be performed in the theater.[26]

I find a souvenir of the Gasparinis' Palermitan sojourn in the name given to their only daughter, born after their visit to Palermo. "Rosalia" is a clear tribute to the holy protectress of the host city, and I interpret this choice as the fulfillment of a pious vow, since until then the marriage of the two artists had not been blessed with children.

In the libretto of *Totila (1696)* Gasparini had already been described as "the new Apollo of our times." In 1705, after referring to the many musical versions of *Alarico* staged in Venice and in other famous theaters of Italy, the Palermo impresarios acknowledged the dilution of the original score with music by Albinoni and other composers of "the most refined taste," admitting that even the comic scenes are by "various, but the most spirited composers of our days." They then declare incoherently:

> to make it more striking and to stand out in our [theater], we have chosen among so many others the music of the celebrated Signor Maestro Gasparini, who years ago already gladdened this Theater with his harmony and his virtuous conduct [...].

"...the prodigious harmony of Signor Don Emanuello Rincon de Astorga..."

At this point another protagonist of our story comes onstage, characteristically alternating between the role of aristocrat and that of profes-

---

[26] Tedesco, *Il Teatro Santa Cecilia,* 207.

sional musician but with a definite preference for the second: Emanuello
Rincon d'Astorga, a composer who is always bracketed with Domenico
Scarlatti for stylistic reasons that were already clear to Padre Martini
and to Burney. We will follow the traces of a possible relationship,
anything but superficial, between this young and enterprising aristocrat
and Domenico. For the moment let us recall an old story collected by
Molitor (at the beginning of the nineteenth century and therefore when
little indeed was known about the events in the lives of all the Scarlattis):
that the Baron of Astorga was instructed in music by Francesco Scarlatti
in his native Sicily. To follow this thread further, it seems to me legitimate to suppose that a prominent young man of the Palermitan upper
class would not have missed the opportunity of learning something from
Gasparini as well, on the occasion of the Master of Camajore's Sicilian
sojourn. In any case, let us look more closely at how noble rank and musical professionalism could coexist or alternate in the life of our young baron.

The relationship between aristocrats and musicians follows a
curve which does not always coincide with the network of balances to
which I have already referred. In the sixteenth century, poetic acad-
emies and madrigalistic diversions could create communication between
aristocrats and poets or musicians. By comparison with more recent
times, however, it was less rare for nobility of birth and real artistic talent
to be united in the same individual.

At the dawn of the seventeenth century the celebrated but unfortunately now-lost madrigal collection *Infidi lumi* had presented aristocrats elbow to elbow with professional musicians (always preserving
certain heraldic or artistic points of superiority). This anthology was
intended to showcase certain trends in the madrigal, as a collective homage to a lady of the highest lineage (even if on the *main gauche)* who
had arrived in Italy preceded by a reputation as a refined patroness of
the musical art: Donna Giovanna d'Austria, daughter of the victor of
Lepanto (Don Juan of Austria, illegitimate son of the emperor Charles
V), married ("by order of king Philip III," Villabianca writes)[27] to
Francesco Branciforte e Barresi, Prince of Pietraperzia and Marchese of
Militello (and the author of plays and moral works). A close relative,
Geronimo Branciforte, Count of Cammarata, combined in his own person genealogical and musical merits that assured him pre-eminence
among the handful of madrigalists in the *Infidi lumi*. It is worth noting
that the elect couple, when they had established themselves at Militello,

---

[27] Francesco Maria Emanuele e Gaetani marchese di Villabianca, *Della Sicilia
Nobile,* Palermo 1754-1759 [hereafter Villabianca, *Sicilia Nobile*],II, 16.

anticipated Carafa's experience at Mazzarino — he was the heir of their best traditions as well as their titles and fiefs—by importing from Venice a printing shop and hosting in the halls of their castle a regular if not intense theatrical activity.

Only a few years later Sigismondo d'India began a successful career as a professional musician, adorning himself with the designation "noble of Palermo" on the titlepages of works which, however, he composed and published far from Sicily. It remains to be known whether, if he had remained in his native land, he would have considered it equally decorous to practice professionally the art in which he excelled.

By the end of the century certain differentiations of caste had become much clearer. The wife and children of the Duke of Uzeda certainly did not mingle with paid actors and musicians in the performances of the little plays written by the viceroy himself, in which they deigned to take part for the pleasure of their noble guests.[28] At the very end of the century, an artistic event of particular importance shows the instant rise of those caste barriers which might have appeared weakened: the performance of a melodrama of Venetian origin, *La moglie nemica*,[29] which Antonio Lucchese, a younger son of the noble family of the princes of Campofranco and future Duke della Grazia, offered in 1698 to the noble guests who thronged the drawing-rooms of his palace. Don Antonio had done things on a grand scale, printing a libretto that transmits interesting information. The drama that was performed "had the good fortune to utter its first cries in the Theaters of Venice," but "as an adult it encountered a brighter star under the sky of Palermo," since the original text of Francesco Silvani, performed with music by Marc'Antonio Ziani at the Teatro San Salvatore in Venice in the 1694 Carnival, had been "enriched with the prodigious harmony of Signor Don Emmanuele Rincon de Astorga," thus becoming worthy of

> sitting [!] on the lips, and on the sonorous right hands of the Nobles, who in the house of Signor Don Antonio Lucchese (where friendship, and the frequency of virtuous exercises entertains them while they are pleasurably joined together) are practicing in order to perform it. In a choreographed dance formed by Gentlemen of the same group you will discover how much the foot can attain by skill. In the sets your will find satisfaction by their suitability to the place: in the costumes by the pleasing fashion of the time.

[28] Guido Di Stefano, "Omaggio alla Viceregina," in *Sicilia Turistica*, Palermo, November-December 1954.

[29] The libretto from which the excerpts are quoted is preserved in the Biblioteca Comunale of Palermo, CXXXVI A 60, 5.

Some young aristocrats, all of the male sex, sing; among them stand out the composer of the music himself and his older brother, Francesco Rincon, Baron of Ogliastro, both of them employed in the only female roles in the cast. Did the Astorga brothers sing in falsetto? I believe so, insofar as their aristocratic status (and the fact that later on Emanuello fathered three daughters) excludes the possibility that they were castrati.

In the preface to the libretto, the figure of Music in person turns "to the noble gentlemen of Palermo who are Lovers of music." Here we find no room for ideas of human brotherhood under the banner of art: the aristocrats were thanked by Music for having "avenged the highest of delights from the degradation of low-class earnings" and because "in the artful song" of their lips they show that "harmonic sweetness" arises only from "nature perfectly attuned in well-composed Souls." It goes without saying that the theatrical poetaster disguised as "Music" (only too obviously the only non-aristocrat in the whole group) glorifies the "Virtude" of the young nobles, worthy of being an example to all the centuries, and is determined to congratulate the artists in advance, before the noise of applause surrounds them, asserting that he has "depicted the height of the Geniuses" of the elect throng "with the rough candor of poverty, so that there may remain for those who hear them the freedom to celebrate it with the ornaments of magnificence."

The information which we can extract from the libretto allows us certain reflections:

1) In the Palermo of the Duke of Veraguas (Uzeda's successor, who in the long run turned out to be a greater lover of works of art, paintings, and rare books—which he pillaged abundantly, especially at the end of his term—than of artists), music continued to be practiced professionally by the members of the Union of Santa Cecilia, but it must also have been a part of the traditional instruction imparted to young aristocrats since that class succeeding in forming an academy capable of supplying all the needs of an opera performance embellished with ballets.

2) From the blue-blooded lovers of harmony there emerges a young man of eighteen who does not limit himself to singing but is also capable of undertaking the tasks, which the practices of the period entrusted as much to little provincial maestri as to celebrated composers, of reworking scores from far away (so I interpret the phrase that the opera was "enriched" by the "prodigious harmony" of the young baron).

3) Even on an occasion so far removed from certain other nefarious doings (to be recounted later), it is the young nobles of the male

sex who mount the otage. Their sisters and female cousins, certainly invited to the party, are seated in the hall to applaud them. This indicates a clear differentiation between the pastime of the nobility and the practice of the professional theater, since in Palermo women had been singing in the theater for a decade, while in Messina a similar novelty would occur only with the so-called Franco-Hispanic era.

What has Francesco Scarlatti to do with all this? His ghost hovers over the little opera performed in Lucchese's palace, since tradition indicates him as the teacher of Emanuello Rincon d'Astorga—that he had learned from him the art that he practised in his homeland without "the degradation of low-class earnings," but by which he would earn his bread elsewhere for a great part of his adventurous life.

The carefree attitude of the young Rincon brothers, so happily included in the "virtuoso" practices of the Palermitan aristocracy, must have been more apparent than real. Before recounting the troubles of the two young men, it is appropriate to spend a few words on the establishment of their family in Sicily, which was reconstructed with great precision by Tiby.

> A Rincon d'Astorga appears for the first time in Sicilian documents in the year 1624, when, on the death of Don Antonio Velez, Royal *Secreto* of the city of Augusta, the office was sold, by a document of 5 January of that year, by the Royal Court to Don Diego Rincon d'Astorga. He was the great-grandfather of our musician.[30]

Tiby continues by explaining what the "secrezie" were. Today the readers of any daily paper know that the Sicilian tax collectorships ("esattorie"), features of the gutter press and of political scandals, have become absolute gold mines. Then also, the secrezie, all too similar to more recent pracices, brought in so much income as to prompt Don Diego to buy an extension of the *diritto percettorio* for his heir. He would also scale the Olympus of nobility by investing further earnings in the acquisition of allodial land which the sovereign made even more attractive by transforming it into a noble fief linked with a baronial title. On 2 September 1633 the Rincon d'Astorga thus became Barons of Ogliastro (their principal fief) and of Millaina (a little property attached to the fief). Five years later the new baron had decided that it was useful to consolidate his territorial patrimony and the aristocratic rights pertaining to it by acquiring Mortilletto, a new fief of lesser importance. It is

---

[30] Ottavio Tiby, "Emanuele d'Astorga—Aggiunte e correzioni da apportare alle ricerche del Prof. Hans Volkmann," *International Musicological Society Congress Report* V. Utrecht, 1952, 398-403 [hereafter Tiby, "Astorga"].

perhaps appropriate to note that in calling themselves "Barons of Astorga" the Rincons manipulated the truth to their own advantage, following a custom widely diffused among the southern aristocracy.

We have already mentioned the income that sovereigns who were undemanding in matters of noble ancestry derived from the transformation of allodial land into fiefs. Other and sometimes more dubious revenues came from the so-called *jus populandi:* a landed proprietor (sometimes an aristocrat still not placed sufficiently high up on the ladder of nobility) willingly paid the fee which assured him the right to adorn himself with the title of a town founded by him and populated by his vassals. Usually these new towns were named after the area in which they arose but, since the practice was not obligatory, there was a rapid escalation in the resonance of such titles, where the size and importance of the fief rarely corresponded with the name chosen. Such a manipulation of reality could only bring a smile to the nobles who were more visible on the pyramid of Sicilian nobility, sure as they were of descent from the loins of Anchises and in certain cases boldly persuaded that they took precedence—morally if not materially— even over a king given to such dubious compromises. For the rest, the boasting was not always competely unfounded. The surname Gioeni proclaimed a connection with the house of Anjou, the Naselli were the lords of a principate of Aragona vaguely traceable to an ancestress but bearing no relation to the homonymous Spanish kingdom. Asti (later called Caccamo) was an important fief but certainly not comparable with the Piedmontese city which it inevitably recalls. Everything was reduced to harmless verbal nonsense that did not impress the Sicilians. The Prince of Aragona would never have dared to assert precedence over the Prince of Butera, but this implicit boasting had an extraordinary effect when the holders of such earth-shaking titles crossed the Strait of Messina. Few Europeans could know that Aragona is a large village a few miles from Agrigento, or that the passage of many centuries had widened the gap between Anjou and Gioeni. And so even an aristocrat of good birth could find himself playing "in the great world-theater" the same comedy that in his own country would have set him snickering behind the back of the last *parvenu* who had just laboriously acquired a coat-of-arms.

Before taking the great leap, the Rincon family had already acted in the same spirit of heraldic imposture: it was sufficient to tack onto their family name "d'Astorga," with its whiff of great Spanish nobility, to prepare the way for the forgery of calling themselves Barons of Astorga. This explains why certain predispositions to adventure did not spring up haphazardly, like mushrooms, in our musician, who would profit greatly from that "Astorga" in the course of his extravagant wanderings—at least when he was not obliged to pretend that he was not himself.

But let us return to the "nefarious doings" that troubled the two young aristocrats who were so broad-minded as to perform the female roles *en travesti* in the operatic performance at Palazzo Lucchese.

A few months after moving to Palermo from Augusta, driven away by the terrible earthquake that had erased from the map half the inhabited centers of Sicily, the Rincon d'Astorga family were involved in a scandal caused by the excesses of their violent father, who had struck *cum ictu carrabinae et cum sanguinis effusione* [with a carbine-shot and with the shedding of blood] his wife the baroness and a woman friend who accompanied her, and had then fled.[31]

While looking for the documents concerning the baronial investiture of our musician, Tiby chanced on the sentence of the Royal Capitanial Court condemning the elder baron. It is interesting to compare the facts already known with the account that I have had the good fortune to dig up in that scrapbook of extraordinary happenings which Mongitore published as *Palermo devoted to the Virgin Mary and the Virgin Mary protectress of Palermo*. Not inclined to gossip, nonetheless the good canon is impelled by the truculent excesses of the wild baron to draw from them the evidence of a miracle. Despite having sworn discretion he drops the name that he had suppressed by applying it to the intended victim and believes that he has sufficiently covered his tracks by not saying that it is a matter of attempted wife-murder.

There arose in Palermo certain serious conflicts between a certain baron (whose name is omitted out of due respect) and D. Giovanna, and D. Tommasa Astorga mother, and daughter, on account of certain interests: the Baron became so angry, and conceived such loathing against them, that he deliberated sacrificing their lives to his rage. When this decision had been fixed in his heart, he bought a firearm, which they call a carbine, well-furnished, with which he appeared at the Convent of S. Niccolò de' Bologni of the Carmelite Fathers, where he took refuge, on the eve of the Holy Birth of Our Lord in 1693; and showing it to those Religious, he said to them, that he ought to make a great hit with it. Since the Fathers knew that he was prepared to carry out some violent plan, they did not fail to apply themselves with all the force of argument, and prayer, to remove all anger from his soul, and from his mind every evil thought that it was hatching. But they labored in vain;

---

[31] Tiby, "Astorga," 97. Mongitore's account says that the baron's daughter was also a victim of the crime.

and remaining obdurate, he loaded his firearm with nine balls. Then having left the Convent about the fifth hour of the night, he went to lie in wait for the two Ladies, D. Giovanna, and D. Tommasa, knowing that they had to go out that night. The devout Ladies had been invited by D. Anna Giaconia in her carriage to attend that night the divine offices and Mass that are customarily celebrated with equal solemnity and concourse of people in the Church of Casa Professa of the Society of Jesus. They went, and when the rites of that holy night were completed, they again mounted the carriage with the said D. Anna to return to their home, situated in the street called "del Celso." But when they had arrived, however, at the alley of the palace of the Count of S. Antonio, their enemy the Baron, who had concealed himself there to await them, came forward close to the carriage and discharged his weapon against them, who not suspecting an ambush were being driven home at a slow pace. The explosion was so terrible that the colonettes of the carriage were smashed, and the roof, which they held up, fell on the terrified women, who were judged to be dead, or seriously wounded. And certainly they would have been killed without fail, if at that sudden shot they had not invoked the Blessed Virgin, and had not found themselves well armed with the strong hauberk of the scapular of Our Lady of Mount Carmel, to whom they professed themselves most devoted. When they reached their house they observed the evidence of the protection of the Virgin; because one of the balls was found behind the shoulders of the said D. Anna flattened against the scapular of Carmel. Another one was also crushed on the scapular that D. Tommasa Astorga wore: and both women without any wound whatever. The mother D. Giovanna was also unharmed, on whom it was observed with wonder by all those who flocked around, that the balls had cut the ribbon by which the holy scapular of the Carmine hung, while her breast remained untouched. The fame of this obvious miracle spread throughout the city: and the devout Ladies, recognizing the miracle of the Virgin of Carmel, gave thanks for it to their loving liberator in the said Church of S. Niccolò of the Carmelite Fathers: and in memory of the wonder, they hung in the Chapel of the Great Lady the said scapular, with its ribbon cut, and the flattened balls, where they were seen to hang for a long time: nor do they cease to attest and publish the wonder even to the present time."[32]

I believe that the real beneficiary of a miracle was the bloody-minded baron: despite his aristocratic birth he would have had a hard

---

[32] Antonino Mongitore, *Palermo divoto di Maria Vergine e Maria Vergine protettrice di Palermo* (Palermo: Bayona, 1719-1720), I, 173-174.

time avoiding the gallows if he had obtained his desired result. Combining the data published by Tiby with those that emerge from Mongitore's report, only superficially cryptic, we learn that the violent bully wished to eliminate not only Donna Giovanna Bongiovanni, his wife, but also Donna Tommasa Rincon d'Astorga, his own flesh and blood. I shudder when I think of those Carmelite bigots who attempted to convert this evil soul instead of rushing to warn the police so that his proposed slaughter could be avoided.

The sequel of the story has the mechanical quality of a Bergsonian sequence and is endowed with its own private humor. The fugitive had a third of his fortune sequestered, with the threat of complete confiscation of his goods if he continued in hiding. Tiby maintains that the elder baron remained concealed while awaiting the natural "cooling down" of the affair; if we remember that a similar strategy had proved fortunate for certain Neapolitan courtesans, we might be inclined to consider it sufficient to solve Astorga's problems. But the courtesans did not risk sequestration, and in these matters the financial authorities did not go in for half-measures; so I maintain that the baron finally appeared, having assured himself that scorched scapulars and the flattened balls of that ineffective shotgun were well displayed in church in order to minimize his attack by demonstrating —miracles apart—that all the *effusio sanguinis* could be reduced to a few scratches and a considerable fright.

The next move in the astonishing sequence which the documents reveal was the turn of Francesco junior. The wild man's first-born son was not behaving like a Metastasio hero *ante litteram* in offering to substitute for his father by serving his punishment. The young man simply claimed the investiture of the barony, which had lapsed *ob mortem civilem* of the criminal. His request was granted promptly on 21 June 1694[33] (N.B.: the Exchequer collected a tax on every investiture).

An unfortunate typographical error, which Tiby missed, has altered the succession of events, substituting 1709 for 1702, permitting biographical reconstructions that border on the ridiculous. Perhaps the baron spent a few years in a castle (not his own: he had none) to work out his punishment *more nobilium*. In one way or another he had paid his debt to society and in 1701, when the Exchequer requested an account of some munitions which had been entrusted to his father, he was able to turn directly to the viceroy to ask—and obtain from him—not to be "bothered." In the early years of the new century his rehabilitation

---

[33] Ibid., Processi Investiture 6827, quoted by Tiby, "Astorga," 97.

was complete, since on 19 January 1702[34] (and not 1709, as we read in Tiby[35]) he was reinvested with his baronial title, a procedure perhaps facilitated by the death of Francesco the younger, of whom I have found no further trace. Only Mongitore preserved a discreet memory of the attempted slaughter. If his sons had been the focus of the operatic celebration in Palazzo Lucchesi, soon their braggart father would see himself named senator of the city of Palermo, while Emanuello himself at the age of barely twenty-five became a member of the trio of Governors of the Finance Committee [Tavola nummularia], in office from 1705 to 1706. This information strengthens the hypothesis that his elder brother had died, since the custom of the period would have reserved that office to him.

[34] Volkmann cit., I, p. 39.
[35] Tiby, p. 97.

VI

"...an Eagle, whose Wings are grown"

The necessity of dealing at the same time with the vicissitudes of Francesco Scarlatti and the debut of Emanuele d'Astorga has made me lose contact with the Scarlattis who remained in Naples. Since our narration has carried us to the edge of the new century, it is time to take note of an important novelty, to which I have already referred in passing while speaking of Barbapiccola. Domenico, the son whom Alessandro Scarlatti had named in honor of the Duke of Maddaloni, was clearly detaching himself from the average level of his family by a strong disposition for music and would soon be revealed as an authentic genius. We lack the evidence of his contemporaries, precise and copious in so many other cases (Mozart and Beethoven, to cite the most famous ones). In Naples the *musicalissima,* there was not in this case a Mongitore, ready to attribute the miracle to the Madonna, San Gennaro, or Santa Cecilia in person. The diarists were too busy following "festa, farina, e forca" ("bread, circuses, and gallows"), the three essential currents of the political and social life of the time, to pay attention to an *enfant prodige.* The predominance of interest in vocal music rendered it almost unthinkable to display a keyboard prodigy in public, to which I think Alessandro would have been opposed in any case.

I have already noted Alessandro Scarlatti's particular capacity for singling out musical talent wherever it was found and his willingness to recognize the merit of illustrious colleagues. In the case of Domenico, it was not just fatherly affection that guided his hand when he wrote to Ferdinando de' Medici: "My son is an Eagle ..." He had not done so for Pietro, in spite of the importance that primogeniture must have had for a man of his mentality; how acutely prescient was his judgment on the first of his Neapolitan children is revealed by the fact that Alessandro would never know the greatest part of the inspired harpsichord works for which Domenico is justly famous. It should be said, however, that we do not know the first manifestations of his talent, and that the accounts of his prowess as a harpsichordist come later, while the vocal music traceable to these earlier years does not differ much from that of most of the hack-composers of the time.

The years in which Domenico's talent must have begun to manifest itself unmistakeably were those splendid ones for music when Naples
had as viceroy the Duke of Medinacoeli (the ex-Marchese of Cogolludo,
General of the Galleys). Since only the distant sovereign could have
checked his mania for sumptuous display, the duke had given himself
full rein to flaunt a procession of magnificent carriages on the occasion
of his solemn entry into the city of Naples, thus announcing to everyone
that there would be a good deal of *festa*. The situation vis-à-vis the *forca*
was destined to remain stable since in the absence of bandits or murder-
ers it was customary to send to the gallows even some unfortunate who
was guilty only of having stolen a candle. A real breakdown occurred
instead in the area of *farina,* insofar as the carelessness of the viceroy
allowed other profiteers to carry on the same smuggling operations that
according to popular opinion had enriched the Duke of Santo Stefano,
Medina Coeli's predecessor. And since the "excellent singer" whom he
had transformed into a grande dame was always at the center of Medina
Coeli's attention, a bold Neapolitan opponent dared to attach to the "Giant in front of the Palace" a placard with a quatrain that was doubly
cutting because it changed his former title (*Cogolludo)* into an insulting
epithet (*coglione): "*The swindler has gone off,/The balls-head has ar-
rived/Who keeps Miss Giorgina/And forgets the *farina.*"[1]

Among the accomplishments of the new viceroy was a notable
relaunching of theatrical activities. It would be wrong to think that he
was impelled by a desire to employ Giorgina, who was condemned instead to appplaud from her box "the best singing actors who could be
found in Italy, brought with large salaries by this viceroy,"[2] as Confuorto
says. We must believe him after reading their names, among which
stands out Vittoria Tarquini called "La Bombace," the future "Bambagia"
of Ferdinando de' Medici.

Weary of the endless restrictions on theatrical ventures, the viceroy decided to support the realization of his follies, abundantly subsidiz-
ing the able impresario Serino who had shown himself capable of mounting spectacles of the required level. Like Uzeda in Palermo, Medina
Coeli made a fine impression with little personal sacrifice. Prota Giurleo[3]
discovered from the duke's financial documents that he drew freely on
the coffers of the Exchequer to meet the enormous expenses that were
not restricted to the theater but were extended, in fine weather, to the

---

[1] Confuorto II, 236.
[2] Confuorto II, 250.
[3] Prota Giurleo, "Breve Storia," 60.

production of splendid serenatas (*Il Trionfo delle Stagioni* was performed in the piazza in front of the Royal Palace with 150 instrumentalists and 50 choristers), until Naples in those years became a sort of promised land not only for musicians but for artists in general: consider the arrival of the most famous scene-designer of the time, Ferdinando Galli, called "il Bibiena." For once, Alessandro must have been occupied full-time: all to the good, since in the Rome of the Pignatelli pope the destruction of the Teatro Tor di Nona left no hope for anything profitable. Not that everything went well for Alessandro, however, since he was constrained to put together the petition already mentioned "in order to obtain [...] four months' salary" that had not been paid to him. If he managed to remain in difficulties even in Naples, where gold was squandered on music and musicians, Scarlatti was indeed persecuted by an evil fate (and by the "pressing urgent needs of his own numerous family" to which he makes his unfailing reference in the petition).[4]

Above all, the splendors of Medina Coeli did not succeed in driving from the minds of the Neapolitans the nightmares of the war of succession, which would break out at the death of Charles II, sickly and without direct heirs. News of the king's health arrived from faraway Spain, spreading alternating waves of optimism and depression. It goes without saying that a cynical voluptuary like the viceroy was inclined toward optimism, since mourning of that importance would have resulted in a long suspension of his theatrical pleasures, together with many other privations. In this spirit, it was possible to reach the height of the ridiculous by prefacing a new (so to speak) opera of Alessandro, *Gli inganni felici,* with a prologue in which Peace (a significant choice for a personification) pretends to forget the state of the king's health in order to phrase an idiotic prophecy: "Oh, if one day the lovely womb of the Royal Bride of the great Hercules of Spain should show itself fruitful! What good fortune it would be for the World if that fateful day arrived, but perhaps it is not far off!"

At the tag-end of the century, Alessandro's connection with Palermo becomes clearer and unequivocal: obviously, the branch-office of the workshop did not remain inactive. After Gasparini's visit, Francesco Scarlatti must have returned to his role of mysterious emissary, if *La caduta dei Decemviri,* "a new opera in music" by Alessandro performed in Naples on 15 December 1697, could be repeated a few months later in Palermo, and if *I rivali generosi* completed a reverse crossing (Palermo, 1699; Naples 6 November 1700, "outstandingly set

---

[4] Prota Giurleo, "Breve Storia," 61.

to music by the virtuoso Filippo Maria Collinelli"). In 1700 *Gli inganni felici* was presented in Palermo for the queen's birthday, with the same prologue as in Naples: it had been necessary to replace the original Alcide with an "Iberian Juno," but the references to the Hercules of Spain were more than ever inappropriate to a dying king. When the Palermitans, encouraged by the arrival of yet another bit of good news, gave the poet Nicola Prescimone the task of hymning the "recovered health" of Charles II, the new prologue, prefaced to the repeat of the *Inganni felici,* betrayed the over-zealous subjects, who, owing to the slowness of communications, found themselves celebrating the convalescence of a dead man!

Even if the tendency to recognize the Bourbon Philip V as the new king was immediately apparent in southern Italy, in Naples there were partisans of the Habsburg Emperor Charles VI so bold as to leave seditious and satirical posters for the Duke of Medina Coeli inside the Royal Palace; one of these posters dared to proclaim: "Non habemus Regem, nisi Caesarem!" ("We have no King but Caesar/Kaiser!").[5]

In Palermo as well, where the hatred of the French went back to the Sicilian Vespers, Imperial agents were scheming in the shadows, but the Viceroy Veraguas kept the situation under control and, having declared that "the old prejudices [...] had ceased,"[6] he could schedule the ceremonies for the acclamation of Philippe d'Anjou (this time an authentic Anjou). Outstanding in the panorama of the festivities was a serenata (eloquently titled *La gara concorde dell'Universo)* performed with an unusual display of musical forces: 32 voices and 100 instruments, literally jammed into the gallery of the Royal Palace, which also had to contain the select audience that was invited.[7] In Naples, even if the same general line prevailed, the pro-Austrian noble party was plotting behind the scenes, and the conspiracy of Macchia attempted to eliminate the Viceroy Medina Coeli by taking advantage of his well-known habit of spending the night in the arms of a *real* singer, now that Giorgina had become a great lady!

---

[5] Prota Giurleo, "Breve Storia," 63.

[6] Giovanni Evangelista Di Blasi, *Storia Cronologica de' Viceré, Luogotenenti e Presidenti del Regno di Sicilia* (Palermo: Edizioni della Regione Siciliana, n. d. [1975] [hereafter Di Blasi, *Viceré*]), IV, 13.

[7] Mongitore, *Diario* (in Di Marzo, *Biblioteca,* VII, p. 285) speaks of a "noble serenade [...] sung by all the musicians of Palermo together"; Giuseppe Sorge, *I Teatri di Palermo nei secoli XVI, XVII, XVIII* (Palermo: IRES, 1926 [hereafter Sorge, *Teatri*]), 292, lists a group of 32 violins, 8 violas, 8 contrabasses, 4 flutes, 2 bassoons, 2 trumpets, 1 archlute, 1 cornett, and 8 harpsichords. This reduces the number of performers to a bit less than a hundred, singers included.

In these same years the development of Domenico Scarlatti's musical talent ceased to be a cause of satisfaction limited to his own family, allowing the young man to enter openly into the crowded musical arena of Naples. It is not difficult to imagine that Domenico gave the first unmistakable signs of his talent by employing the medium that would remain the most congenial to him: the keyboard. What all children do when they are gifted with a good ear, amusing themselves by strumming a melody after having heard it, Domenico must have done with such ease and precision as to alert the antennae of the paternal "talent detector."

The Scarlatti household was indeed the musical factory that we have described: opportunities to hear music were certainly not lacking, and I do not find it difficult to go back to imagine the surprise of the bystanders at some striking musical intervention on the part of the child in a rehearsal, or even in a performance otherwise assigned to experienced professionals. Even Kirkpatrick,[8] generally so prudent in reconstructions not based on explicit documents, cannot resist the temptation to imagine young Mimo—his family's nickname for Domenico—in the midst of a veritable bustle of singers and instrumentalists who have come to rehearse, of librettists and scenographers flocking to consult Alessandro, of poets and painters visiting the illustrious personage. The comparison with the Bach family is more than obvious, although Kirkpatrick wisely observed that the life of Johann Sebastian was based on a regularity of habits and occupations simply unthinkable in the family of a musician connected with the uncertainties and turmoil of theatrical life. For this reason, by a happy hypothesis he assigns to some member of the family other than Alessandro the task of harnessing the free imagination of the child to the yoke of traditional instruction: papa, too busy, lacked above all the necessary patience and would be the first to recognize this, at the proper time and place.

When Kirkpatrick then supposes, as an alternative to the previous hypothesis, that the child limited himself to repeating what he heard every day, the usual fascination of literary reminiscences reminds me of a page of Edmund Gosse, in which the first manifestation of a child's intellectual capacities is recognized in his attempt to imitate what he sees around him.

But it seems to me absolutely unthinkable to apply to Domenico Scarlatti the principle invoked by Gosse, according to which the child of a great sculptor might not become a sculptor himself, after having tried

---

[8] Kirkpatrick, *Scarlatti,* 22.

as a child to sculpt a head employing a nail and a fragment of marble thrown away by his father. In our case, fate left no other avenue open to Domenico: he would be a musician. Above all, I maintain that only with great difficulty would papa Alessandro have allowed him to disperse in other directions a talent that his capacity for judgment (sovereign, in every sense) told him was already directed for the best.

The pathetic aspect—and a very Sicilian one—of the whole affair is that Alessandro clung to the necessity of displaying in everything that authority in which he firmly believed, without foreseeing that the impact of a fatherly personality that was so strong and so haloed by prestige would impede his son from expressing his full artistic possibilities. Gosse wrote:

> I was like a plant on which a pot has been placed, with the effect that the center is crushed and arrested, while shoots are straggling up to the light on all sides. My father himself was aware of this, and in a spasmodic way he wished to regulate my thoughts. But all that he did was to try to straighten the shoots without removing the pot which kept them resolutely down.[9]

In the present case, the fanatical delirium that drove papa Gosse only peeps out from the background in the guise of a sincere religious feeling; and the "study of two temperaments" (necessarily with gaps, since Domenico left no document comparable to *Father and Son)* must be conducted recognizing the Biblical infallibility that Alessandro attributed to his own authority over all his children, especially over the most gifted of them. If I close my eyes and immerse myself in that situation, it is all too easy for me to reconstruct the moralizing sermon that the elder Scarlatti must have often administered to the unfortunate genius whom he had brought into the world: it is the same one that certain Sicilian educators—even in times close to our own—have delivered to the promising young men whom Providence entrusted to their care. These observations may perhaps appear premature, since I have not yet recounted anything of the debut and the first stages of the younger Scarlatti's career, but it seemed to me appropriate to offer the readers my keys to the interpretation of events before employing them.

In the Naples of the Viceroy Medina Coeli we have seen Alessandro employed as never before in composing operas and serenatas, in patching up the operas of others, in writing cantatas for the rare occasions when Giorgina was allowed to remember that she was a great singer, in "supplicating" for the payment of salaries in arrears. Nonetheless,

---

[9] Edmund Gosse, *Father and Son* (Boston: Houghton Miflin, 1965), 185.

Alessandro did not weaken his contact with other centers and with the provincial areas that contributed to balancing his slender budget. Turin, Genoa, Parma, and Bologna had been added to the Tuscany of Ferdinando de' Medici and the Rome of cardinals Ottoboni and Pamphilj in order to ensure the circulation throughout Italy of Alessandro's productions and those of his Neapolitan workshop, although such circulation was momentarily threatened (except in the area of sacred music and oratorio) by the deaths of Charles II and pope Pignatelli.

Operas were prohibited at Naples in the Carnival of 1701, but the skill of making-do suggested to the theater people a humble substitute: the operas were performed onstage by actors who manipulated *bambocci,* marionettes, but were sung by offstage performers. A typical phase of the workshop's activity begins here, but Alessandro is very circumspect about coming out into the open: he fears that certain undertakings might be considered inappropriate to his dignity as the famous master of the Royal Chapel. Even if his name never appears in libretti and various documents, the members of his household seem already busily employed in this mixture of Carnival operas and Lenten mourning. There is sufficient evidence that the Scarlatti workshop had reacted promptly to the crisis caused by official mourning. *La donna sempre s'appiglia al peggio* is the work of "Signor Carlo de Petris" set to music by "Signor Tomasso di Mauro;" Nicola Pagano signs the dedication to the Duchess of Maddaloni, and its performance is expected "in this present year of 1701 in the Theater called 'of the puppets' by certain Gentlemen and Ladies, Neapolitan virtuosi," although the male and female virtuosi may incur the viceroy's anger for their conjuring trick. Particularly eloquent is the invocation for protection to the Duchess of Maddaloni, a tried and true lightning-rod to deflect the possible anger of the viceroy. The fact that only the *bambocci* appear on stage allows the singers to conceal their identities, leaving visible the enterprising Nicola Pagano, the librettist de Petris, and Tomasso di Mauro, who is described provocatively in the preface to the libretto: "of whom I do not speak, because you know who he is, and in what consideration he lives before the entire city. He is young and the elders of his profession would be content to imitate him, let alone to equal him!"[10]

The description of Tomasso di Mauro (or *de* Mauro elsewhere) too closely coincides with what we know of the sixteen-year-old Domenico not to have aroused my curiosity. "You know who he is" could have been justified by the impudent employment of a pseudonym;

[10] Croce, *Teatri* I, 184.

"in what consideration he lives before the entire city" seemed to me a certificate of merit that the Scarlatti clan would not have issued light-heartedly to outsiders when they had at home the prodigy Domenico. Unfortunately, de Mauro appears elsewhere in the busy musical life of Naples, and my doubts are definitively buried when I read that in 1716 a musician of that name competed unsuccessfully to succeed Gaetano Veneziano.[11]

From this point on it seems that Alessandro began to distance himself from the sorcerer's apprentices who surrounded him, fearful that all his family's goings-on might damage his career or that of his son.

Domenico had certainly not fallen into disgrace with the vice-roy, since on 13 December 1702 the latter named him "organist and composer of music" in the Royal Chapel, assigning to him in addition a salary from his discretionary funds as "chamber harpsichordist" in his personal service. In reporting these appointments Prota Giurleo[12] commented that the salary granted to the fifteen-year-old boy (eleven ducats and one *tarì* a month) was "a sum indeed fabulous for those times," but Alessandro must not have been of the same opinion, since only four months later he had the nerve to ask for "a leave of absence for ten months to leave the Kingdom, he and his son Domenico, continuing to both, in their absence, the enjoyment of the payment that they received as musicians of the Royal Chapel."[13] It is astonishing that the viceroy had nothing to reply and that the leave, which had been granted, was cancelled only because the rumor had spread of the imminent arrival of Philip V. His visit was intended to dissipate the discontent caused by the bloody repression of the Macchia conspiracy and to present to his sub-jects the image of a king whom not all of them accepted.

Thus father and son remained momentarily chained to their du-ties in a Naples that finally could experience again a spectacle worthy of its traditions as a capital. On 28 February 1702 Francesco Pacheco de Acuña, Duke of Ascalona, formerly viceroy of Sicily, had come to re-place Medina Coeli, leaving in his stead in Palermo a personage whom we have already encountered: "Monsignor di Giudice," who had been made a cardinal by pope Ottoboni thanks to the intrigues of the Spanish ambassador. It is sufficient to recall that the intriguer in question is Medina Coeli, who had just left Naples, to show once again that by

---

11 J. L. Jackman and P. Maione, "Mauro, Tommaso de," *New Grove* 2, 16, 162.

12 Prota Giurleo, "Breve Storia," 64.

13 Prota Giurleo, "Breve Storia," 65-66.

comparison with the geographic expansion of our story the number of its protagonists tends to remain limited.

Not too sure of liking the music that he would hear (let us not forget that the king came from Paris, where in the same year the publication of a eulogy of Italian music by the Abbé Raguenet had stirred up a hornets' nest), Philip V, in an outburst of royal sadism, "ordered, that all those Knights who were present in his apartments should enter: when they had told the King that it was not known how much the said Knights enjoyed music, His Majesty said in reply that if they did not enjoy music, they would perhaps enjoy the fact of being in his presence [...]."[14]

The evening of May 1, again in the Stanza del Belvedere, there was another "most lovely serenata," followed at nightfall by the explosion of a "new fireworks display, which was made by the Marchese di Vigliena the viceroy."

Then, on May 8,

> Around the twenty-second hour there began the Opera in music entitled Tiberius Emperor of the East, in the Hall of the Royal Palace, where the King went to hear it in private; for which purpose they built a room of wood, from which His Majesty could easily see and be seen. The Ladies who were present at the very beginning had the honor of kissing the King's hand. They appeared on that occasion in black court dresses of French cut, but resplendent with the great quantity of jewels which adorned them.[15]

The Viceroy Ascalona had done things on a grand scale, although he was badly informed about the king's taste. Applying to Cardinal Ottoboni or to the Duke of Uzeda (who in the meantime had become Spanish ambassador in Rome), he had summoned to Naples Corelli and Matteo Fornari in order to reinforce the assembled violinists of Naples. Geminiani's account allowed Burney to transmit a story that renews in the Corellians of today the displeasure that their idol must have experienced, although Alessandro Scarlatti restrained himself, as I have already noted:

> At the time that Corelli enjoyed his highest reputation, his fame having reached the court of Naples, and excited a desire in the King to hear him perform; he was invited, by order of His Majesty, to that capital. Corelli, with some reluctance, was at length prevailed

[14] Antonio Bulifon, *Giornale del viaggio d'Italia dell'Invittissimo e gloriosissimo Monarca Filippo V Re delle Spagne, & di Napoli, &c.,* (Naples: Nicolò Bulifon, 1705), 23

[15] Ibid, 53-54.

on to accept the invitation; but, lest he should not be well accompanied, he took with him his own second violin and violoncello. At
Naples he found Alessandro Scarlatti, and several other masters,
who entreated him to play some of his concertos before the King;
this he for some time declined, on account of his whole band not
being with him, and there was no time, he said, for a rehearsal. At
length, however, he consented, and in great fear performed the first
of his concertos. His astonishment was very great to find that the
Neapolitan band executed his concertos almost as accurately at sight,
as his own band, after repeated rehearsals, when they had almost
got them by heart. *Si suona,* (says he to Matteo, his second violin)
à Napoli! ["They can play, in Naples!"].

After this, being again admitted into His Majesty's presence,
and desired to perform one of his sonatas, the King found one of the
adagios so long and dry that, being tired, he quitted the room, to the
great mortification of Corelli. Afterwards, he was desired to lead in
the performance of a *masque* composed by Scarlatti, which was to
be executed before the King; this he undertook, but from Scarlatti's
little knowledge of the violin, the part was somewhat awkward and
difficult: in one place it went up to F; and when they came to that
passage, Corelli failed, and was not able to execute it; but he was
astonished beyond measure to hear Petrillo, the Neapolitan leader,
and the other violins, perform that which had baffled his skill. A
song succeeded this, in C minor, which Corelli led off in C major;
ricominciamo ["let's start again"], said Scarlatti goodnaturedly. Still
Corelli persisted in the major key, till Scarlatti was obliged to call
him out, and set him right. So mortified was poor Corelli with this
disgrace, and the general bad figure he imagined he had made at
Naples, that he stole back to Rome in silence.[16]

The historical foundation of the anecdote, which has aroused a
great variety of comments and interpretations, is disputable at least in
part. First of all, Burney speaks of Philip V as a king residing permanently at Naples, rather than a transient visitor. Given the uncertainties
and the actual ceremonies of the young ruler's Italian journey, Corelli
could not have hesitated, since his presence in Naples had to be decided
upon within the space of a few hours. That it was Ottoboni who induced
him to go there I do not doubt. Let us turn to the king's reaction. Philip
V had every reason to have come from Paris with a desire to hear Corelli:
before leaving for Spain, the Sun King's grandson had time to hear those
premières Sonades Italiennes that François Couperin tells us had just

---

[16] Charles Burney, *A General History of Music from the Earliest Ages to the Present
Period,* ed. Frank Mercer (New York: Dover, 1957 [hereafter Burney, *General*]), II,
439-440.

arrived in the French capital, exacerbating certain divisions in the
République de la Musique. But the balanced synthesis worked out by
Corelli in the violin style of the seventeenth century gave results that
were not showy and virtuosic and were thus incapable of arousing a
young monarch who was never very inclined towards music.

By involving his faithful Matteo Fornari and a violoncellist
(Giovan Lorenzo Lulier?) in his Neapolitan trip, Corelli did not show a
distrust in the local instrumentalists. Rather, he wished to assure himself
of a stylistically consistent *concertino* ensemble, capable of adequate
execution. With Alessandro or Domenico Scarlatti at the harpsichord,
those *Sonades* that should have aroused the curiosity of the king instead
induced him to leave the concert.

Corelli was surprised to discover that the Neapolitan instrumentalists not only deciphered his music with ease, but also the music, unorthodox in violinistic terms, of his illustrious colleague and friend. That
Alessandro Scarlatti was not a born violinist is obvious; but to attribute
to him the "little knowledge" of which Burney speaks is a long leap.
The example cited by Pincherle[17] concerning this episode would be
enough to evaluate as ill-judged impetuosity what certainly did not come
from an inadequate knowledge of the medium. Certain "routines" practiced at higher levels freed the Neapolitan violinists from the instrumental formulas in whose ruts the Corellian school moved; I may be permitted to see in this attitude a significant anticipation of that phrase in the
preface to the *Essercizi* in which Domenico Scarlatti will indicate "freedom on the harpsichord" as the objective to be gained. "They can play,
in Naples!" said by a Corelli is high praise for the accomplishments of
the city's cultural isolation.

These experiences of Alessandro Scarlatti anticipate those that
Domenico would be able to mature in the "splendid isolation" of a royal
boudoir. For the moment, we are far from such brilliant results. Even
the instrumental components of scores that Alessandro Scarlatti composed with an eye to the predominance of vocal style reveal attempts
towards the concertante juxtaposition of voice and instrument; but he
was certainly not interested in the virtuosic possibilities of instrumental
technique.

It is ironic that Corelli sent the young king to sleep since Philip
V was later destined to find in the virtuosity of Farinelli the antidote for
his own suicidal depression. The fault was certainly not that of the great
violinist, but of his *Adagio.* It is strange that Corelli did not choose the

---

[17] Marc Pincherle, *Corelli et son temps* (Paris: Plon, n.d. [1954]), 24.

famous *Sonata* which, was in homage to an old Spanish dance, closes the Opus V, at that moment hot off the presses; but perhaps an obscure foreboding suggested to everyone that a series of variations on the *Follia* might be an imprudently prophetic metaphor.

The entrance of a personage as important as Corelli onto our stage has led us to neglect our previous protagonists: a company of singers among the best that could be found in Italy. It may have been accidental, but it makes a certain impression on one familiar with the New Testament to read in the libretto of *Tiberio Imperatore d'Oriente* a list of singers that opens with two Mary Magdalens: Musi, "called the Mignatti," and Manfredi, who boasts the title of "chamber virtuosa of His Highness of Savoy." With them sing Isabella de Piedz, Nicola Paris, Nicola Grimaldi, and Antonio Lauri (all virtuosi of the Royal Chapel of Naples); and then Giulio Cavalletti (virtuoso of the Duchess of Laurenzana), Livia Nannini, "called the Polacchina," and Giovan Battista Cavana. The libretto that I consulted in Bologna tells us that the sets were in part by Bibbiena and in part by Sig. Giuseppe Cappelli. That the music was by Scarlatti has been deduced from a manuscript preserved in the library of the Naples Conservatory. In reality, this manuscript contains only forty-four arias that Alessandro wrote for the occasion, and it is worth noting that in the same year, 1702, a *Tiberio Imperatore d'Oriente* marked the Venetian opera debut of that same Gasparini whom we have seen insinuating himself into the musical fiefs of the Scarlatti family in Palermo.

The music of the serenata *Clori, Dorino e Amore,* whose score is dated 2 May 1702, and the indication "in the presence of Philip V of Spain,"[18] was certainly by Scarlatti, but if I consider his need for additional earnings, and I read Bulifon's account of the entire musical component in that month's ceremonies, the suspicion arises that Alessandro also had other tasks, apart from his official duties as *maestro di cappella.*

On June 2, when Philip V had left, Scarlatti was able to return to his post. The leave of absence that he had previously requested was now granted to him and to his son, but only for four months. If I were not certain that their destination was the Tuscany of Ferdinando de' Medici, I would be seized by one of my Sicilian doubts: never as in this and the following season would the operatic activity of the Teatro Santa Cecilia in Palermo be so centered on the work of Alessandro, enriched by the participation of some of the singers whom we have already met in Naples, now attracted to Sicily by the blandishments of a new siren of patronage: Cardinal del Giudice.

[18] Indications drawn from the manuscript scores: see Rostirolla, Catalogue, in *Scarlatti* ERI, 370.

From the duplication of opera titles we learn that this activity in Palermo was a matter of systematic and organized importations:[19] *Il pastor di Corinto* (with the same intermezzi as in Naples), *Bassiano o vero Il Maggiore Impossibile*, *Il prigioniero fortunato*, *Tito Sempronio Gracco* (all very Scarlattian, even if Alessandro's name no longer appears on the Palermo librettos), as well as a *Ripudio di Ottavia* which must be a reworking of the opera by Pollaroli performed in Venice in 1699. The libretto of *Tito Sempronio Gracco* follows the Neapolitan original so literally as to specify that the sets are those "of the famous Signor Ferdinando Galli called Bibieno, Engineer of the Most Serene [Duke] of Parma." This might suggest an importation of the complete Neapolitan productions, but it does not allow us to assume that the set-designer came to Palermo, as certain art and theatrical historians, insufficiently informed about customs of the time, have done. We shall see why the relationship between the theater in Palermo and the Neapolitan headquarters of the Scarlatti workshop appears so intensified.

We have already recorded the galaxy of important personages who had brought Cardinal del Giudice to the post of viceroy of Sicily. By his Neapolitan origins (he was the brother of the Prince of Cellamare) and by his friendship with Cardinal Ottoboni and with the Duke of Medina Coeli, Francesco del Giudice (destined to become Archbishop of Monreale and finally Grand Inquisitor of Spain) was a truly worthy prelate and a rabid Scarlattian.

In Messina, a chronicler attributes to del Giudice's personal initiative the radical change of customs that came about with the passage to the so-called Franco-Hispanic era:

> The brilliance, the pomp which this prince introduced were extraordinary, and from this time on the Italian manner of living was introduced into Messina, which indeed abandoned that gravity and lifestyle introduced previously by the ruling nation."[20]

But Cardinal del Giudice certainly had not been able to indulge his predilection for Scarlatti in Messina. Alessandro had an original sin—that of having been born in Palermo, which rendered it impossible to import his operas to the city which coveted the title of capital of Sicily. In Palermo as well, the cardinal wished to multiply musical festivities, and the topical prologues that prefaced Scarlatti's operas could not exhaust the calendar of occasions to be celebrated. There was thus a

---

[19] Data from my inventory of musical activities in Palermo.
[20] Caio Domenico Gallo, *Gli Annali della Città di Messina* (Messina: Filomena, 1882), IV, 25.

proliferation of serenatas, in which we find the praise of the unhappy
Hercules of Spain replaced by unending hymns to the "Happy offshoot
of the Gallic Thunderer."[21]　But theatrical music or the music of the
official festal apparatus was not enough for Cardinal del Giudice, and he
continued to enjoy music even during a dinner (it goes without saying
"in the French manner")[22] offered by him to the most important personages who had taken part in the ceremony which had consecrated him
Archbishop of Monreale. And the music must have been most select for
the sumptuous celebration that the Prince of Villafranca prepared for the
baptism of his first child (we must trust the assertions of contemporaries, since not one note of those unlucky scores has survived).

　　The Polish scholar Michele Bristiger discovered that one of the
serenatas provided for the occasion was set to music by Domenico
Scarlatti;[23] the other, already cited by Sorge, was by Domenico Sarro.
We are in the circle of the Neapolitan Royal Chapel, and it is more than
evident that the prince had gone to all that trouble in the hope of a male
child. When a girl was born he was unwilling to retreat, and the great
celebration took place all the same. The *Ceremoniale de'Signori Viceré*
transmits a savory account of it, which shows our worldly cardinal involved in various ways in the complicated festivity:

> The Sig. Cardinal baptized the daughter of the Prince of
> Villafranca in this form: the Prince of Villafranca and the Prince of
> Roccafiorita went to the Palace and said that everything was ready
> when His Eminence wished to favor them, and then His Eminence
> got into his sedan-chair, and when he arrived at the House of the
> Princess he was met by the Nobility in the Sala; and when he got
> out of his chair he entered accompanied by the Prince of Villafranca
> and Relatives to the second antechamber, at the door of which he
> was received by the lady most closely related to the Princess, ac-
> companied by others, without His Eminence having accepted the
> right side; when the Signor Cardinal entered the Chamber where
> the Bed was, the Princess reclined in the seat that was prepared,
> having wished however that the ladies sit first: when the greetings
> were finished, Monsignor della Monarchia vested to celebrate the

---

[21] *Gli Arbitri del Tempo e della Fortuna inchiodati a'piedi di Filippo V, re delle
Spagne e delle due Sicilie...* (Palermo, 1703): a libretto inserted by Mongitore in his
Diario and reprinted by Di Marzo in *Biblioteca Storica e Letteraria di Sicilia,* VIII,
15ff.

[22] *Ceremoniale de'Signori Viceré,* III, 23.

[23] *Il Concilio degli Dei.* The titlepage of the libretto is reproduced in Wladislaw Malinowsky, "O teatrze Krolowej Marii Kazimiery Domenico Scarlattim u kilku innych
sprawach Michalem Bristigerem," *Ruch Muzyczny* XX (1976), 13, n. 6.

Office, in the large Chamber, where tho font was prepared, whence having informed His Eminence that everything was in order, he exited with the Lady most closely related, who was to participate as Godmother, and the baby girl was given into the arms of His Eminence by the Signor Prince, who received her from one of his gentlemen. When the Ceremony was finished a little cross of Diamonds with a rich ribbon was put on the Baby by His Eminence from whose hands the Baby was received by the Prince and Father: Who in the act of thanking the signor Cardinal wished to kiss his hand, and was tenderly embraced by him. His Eminence entered the Princess's chamber and when the courtesies were finished he was begged by her that he lay aside his purple to amuse himself at Gaming; whence when he had divested himself without accompaniment in the Gallery, he returned to the chamber, to amuse himself; they first performed a Serenata, and distributed waters, and sweets, and having passed several hours in Gaming His Eminence took his leave and accompanied by the closest lady relative and the group as far as the door of the large chamber, or second antechamber, he was served by the prince and knights as far as the door of the hall, where when he had got into his chair he took leave of them, six pages with torches accompanying the Cardinal as far as the door of the house.[24]

When I read to Kirkpatrick the passage of the *Ceremoniale* that I have just quoted, the Maestro was quick to pick up a coincidence between the date of the Palermitan festivity (26 October 1704) and that of the nineteenth birthday of Domenico Scarlatti. Having pointed out to Bristiger (who, acting on the typographical indications assigned the serenata to Naples) the possibility that the libretto that he had discovered corresponded to an event in Palermo or in Sicily, I will play devil's advocate by suggesting that the serenata with music by Domenico Scarlatti could have been destined for a Neapolitan echo of the celebration (which perhaps fell through because of the failure of the male baby to materialize), or for an equivalent in Messina, rendered probable by the fact that the Prince belonged to the Messinese aristocracy.

I find an indication that Scarlatti's serenata was a reworking in the hurried corrections of the libretto to fit the circumstances by some changes of gender. In the dedicatory preface, free from the straitjacket of verse, the same sentence speaks of the "most happy baby girl" and of a "worthy [male] offshoot."[25] The libretti of the two serenatas, works of the same poet (a Don Pietro Riccio who emerges from total obscurity to

[24] *Ceremoniale* III, 27.
[25] Information from the unique copy of the libretto: I-Rc.

appear in these occasional compositions) bear different typographical indications: the one printed in Palermo (*L'Oreto festivo*) indicates Domenico Sarro as the composer; the one printed in Naples ("For Michele Luiggi Muzij," bears a dedication addressed to the father of the newborn girl, and the title page states that the serenata is "composed by D. Pietro Riccio" and set to music by Domenico Scarlatti.The serenata is entitled *Il Concilio degli Dei Radunato in occasione del Parto dell'Illustrissima, ed eccellentissima la signora D. Giovanna Alliata, e Bonanno, Principessa di Villafranca e Duchessa de la Sala di Paruta &c.* (*The Council of the Gods assembled on the occasion of the Childbirth of the Most Illustrious, and most excellent Donna Giovanna Alliata, and Bonanno, Princess of Villafranca and Duchess of Salaparuta &c.).*[26]

In the dedication Don Pietro Riccio addresses the prince-father in these terms:

Most Illustrious Most Excellent Lord / It was the invention of the ancient mysterious tellers of fables, that when Pandora was born she was by special care of the Gods enriched with gifts most rare and appropriate to their virtue and power. Thus they wished to give us to understand, that when some singular and unusual birth is to take place it appears that all the Deities commit themselves with special providence to adorn it with the rarest and most prized prerogatives. Such is precisely the most happy baby girl, worthy offshoot of Your Excellency, in whose birth the great COUNCIL OF THE GODS is meeting (which furnishes the subject for the present Serenata) to endow her with those excellences which are fitting not only to herself, but also to her noble Parents. Here, my Lord, I might extend myself in the praises owed to Your Excellency and to your Most Excellent Bride whether I regard the merit of your noble Forebearers or if I consider the particular merits of each: but it would be undertaking so difficult a task, that would far surpass my weak powers, and would get me accused not of zeal, but of rashness. Therefore I pass over in silence the infinite merits of Your Excellency since they are so clearly registered in the annals of glory, and live so imprinted in the memories of Men, that I could not with the shadow of my ink add a point of light to that which Your Excellency dispenses copiously with your generosity, and the greatness of your thoughts, and with the deeds of your great liberality and magnificence. I only beg for Your Excellency's kindness in welcoming with pleased countenance, as is your custom, this homage, although slender, of my Muse, and to consider it worthy of your high protection against the tongues of ill-speakers; while with most

---

[26] Domenico's operas performed in Naples between 1703 and 1704 are "For Parrini, & Mutio."

reverent homage I dedicate myself eternally. / Most Excellent Lord
/ Your Excellency's / Most Humble Devoted and Obliged Servant /
Don Pietro Riccio. "

The speakers are Jove, Pallas, Juno, Venus, and Apollo, gathered together when necessary into a Chorus of Deities. The text alludes
to the noble families of the parents, and in certain cases it is clearly
impossible that the poet was radically modifying texts already set to
music by distant composers. In the Villafranca baptism I find, perhaps
for the first time, a custom that aristocrats, civic institutions, and confraternities in Sicily follow when it seems appropriate to stress the exceptional character of certain festivities: texts of local poets will cross the
sea to be set to music by distant composers, illustrious or considered to
be so, and to be printed in Naples, Rome, or Venice. In the case of the
performance in Messina that I have hypothesized, printing the libretto in
Naples would have made everything easier. It was much more practical
to print the text in the same city where the composer who wrote the
music resided; given the rivalry between the two cities, one could not
even think of distributing to spectators in Messina a libretto published in
Palermo. And this the Prince of Villafranca must have known all too well.

To complete the story of the relations between Cardinal del
Giudice and the musical activities of Palermo, it only remains for me to
give him credit for the arrival in Sicily of famous singers: first of all that
Antonio Lauri whom we left as "virtuoso of the Royal Chapel of Naples"
in the extraordinary cast of the *Tiberio* performed to celebrate Philip V.
Roman by birth, Antonio Lauri (or Lauro) was a tenor in the chapel at
Naples, as well as in the theater. We find him on both personnel lists as
published by Prota Giurleo (June 1702 and December 1704, paid almost
double what the other tenors were getting). Cardinal del Giudice succeeded in bringing him to Palermo, first to sing at Santa Cecilia, then as
a virtuoso in his own service (with what results on his attendance in the
Neapolitan Cappella you may imagine). Lauri was an outstanding figure in the musical life of Palermo, a real master of the stage who could
work himself so felicitously into the local scene that he got away (through
the customary protection of a magnate) with a grim crime of honor. The
Marchese of Villabianca, who remembered the episode at a distance of
more than half a century, tells us how lasting was the memory that the
bloody deed had left on the aristocracy of Palermo:

> [...] in my earliest years, before I was five, there flourished
> among the men [singers] Antonio Lauro, Roman, and Francesco
> Ferrazzano, Palermitan, and the Turcotta and the Manfré among
> the women. Some of our nobles committed themselves to the wor-

ship of these ladies with such ardor that they came to squander thousands of scudi in picking favorites, I imagine with great loss to their families. And then through these competitions these ladies returned home quiet as mice, with the gold in their pockets and embellished by the silver of Palermo. Their [the nobles'] folly reached such a point, that to distinguish one from another in the strength of their partisanship, they allowed themselves to wear in public the amorous emblems of the *jasmine* and the *anchor,* hanging from their breasts by *vermillion* and *green* ribbons not otherwise than if they had been honorable emblems of Knightly Orders.

Meanwhile, by these doings Palermo was burdened with the infamous reputation of being believed by foreigners to be a country of asses and low buffoons who let themselves be made fools of by women. And what is worse, this disorder of idolizing the fair sex was followed by a sad accumulation of serious disturbances, famous among them the double homicide committed around 1710 by the aforesaid fine actor Antonio Lauro, who with the scepter in his hand as he acted the role of a prince, had a low Assassin (a butcher by trade, whom unfortunately he encountered in the street in the dead of night while returning from the theater) massacre his wife and his mother-in-law, who were found at home in sin with the lawless late Duke of Serradifalco, Francesco lo Faso e Gaudioso.[27]

Although describing an event of which he certainly was not a direct witness, Villabianca increases the dose, taking as his starting point the scandalous protection of a prince to lament the passing of the good old days in which a magnate could dictate laws to the "white collars" (that is, the judicial class, from which came the Viceroy Caracciolo, the hated adversary of aristocratic privileges) and annotates the account with details that anticipate the *Henry IV* of Pirandello or *Hamlet,* where theater bloodily erupts into real life:

> With the scepter in his hand the enraged Lauro said to the pitiless outlaw: 'Kill this one, kill that one!' He would have died on the gallows for such a crime, if the protection of the Prince of la Cattolica, Giuseppe lo Bosco, one of the magnates of Palermo who in those days made himself much feared and much respected by the Government, had not saved him. The white collars [*collaretti*] did not have so much scope then.

I have quoted the episode at length to connect it with the other bloody crime of Astorga senior. Both the murder attempted by a baron

---

[27] Francesco Maria Emanuele e Gaetani, marchese di Villabianca, *De' Teatri Antichi e moderni della Città di Palermo,* "historical commentary" included in the manuscript of the *Diario palermitano,* 2 June 1787; later copied among the manuscript *Opuscoli palermitani* of the marchese (Palermo, Biblioteca Comunale), 2-3.

and the one carried out by a singer (who after a brief interruption of his long Sicilian season returned to being literally all the rage on the stage) went unpunished. As always, the standards which defer to certain hierarchies remain intact, and the musician can get away with it because the aristocrat who protects him is higher up than the "lawless duke" for whom, it seems, the dangerous incident had resolved itself into a *coitus* badly *interruptus.*

Villabianca also mentioned one of the Magdalens whom we last saw singing in *Tiberio* for Philip V at Naples: the Manfredi (her real name, confirmed by all the Palermitan libretti) who, at Palermo as at Naples, continued to title herself "chamber Virtuosa of His Highness of Savoy" until the coronation of Victor Amadeus allowed her to style herself in Naples "chamber virtuosa of His Majesty."

Some of the operas performed in Palermo had already been undertaken in Naples by Manfredi and Lauro, but these importations did not signal a passive recycling, since in those brilliant years even the so-called "name" singers abandoned their proverbial laziness to adapt themselves to new distributions of roles. For example, in *Ariovisto o vero l'Amor fra l'armi,* Lauro, who had been the hero in Naples, in Palermo sang the role of Valerio Procillo, formerly Manfredi's, while she returned to female attire to sing Elimene. In the same opera another singer (Anna Maria di Piedz) sang the comic role of Bellina in both cities. Although the opera was performed at Naples in 1702 with music by Francesco Mancini, there also exists in the Santini Collection in Münster (MÜp) a group of arias from *Ariovisto* attributed to Scarlatti (it does not specify Alessandro, Francesco, or another) that might be related to the Palermo performance. The libretto is dedicated, it goes without saying, "to the Most Eminent Signor D. Francesco Cardinal Giudice, by Divine Pity Titular [Cardinal] of Santa Sabina, of the Council of State of His Majesty, Archbishop and Lord of the City of Monreale, Viceroy, Protector, and Captain General in this Kingdom of Sicily."[28]

---

[28] Palermo, Biblioteca Comunale.

VII

Fugue for two voices, with some liberties

We left Alessandro and Domenico en route, headed for Florence, while we followed our Sicilian thread once more. The Duke of Ascalona had allowed only four of the ten months' leave previously requested by Scarlatti. Alessandro probably did not have sufficient artistic obligations to cover so long a period but he was certainly planning to display his Mimo on tour, prefiguring the career-launching jaunts of papa Mozart.

Father and son did not go to Florence alone.[1] At the end of the journey, thanking the Grand Prince from Rome, Alessandro informed him of the good health of the family members who accompanied him. However, Domenico was no longer among them if, as I believe, he had returned to Naples, respecting the terms of the leave which were disregarded as usual by his impatient father.

Datings and geographical references in manuscripts that transmit several cantatas (*Dopo lungo servire*, 2 July 1702; *Care pupille belle*, July 1702; *Ninfe belle, e voi pastori*, "written in Livorno") show that these pieces were composed on the journey to take advantage of the sixteen-year-old musician's capabilities as a vocal composer, to which Alessandro attached particular importance. Even if Domenico's excellence as a keyboard performer (testified by his Neapolitan appointments) could not escape his father, Alessandro refused to accept the idea that Domenico could follow a path other than the one that had brought the older man celebrity and honors. It would also have given him riches if only the "heavy weight of a numerous family" had not distanced him from the objectives that he had perceived from the first stages of his strange career, made up of both glory and privation.

But the edifice conceived by Alessandro rested on foundations of "virtù" and not of "virtuosity," which placed an established composer

---

[1] The discoveries communicated by William C. Holmes at the International Congress in Naples in 1985 (later published as "Lettere inedite su Alessandro Scarlatti," *La musica a Napoli durante il Seicento: Atti del Convegno Internazionale di Studi, Napoli, 11-14 aprile 1985* [Rome: Torre d'Orfeo, 1987], 369-378) revealed that father and son were anything but alone: Alessandro had the temerity to bring his entire "numerous family" to Florence.

far above a good performer, even if the former earned less than the latter. It was necessary for Domenico to conform to this pattern, even at
the risk of repressing his own natural tendencies. Eventually, his father's
bitter experiences would show him the right path, helping him avoid
obstacles and flee compulsions.

It is all to easy for an experienced musician to make his son
aware of certain values; and it is all too easy for a moralistic father to
open the eyes of a young man to all the corruption in the world of the
theater. Here also we anticipate the experience of the Mozarts, although
we lack the correspondence between father and son, since the Scarlattis
had the inconvenient habit of resolving verbally certain problems that
Leopold and Wolfgang Amadeus debated at length in their letters. Who
knows how much of the long journey to Florence was spent by Alessandro
in a detailed catechism of his son. Wedding his own expert wisdom to
his son's youth, papa Scarlatti was sure that he would obtain the intended results.

Even poor Corelli's bad showing could furnish useful elements
for Alessandro's moralizing. No matter how accomplished a performer
was, he always ran the risk of ruining in a single moment results that had
taken an entire lifetime to build. The fate of a composer of solid training
was different: only a king little disposed to music could have deserted a
concert in which Corelli performed one of his magnificent *Adagios*. In
compensation, musical Europe bowed before the magisterial learning
that the five collections already in print delivered to the admiration of
posterity (even if, after all, it was not vocal music ...). Certainly,
Domenico had excellent inclinations; but the necessity of aiding the family with his own earnings had already induced him to trust his own im-
provisational gift without investigating forms and structures that required lengthy experience before being practiced knowledgeably. In
the meantime, the journey would have put Domenico in contact with a
reality different from the Neapolitan one to which he was accustomed. Perhaps more than the other cities of Italy, Florence lent
itself to that experience, beginning when musical activities were sifted
through the "purified understanding" of the Grand Prince.

Assuming that the Scarlattis had arrived in Florence at the beginning of July,[2] Fabbri considered that Domenico's cantatas were composed for that occasion. Boyd[3] connects the works more reasonably

---

[2] Fabbri, *Scarlatti,* 44.

[3] Malcolm Boyd, "Domenico Scarlatti's *Cantate da Camera* and their Connection
with Rome," paper read at the international meeting on "Handel and the Scarlattis in
Rome" organized in June 1985 by the Accademia Nazionale di Santa Cecilia.

with Rome, where the Scarlattis had remained until the middle of the month, performing in the house of Marchese Ruspoli. The first evidence of Alessandro Scarlatti's activity in Florence is the letter written by the contralto and composer Antonio Pistocchi to the Bolognese Antonio Perti to inform him, in terms of acid disapproval, of the performance of the motet for four voices composed by Scarlatti for the thirty-ninth birthday (9 August) of Ferdinando. According to Pistocchi, Alessandro had written the motet "in a curious manner that never in our days would I have dreamed of such a thing" and had disappointed "the Virtuosi, Musici and *Geniali*" of the city, who had thronged the church to hear the music of Scarlatti and the singing of Matteuccio, come expressly from Naples after his triumphs in Madrid and Vienna. (Those in Madrid were particularly important, although the musical therapy that would later give momentary relief to the crises of Philip V, and would transform Farinelli, the greatest singer of the century, into a powerful minister in his new role of magic carillon, had failed with Charles II).

"The Motet did not please in general, nor Matteuccio, and not at all to the professionals." However, when we read that the major part of the spectators' praise went to Pistocchi himself, while Scarlatti received "a gold snuffbox, of the value of 18 or 20 dobles," and "Matteo a world of gifts from Checco" (our friend de Castris, Ferdinando's *mignon),* and "I, nothing," we understand that it is jealousy that guides the hand which wrote: "For that reason I consider that all my glories are covered with shit."[4]

Pistocchi says not a word about Domenico. Even if it is certain that his performances were reserved for a more select circle of listeners, one of the cantatas that I have already mentioned (*Dopo lungo servire,* dated 2 July) is for contralto and might have been performed by Pistocchi himself. But the boy was not yet writing anything challenging, and for that reason the singer-composer did not consider him a worthy target.

This letter shows us the snake-pit in which the prominent musician found himself working. Too proud to descend to direct polemic, Alessandro sought an antidote to the poison of the envious in his own studied and austere music. He erred, since such poison would be insinuated even into the "most purified understanding" of the Grand Prince, who would finally dismiss Scarlatti and turn to Perti, the recipient of the letter just quoted. From this point of view, Domenico would have done better not to learn proud discretion from his father and to choose other, less prejudiced and more realistic teachers of life.

[4] Fabbri, *Scarlatti,* 44-45.

When Alessandro left Florence at the end of October, the leave of absence from Ascalona for that first visit had already expired two weeks earlier. Don Geronimo della Marra had been dead for several years, but Scarlatti senior felt as though he had returned to the grand chaplain's times. He experienced his old psychological resistance to the reality of Naples. I maintain that Domenico returned punctually. In this also there might be some strategic design on the part of his father: that of putting himself aside in the hope that his son would succeed him. And the welcome he had received in Florence aroused the rosiest hopes. Ferdinando, a contemporary symbol of the cultivated patronage that Alessandro had always worshipped, resurrected Christina of Sweden, even if the Grand Prince lacked the impulsive frankness that marked the human side of Gustavus Adolphus' daughter. In truth, Alessandro's understanding with Christina had been immediate and remained deeper. Ferdinando announced himself pleased with the music that had been sent, but in commissioning new music he suggested and had others suggest to Alessandro something that should have put that seeker of utopian artistic dialogues on his guard: "Some rather easy and noble Music, and which, in the places where it is permitted, should be rather lively as well."[5] Thus Ferdinando called on Alessandro, not to write for connoisseurs, but to entertain his guests at Pratolino, not all of them disposed to Pindaric flights of the ear. Alessandro might amuse himself by sending Ferdinando archeological imitations and rarities, but not when the courteous host's principal aim was to avoid provoking yawns from the crowds who flocked to his parties.

At this point the reference to Christina of Sweden shows us how far Scarlatti was off the track. In 1706, he sent the Grand Prince a "madrigal for the table" (*Madrigale a Tavolino,* an unaccompanied madrigal), a genre that everyone considered completely outmoded by then.

The letter that accompanied the madrigal clarifies the intent of the donor:

> Taking the time for the production of Madrigals at Table (a pleasure of the most purified knowledge of the speculative Art of composition which, from the Prince of Venosa on, the late Queen of Sweden, who was my Patroness, took pleasure in more than any other composition, and Your Royal Highness has confirmed it) which gives me the boldness to present one to you at your royal feet [...] that it might have the fortune to be kindly pitied and corrected from its errors by the profound understanding of Your Royal Highness [...]."[6]

[5] Letter of Ferdinando, 8 April 1706, quoted by Fabbri, *Scarlatti,* 69.
[6] Letter of Alessandro, 28 August 1706, quoted by Fabbri, *Scarlatti,* 83.

The temptation to provoke Ferdinando to correct his music was a constant and malicious one; perhaps Alessandro did not realize that a patron of that importance does not waste his time correcting errors: he turns to others. But this type of *gaucherie* was innate in Scarlatti's character; he was ready to protest his inferiority in terms of the most shameless adulation but was capable of asking a Medici to descend to his own terrain. The Grand Prince must have read in these continuous requests a real challenge to which, for many reasons, he did not deign to reply.

Another nuisance in the correspondence was the proliferation of prayers, petitions, and heavenly benedictions, which— appropriate if aimed at Cosimo III—appear misplaced when directed to Ferdinando, that happy unbeliever. But Scarlatti himself gives a name to his unfortunate manner of behaving when he speaks euphemistically of the "composition of my own particular horoscope."[7]

Ferdinando appeared to play the game: in the correspondence the advice already mentioned seems more than amply balanced by exaggerated praises which only multiply after the arrival of the *Madrigale a Tavolino*. In the meantime, Alessandro continued to cultivate a fantasy, dreaming that sooner or later (and perhaps when the Grand Prince's father was dead, since for the moment Ferdinando remained dependent on his family) his favorite patron would summon the musician to himself once and for all.

Alessandro completed his journey back to Naples in a bit less than two months. We might believe that he walked, if it were not all too easy to understand that his reluctance to return to the Neapolitan routine made it natural for him to linger in Rome, which was beginning to rouse itself from the crisis of Innocent XII's reign. Here, to the splendor of Ottoboni, to the more discreet entertainments put on by Pamphilj and other cardinals or ambassadors, there had been added the life the miniature court of a new queen in exile. Not always solidly based financially, she desired to collect the spiritual inheritance (and the temporal one as well in the rank and esteem that she had enjoyed) of Christina of Sweden.

It is worth dedicating a parenthesis to this singular personage, destined to play an important role in the Roman vicissitudes of the Scarlattis. Maria Casimira of Poland serves as a link between father and son, who will succeed each other as *maestri di cappella* in her service. The Romans immediately sensed the worthlessness of a queen who was

---

[7] "Costituzione del mio particolare ascendente," letter of Alessandro, 18 April 1707, quoted by Fabbri, *Scarlatti,* 85.

"Christian" but not "Christine." Only the hope of reviving the happiest and most fortunate phase of his career could have induced Alessandro Scarlatti to prefer the dreams of Rome to the certainties of Naples, which had left him embittered and unsatisfied.

In addition, his earlier Roman patrons were ready to offer him further encouragement and to promise him additional earnings. Among them were Benedetto Pamphilj (we know cantatas of Scarlatti, dated 1702, on texts by the cardinal) and Ottoboni, who had not yet reached the bottom of his riches and credit. In short, Alessandro needed to believe in something that would keep him far from the yoke of Naples, and if the appointment to Florence continued to occupy his daydreams, other castles in the air kept him in Rome— until his lengthy absence turned into a genuine desertion. Current history would have us believe that Scarlatti senior did not return to Naples at all that year; in fact, he arrived in December, but only to pack up part of his family, and then head off to Rome.

Apparently Alessandro said nothing to the new grand chaplain or to the viceroy, since these two waited a good nine months before deciding that he had resigned and advertising a strange competition for the vacant post.[8] Why "strange"? Quite simply: the accounts tell us that the viceroy wished to be protected against local cliques and demanded that the qualifications of the four candidates be judged far away, in Venice. His suspicions were legitimate, but his choice of judge was absurd since the viceroy asked that Legrenzi—dead for almost fifteen years—evaluate what today we would call the written exams. Actually, there was great confusion in Naples between Legrenzi and a nephew of his, the much more humble Giovanni Varischino. This is confirmed by the preface to the old libretto of the *Odoacre,* which Alessandro had been obliged to modify, containing a tribute of praise to Legrenzi that turns out to be even more inappropriate when we learn that the original opera was written by Legrenzi's nephew and student!

If Alessandro hoped that his flight would favor his son he must have been disppointed, since Domenico kept out of the competition, and the lot fell to a Veneziano—one by name rather than by birth. In fact, the response from Venice designated the aged Don Cristoforo Caresana together with Don Gaetano Veneziano, but the final decision was subject to hearing their pieces performed and this favored Veneziano. In the same competition another young maestro emerged: Domenico Sarro, named vice master of the Royal Chapel at the end of 1702 and later the composer of the other Villafranca serenata.

---

[8] Prota Giurleo, "Breve Storia," 70ff.

But let us return to Domenico. First of all, we should ask what had been the consequences for him of the Florentine visit. It would be necessary to know the music that Mimo could have heard in Tuscany much better, in order to point out some influence of its style in the pallid copies of his father's vocal music that the obedient young genius continued dutifully to produce. But there is a circumstance important for the distant consequences on the "real" Domenico Scarlatti—that is, on the colorful butterfly who thirty years later would emerge from the cocoon where it had dozed.

We cannot verify the praises historians have offered to the musical taste of Ferdinando de' Medici, whose more than professional ability made him "the Orpheus of Princes," by examining his compositions; none have survived. Nor is it possible for us to judge his competence from a correspondence in which concepts and opinions of some importance are drowned in a sea of expressions of the most conventional and redundant courtesy. When he chose Alessandro Scarlatti in far-off Naples, Ferdinando showed that he was a most up-to-date connoisseur of opera fashions; one must admit, however, that he would also show himself equally sensitive to changes in fashion by his later desertion of an Alessandro who was no longer à la page. In all these choices, the Grand Prince is not exempt from the suspicion of aesthetic snobbery. This gives way to admiration when we consider that under his patronage Bartolomeo Cristofori invented the instrument destined to revolutionize domestic music making for the next two centuries: the harpsichord "with soft and loud," "il gravicembalo col piano e col forte."

The confrontation between the persistence of certain vocal stereotypes and the independent evolution of instrumental music offers a fascinating investigation for those with direct access to texts that document the change of taste and style from the so-called "Baroque" to the so-called "Viennese Classicism." I have scattered the "so-called's" around because today we are rethinking certain schematizations that had been quietly accepted until a few years ago, although in the case of Domenico Scarlatti the final outcome of this evolutionary process interests us only marginally. At the beginning of the eighteenth century the problem of rendering the harpsichord, an "instrument that can neither swell nor diminish sounds" into one "capable of expression" troubled Couperin,[9] who promised his gratitude to whoever could achieve so utopian a result. In fact, Couperin himself was the repository of that *art infini* necessary for the miracle, but his employment of *rubato* and some conventions of phrasing had illustrious precedents in the tradition of Frescobaldi. No matter what certain fashionable scholars maintain, the aesthetic of *one* instrument could not be before the Romantic era—the aesthetic of *all* instruments. There was, however, the custom of *transference* (calm yourselves: I am not speaking of psychoanalysis), to keyboard instruments of formulas usually belonging to other instruments and especially to instrumental ensembles. Nonetheless, pragmatic solutions could not furnish the exact sonorous equivalents, demanded by the impulse toward a uniformity of means destined to transform itself, with the advent of Classicism, into a uniformity of language. Thus the invention of an instrument with struck strings rather than plucked ones dealt a heavy blow to Couperin's *esprit de finesse* but smoothed the way for the realization on the keyboard of the *crescendo* effects with which the new orchestral technique was experimenting. Try performing a piece like *L'âme en peine* on an antique fortepiano: it is a real blasphemy, like adapting a Debussy *Prélude* to the harpsichord, or even to the clavichord.

Yes, the clavichord: strongly influenced by Kirkpatrick's categorical rejection of the instrument as a performing medium for Scarlatti's sonatas, based on the conspicuous absence of clavichords in the inventories of the Queen's and Farinelli's instruments, I considered it completely out of place in the Scarlattian panorama and described it as a "myth of musicological science-fiction." Kenyon de Pascual's discoveries[10] testify to the presence of clavichords in Spanish eighteenth-century musical life. So I must give some credit to occasional performances of Scarlatti sonatas on this medium, without forgetting that the clavichord is more suited to a single person than even to small domestic audiences. In Florence, Domenico had the good fortune to encounter, well before so many harpsichordists of the period, a new medium destined to follow him during all the last, incomparable phase of his career as a musician. Mimo Scarlatti was able quickly to profit from his technique as a keyboard player on this instrument with its unusual and still imperfect mechanical requirements. The impact that Johann Sebastian Bach might have had with Silbermann's instruments, Domenico had with Cristofori's prototype. Unlike his great contemporary, who was skeptical about this novelty, Mimo must have immediately understood that the Cristofori fortepiano would give him the means of realizing better certain vocal models of his inspiration on the keyboard.

---

[9] François Couperin, *Pièces de clavecin, Premier livre* (Paris, 1713), Préface.

[10] Beryl Kenyon de Pascual, "Harpsichords, Clavichords and Similar Instruments in Madrid in the second half of the Eighteenth Century," *Royal Musical Association, London, Research Chronicle* 18 (1982), 66-84.

I confess that I have allowed myself to anticipate matters that should not be confused with my biographical narrative, but I wanted even readers not specifically interested in the "fugue"that I promised, to notice a detail of extreme importance: the artist whom we continue to consider the greatest harpsichordist of all time was among the first to know this revolutionary development, destined a century later to eclipse the aristocratic instrument to which we wrongly ascribe too exclusively Domenico Scarlatti and his music. When the young genius arrived in Florence, for him the "piano" and the "forte" existed only as opposed sonorous entities on the keyboards of those instruments with which he had a marvelous familiarity. The possibility of obtaining a gradual passage from one to the other dynamic level involved the progressive abandonment of a very narrow repertory of rhetorical formulas: that of the so-called *Terrassendynamik* (terrace dynamics, conceived by the opposition of clearly-differentiated sound masses). For the moment Domenico remained bound to tradition, but the seed of such an upsetting novelty had been planted in the fertile soil of his imagination.

Despite these new experiences, which he could have investigated thoroughly only by remaining in Florence, Domenico returned to Naples. My departures from the chronological exposition of events have already anticipated part of what remains to be told about the young musician's last stay in his native city.

Domenico returned to a city where the previous opera season had celebrated, with splendid festivities, the arrival of Philip V. On that occasion the Viceroy Ascalona must have made the greatest possible effort to obtain subsidies for theatrical activities, but now it seemed that he would be much less courageous and unprejudiced than his predecessor Medina Coeli. Discouraged by such dark prospects, the impresario Serino must have shown his intention of giving up his activity, at least for the moment. At this point there enters the story of the knavery of the Pagano-Scarlattis vis-à-vis Barbapiccola, the rich relative whom they induced to pledge his own credit in a theatrical venture that would provide work for the whole family. In Alessandro's absence without leave, young Domenico was permitted to emerge from obscurity. This move has been seen as one more pressure on the viceroy to give the young son the post the father had deserted, but the precedents did not favor this. The "patriot virtuosi" were much more resolved not to be tricked, and there were no "whore actresses" involved. (While the preparations for the season were in full swing, Anna Maria Barbapiccola, seriously ill, was experiencing the far-from-disinterested hospitality of her sister and brother-in-law.) This time, the second-hand attractions and the pseudonyms employed on the preceding occasion (the opera with the *bambocci*) were abandoned. Instead, Domenico was called upon to carry out the same task that had been his father's: to rejuvenate the music of earlier operas by the addition of new arias adapted to the current singers. They were then declared to be operas "by Sig. Domenico Scarlatti;"[11] although he protested *sotto voce* that he did not wish to "cheat" his predecessors "of the praise (worthily due to the [...] original Composer of the Music)." In fact, for only two of the three operas is there a definite pre-existing source (*Il Giustino,* by Legrenzi, and *L'Irene* of Carlo Francesco Pollarolo, transformed for the occasion into "Sig. Gio: Battista Pullaroli"). *L'Ottavia ristituita al trono,* which is presented on the titlepage of the libretto as an "opera of the Abb. Giulio Convò" (the same poet employed for the reworking of the other texts) would seem to have been set to music by Domenico alone, but the existence of one of the customary anthologies, which adds thirty-three "Arias with instruments from the Opera entitled *Ottavia ristituita al Trono.* Of Sig.r Domenico Scarlatti" to those which must have been the original interventions of the young musician in *Giustino* arouses my distrust. I admit that I exaggerate in such suspicions, but everything that I know of the *modus operandi* of the Scarlatti household induces me to see falsifications and workshop labor in several of the products attributed to one of the "authors," or in other products more conveniently left in anonymity. In formulating these accusations I find myself in excellent company, since forty years before me the late Claudio Sartori, the most acute expert on the historical data of Baroque opera retrievable from libretti, had reached similar conclusions.[12] Indeed, we owe to Sartori the first intelligent, detailed information on certain mysterious traits in Alessandro's behavior and that of his relatives/subjects in Naples.

In 1942, when Sartori was writing, Prota Giurleo had not yet published the documents relating to the wills of Anna Maria Scarlatti and the controversies following her death.[13] For this reason, having duly pointed out that Domenico's debut has the air of "a family party" in which Giuseppe Scarlatti participated as "Engineer and Painter" (in *Giustino*) and Tommaso Scarlatti as singer (he has a determining role in

---

[11] Claudio Sartori, "Gli Scarlatti a Napoli: Nuovi contributi," *Rivista Musicale Italiana* XLVI (1942), 374, 390 [hereafter Sartori, "Scarlatti"].

[12] I also render admiring tribute to this musicologist, also because I have never forgotten the affectionate letter that he wrote me after having read my biography of Alessandro. He approved *toto corde* the re-appraisal of its protagonist which had so annoyed others.

[13] Prota Giurleo, "Anna Maria," *passim.*

consolidating a tenor tradition characteristic of Neapolitan opera), was Sartori unaware that the impresario was also a member of the family, and that just at this time he had no reason to congratulate himself on the fact.

In viewing Domenico's debut, no contemporary witness acclaimed the miracle; rather, the chroniclers allowed the novelty to pass in silence, perhaps in expectation of developments in a situation that was quite different from the one hoped for by papa Scarlatti. The prestigious widower Barbapiccola had continued to sign the dedications to the viceroy or to his nearest relatives. However. no one could have induced him to embark on a new theatrical venture, especially after many of those who had taken advantage of him had summoned him into court to harass him by a sequestration of his fortune that smelled of blackmail. We may well believe that, in addition to the dedications, Barbapiccola had sent the viceroy his complaints about the persecution that he underwent from those jackals. The facts remain that the regained respectability of the Scarlattis must have been compromised by the new scandal, and that the new plan for the Royal Chapel, launched by the Viceroy Ascalona after the appointment of Veneziano, did not assure for Domenico any of the advantages hoped for and even lost him the post of "Chamber Musician to His Excellency"[14] and the salary which went with it. Since other young musicians were promoted to important posts on the same occasion, it was easy to see these new events reflected a change in fortune. Alessandro must have been consulted with all possible haste, but the moment was not favorable to him either, since he had been obliged to accept a modest settlement, decent but far from worthy of his own merit: the appointment of assistant to the *maestro di cappella* of Santa Maria Maggiore in Rome, obtained for him by Cardinal Ottoboni. Alessandro still had with him Pietro, his first son and a millstone around his neck (a year later Alessandro would finally succeed, with the help of the pope, in having Pietro named *maestro di cappella* at the cathedral of Urbino); but the mortification of Naples could not be suffered without reacting. Thus, on 5 January 1705 the Viceroy Ascalona had to reinstall the elderly Cristoforo Caresana, already retired, since "the organist Domenico Scarlatti had resigned of his own free will."[15]

For Alessandro, it had been a real catastrophe.

It must have seemed to Alessandro that he had planned everything carefully (including satisfying his unwillingness to return to Naples). Now, instead, a certain Mancini—an adroit but not completely negli-

14 Prota Giurleo, "Anna Maria," 74.
15 Prota Giurleo, "Breve Storia," 74.

gible *homo novus*, prepared to seize the favorable occasion—had even succeeded in having assigned to himself the supplement that had been taken from Mimo.

We can be sure that not even so unhappy an outcome of what should have been the validation of Domenico's genius suggested to the proud Alessandro that he had erred, that he had directed his son badly, that he himself was the most cumbersome obstacle to accomplishing those goals that were inevitable for Domenico. The authoritarian *religio* in his blood must have held out the only possible hope: to admit that he had erred would have been to confess that he could still err. No: the fault was all that of the Neapolitans who had been incapable of understanding the young genius or who, worse still, understood him only too well but profited by his weakness to make him pay, at twenty years' distance, for what they had had to put up with from his father.

If all hope was lost in Naples, Rome in those years certainly could not offer a worthy revenge to the ill-treated young man. Alessandro knew this well, since all that the protection of the powerful Ottoboni had been able to secure for him—one of the most famous musicians of the period—was the post of assistant, good only for saving him from the necessity of returning to Naples. It was in Rome, however, that his son was soon to rejoin him. The real error—but this, Alessandro could confess only to himself—had been that of leaving Domenico without support and fatherly counsel in all that Neapolitan mess; exposed, moreover, to the resentment aroused at every level by the manoeuvres of the Pagano gang.

But had the viceroy of Naples acted without consideration and in bad faith? I do not think so. Not having the intuition that allowed Alessandro to divine the talent of his son even in the vocal compositions of those years, the Duke of Ascalona stuck to the facts, and these, as we have seen, were not encouraging. The three operas performed during the following season had not been real fiascos, but the comparison with the musical display organized in honor of Philip V certainly was not in their favor. Moreover, the hidden pressure exercised by the delinquent Alessandro was not only gauche and indiscreet, but also particularly irritating. He had asked Ascalona to oblige a proverbial absentee by assigning his post to a young man who a short time after his first appointment had already requested ten months' leave without even giving up the salary that, in his absence, would have had to be paid to a substitute.

The arias composed by Domenico in that unhappy season show that the Duke of Ascalona acted wisely in insisting upon a competition to find a replacement for the obstinate Scarlatti senior. He certainly erred, however, when he inflicted on Domenico's self-esteem the humiliation of a pay-cut that deprived His Excellency of the possibility of enjoying the best part of young Domenico's musical talent: the exercise of his functions as "Chamber Musician" of which he had been relieved unexpectedly.

Everything inclines me to limit the first unmistakable manifestations of Domenico's talent to the keyboard . Given the lack of harpsichord compositions attributable with certainty to those years, it is likely that genius found its outlet in improvisation. This must have been rooted in a Neapolitan tradition since a half century later Francesco Milano, Prince of Ardore, an excellent amateur of music and the Neapolitan ambassador to France, could eclipse Calvière and Daquin, considered by everyone as the French specialists in the *grand Art de Préluder.* The source of this information might render it suspect, since it is the great francophobe Jean-Jacques Rousseau who swears that the prince-ambassador had surpassed the most illustrious artists "by the vivacity of his invention & the force of his execution."[16]   But we realize that we are not talking about the usual amateur when Francesco Durante, "Formerly Cheiron to this Achilles," forgets the customary golden trumpets of fame to dedicate his *Sonate per Cembalo divise in Studii e Divertimenti* to his ex-pupil, Ardore, who "In the manner of the famous heroes of Greece/Is Pleased to bring marvelously/The Study of Music/Powerful Medicine for the Soul/And noble Ornament of well-born and cultivated Spirits/To the Highest Rank of Perfection [...]."[17]

Francesco Durante. See whom I encounter just when I am maintaining that Alessandro should have encouraged his Mimo's propensities for the keyboard. An inconvenient encounter, insofar as the entire biographical and artistic career of the musician whom the same Jean-Jacques had called "the greatest harmonist of Italy, that is to say of the world,"[18] demonstrates that in Naples true glory could not be separated from the operatic stage. In 1744, on the death of Leonardo Leo, the now sixty-one-year-old Durante wished to participate, together with eight other less famous musicians, in the competition for the post of first master of

16 Jean-Jacques Rousseau, *Dictionnaire de Musique* (Paris: Veuve Duchesne, 1768), 389, s.v. *Préluder.*

17 Dedication of the *Sonate per cembalo,* reprint (Bologna: Forni, n.d. [1974]).

18 Rousseau, *Dictionnaire,* s.v. *Composition,* which Francesco Degrada quoted from the 1762 edition. In the 1768 edition I find a reference to Durante only under *Compositeur,* 109: the author compares Durante to "Corelli, Vinci, Perez, Rinaldo, Jomelli" and judges him "more knowledgeable than them all." Degrada's citation matches the one that Burney (*Present State,* 315 n.) refers to the same source.

the Royal Chapel. None of the four examiners (Hasse, Perti, Costanzi, and Jomelli) found his examination-piece worthy of consideration. If Domenico had remained in Naples, free to follow his own vocation, probably he would have come to the same end as his contemporary, only seemingly fortunate; paradoxically, Francesco Durante's career justifies the firm attitude of Alessandro.

We have little information about the beginnings of Durante's career. He held teaching posts in three of the four famous Neapolitan conservatories; barely six months in 1710 at Sant'Onofrio a Capuana, eleven years (1728-1739) at the Poveri di Gesù Cristo, two years at Santa Maria di Loreto (1742-1744), and again at Sant'Onofrio for thirteen years (1742-1755). The fact that he was employed at the same time, and for so long at two conservatories shows the prestige which he enjoyed as a teacher. Almost all the composers who spread out over Europe from Naples during the eighteenth century were pupils of Durante, and his teaching is an indispensable point of reference for the adherents of the venerable conception of a "Neapolitan School." As I have already said, Durante remained excluded from the opera "business." The time that he did not devote to teaching he employed in composing sacred music, collections of basses for his students to harmonize, and toccatas and sonatas for harpsichord. These he conceived as halfway between the "study" and the "divertimento" (the titles he gave to the two sections of each of the six sonatas dedicated to Ardore, a prince and the improviser of preludes).

Durante's *Sonate* have to be placed in a very special area of keyboard music: that in which "study" becomes "diversion," and traditional teaching is crystallized into geometric aggregations of sound, dictated half by the agile play of the fingers and half by normative harmonic schemes already consolidated in a multi-century process.

Francesco Degrada[19] has stressed that the reality of the Neapolitan conservatories was "provincial by definition" to justify emphasizing other traditions claiming that Durante moved to Rome for five years in his youth in order to profit by the teaching of Pitoni and Pasquini, or that he even visited northern Europe. For Degrada, such experiences far from Naples suggest that Durante absorbed from Pitoni, an heir of the Palestrinian tradition, or that the contact with northern orchestral conceptions destined to find their outlet in the *Concerti* for strings. To me the obscurity of the data concerning Durante's apprentice years sug-

---

[19] Francesco Degrada, Preface to Francesco Durante, *Sonate per Cembalo divise in Studii e Divertimenti* (Milan: Ricordi, n. d. [1978]).

gests a widening of keyboard experiences, different from the balanced universe of Pasquini, with distant roots in those Neapolitan pioneers of keyboard music who have recently aroused the interest of young musicologists.

It is more than logical that the priceless Villarosa[20] or the partisan Florimo[21] should resist biographical hypotheses that weaken the Neapolitan quality of Durante. Nonetheless, there remains a real black hole to fill. Today no one wishes to consider seriously the hypothesis that Durante was a pupil of Alessandro Scarlatti. However, there remains the possibility that in Naples or in Rome Domenico encountered Durante, who around 1732 would publish in the city that Scarlatti junior had left forever the harpsichord sonatas that were perhaps the closest to the anticonformist boldness of Domenico's *Essercizi*.

The Durante of those years is the super-bourgeois musician whom Villarosa and Florimo have described. By remaining in Naples, Domenico would have possibly surrendered to the progressive coarsening of Durante by three unstimulating marriages, or by those listeners who, having requested him to "perform one of his sonatas for harpsichord," ended by finding them "of long duration and always of the same kind."[22]

"He went all red," Florimo recounts, "and showed the effort that lasted while he performed them, and as soon as he had finished, he found relief only by gulping down a glass of wine."[23]

We are far indeed from the astonished enthusiasm aroused by Domenico when he sat down at the harpsichord. At the risk of appearing inconsistent, I remain thankful to Scarlatti senior for having "detached" his son from Naples "by force."

---

[20] Carlantonio de Rosa marchese di Villarosa, *Memorie dei compositori di musica nel regno di Napoli,* (Naples: Stamperia Reale, 1840 [hereafter Villarosa, *Memorie*]), 70-74.

[21] Francesco Florimo, *La Scuola Musicale di Napoli e i suoi Conservatori* (Naples, 1882 [hereafter Florimo, *Scuola*]), II, 178-184.

[22] Florimo, *Scuola,* II, 181.

[23] Ibid., II, 182.

VIII

Polish Intermezzi - 1

"I was born of a Gallic cock a simple hen,
Lived among the Pole-try and then a queen ..."

One cannot say that the biographers of the Scarlattis—including me, I admit—have gotten the ex-queen of Poland in correct focus. Kirkpatrick made an error of fact in believing that the Polish monarchy was hereditary and in speaking of a son of Maria Casimira who, when he had ascended the throne, got rid of his mother by exiling her to Rome.[1] The truth is different, and the protagonists are so picturesquely placed in a well-defined historical reality as to deserve a closer investigation.

The Mémoires of Saint-Simon describe at great length a certain event at the end of the seventeenth century, but one cannot say that the fascination of prose and the sharpness of judgments of his are complemented by his sufficient precision in his information. This source is precious rather for its reconstruction of the humors of the French faction and of a political and courtly mentality that not all historians have been able to render in adequate terms.

Saint-Simon allots a few scraps of attention to Henri de la Grange, Marquis d'Arquien, a very marginal figure in his vast fresco, describing him as

> a man of wit, of good company and very fashionable in society,
> where he was greatly helped by the Duc de Saint-Aignan and by
> his sister, the Comtesse de Béthune, a lady-in-waiting of queen Maria
> Theresa.[2]

According to this source, such powerful protection had not succeded in assuring sufficient income for d'Arquien's career. Having become a widower with a son and five daughters in 1672, he managed to send two of the girls off to the cloister but remained "hindered in marrying the others,"[3] so that he decided to follow a friend who was ambassador to

[1] Kirkpatrick, Scarlatti, 55.
[2] Saint-Simon, Mémoires, VI, 29.
[3] Ibid.

Poland, with his cargo of marriageable daughters. To avoid confusion, I will specify that the Comtesse de Béthune (the sister of Saint-Aignan) is not the *Marquise* de Béthune, Maria Casimira's sister, whom we shall soon encounter in a state of absolute hostility toward her dissolute father. Saint-Simon is fantasizing when he claims that the first positive result of Arquien's move to Poland was the marriage of Maria Casimira to Jacob Radziwill, Prince of Zamosli and Palatine of Sandomir, a man who joined good fortune to sufficient discretion to leave her soon a widow. According to Saint-Simon the enterprising young French woman was now rich and childless, quite disposed to transform herself into an appetizing "tidbit"for more than one reason.[4] The reality is very different, as Waliszewski tells us in his colorful but well-informed *Marysienka*.[5]

Maria Casimira, who since 1657 had been married to Prince Zamoyski (this is the correct spelling of the title mangled by Saint-Simon), could not have been part of the picturesque baggage of marriageable daughters transferred to Poland after 1672 by the marquis. "Marysienka" had already reached her adoptive country in childhood as part of the suite of Maria Gonzaga, who in 1645 had married the aged and gouty king Ladislas IV. In bringing her along as an act of charity, the queen had defied the spiteful gossip aroused by the undefined role of a four-year-old girl in the suite of a woman with a lively romantic past.

On 9 August 1647 the only heir of this royal marriage died, and a year later his father followed him to the tomb. To remain on the throne, Maria Gonzaga had to marry John Casimir, Ladislas's successor. Do not forget this precedent: we will encounter an unfortunate attempt to repeat this curious maneuver.

The intrigues, the wars, and the struggles that formed the background of the adolescence and the early maturity of Maria Casimira are described by Waliszewski in terms that confirm certain dubious aspects of that personage. However, her biographer finds the negative judgment on Marysienka formulated by most Polish historians unjust and on the whole exaggerated. Nonetheless he furnishes us with all the ingredients to render the "Arquien queen" a commonplace busybody basically in love with her Sobieski, but not sufficiently so to sacrifice to him her personal ambitions (all too often unsuccessful) and a desire for preeminence with insignificant and sometimes downright ridiculous results.

---

[4] Ibid.

[5] Kazimierz Waliszewski, *Marysienka, Marie de la Grange d'Arquien Reine de Pologne femme de Sobieski 1641-1676* (Paris: Plon, 1896 [hereafter Waliszewski]). Except where otherwise indicated, all the information on the Polish sojourn of Maria Casimira is drawn from this source.

The riches of the widow Zamoyoki which, according to Saint-Simon, must have been the deciding force in Sobieski's choice—were somewhat uncertain, since the relatives of the deceased contested her possession of the family goods. Beyond that, the proud warrior was an old acquaintance of Maria Casimira, who was only fifteen when her glance crossed Sobieski's for the first time; he was then still far from the successes that would make him the defender of Christian Europe against the Ottoman peril. Maria Gonzaga must have given excellent advice to her little maid of honor. Maria Casimira was joined in marriage with Prince Zamoyski only a year later; she put on her bridal gown in the queen's apartment before a table on which were displayed "lakes of love" formed by the great pearls given by the bridegroom. On this occasion the handmaid already seemed to follow the example of her august protectress. Her bridegroom was a magnate and a tippler, gouty and gross; from him Marysienka would have riches and jewels but not joy. The three sickly children born of their union died in early infancy.

The protection of the queen allowed Maria Casimira long and brilliant sojourns in Warsaw; her husband grumbled in the country but refrained from joining his wife. Quite soon Maria Gonzaga had proof of certain indiscretions: while waiting to become famous in more important battles, Sobieski had emerged victorious from certain love-skirmishes with the lovely princess. At first it must have been a question only of playful re-enactment of the two lovers as Astrée and Celadon, the protagonists of Honoré d'Urfeé's lengthy pastoral novel. Then the skirmishes were transformed into a turbulent passion, destined to cultimate in not one but two weddings and a long married life.

The unusual fact of two weddings deserves some clarification. After the unexpected and providential widowing of Maria Casimira, Celadon got cold feet, but Maria Gonzaga considered it indispensable to bind him to certain of her political designs by means of the lovely Astrée. The trap into which Sobieski fell remains perhaps the darkest page in the entire military record of the hotblooded warrior. Astrée attracted her lover to the royal palace for an encounter of gallantry—but here it is worth turning the pen over to Waliszewski:

> It was mid-May; the windows opened on a park that was perfumed and resounded with the songs of birds in love. You can guess the rest. At the appropriate moment Maria Gonzaga made her sensational entrance.
>
> Surprise and well-simulated anger, an explosion of reproaches and high-sounding words: scandal, outrage to God, and the crime of lèse-majesté!

Sobieski crumbled. Although very astute, this great man had never lost a certain amount of ingenuousness. He was scolded, reproached, sermonized; they spoke of honor, of religion, of necessary reparation. He surrendered. It was eleven o'clock at night. At midnight a priest appeared, perhaps the king's confessor [...]. A quarter of an hour later Sobieski left the castle, somewhat dazed by his adventure and more or less married according to the rules."[6]

For the moment it was to have been only a secret marriage; but the fat was in the fire, everyone knew, and the scandal was enormous. There were those who went so far as to suspect Maria Casimira of having poisoned her husband. In addition, Zamoyski was not yet buried, and his relatives refused to be present at the solemn funeral, protesting that they were offended because they had not been invited to the new wedding! The marriage was re-celebrated in great style (by the future Innocent XII, at that time nuncio to Poland) on 6 July 1665, with festivities and a ball commanded and presided over by the king in person. The Austrian resident commented on the ceremony without mincing words, calling it "a farce between persons already married for a long time."

Far from having moved to Poland as Saint-Simon would have us believe, the Marquis d'Arquien had remained in France. His wife was still alive, and the couple had barely replied negatively to a letter from Maria Gonzaga requesting their pleasure in the new union when a new missive exploded like a bolt from the blue with the news of the secret marriage. Waliszewski regales us with a real gem by publishing the letter to Maria Casimira in which the marquis declares himself appalled, disappointed, and saddened by the new Polish marriage of the young widow whom he had wished to recall to France, given the unfortunate result of her preceding experience. Evidently no one in Paris had any clear ideas about the brilliant prospects that the protection of the queen assured to Sobieski, the Grand Marshal who had succeeded the rebel Lubomirski. The facts soon belied such pessimism, even if at the deaths of Lubomirski and Maria Gonzaga the feeble John Casimir saw no further obstacles to his own abdication, with the prospect of selling to the Sun King for a high price his own support for the election of a French prince to the Polish throne.

Maria Casimira believed it the moment to insinuate herself into this complicated situation by returning to her own country, unbeknownst to Saint-Simon and officially justified by the desire to give birth to Sobieski's first child on her native soil. In reality she was bored to death

6 Waliszewski, 135-136.

in Poland and hoped to reap advantages for her husband, for herself, and for the Arquien family from the election of the new king of Poland. Louis XIV was displeased by her continuous requests for his intervention in favor of the litigious and ruined Marquis d'Arquien, by her claim to barter Sobieski's influence in Polish affairs for benefits of every sort, but above all by Maria Casimira's aspiration to the *tabouret,* that is, to the right of remaining seated in the presence of the sovereigns. In 1669 the Sun King would write to one of his ambassadors:

> the behavior of the *grande maréchale* who was born my subject and has kept her foot firmly on my throat, in the absolute need that she saw or believed that I had of her husband, and all her indiscreet, imprudent, and impudent expressions have remained in my spirit and in my heart [...].[7]

A real success, for a woman who was convinced that she had been cut out for the management of delicate diplomatic affairs! This explains the origin of Saint-Simon's unfavorable appraisal.

Having given him an heir, Maria Casimira informed Sobieski that she did not want any other children. The angry satrap continued to proclaim that he was ardently in love with his wife. He lamented her long absence, and he saw in an abundant progeny the symbol of the vitality of a union that had undergone a thousand tests, especially from the capricious and obstinate character of Astrée. In this case, the warrior won the game: after the first birth in 1667 Maria Casimira brought into the world at least another eleven or twelve children, in addition to the three Zamoyskis who died as infants. Half of the little Sobieskis suffered the same fate: only three males and three females reached maturity.

At this point in our story an event occurred that Maria Casimira would never have dared hope for at first. To visualize the background of the events that were maturing it is timely to reread a page of Voltaire dedicated to the kings of Poland. He depicts the contradictions threatening the political balance of a nation that for centuries claimed to be able to combine the institution of monarchy with a republican mentality always, if disputably, ascribed to Roman *civitas:*

> Anyone who saw a king of Poland in the pomp of his royal majesty would believe him the most absolute ruler in Europe: he is, however, the least. The Poles in fact make with him the contract between the sovereign and his subjects which one could only imagine in other nations. At his coronation itself, while swearing the

---

[7] Quoted by Waliszewski, 229.

pacta conventa the king of Poland dispenses his subjects from their oath of obedience in the case that he violates the laws of the state.

He nominates all the offices, and confers all honors. Nothing is hereditary in Poland, except land and noble rank. The son of a palatine and that of the king have no right to the dignities of their father; but there is this great difference between the king and the state, that he cannot take away any office after having bestowed it, and that the state has the right to take away his crown if he transgresses its laws.

The nobility, jealous of their liberty, often sell their votes, and rarely their affections. They have barely elected a king than they fear his ambition, and oppose to him their conspiracies. The grandees whom he has made, and cannot unmake, often become his enemies instead of remaining his creatures. Those who are attached to the court are the object of the hatred of the rest of the nobility: which always forms two parties: an inevitable division, and even a necessary one, in countries where one wishes to have kings, and to conserve one's liberty [...].[8]

This division between court and nobility disappeared after the abdication of John Casimir. While Condé, Bavaria, and Lorraine competed for the favor of the electors, the Bishop of Culm had the idea of promoting a national alternative: they must acclaim as king a *Piast,* a Polish aristocrat. The idea began to catch on, and when in a full session of the parliament someone had the courage to shout the magic word, making some allusion to Sobieski, the latter witnessed the strange plebiscite/election of Michael Wisniowieski, whom he considered "a fool, an ape, an imbecile, a beggar to whom the late queen gave four thousand lire a year so that he could study in Bohemia."

The new king was the son of Maria Casimira's former sister-in-law. After so many disputes about the Zamoyski inheritance, it was necessary to reach an understanding; malicious gossips said that Maria Casimira attempted to seduce her ex-nephew, but Sobieski made no secret of his rage at seeing the "ape" on the throne. A serious conspiracy developed, exacerbated by Wisniowieski's marriage with an Austrian archduchess, which placed the French party in crisis. Other intrigues, open rebellion on the part of the Grand Marshal; Louis XIV, ever less disposed toward the intriguing Maria Casimira (who in the meantime had returned to France), refused his support.

---

[8] Voltaire (François-Marie Arouet), *Histoire de Charles XII* (Paris: Bry Aîné, n. d. [1856]), 40-41.

"Thus my last and firm resolution is to leave them in the mortification where they now are [...],"[9] wrote the Sun King about the
Sobieskis. It appeared to be the end, but the death of king Michael
solved everything.

Sobieski's first important military victories had already made him
a beloved hero. The usual foreign candidates were easily eliminated,
and on 21 May 1674 Maria Casimira found herself queen of Poland.

In spite of everything, at the beginning of the Sobieski reign, relations with the crown of France seemed idyllic. The Sun King had let it
be known immediately that he would never address his new "brother" as
"Majesty," but in compensation he consented that at his coronation Maria
Casimira should receive the treatment reserved to a daughter of a king
of France. If, as wife of the Grand Marshal, Marysienka had believed
that she could profit from political negotiations with the crown of France,
as queen she induced her husband to widen the scope of his claims:
subsidies for the war against the Turk, an alliance with Sweden against
Brandenburg, military aid to reconquer lost territories. But in the midst
of all these requests dictated by reasons of state, at the head of the line
were Marysienka's old aspirations, exacerbated by previous refusals;
her father, the marquis, must be made a duke and promoted to the rank
of peer of France, for his second son she asked a regiment. As if all this
were not sufficient, the Sun King's intervention was solicited even in
domestic matters of minor importance, such as the dismissal of a German servant who was robbing the Marquis d'Arquien, or the relegation
to a convent of a prostitute intent on appropriating for herself some of the
last crumbs of the fortune already depleted by drunkenness and lawsuits.

Such vulgarity must have turned the stomach of Louis XIV, but
politics demanded compromises, and when the Sun King was obliged to
sign a patent *carte blanche* for a dukedom and a peerage of France, he
believed that Maria Casimira had employed that means to extort from
him the hoped-for advancement of her father. The king's anger knew no
bounds when he found out that the Sobieskis had betrayed his trust by
elevating to that dignity an imposter called Brisacier, who had succeeded
in worming himself into their good graces by displaying false documents
proving his distant Polish origins and the high lineage of his ancestors.

That was more than the great Louis could bear. It is not surprising
to read in Saint-Simon that Maria Casimira, "carried away by seeing a
crown on her head [...] had a burning passion to come to display it in
her own country, which she had left as so unimportant a private per-

---

[9] Quoted by Waliszewski, 229.

son."[10]   When she proposed to take the waters at Bourbon, her sister
Béthune informed her that the queen of France would not treat her as an
equal, insofar as the non-hereditary character of the Polish royal dignity
could not be equated with one solidly rooted in a dynastic tradition.
Rage of Maria Casimira: voyage cancelled, a plot of alliance with the
court of Vienna and all the enemies of France, pressure on her husband
to abandon his previous francophile stance by strengthening relations
with Austria. This was destined to result in the liberation of Vienna
that in 1683 would transform Sobieski into a champion of victorious
Christianity.

Saint-Simon claims that Sobieski's momentous rescue was not rewarded with appropriate gratitude, and he is right. Embarassed by the
weight of his moral indebtedness, the emperor Leopold I took refuge in
haughty superiority and did not deign even to glance at his savior's eldest son, whom Sobieski had wished to present to him.

Since the attempts to obtain French acknowledgement for her father were in vain, Maria Casimira decided that it was preferable to summon him to Poland. As soon as the news of his departure spread in
Paris, the creditors of the old toper secured his precautionary imprisonment. D'Arquien's only recourse to extricate himself from this mess
was to sell his post of captain of the guard of Monsieur, but just when
the matter was about to be concluded there arrived from far off the opposition of Mme. de Béthune who, claiming that she had been defrauded
of the small inheritance that she hoped for from her father, succeeded in
keeping him in jail for some time longer.

Finally the marquis could undertake the journey so inaccurately
described by Saint-Simon. From Louis XIV he had been able to obtain
only an honorarium that had all the flavor of a peremptory dismissal,
since the king did not wish to hand it over in person and charged
Sobieski with it, perhaps to be certain of getting rid of so inconvenient a subject.

For the savior of Christianity it was not too difficult to obtain a
singular consolation prize for the man who had not wanted him as a son-
in-law: a cardinal's hat, which descended on the dissolute unbeliever
without arousing in him the doubt that his decrepit age (eighty-two) and
his new condition might prompt changes of life and mind. The creation
of the new cardinal was one of Sobieski's final exploits. Bloated, dis-
gusted with everything and everyone, the aged hero sent to the devil
anyone who encouraged him to make a will; he could foresee what would

10 Saint-Simon, *Mémoires*, VI, 31.

happen at his death and cursed: "Let fire devour the earth [...] there is not a single good man, not even one [...]."[11]

On 17 June 1696 Maria Casimira again became a widow, but with an unshakable intention of remaining in command. Less well-informed than Voltaire, Saint-Simon attributes to the Poles the tradition of electing the heir of the deceased king and charges Maria Casimira with having compromised this possibility by damaging the relationship between Sobieski and his subjects.[12] In reality, even if the ex-queen did do everything to undermine the chances of her hated first son, we have already seen that the tradition invoked by Saint-Simon is simply imaginary.

What guided Marysienka in her injudicious behavior was the mad hope of remaining queen. I do not believe that Saint-Simon knew this aspect of the matter when he wrote that "the public aversion which she showed without measure to prince James, her elder son, cost her family the crown."[13] It is strange to learn that what did not reach Paris was known in Naples. I find in the *Giornali* of Domenico Confuorto:

> On the eleventh of the same [July 1696], Wednesday, we had with the public notices the news of the death of the king of Poland; and that among those who aspire to the crown of the said kingdom there are three, and that is the son of the late king, the Duke of Lorraine, and Teblonewschki, one of the palatines of the kingdom, who is favored by the queen mother even against her own son, since, by taking him as her husband, she would remain in first place, that is, with the crown on her head."[14]

If not all their news was consistent, Paris and Naples both underlined with the same words the fervid craving to keep "a crown on her head" that inspired Maria Casimira in her follies.

"What follows is not very pretty," writes Waliszewski, and he seeks to spare his readers the details of the new intrigues which the queen wove in favor of one of her younger sons or Jablonowski (the Teblonewschki of the Neapolitan *Giornali)* against her older son and the other candidates. The burial of Sobieski had already been the occasion of terrifying scenes, which the biographer summarizes in these terms:

> To start with, they argued about the corpse. Together with an address of condolence, Marysienka received from her eldest son

---

[11] Waliszewski, 344.
[12] Saint-Simon, *Mémoires,* VI, 32.
[13] Saint-Simon, *Mémoires,* X, 248.
[14] Confuorto, II, 227.

the notice that access to the castle of Warsaw would be forbidden
to her. She paid no attention: the dead man was in her hands. When
she presented herself at the gate with the coffin, she cried: 'Make
way for the King!' The common people in an uproar agreed with
her in this matter. Arguments of this type always have a hold on
crowds. The gate opened and James, dismayed, threw himself at
the feet of his mother. Never had he spoken to her with such ten-
derness. Maria Casimira remained cold, her lips tight, her eyes
dry. She was pursuing an idea of hers, that of reigning still, in her
own manner, in the shadow of the cadaver. But outside the crowd
also followed its own thoughts: the dead man had been allowed to
enter his home; now they wished to see him on his catafalque. The
dead man was not vested. In the wardrobe of the castle were found
a mantle lined with ermine, a scepter, but not the crown. Who had
it?—The Queen.— Would she give it over?—No! Prince James would
never get possession of it!—Matczynski, faithful companion in arms,
ran to an armorial trophy to take down an iron helmet. In this manner
the people of Warsaw saw the soldier of Vienna for the last time.

   During the cortege, prince James disappeared. It was discovered that he was galloping toward the castle of Zolkiew, where it
was said that the departed had amassed an immense treasure.
Marysienka had a sinister smile: she was forearmed. A few days
later, James had returned with his tail between his legs, to offer her
five million for her part of the treasure, which he had found well
guarded. His mother accepted, but without disarming [...]."

   The Neapolitan *giornali* give us a summary of the events that
followed. Poland is ever more troubled and divided; Augustus of Saxony
prevails (but only for the moment), and Prince Conti, previously elected,
is obliged to return to France with his bagpipes in their bag, in the face
of new and unforeseen developments of a situation further complicated by the opposing interventions of Charles XII of Sweden and
Peter the Great.

IX

Polish Intermezzi — 2

"To Rome I came, Christian and not Christine"

Maria Casimira continued to attempt to copy the model of Maria Gonzaga after the death of Sobieski. When her maneuvers failed she imagined she could follow the example of a yet more illustrious queen. Uneasy in the country over which she had wished to continue to rule—"hated, misunderstood, a foreigner, and without support because of the division of her children,"[1] writes Saint-Simon—Maria Casimira turned toward Rome, deluded into thinking she could repeat the golden sunset of Christina of Sweden. According to the French memoirist, in Rome the truth was already out about the dubious status of the queen without a kingdom and her unruly sons. It should be said, however, that this does not appear from the Roman documents known to me, neither under the pontificate of Innocent XII (who was in any case an old acquaintance of Marysienka, having blessed her "official" marriage with Sobieski), nor under Clement XI.

Under the date of 6 September 1698, we read in Confuorto's diary that Don Livio Odescalchi is preparing to receive and entertain in his own palace in Rome the "widowed queen of Poland." The stages of her voyage follow: Vienna, Venice, and Bologna. Finally, a Roman broadsheet for 28 March 1699 reports Maria Casimira's arrival:

> on the 23rd of the said month there reached this city the queen of Poland with the cardinal her father, and she went to live in the house of prince Don Livio Odescalchi, who received her at the foot of the staircase, which house had already been decorated for the said occasion; and on the 25th His Holiness sent her as a gift sixty loads of various fruits, wines, wax, a sturgeon, and many other pretty things and precious objects; and then the next day, the 26th, the said queen, with the princess her niece, went privately to reverence His Holiness; and first there had been Cardinal Archin [sic], her father.[2]

[1] *Mémoires,* X, 248.
[2] Confuorto, entry for 28 March 1699.

If I have previously found fault with Saint-Simon, now I must part ways with Waliszewski. In softening the story of his heroine's descending spiral he incurs some mistakes, such as believing that Christina of Sweden lived in Palazzo Odescalchi or considering Maria Casimira's installation in the house of Don Livio permanent.

Don Livio Odescalchi, the nephew of Innocent XI, during the years marked by the guerilla war between Christina of Sweden and his bigoted uncle had defied the pope's anger by joining the nobles in a sort of Fronde against Innocent as an enemy of the theaters. The pope might redouble persecuting edicts and dire threats, but when his informers told him that his own nephew was one of the financiers of the hostile theatrical undertakings, he could only raise his eyebrows, swallow the bitter pill, and pretend it was nothing.[3]

Other "nipoti" were threatened by the loss of powerful support when an uncle-pope went to his eternal rest. A decade after Innocent's death in 1689, Don Livio still preserved all his power and had even succeeded in increasing his riches by heavy investments in land reclamation. Certain comments by Valesio reveal Don Livio's fundamental avarice, but like many Arpagons of high lineage he knew that on certain occasions one must not consider the expense. And so we find him at the foot of the staircase of Palazzo Chigi in Piazza Santi Apostoli, where he lived, to welcome Maria Casimira and to accompany her personally to the magnificent apartment prepared for her. Among Roman aristocrats, Odescalchi was the one most qualified to open his own palace to the exiled queen. Together with Sobieski, Don Livio had distinguished himself in chasing the Turks from Vienna. More fortunate than the Polish *condottiere,* he had received from Leopold I considerable rewards and honors and in 1697 had advanced his own candidacy—unsuccessfully— for the Polish throne. In any case, his hospitality could not be permanent. The queen was too determined to copy Christina's establishment not to seek a royal palace for herself in which to revive, even if at a reduced outlay, the splendors of Christina's Palazzo Riario on the Lungara.

Contrary to Saint-Simon's assertions, Innocent XII and his successor did all they could to please Maria Casimira. They even tolerated certain of her poses—a pretentious upstart masquerading as a queen— as well as the not-always commendable enterprises of her empurpled father or the extravagant exploits of the two Sobieski princes. The younger of the two was completely out of control, good only for enlivening Roman gossip by his blatant liason with the singer-courtesan

---

3 Ademollo, *Teatri,* 156.

Vittoria Bocca di Leone, called "Tolla."[4] Innocent XII, who was extremely ill, was kept in the dark about the libertinage of Constantine Sobieski. The prince had secured the exclusive enjoyment of the lovely Tolla's favors at the price of costly gifts acquired by pawning the family jewels, incuding a jewelled sword he had received from the queen of England. Accustomed to the Tolla's compliancy, certain of her *aficionados* did not resign themselves to so unexpected a change. One day Duke Cesarini's son disfigured the shameless woman with a sword while she, *en travesti* as a coachman, was performing in a serenata *comme il faut,* sung to her protector from the piazza while the queen listened as she dined with her children.

The *sérénade* so violently *interrompue* gave way to a sequence worthy of the best Feydeau farce: cries from the attacked woman, the flight of the bloody braggart, the capture of an unfortunate gentleman from Spoleto who happened to find himself in the assailant's company. No one dared explain the event to Maria Casimira who, scenting the danger of a brawl, had staged a faint in order to prevent her enraged sons from descending into the street. Finally someone had a brilliant idea: a certain Capuchin father was the only one who could make clear to the queen, with all the necessary respect, the outrage that she had suffered. The height of this grotesque comedy was reached with the arrival of the holy man. The Spoletino knew how Maria Casimira emulated Christina's example and was aware of a dark precedent: the murder of the traitor Monaldeschi, barbarously executed at Versailles while the queen of Sweden and her unfaithful ex-lover and advisor were the guests of Louis XIV. Thinking that the Capuchin had been called in to comfort his final moments, the unfortunate prisoner from Spoleto guarded by the Polish "Spahis" fainted in his turn.

When the plot of this exhilarating drama had been played out, there remained the comedy of *lèse-majesté.* Scenting the possibility of a bloody vengeance on the part of Sobieski, the elder Duke Cesarini sought a peacemaker pleasing to the queen, whom he immediately found in Cardinal Ottoboni. The latter, however, limited himself to testing the waters with Maria Casimira, entrusting the "settlement" of everything to the Count of San Martino.

---

[4] E. P. Rodocanachi dedicated a volume to the exploits of Vittoria Bocca di Leone entitled *Tolla la courtisane,* quoted by Waliszewski, but I have not succeeded in tracing it. I take my information directly from the *Diario di Roma* of Francesco Valesio, which I quote in the modern edition made by Gaetano Scano with the collaboration of Giuseppe Graglia (Milan: Longanesi, 1977-1979).

Maria Casimira rained her magnanimity down from on high, but this did not prevent her from claiming complete submission and embarassing apologies from those Germonts before the fact. If it were only a question of diarists' gossip, it would be amusing to read. However, offended honor—worse, if royal—demands formal statements of the humiliations inflicted on the guilty one. Thus, Valesio diligently copies page after page of a *Relation of the matter of signor Gaetano Cesarino which took place before the palace of the queen of Poland (mediated by the count of San Martino)*. I will spare you its prolixities, but not its happy ending, which is a real triumph of Ottoboni's diplomacy. The guilty man was finally admitted to the royal presence following his release from Castel Sant'Angelo. After laborious negotiations, the duke had been obliged to have his son shut up there "at the disposition of Her Majesty, so that she might have him punished as was pleasing to her, while he [the duke] forgot that he possessed him [the son] any longer in this world." Young Cesarini found himself facing something between a Christmas crèche and a *tableau-vivant*.

> Maria Casimira was seated on the throne with prince Constantine on her right hand and the little princess her niece on some cushions on the left, in the company of her ladies and many gentlemen. When the said gentleman appeared in the doorway of the room, Her Majesty immediately rose to her feet and, removing her glove, gave him ["her" in the original] her hand to kiss. When Don Gaetano had done that, she pronounced the appointed words, and in naming the prince, she turned with a bow toward him, to which he responded politely. The queen with a most courteous manner then said to him that she was very sorry about the event that obliged him to come into her presence in such circumstances, but after all she was not at fault. After which, when she had again given him her hand to kiss, Don Gaetano Cesarini left and she immediately turned to the Count of San Martino, saying to him: 'Did you hear how I responded to the event?' and he replied: 'On every occasion Your Majesty wishes to make your benignant clemency shine as the true dowry of your great soul, and I shall not fail to bear witness of it to Cardinal Ottoboni and to any other who asks me.'[5]

It is interesting to note that the mistakes in the text restore the guilty one to the male sex only after the royal pardon, but anyone who is familiar with Valesio's prose knows that confusions of this kind appear frequently.

---

5 The complete text of the *Relazione* is the first of the documents published in the appendix to vol. I of the *Diario di Roma*, 195-205 of the printed edition [hereafter Valesio, *Diario*].

I have mentioned Foydeau because of the irresistable theatrical rhythm of the farcical contrast between the pretensions of the Poles and their actual behavior. In Rome there was Pasquino, a connoisseur of men and things (and certainly not a forbearing judge), with a nose too experienced not to scent the disparity that impelled him to produce a killing terzet:

> *I was born of a Gallic cock a simple hen/I lived among the Pole-try* [*pollastri* = young fowls and *polacchi* = Poles] *and then/To Rome I came, a queen, Christian and not Christine.*

Valesio annotates: "It alludes to her having been born a private woman in France, having been queen of Poland, and having come to Rome without the greatness of spirit of the queen of Sweden of glorious memory."[6]

Valesio's diary interweaves this farce with the long and painful physical decline of Innocent XII, and with the torturous conclave from which pope Clement XI would emerge. The death of Charles II of Spain made war almost certain, but the Romans could not foresee the natural calamities (earthquakes and floods) which, inevitably interpreted as heavenly chastisements, would furnish the new pope with pretexts for a radical movement away from "la dolce vita" in the years ahead.

Prince Constantine continued to commit follies for Tolla. She must have committed worse ones, since a miscarriage of hers prompted a sonnet by Pasquino full of sinister implications at a time when the bloody claims connected with the Spanish succession would have prevented any person of good sense from joking about the failure of a pregnancy and its dynastic consequences. With an appetizing target for his arrows, Pasquino did not mince words. The sonnet depicts Poland afflicted "because its future king has been aborted," Europe in despair, and Germany torn by grief, claiming that "if one day the mother with all the honors/ from a low whore became a countess,/her son could become emperor." [7]

After the death of the pope, satirical sonnets continued to target Tolla, but Pasquino had other, more pungent provocations. The decrepit Arquin was involved in the intrigues of the papal conclave. As ignorant of certain customs as he was of the religious practices customarily connected with his rank, he did not bother to announce his arrival. His appearance was particularly theatrical, since his daughter accompanied him "to the stair of Constantine," taking her leave of him with a moving

---

[6] Valesio, *Diario,* I, 15.

[7] Valesio, *Diario,* I, 72. Waliszewski cites from Rodocanachi the information that the title of "comtesse de la Paille" had been bestowed on Tolla by Maria Casimira.

embrace. He then had the unpleasant surprise having to wait for some time in the rooms of Prince Savelli until the cardinals could assemble to welcome him.

After many false starts and intrigues, the "young" Cardinal Albani was elected pope. Dismayed by the dark political prospectives looming over his pontificate, Clement XI initially attempted to keep his relatives far from the prospects of nepotism. His resolve was later weakened by the maneuvers of numerous interested parties. He ate his first meal as pope in the cell of Cardinal Ottoboni (although only four days later he reprimanded Ottoboni "for living little like an ecclesiastic"). To Maria Casimira alone he conceded the honor of a box in St. Peter's for the ceremony that consecrated him Bishop of Rome.

Impatient to extract from every important occasion some pretext for displaying her own preeminence, the queen rushed to the Vatican, anxious to be the first to kiss the foot of the new pope. Occupied at table with Ottoboni, Clement XI informed her that he would not receive her until he had rested, obliging her to disguise her wait by dining with her father in his cell. Returning home was unthinkable, since she ran the risk of being forestalled in her homage by some Roman princess.

The events behind the scenes of the conclave kept Pasquino busy without distracting his attention from Tolla. His poisoned pen was quiet, however, when on 19 December the church of San Luigi dei Francesi filled up for a sumptuous ceremony that would seem to give the lie to Saint-Simon. The French ambassador solemnly conferred "the Cordon bleux [sic] granted by His Majesty Louis XIV king of France to the princes Alexander and Constantine Sons of the Queen Widow Maria Casimira of Poland."[8] Saint-Simon himself, however, makes it clear that the Roman ceremony was an expedient thought up during the pilgrimage to France of the two high-spirited princes. They had claimed the Order of the Saint-Esprit, which their father had obtained for them, along with a whole string of honors the Sun King was unwilling to concede to princes of a non-hereditary monarchy.[9] After months of uncomfortable incognito, spying out the land and accumulating rebuffs, the two Sobieskis resigned themselves to taking leave of the king, with the excuse that they wished to return to Poland before their father's successor was elected.

Pasquino certainly did not know this inside information. On the other hand, if the ceremony was an expedient, appearances had been

---

[8] Valesio, *Diario,* I, 176.
[9] Saint-Simon, *Mémoires,* II, 155.

saved in the best of fashions. The music included a "well-regulated en-semble of one hundred and more stringed instruments concerted by Arcangelo Corelli,"[10] and the motets of Paolo Lorenzani, whom the French ambassador esteemed as a maestro of the Cappella Giulia who had been *surintendant de la musique* in Paris to the queen of France.

The two princes had chosen to wear garments

> in ancient style, or Royal style [...] with Hats of black velvet with white plumes girt with rich pearls and diamonds, with the brim embroidered with inestimable jewels [...].[11]

A plunge into respectability, we may say; but one of brief duration, at least for the fiery Constantine.

Although Valesio pointed out that the beginning of Carnival seemed dampened owing to "the scarce merriment and money among the people," less than a month after the ceremony, a sumptuous celebration ended in an enormous scandal. Maria Casimira offered one of her customary entertainments and Tolla dared to mingle with the ladies who had been invited, insulting them when they showed that they did not enjoy her company. Informed by one of her gentlemen, Maria Casimira ordered her inconvenient quasi-daughter-in-law "not to incur similar errors any more." But she then denied it to the papal envoy who had come to con-dole with her, assuring him that they were "evil suppositions against a woman who never left her house." In fact, the incorrigible Tolla con-stantly disobeyed the order that forbade masked women to walk in the Corso. Unaware of such doings, Maria Casimira imprudently autho-rized the singer's arrest if she were caught in the act. Later, being better informed, she retracted everything in a letter to Cardinal Sacripante, prom-ising to find a husband for Tolla or send her away at the end of Carnival.

An oversight on the part of the abatino Scarlatti (nephew of the powerful abate Pompeo Scarlatti in the service of the Elector of Bavaria, brother-in-law of Maria Casimira) delayed the letter from reaching its destination. Tolla was arrested by the *bargello* and forty policemen while she was riding masked in her carriage and was then shut up in the mon-astery of San Giacomo of the Convertite on the Lungara, a foundation for repentant prostitutes. Valesio notes Maria Casimira's anger, adding:

---

[10] *Raguaglio di quanto si è fatto di solenne nella Chiesa di S. Luigi della Nazione Francese in occasione della cerimonia pratticata nel conferirsi ...* (Rome: Eredi del Corbelletti, 1700). The pamphlet, included in Valesio's manuscript, is reproduced on 169-175 of vol. I.

[11] Valesio, *Diario,* I, 176

It is certain that the queen viewed with disapproval the continuing familiarity of her son with the said Tolla, as well as the fact that, to maintain her in that state, he gave the city occasion for gossip by selling many of her [the queen's] things, and most recently he sold two buckles with diamonds for six hundred scudi, but they were of greater value [...].[12]

A few days later "the commotion made about the imprisonment by the queen and her sons and especially by Cardinal d'Archien" obtained Tolla's removal from the monastery by Maria Casimira's factotum, *maestro di camera* Count d'Alibert. Tolla was transferred to the house of a lawyer, where she was entrusted to an honest woman, "since it was certified that within two weeks Tolla would marry so as not to make so tumultuous an imprisonment end in a ridiculous outcome."

But what could be more ridiculous than a marriage in the situation described? It would be naive to consider a shot-gun wedding: naturally, the prince responsible for the scandals was out of the question. Only a few years earlier in Naples an arranged marriage had snatched the singer Ciulla de Caro from the clutches of justice. She had turned the head of a viceroy (who of course had been replaced for some time when the police finally dared to take notice of the scandal) and those of a good many other aristocrats. The malicious Muscettola accused Ciulla of having been "the support of the Naples bordello." Croce[13] and Prota Giurleo,[14] who wrote about this enterprising harmonist, claim that the harsh lesson which she had learned induced her to change her way of life (although in Neapolitan tradition the name of her husband/savior—Carlo Mazza—still remains, after three centuries, a synonym for the complaisant cuckold).

In Rome, however, no one could be found to emulate Carlo Mazza, and Maria Casimira knew that in her son's interest it was preferable to get Tolla out of circulation rather than to leave her in his arms. To revenge herself on those who had dared to imprison someone under her protection, Maria Casimira broke her agreements with the Curia and welcomed the shameless woman under her roof. Only after the indignant protests of the pope did the queen "have the said Tolla accompanied with a coach and six to Acqua Santa, where a Polish carriage with four horses was ready, and she was conveyed to Naples, having been given one thousand *ungari* and letters of recommendation for the viceroy there."[15]

---

[12] Valesio, *Diario*, II, 292.

[13] Croce, *Teatri*, I, 143-153.

[14] Prota Giurleo, "Un po' d'indulgenza per Ciulla...," *Nostro Tempo* IV, nos. 6-7.

[15] Valesio, *Diario*, I, 297.

Before taking leave of Tolla ourselves, we can summarize her further adventures through the continuing reports in Valesio's diary. At the
beginning of April the news arrived from Naples that the Duke of Mantua,
the famous collector of female singers, had not given up on assuring so
exceptional an exhibit for himself, and that Tolla had been "declared his
foremost *virtuosa* of song by that duke."[16] A month later, however,

> we hear from Naples that the famous Tolla Bocca di Leone [...]
> has returned to that city, not having been accepted by the Duke of
> Mantua, who perhaps, considering the emergencies of these wars,
> did not wish to burden himself with new cows.[17]

In spite of Maria Casimira's recommendation to the viceroy, no
good wind blew for Tolla even in Naples, and at the end of June Valesio
writes: "We hear that contessa Tolla Bocca di Leone has passed on her
way to Palermo from Benevento, where she was staying."[18]

I have accompanied Tolla to my own city, where I find no news of
her. I am not surprised, since the diarist of the period is the bigoted
canon Mongitore, fascinated by miracles but completely uninterested in
the intrusion of lively personalities into the façade of respectability that
he describes. I can now return to Rome.

Although she had every reason to be content with the hospitality of
Don Livio Odescalchi, Maria Casimira must have secretly cherished the
desire for a palace where she could relive the experience of her great
Swedish precursor. Starting with the idea of passing her summer vacation there, the queen soon decided to inhabit permanently "the casino
de Torres, on Mount Pincio with a garden abutting another one belonging to the Medici." However enlargements were necessary to transform
it into the palace of her dreams. Valesio's diary furnishes precise and
cirumstantial information, either misinterpreted or even unknown to those
who have concerned themselves with Maria Casimira's Roman sojourn.
On 7 July 1701, the diarist specifies that the casino "has its entrance
next to the last house on the right going toward Porta Pinciana and, since
it is small for her numerous suite, the queen has rented two contiguous
houses having obtained from Our Lord [the pope] a faculty for evicting
the inhabitants of the same from the houses deemed appropriate for her
service and placed in those surroundings."[19]

---

[16] Ibid., 341.
[17] Ibid., 385.
[18] Ibid., 409.
[19] Ibid., 432.

On July 8 Maria Casimira took a carriage-drive with her father, her son Alexander, and her little niece (the daughter of her detested eldest son, who apparently hated the little girl in return) to "see the new little palace at Porta Pinciana, which had been taken to live in."[20]

Don Livio's palace was no longer appropriate for Maria Casimira, now that Odescalchi had openly declared for the imperial side and she wanted to preserve an appearance of political impartiality. Her enthusiasm for her new residence was soon combined with her proclivity for monastic retreats.

On 3 August 1702, Maria Casimira expounded to the pope her project of founding a monastery attached to the palace that was being constructed and enlarged. For that purpose, several nuns would come from France. With papal approval there were no other obstacles, and on September 30 Valesio wrote:

> The Queen of Poland is having built with all speed the monastery that she intends to found in the last house of the Zuccari, the one that forms the two streets Gregoriana and Felice on the piazza of Trinità de' Monti and, with the masons working on this, covering it with whitewash on the outside, Zuccari, the owner of the house, who knew nothing of these doings, has arrived from Sora, and when he had complained about it to Her Majesty, he was assured that the rent would be paid to him punctually. Her Majesty has also obtained permission from the *maestri delle strade* to build an open bridge on the strada Felice in order to pass from the former casino de Torres, bought and inhabited by Her Majesty, to her contiguous houses and to that of the Zuccari, which will be converted into a monastery.[21]

Valesio's topography of the area occupied by Maria Casimira's court seems to reverse the locations described by previous scholars. (For those unfamiliar with old Roman place-names, the Strada Felice is the present Via Sistina: the old name referred to Felice Peretti, pope Sixtus V.) The "casino formerly de Torres," with all the enlargements that had been carried out, houses the principal body of the palace and coincides with one or more of those buildings that in more recent times have been transformed into grand hotels. Other passages from the diary confirm that this was the principal body, reserved for habitation. Palazzo Zuccari, the house "that forms the two streets Gregoriana and Felice on the piazza of Trinità de' Monti," was initially destined for the proposed mon-

---

[20] Ibid., 436
[21] Valesio, *Diario,* II, 292.

astery and then for a theater and other incidental uses. I had previously maintained that the theater was built in the ex-casino, but the diary confirms its traditionally accepted location in Palazzo Zuccari. The large bridge that joined the two bodies (and which the Romans soon called "the queen's Arch") must have been conceived to allow Maria Casimira to reach the peace of the cloister whenever she was overcome by mystical rapture. In practice it would be reserved for the semipublic performance of serenades and motets offered to passers-by—a format that eliminated many problems of etiquette, as well as those expenses for refreshments, which on similar occasions ruined the super-rich Ottoboni.

The Pincio and Trinità de' Monti had rather doubtful traditions in the matter of "casini." This was perhaps unknown to Maria Casimira but not to her decrepit but lively father, who had done everything possible to adapt himself to them. On 2 September 1701 Valesio had written:

> Prince Tassi of Naples, post-master of Spain, inhabits a casino on Monte della Trinità next to the said church, in which he lives like Nebuchadnezzar among the animals, keeping a great number of goats, stags, monkeys, and parrots, which he claims are his vassals, since he has no princely fief; in addition to which he constantly has billy-goats and cows, *id est* singers, whom he maintains in the adjoining houses in great numbers, amusing himself every day between songs and sounds surrounded by his mules. When His Holiness found out about it, he sent someone to admonish him more as viceregent than as pope that, since this prince is old, he ought now to apply himself to a good life and to that end dismiss his lady singers; whence, to carry out this pontifical correction he evicted his ladies of the *solfa* from the pen which he kept next to his house."

It is amusing to find this picturesque pigsty, a worthy substitute for a fief for an old debauched prince, next to the pretentious palace of a queen without a kingdom. The more so, since Tassi's casino defied the building expansion promoted by Maria Casimira: the pope could inflict his own moral reproofs on the rich and powerful "post-master of Spain," but he would have considered it imprudent to extend to Tassi's loss the faculties conceded to the queen.

The collapse of the international situation made the last months of 1702 a fitting prelude to the long Lent that the Romans would undergo after the floods and earthquakes of 1703. At the end of 1702 Cardinal d'Arquien moved from his rented palace in Piazza Santissimi Apostoli, next to the one where Don Livio had housed Maria Casimira, to the new casino on the Pincio.[22] His lively temper resisted the discom-

22 Ibid., 361.

forts of moving and of establishing himself in surroundings where the plaster was still damp better than the French nuns, who had moved into their new convent too soon and were obliged to seek refuge with the queen.

Only a few months had passed since the providential arrival of a thousand doubloons from France had allowed the decrepit reveler d'Arquien to rehire the musicians (and the lady singers) whom, like Prince Tassi, he had been constrained to dismiss. I cannot refrain from reading in a malicious light the following entry of Valesio:

> whence the French nuns destined for the new monastery, who live in the upper apartment of the said palace, will also enjoy that music.[23]

But life was also not going well for Maria Casimira. If the convalescent nuns cold be easily distracted by a ride in a closed carriage, things were not so simple when her guests had little connection with the Church. When there arrived in Rome "the beautiful madamigella di Tornelle of Venice with a little baby that she had had by prince Alexander her [the queen's] son when he was passing through that city," Maria Casimira risked a renewal of the scandals that she had overcome by sending Tolla away.[24] The queen could not think of anything better than entrusting mother and child to the ubiquitous d'Alibert. To everyone's good fortune, the damoiselle returned to Venice after ten days, while the little baby remained in Rome, confided to the doubtful pedagogic capabilities of the count-factotum. During the beautiful madamigella's Roman vacation d'Alibert's palace was enlivened every evening by music and song, "with an incredible concourse of foreign and local gentlemen intent on gazing at so lovely a woman."[25]

All this must have been costly for Maria Casimira at an unpromising moment for her finances. The buildings on the Pincio had used up all her available cash just when misfortunes in Poland threatened the enjoyment of her previous income. Some economies were necessary. "Perhaps in order not to assume any further obligations,"the queen adopted an expedient that gave some "inconvenience" to her courtiers and to the clergy assigned to the service of her churches: that of going to perform her own devotions four hours after the sunset Ave Maria.[26]

In this darkness, the symbol of the harsh times that were preparing, the first phase of Maria Casimira's Roman sojourn closes.

---

[23] Ibid.,. 325.
[24] Ibid., 307.
[25] Ibid., 311.
[26] Ibid., 321.

X

A time of penitence and of darkness

Alessandro Scarlatti had ample opportunity to draw up a balance-sheet of his life during the years he spent in the papal city after his journey to Florence. The Rome of that period encouraged this type of meditation. As soon as he had been elected, the young pope Clement XI declared himself worried by the grave responsibilities that had fallen on his shoulders in such difficult years. He wished to keep his own relatives far away from the temptations of nepotism and could not conceal the tears that streaked his face on every solemn occasion. In response to the threatening claims of the Franco-Hispanists and the Imperialists, the pope made it known that he was invoking divine assistance "in certain serious and important deliberations regarding his apostolic ministry." He then proclaimed a special jubilee, accompanying it with a "most strict edict prohibiting masking, comedies, and performances, whether memorized or improvised, banquets, merrymaking, and any other liberty of carnival." The severity of the threatened sanctions was enough to dissuade even the poor buskers of Piazza Navona from earning their living with their instruments and their usual puppet-plays.

The queen of Poland also adapted herself to such austerity and on more than one occasion indeed displayed a "singular modesty" sufficient to induce Valesio to change his tone:

> This royal lady also edifies the city by the devotion with which she visits every day the churches in which the Venerable [Sacrament] is exposed, and in the processions for the deposition from the said churches she follows the Most Holy Sacrament with a torch in her hands.[1]

Perhaps Maria Casimira was unaware that Christina of Sweden had behaved in a very different manner, obliging the pope to tell her that there could be more devotion in an Ave Maria recited in public than in an entire rosary said in private (not surprising at the height of the

---

[1] Valesio, *Diario,* II, 21.

Counter-Reformation, especially since the objection was addressed to an ex-Protestant).

During Carnival Maria Casimira multiplied her works of devotion, serving dinner in her palace to thirteen poor people newly clothed by her. Since every reason for disagreement with the pope had been eliminated, after the exile of Tolla the comic pretensions of the queen without a kingdom again emerged. As if to seal the reentry of the whole Sobieski clan into the ranks of respectability, Clement XI made his most coveted gift to the queen: a private visit. Saint-Simon would perhaps have turned up his nose at certain details, but in Valesio's account, the ceremony seems to repeat, with changed roles and protagonists, the *tableau-vivant* of Gaetano Cesarini's pardon. This time the pope is on the throne while Maria Casimira sits in a corner at his feet. Only the "little niece" maintains her former place "on a cushion." "The princes her sons"are conveniently absent. Don Livio Odescalchi is nowhere to be seen.

By sending her son's trollop away from Rome and packing madamigella Tornelle and her little bastard off to d'Alibert, Maria Casimira had recovered the pope's entire favor. This is shown by his gift of a

> most beautiful *trionfo* [table decoration] carried by twelve porters
> [...] composed of fruit and a quantity of citrons of singular size
> with two cages of live pheasants, twelve in number, and the other
> of partridges in equal number, adorned with gold ribbons [...].

Proud of so sensational a gift, Maria Casimira ordered that the trophy be immortalized in a drawing to send "to the Galleries of Poland."[2] Perhaps she was unaware that the pope had merely recycled a gift from the spendthrift Ottoboni, who had barely recovered from the economic difficulties that only three months earlier had obliged him to pawn tapestries and precious vestments ("for exorbitant expenses made continually by His Eminence for music and similar vanities," Valesio specifies.)[3]

Of papal protection—and divine protection, if we take all her displays of devotion seriously—the ex-queen had great need. By June 1701 prince Constantine had left for Cracow, summoned to his fatherland by the complications of a political situation that left ample room for intrigue. In September his brother also joined him, dreaming of unlikely vindications which were to have a tragicomic outcome. Maria Casimira passed the evening of his departure in the Monastery of the Virgins, in meditation and prayer.[4] As time went on, these retreats of hers would

2 Ibid., 458-459.
3 Ibid., 393.
4 Ibid., 486.

intensify, since the queen soon found a way of combining her own interest in monasteries with an explicit homage to the pope.

Anxious to keep his relatives far from the blandishments of courtiers of every rank, Clement XI had ordered the abbess of the convent of the Barberine, in which one of his nieces was a pupil, to allow no one to visit her. Maria Casimira succeeded in overcoming the resistence of the abbess, and Valesio supposes that the pope was finally pleased "within himself [...] by such an act of esteem toward his own family." Not surprisingly, the ceremonial adopted on that occasion was the one established by "the former queen of Sweden" for her encounters with "the nieces of reigning popes."[5]

The news from Poland was ever more worrying. Charles XII of Sweden had entered Warsaw, imposing a new parliament in order to depose Sigismond Augustus of Saxony and to name another king. The cardinal primate of Poland, warned in vain by the pope, allied himself with Charles, and other palatine princes followed his example. Is it necessary to ask which side the Sobieski princes took?

As I have already recorded, between the end of 1702 and the beginning of 1703 several violent earthquakes and other calamities transformed the prospects of the Carnival diversions the Romans had promised themselves at the end of the jubilee into dismay and terror. Early in February cardinals and Roman nobles met to consider the undertaking of some solemn vow by the people. Some spoke of building a church, some of cancelling Carnival for ten years, some of making women dress in black for three years. On February 14 a printed leaflet established the procedures of this exemplary penitence: black clothes, undecorated, for both sexes, other pious practices, but above all:

> That for the next five years there be totally prohibited from the City of Rome at any time, even in Carnival, Masking, Horse races, Banquets, Dances, and Performances, of Comedies as well as Tragedies, Representations, and the like, even though in music, & also in the Colleges, Seminaries, Monasteries, and Sacred and Profane Places.[6]

Valesio supposes that the pope did not intend to prohibit Carnival for more than a year, since the merchants would have suffered enormously from the diminished influx of visitors and from all that austerity. According to the diarist, however, it only took a new earthquake at the end of the year to renew fears and devout renunciations.

---

[5] Ibid., 562.
[6] Valesio, *Diario,* II, 532.

So began the long Roman Lent in which Alessandro Scarlatti's usual unfortunate instinct landed him, under the illusion that Maria Casimira could overcome every obstacle and revive the splendors of Christina. In truth, the ex-queen and his other patrons indeed did everything possible to elude the papal prohibitions more or less gracefully, but they did not always succeed.

With the arrival of summer, serenatas offered those enthusiasts the most elegant of expedients. Perhaps his usual caution suggested to the "celebrated *maestro di cappella* Scarlatti" that he stage his new Roman debut in a more orthodox setting, choosing the celebration sponsored by Monsignor Colonna for the Madonna of Montesano, 16 July 1703.

On August 5 Maria Casimira had a serenata sung "at the third hour [after sunset] on the bridge of her palace that crosses the strada Felice." We do not know who composed the music of the serenata that the queen presented, but Valesio describes Cardinal Ottoboni's gallant and sumptuous reply four evenings later. Another "noble serenata" was performed before the queen's palace:

> The singers and players were brought in an open coach and six, to which the two counts Spada, maestro di camera and cupbearer of the said cardinal, served as outrider and coachmen, with sumptuous country outfits and a white plume in their hats. These were accompanied by five other carriages and two likewise open, also full of singers and players, who were driven by the gentlemen of His Eminence, the night was lighted up by seventy torches of white wax [...].[7]

The usual "oblique fury of the coaches," Parini would say; the usual disputes about precedence; the usual reconciliations.

> The serenata was full of instruments and voices, with the music of the four carriages being echoed by four other choirs placed on the loggias of the surrounding houses. The words had been composed by the cardinal himself, and the music was by the famous Scarlatti. There were present to hear the serenata Cardinal Ottoboni in a little carriage with Cardinal Cenci, Don Orazio Albani brother of the pope together with his son Don Carlo, and in the casino of Prince Tassi there were the ambassador and ambassadress of Spain."[8]

The queen presented a new serenata "on the bridge" (12 August) for the feast of the Assumption at the Collegio Clementino (the

---

[7] Valesio, *Diario,* I, 670.
[8] Ibid., 671.

same Collegio in which the sensational career of Alessandro had taken wing twenty-four years earlier). Afterwards an oratorio was performed that repeated the collaboration between Ottoboni as librettist and Scarlatti as composer. The "celebrated Scarlatti" was also engaged by the Venetian community (here again we see the fine hand of Ottoboni) to direct the music for the feast of San Lorenzo Giustiniani in the church of San Marco, which "succeeded nobly and [was] full of voices and instruments."[9]

It was the oratorio, naturally, that offered to musicians and melomanes the pleasures which most nearly approached those of the forbidden operas. From the time of his return to Rome, Alessandro's protectors had moved in this direction to assure a worthy employment of his talent.

Despite the support he enjoyed (or perhaps because of it, since the local musicians were not all as magnanimous as Corelli and Pasquini), Alessandro did not meet with the unanimous approval he expected. I do not believe that his qualities as a musician were in doubt. Some of the obstacles must have been created by his well-known disregard for others; as a man in constant pursuit of positions and commissions, he was not very punctual in fulfilling his official duties.

An old reference of Gasbarri,[10] cited by Bertini,[11] put Arnaldo Morelli[12] on the track of documents that establish a surprising background for Alessandro's appointment in 1703 at the Chiesa Nuova, S. Maria in Vallicella. Giovanni Bicilli, titular *maestro di cappella* of the church, was decrepit: his coadjutor would soon succeed to the coveted position. With this expectation, Alessandro proposed himself. He had the unpleasant surprise of learning that, despite the support of Marchese Ruspoli and Cardinal Marescotti, the select committee to which his proposal had been entrusted had shown a "positive aversion" to accepting him. It took the intervention of Ottoboni, the customary *deus ex machina,* to resolve everything positively by means of a "general congregation" that on 9 January 1703 named Alessandro coadjutor and successor to Bicilli, with twelve votes in favor and five against.[13]

Morelli's researches allow me to remind those who promote an optimistic picture of Alessandro as a human being that "the knots would

---

[9] Ibid., 690-691.

[10] Cf. Carlo Gasbarri, *L'Oratorio Romano dal Cinquecento al Novecento* (Rome, 1962), 90.

[11] Cf. Argia Bertini, "La Musica dell'oratorio dalle origini ad oggi," *Quaderni dell'Oratorio* 11, Rome, 1966, 24-26.

[12] Morelli, "Scarlatti," 117-144.

[13] Ibid., 122.

come to the comb at the Vallicella also." (The Italian equivalent of "the chickens would come home to roost.") Two years later, in the face of Alessandro's insistence that he participate "only at feasts of the first rank"[14] of the chapel, the Congregation was obliged to ask respectfully that Cardinal Ottoboni offer his protégé a reasonable choice: either provide the promised services or resign. "Owing to the many occupations which he had in composing music for the service of various important persons," Alessandro saw that he was obliged to give up the post. We shall soon see that he would find himself in the same imbroglios at the Basilica Liberiana.

The abate Pompeo Scarlatti, the Roman agent of Maria Casimira's son-in-law the Duke of Bavaria, died on 12 September 1703. We have already encountered this powerful personage. Perhaps he had aided Alessandro's Roman career, but certainly he did not oppose it as he would have done if he had been annoyed by the *parvenu* whose encroachment attempted to link their family names.

Abate Pompeo's connection with Bavaria supports the hypothesis of Scarlatti kinship. The journey to Munich and Vienna suggested by Eva Badura Skoda, which Alessandro Scarlatti would have made in the period immediately following his first Roman successes, may have been due to the involvement of this personage, whom Valesio loses no opportunity to call "most powerful."

But other connections between Maria Casimira and Alessandro Scarlatti were not lacking. One of these was certainly Count Giacomo d'Alibert, the unfortunate and incurable entrepreneur whom Christina of Sweden had already employed in a more or less permanent capacity. This adventurer of high rank had plotted with Retz at the time of the Fronde. After shuttling between France and Italy, he had plunged into intrigues which brought him to the Bastille. Moving to Italy, he had been taken on by Christina of Sweden at the request of Cardinal Azzolini. There is an excellent summary of his convoluted biography in a note by Jeanne Bignami Odier and Giorgio Morelli to the manuscript on Christina that they published.[15]

These past good offices rendered d'Alibert particularly acceptable to Maria Casimira, who kept him in her own service as a gentleman in waiting. The count's son (future builder of the "Teatro delle Dame") also began to be active, since Valesio noted on 27 August 1702 the news of a serenata that the young d'Alibert had presented "toward midnight" in the queen's casino on the Pincio, with many instruments and the celebrated

---

[14] Ibid., 127.

[15] *Istoria Secreta,* 59, n. 67; Bignami Odier, 30, n. 8.

Faustina Perugini (This is not, as some have believed, Faustina Maratti-Zappi, who was famous but as a poet, not a singer.)

And there was Carlo Sigismondo Capeci, alias Metisto Olbiano, the Arcadian poet whom Maria Casimira took into her service in 1704 as secretary and who would be the principal librettist of all the musical activity supported by the queen of Poland.

Meanwhile, the life of the papal city continued to reflect the relentless struggle between Franco-Hispanic and Imperial forces, who were preparing to bathe Italy in blood. The Papal States and Rome itself would be threatened by the passage of the Austrian armies headed for the conquest of Naples.

The partisanship of the Romans for one or the other faction, nourished by ambassadors and Imperial, French, or Spanish agents, found an outlet in violent polemics that flared up on the arrival of *avvisi* and gazettes, which the pundits of one or the other party duly commented on in the cafés. From time to time the governor of the city prohibited these political discussions, but the prohibition aroused the protests of the proprietors, whose customers were diminishing, afraid of being caught in a roundup. There was even a violent protest by Cardinal Grimani, who objected that such severity was displayed when it was a question of celebrating an Imperial victory, while no one was prevented from rejoicing publicly at the arrival of news favorable to the Franco-Hispanic party. On that occasion the pope, literally terrified by the advances of the Austrians, induced the governor to backpedal and to tell the proprietor of the café "that it had never been his intention to prohibit them from discussing the news in the cafés, but only to impede noisy groups and especially the common people who spoke ill of the princes."[16]

This partisanship infected the craze for games of chance, and there were those who bet ruinously on the outcome of the battles or on the conquest of besieged cities.

The alternating fortunes of war or certain recurring feasts were reflected in celebrations and festal decorations in San Luigi dei Francesi, San Giacomo degli Spagnoli, and San Carlo al Corso for the Franco-Hispanics, and Santa Maria dell'Anima for the Imperial party. This caused serious worries to the governor, since often the opposing party challenged the legality of the festivities and threatened reprisals.

Paradoxically, the duplication of festivities related to the Spanish monarchy increased the employment of musicians and composers. It

---

[16] Valesio, *Diario*, II, 270.

has always reminded me of Voltaire's *Candide,* where the two *Te Deums* are ordered by captains of opposing armies that were butchered in the same battle. But reading Valesio has persuaded me that the ridiculous episode is true to life, revealing the arrogance with which the comuniqués of opposite sides—worthy forerunners of certain modern war-bulletins—transformed uncertain outcomes into brilliant victories.

Without this increase in festive demonstrations the poor musicians would virtually have gone hungry. Traditional patronage was also threatened by the fortunes of war, as well as by its customary tendency to dissipate funds. Ottoboni, for example, had been obliged to borrow at least 100,000 *scudi* to silence his creditors. In order to repay the Sinibaldi brothers their capital plus interest he had to cede to them ten years of income from the rich abbey of Chiaravalle (and the pope had given his *placet* to the operation, scandalously guaranteeing that even in the case of the debtor's death his creditors would not be disturbed).[17] To get some idea of the prodigality of these famous cardinals, it is sufficient to learn that when Cardinal Pamphilj decided to change a few lines in one of his oratorios he ordered the reprinting of the entire libretto, tearing up the two thousand copies that were ready to be distributed.[18]

Perhaps as divine punishment for having eluded the anti-Carnival edicts by performing an improvised comedy with musical interludes, Maria Casimira suffered a whole series of severe blows in 1704. Immediately after hearing from the primate of Poland the news of her sons' rebellion against Sigismund Augustus of Saxony, the queen learned that during a hunting party the princes James and Constantine been ambushed by Saxon knights, who had captured them and brought them prisoners to the castle of Dresden.

"[...] rendered inconsolable, Her Majesty swooned and immediately sent to inform His Holiness,"[19] writes Valesio, who then tells us of her feverish attempts to obtain the intercession of the pope with the king of Poland to free the unlucky hunters, whom he considered rebels. The queen even planned a trip to Vienna to obtain from the emperor support that would be more effectual than that of the pope. Waliszewski publishes Maria Casimira's letter to her son Alexander, perhaps the only human document left by Marysienka. Even here, she cannot forgo a theatrical gesture by offering herself as a hostage for the liberty of the princes.[20]

---

[17] Valesio, Diario, III, 101.
[18] Ibid., 339.
[19] Ibid., 48.
[20] Waliszewski, 360-361.

In addition, the political troubles in Poland continued to deprive the queen of much of her income, forcing her to adopt emergency measures such as suspending the salaries of her gentlemen, who nonetheless continued gallantly to serve her without pay. The annual celebration of the liberation of Vienna could not be compromised, because the sparkling illumination of the casino on the Pincio and the singing of "various prayers" on the bridge served to refresh the memories of those whose duty it was to remember.

Such woes ran like water off the tough hide of papa Arquien who, despite his "decrepit age," did not give up his erotico-musical delights ("which the queen his daughter found very bad," pronounces Saint-Simon).[21] In competition with the imperial ambassador (who had engaged in his service a "beautiful young singer, niece of the famous Swiss colonel Cluter"), he hired another singer, "the daughter of Massimo Ugolinucci, a gravedigger." However, her father's profession did not lead him to any timely reflections.[22]

In order to negotiate the liberation of her sons, Maria Casimira had to borrow 40,000 *scudi* for the journey from a Genoese merchant, "giving him many jewels in pawn."[23] These were only a part of those she possessed, since a few months later she could go off

> with all pomp to His Beatitude's audience [...] in an outfit in Polish style [...] with belt, necklace, and headdress adorned with precious jewels and, among others, the famous pearl called *la pellegrina* hung on her forehead [...],[24]

and later she could give a cross studded with diamonds, valued at 60,000 *scudi*, to Cardinal Sacripante, who was assigned to her by Innocent XII as "director of her affairs and protector."[25]

Such magnificence contrasts with another item from Valesio, which reveals a profitable operation that she carried out with papal authorization. By depositing furniture in the government pawnshop, she drew from it 10,000 *scudi* exempt from the usual interest rate of two per cent.[26]

When Maria Casimira finally left on February 14, her servants had been paid in advance for two months, with the understanding that they were to consider themselves dismissed if the queen had not returned to

---

[21] *Mémoires,* VI, 32.
[22] Valesio, *Diario,* III, 179.
[23] Ibid., 204.
[24] Ibid., 299; the pearl now belongs to Elizabeth Taylor.
[25] Ibid., 305.
[26] Ibid., 309.

Rome by that time. Even if she did return, however, the fate of her staff remained uncertain, since Valesio could comment:

> it is believed that when she returns she will enter a convent, since she is not able to overcome the expenses of maintaining herself in public by reason of the wars that afflict Poland, through which the income that she has in that kingdom is blocked.[27]

Contradicting such catastrophic predictions, Marysienka returned on May 21, welcomed by a serenata performed by the cardinal's lady singers to celebrate her arrival. On her journey the incorrigible intriguer had been able to combine her undertaking in favor of her sons with a plot intended to restore Bavaria to her son-in-law.

In the absence of operatic performances (but not of the usual scandalous episodes occasioned by the behavior of female singers), serenatas and oratorios continued to punctuate the musical life of Rome. The customary cardinal-patrons, also occasionally authors of sung poetic texts, displayed their love for sumptuous entertainments. Year by year the Carnival prohibitions were repeated, even if the Romans had wished to shake themselves out of their penitential lethargy; infractions were ever more frequent, followed by punishments, which in some cases involved members of the Capitoline aristocracy. Only Ottoboni dared challenge the anger of the pope openly, but he knew how to steer his course. On the one hand, he ran with the hare. Two acts of his opera libretto *Statira,* set by Alessandro Scarlatti and entrusted to the best singers of Rome with a large orchestra, were performed on 10 February 1706 in the little theater of the Cancelleria. Extensive invitations were issued to the nobility, who were further regaled with a fabulous dessert table. On the other hand, he hunted with the hounds. (Ottoboni presented a "most beautiful sinfonia" for the pope's enjoyment when he came to pray at San Lorenzo in Damaso before the "sumptuous apparatus [...] set up on 11 February 1706, Giovedi Grasso, for the solemn exposition of the venerable Sacrament").

In the meantime things were going better for Maria Casimira. The complex developments in the Polish situation had eliminated Sigismund Augustus of Poland and had brought Stanislaus Leszczynski, who was supported by Charles XII of Sweden, to the throne. Some months before, the emperor of Austria had obtained a promise that the two Sobieski prisoners would be consigned to one of his gentlemen and taken to Graz. In December of 1706 a letter arrived in Rome with the news that

---

[27] Ibid., 314.

the new king joined in Maria Casimira's rejoicing for the liberation of her sons. This was followed by another letter that provides a happy ending to the whole Polish experience, with great harmony and a dinner of the "three kings, the Swedish, Augustus, and Stanislaus" together with the Sobieskis. Communication of the happy news to the pope, to the Sacred College, singing of the *Te Deum* in the little church of the monastery, the sound of trumpets, illuminations and mortar-salvos in the casino. When the *Te Deums* were finished in the churches of Trinità dei Monti and San Stanislao, Cardinal d'Arquien celebrated the liberation of his grandsons in his own way—with a sumptuous banquet.[28]

In spite of these signs of rejoicing, on January 19 "there was seen posted the usual rigorous edict prohibiting Carnival and any other amusement even if allowed at other times."[29] Cardinal Grimani bestirred himself to oppose the Duke of Uzeda's claim that at the feast of Candlemass a portrait of Philip V should be hung up in the church of Monserrato, but more and more the cardinal dedicated himself to planning and carrying out the invasion of Neapolitan territory. Despite the tension, Maria Casimira and the Spanish ambassador defied the pope's anger with an improvised comedy (in the "little theater at Trinità dei Monti") and with a "fine banquet with lavish refreshments, in which there appeared many gentlemen and ladies, French and Spanish, in masks."[30]

The Romans were chafing at the bit: "to flee the melancholy that reigns here, many gentlemen have left and gone elsewhere to live happily," Valesio writes.[31] But he also reports that in dealing with the Carnival floats organized by Maria Casimira and Cardinal Grimani, the Curia had dissuaded the performers, with the customary threats, from continuing to offer their work. The rebellion against the edicts spread, and even "many honored and well-brought-up young women" showed themselves at windows, "dressed as men,"[32] while the most courageous ventured masked into the areas of Piazza di Spagna and the Lungara, counting on the protected status of those places. Repression was not delayed: when the police had news of a banquet they broke into the house where it was being held, arresting the men and leaving the women shut up there. Against this turbulent background, the progress of the Austrian armies met with popular approval, which was particularly displeasing to the pope.

[28] Ibid., 753.
[29] Ibid., 756.
[30] Ibid., 768.
[31] Ibid., 768-769.
[32] Ibid., 776.

On May 2, while Grimani saw to the final phase of enrolling troops, Maria Casimira decided to go to Naples (under the name of Countess of Marienburg) to be present at the miracle of San Gennaro, thereby keeping a vow made during the imprisonment of her sons. She had not reached Frascati when news of her father's serious illness arrived from Rome. By dying at the age of ninety-seven (some in Rome said one-hundred-and-seven), Cardinal d'Arquien prevented his daughter from being present at the Neapolitan triumph of the Imperial forces. But there were bitter pills to swallow for the impoverished Cardinal Grimani as well: yielding to jealous courtiers, the emperor reneged on his promise to appoint Grimani viceroy, consoling him for his disappointment with a "most polite letter in his own hand."[33]

Rome was almost in a state of war. The Imperial plenipotentiary, the Count of Martinitz, could not expect a cordial welcome from Grimani. The Cardinals del Giudice and La Trémouille complained to the pope about the presence of so many enemies of the crowns of Spain and France in Rome. Fearful of being attacked, they kept their palaces in full readiness for war. Maria Casimira did the same, with sixty fusiliers on guard in her mini-palace. The news of the entry of the Imperial forces into Naples (7 July 1707) overjoyed the pundits of Austria but did not improve the situation in Rome.

Reinhard Strohm's clarifications concerning Handel's long sojourn in Italy[34] have made many composers of the period appear to be weather-vanes waving obediently to winds determined by their patron-commissioners' adherence to this or that political faction. I have greatly enjoyed the idea of a political map of the situation, but my knowledge of the protagonists leads me to disagree with categorical placements. Ottoboni, for example, is described as clearly francophile, when his final choice was clearly opportunistic. His friendly relations with his compatriot Grimani, recognized leader of the Imperial party, influenced his attitude in early years. That the Medici were francophile I might attribute to a centuries-old tradition rather than to their more recent connection with the Most Christian Kings through the ever-embarassing Marguérite-Louise d'Orléans, although the financial as well as political blackmail of the imperialists weighed heavily on the agonized decision of Cosimo III.

Strohm (followed by Giovanni Morelli, who gave rein to his fancy in a typically amusing diversion, significantly titled "Monsù Hendel,

---

33 Ibid., 828.
34 Reinhard Strohm, "Il viaggio italiano di Händel come esperienza europea," in *Händel in Italia,* ed. Giovanni Morelli, Third Venice Festival, Venice, 1981 [hereafter *Third Festival*] ,60-71.

the servant of two masters")[35] tends to present us with one of those lucid maps in which two armies oppose each other in battle order. To me this schematization seems to reflect only imperfectly the reality of positions that were often ambiguous and changeable, and always ill-defined. What our great cities lived through was only the reflection of this situation. We must remember that men and armies were opposed in a well-defined manner only in Spain and the Italian territories directly occupied by the belligerents. Rome, we have already seen, was a sort of Casablanca before the fact, swarming with spies and intrigues. Given their economic dependence on their patrons, it is obvious that the musicians, poor devils, had to remain with their noses in the air, perpetually sniffing the direction of the wind—even more so since, in many cases, it was the patrons themselves who oscillated between the two sides, with effects that could result in sensational reversals of their positions. I have already cited the example of the transition to the Franco-Hispanic period, which was almost painless in Sicily but much more troubled in Neapolitan territory. A few years after the useless visit of Philip V, Naples became Austrian ("without even firing a tercet," poetised Giancola Sitillo, quoted by Croce).[36] Perhaps only in these politically defined areas was it possible for musicians to embrace a political ideal consistently. If we are to believe Francesco Scarlatti, his attachment to Austria had cost him his post as *maestro di cappella* in a Palermo that was clearly Franco-Hispanic. However, in this case his evanescent role suggests that his martyrdom was imaginary, to be changed into hard cash on the counter of Viennese imperial favor. Recent discoveries[37] have instead fully confirmed the Austrophile attitude that forced Francesco Scarlatti and Emanuello Rincon d'Astorga to save themselves by fleeing the persecution of the Spansh viceroy. Often in the musical history of Palermo however—above all where the war did not exercise its bloody pressures directly—even the nobles found themselves in ideological-political difficulties: it was one thing to change a master because of a treaty handed down from above, another to offer one of the contenders one's own loyalty.

In Rome, where a "Catholic King" and a "Roman Emperor" had set off a series of blackmailings disguised as lawful, diplomatic moves,

---

[35] Ibid., 72-82: the reference is to Goldoni's *Arlecchino servitore di due padroni.*

[36] Croce, *Teatri,* I, 192.

[37] Andrea Sommer-Mathis, "Entre Napoles, Barcelona, e Viena. Nuevos documentos sobre la circulación de musicos a principios del siglo XVII," *ARTIGRAMMA,* Revista de la Departamento de Historia del Arte (Zaragoza, 1996-97), n.12, 45-77 [hereafter cited as Sommer-Mathis,"Nuevos Documentos"].

the situation was more uncertain than ever. Only under the pressure of armed threats did the pope decide to swallow the bitter Austrian pill, since his long idyll with the Franco-Hispanics, to whom he had always shown an unmistakable partiality, was brutally compromised. In fact, the whole situation was one of shreds and patches owing to the weakness of the Italian forces, crushed between the two warring colossi.

It is always risky to depend on political abstractions dictated by history when we concern ourselves with its human protagonists. For that reason I extend to the Italian reflections of the War of the Spanish Succession the doubts that I expressed about Arcadia as the mouthpiece of the Curia. I continue, in an attitude of skeptical possibilism, to follow the fortunes of the musicians who interest us, tossed up and down in the cyclone of war without the political or economic sureties that rendered the fortunes of those who employed them less uncertain.

Nostalgia for Christina

Even in these uncertain circumstances, one cannot say that Alessandro Scarlatti remained idle during the time he spent in Rome in the first decade of the century. Despite the closing of the theaters he had been able to continue to produce new operas, since he had received a commission for the Medici theater at Pratolino every year. The request of the Grand Prince was a specific case, but Alessandro also kept himself in touch with the traditional forms of opera by means of the parallel genres of the oratorio and the serenata, not to mention that miniature upper-class domestic surrogate of the opera, the chamber cantata. Scarlatti cultivated the genre with real affection because it allowed him, as we shall see, to pass beyond the boundaries of the *human* in the more recherché investigation of the relationship between word and music, without exposing himself to the snare of pleasing the masses. The pastoralizing poetry that serves as a background for the chamber cantata is the work of the Arcadians, and the flourishing of the form (which only today is beginning to be offered again to the general public) as an alternative to the prohibited opera seems to me as Christinian as one could imagine.

In fact, the Basillissa had not been forgotten by the intellectuals who were close to her in the years of her Roman sojourn. By October of 1690, little more than a year after Christina's death, a group of poets who had met to recite their compositions in the meadows adjoining Castel Sant'Angelo felt that they had "renewed Arcadia." Giovan Mario Crescimbeni, the promotor of these "ragunanze," chose this glamorous label for the academy. Supported by more conspicuous patrons, it would have an important role—if not always a well-defined one—in the development of Italian letters in the following century.

By "more conspicuous patrons," I refer to important prelates such as the Cardinals Albani (later Clement XI), Ottoboni, and Pamphilj; and rulers in exile (Maria Casimira, as usual), or firmly seated on their thrones and disposed to favor the expansion of the "colonies" of Arcadia. João V of Portugal handed out the pharaonic sum of four thousand *scudi,* which made it possible for the Arcadians to acquire land and to construct an amphitheater, thereby creating headquarters for their "Bosco Parrasio," their meetings, and their "Olympics." So farseeing a promotional campaign strengthened the Academy. Its truly international proliferation should be seen in relation to the hypothesis of Amedeo Quondam, who pointed out the "effective organicity" of the institution "for the historical necessities of the political strategy of the Roman Curia, which constitutes its real point of reference."[38] To me, however, it seems that such an hypothesis should be related to the whole time-span of the Arcadia rather than to its first manifestation. This was characterized by the personal influence of Ottoboni, who lived the human adventure too much in the first person to be the bearer of any precise political design of the Curia.

I have already recorded that the *nipote* of Alexander VIII came to his privileged situation at all too young an age. It was not soon enough, however, to allow him to enter the world of Christina of Sweden before her death. On the other hand, many of the Arcadians had been members of the Royal Academy operating out of her palace on the Lungara. The direct connection with that tradition is assured as much by the presence of several *fidèles* of the royal *noyau* in the historic "ragunanza" of Prati as by the interesting document that Della Seta published. From this we discover the project of creating a proper artistic university to fill a notable lack in Roman cultural life.[39] It is Ottoboni who turns directly to Clement XI (and to the pope who, as a cardinal, had attempted to mediate between Christina of Sweden and Innocent XI to end their guerilla war). He requested the pope to transfer the Academy of Design dedicated to Saint Luke from the halls of the Campidoglio to a "more convenient and proper place:" Christina's Palazzo Riario on the Lungara. This suggested enlargement would have transformed aristocratic Roman

---

[38] Quoted in Fabrizio Della Seta, "La Musica in Arcadia al tempo di Corelli," *Nuovissimi Studi Corelliani,* Proceedings of the III International Conference (Florence: Olschki, 1982 [hereafter Della Seta, "Arcadia"]), 123-150, 124.

[39] Ibid., 133.

youths into "perfect gentlemen" through a complex of studies "appropriate for deterring [them] from any other useless or base entertainment."

It is striking to see the criteria proposed by Saint Philip Neri for his "exercises of the oratorio" transferred to this preoccupation with the highest social classes. Although it may surprise us to find personages as different as Neri and Ottoboni holding the same positions, we should not forget that they were both notable men of the Counter-Reformation. Ottoboni then lists the proposed studies:

> They would be these: literature, riding, dancing, fencing, and music; which professions not less than the first ones, demonstrated by famous and able instructors would remedy the only defect of this great Court, that because it is applied only to teaching Ecclesiastics, it appears, that the good education of the seculars is completely neglected.

Here our reasons for amazement multiply. It is already sufficiently surprising to find a cardinal who takes it on himself to remind the pope-king that his subjects are not all priests, and that the gentlemen of Rome threaten to remain louts, but the polemic thrust that challenges the Church on the excessive—indeed exclusive—care it dedicates to turning out priests is breathtaking. The economic project is clearly utopian: lessening the financial burdens of the venture by promising a sufficient income, assured either by the payment of admission fees to the academy or by the performance of work by the students for the benefit of the college. However, we know that yesterday as today anyone who hopes to execute an ambitious program can hardly tell the truth about the expenses it entails.

This intriguing project was never carried out, but the fact that Della Seta found a copy of Ottoboni's letter in the archive of the Arcadia shows the pre-eminent role that the academy would have played in this splendid operation of secularizing studies.

What remains mysterious to one who distrusts conventional and overly general labels is the real depth of the aesthetic-ideological link that could exist between poets like Vincento da Filicaja or Francesco Redi and the more evanescent and languishing Crescimbeni, Felice Zappi, Silvio Stampiglia, and Carlo Sigismondo Capeci. This school was scourged by Giuseppe Baretti (1719-1789), who in 1763 founded *La Frusta Letteraria* ("The Literary Whip"), a polemical journal against the Arcadians and their poetry. Christina of Sweden had certainly exaggerated when she celebrated Filicaja as Petrarch reborn ("without his defects!") or as the potential rival of Tasso. But the Basilissa might not have shown similar enthusiasm for the mincing attitudes of certain

Arcadians intent on the dream that a now *Deus* would restore to them the *otia* of Tityrus and Meliboeus (asking nothing in exchange, naturally), or on remasticating Horace's "O rus, quando ego te aspiciam!" To define the first Roman Arcadians, I would say that they were more or less illustrious personages, given over to poetizing, sworn enemies of the Baroque poetics of Giovanni Battista Marini, devoted to the classics and applying themselves more to searching for than to practicing "good taste."

...escorted only by his ability (which is greatly advanced ...)

To expiate the sin of pride that he had committed in Naples, Domenico Scarlatti followed his father to Rome, a city of penances symbolized by the absence of theatrical activity, and one given to Arcadian longings. If his father had been obliged to content himself with the makeshift expedient already described, there were surely no great prospects for the prodigal son. After the failure of his Neapolitan experience, Domenico was like one of those boys who grow too fast, who seem to burst out of clothes that are no longer the right size. This is the moment of Domenico's first superficial inclusion into Roman musical life. It raises one of the crucial problems of the biographer: the relationship between the younger Scarlatti and Gasparini. The oldest tradition would place Domenico's study with Gasparini in Rome, but generally only their contact during the Venetian years (1705-1709) is taken into account. In my opinion Kirkpatrick is correct when he supposes it possible, as well as more logical, to date Domenico's discipleship to a period preceding Gasparini's move to Venice (June 1701).[40] For the overgrown boy fresh from the leadership of the Neapolitan season of 1703-1704 to regress to the role of apprentice would have been something that not even a father as severe as Alessandro could conceive. The mortification would have rebounded on the person who had given his consent to so rash an undertaking. In any case, the tone of the famous letter to Ferdinando de' Medici, which we will re-read in a moment, would still be inappropriate.

Kirkpatrick suggested that Alessandro could have sent Domenico to Rome before 1701. Having discovered Gasparini bent on sacrificing to Santa Cecilia, the patroness of music, and Santa Rosalia, the patroness of Palermo, in 1696, I might extend the same supposition to the city in which Domenico had found hospitality in the house of his uncle Francesco; but I think that an adolescent coming from Naples could be sent more easily to Rome than to Palermo.

---

[40] Kirkpatrick, *Scarlatti,* 37.

In choosing Francesco Gasparini to give a final honing to Domenico's talent, Alessandro Scarlatti showed extreme wisdom. The exploration of Gasparini's work is rather recent, but its first results encourage deeper research. The label of principal theorist of the *basso continuo*—well-merited by the author of the *Armonico pratico al cimbalo*—has wronged a musician of great importance in the early eighteenth-century Italian musical scene. Despite the success of his theoretical work, Gasparini must have been reluctant to accept the role of a teacher, which he considered to be absolutely secondary. He continued to preface the reprints of the *Armonico* with an address to the "Gentle Reader" in which we read:

> You will marvel to see emerging into the light of the World a Work which you never expected. First, because perhaps you did not think that I was an Organist, and consequently not able to treat such material [...]. And if you will be pleased to skim through these pages with a favorable eye, perhaps you will find something new to notice, which will not displease you. If I write simply, and not with the elegance of fine speech, I am satisfied, and it will not be little, if you consider me a Musician, not a Rhetorician [...].

In spite of such a profession of modesty, Gasparini knew that he was a superb teacher, and his little treatise is a compendium of experience ripened in the practice of accompaniment and transferred to the practice of teaching. The Introduction to the work already declares plainly that three things are necessary to anyone who wishes to master Music: "Deliberation, Application, and a Good Teacher." Then he specifies:

> The good Teacher is the rarest thing, because not all good Teachers teach willingly, not all of them partake of a facility in communicating, not all the Scholars of Music have the benefit of being able to have them, and Excellent Teachers are not found everywhere (although today, to tell the Truth, there appear more Teachers, than Students).

He must have been considered a superb teacher by Alessandro Scarlatti, who in the flood of his demanding occupations knew that he did not have the time—or the patience—necessary to the good educator. A few years later (between 1708 and 1709) Cosimo III of Tuscany would send the young Zipoli to Naples to profit from Alessandro's teaching. A note from Padre Martini reveals that "because of sharp differences"[41] the

---

41 Giovanni Battista Martini, *Scrittori di Musica—Notizie storiche e loro opere,* ms. in the Archive of the Convent of San Francesco in Bologna, quoted by Luigi Ferdinando Tagliavini in the Preface to *Domenico Zipoli, Sonate d'intavolatura per Organo e Cimbalo* (Heidelberg, 1957).

young apprentice fled to Bologna, where he found understanding and help from Fra Lavinio Vannucci before passing on to Rome under the guidance of the great Pasquini. It is yet another stroke of clear-sightedness that allowed the possessive Alessandro to entrust to another such a delicate task as the cultivation of a genius.

It is reasonable, then, to place the first encounters of Domenico Scarlatti and Gasparini around June 1701. This supports the version of Burney, who categorically associated the relationship with "the residence of Scarlatti at Naples"[42] and spoke of the student's youth in terms that would exclude a previous Neapolitan debut.

If located in Rome, the relationship assumes more importance. There Gasparini would have stood as an intermediary between the young man entrusted to his care and a glorious tradition that went back to Frescobaldi by way of Pasquini and Corelli, whose student Gasparini himself had been. In the introduction to the *Armonico pratico* the teacher whom Alessandro had selected for his son refers explicitly to the founder of the tradition, declaring that "to become a true, and practising Organist" it was necessary "to make a particular study" especially focused "on the Toccatas, Fugues, Ricercari, etcetera of Frescobaldi, [and] of other Excellent Men."

This recalls—with a more solid historical foundation— the possible experiences of Francesco Durante. Like Domenico, he was trained in Naples and perhaps also came to Rome to draw from fountains of knowledge named Pitoni and Pasquini. Domenico's miraculous displays crowned him prince of the harpsichord well before his written compositions left more unequivocal evidences of his talent for posterity. They must necessarily have been founded on this combination of Neapolitan *gusto* and Roman *dottrina,* integrated by the example and subsequent teaching of his father.

Having made this important point about the formative experiences of Scarlatti junior, let us follow his passage from the penitential Rome that we have described and his subsequent exodus by means of Alessandro's famous letter to Ferdinando de' Medici, dated 30 May 1705:

> Royal Highness,/My son Domenico brings himself, with my Heart, humbly to the feet of Y.R.H., mindful of the debt of my and his profound regards and most humble service.
>
> I have detached him by force from Naples, where, although his talent had place, it was not a talent for such a place. I now send him

away from Rome, because Rome has no roof to welcome Music, who lives here as a beggar. This son who is an Eagle, whose Wings are grown, must not remain at ease in the nest, and I must not impede his flight.

On the occasion that the Virtuoso Nicolino of Naples is passing by here on his way to Venice, I have decided to send him off with him; and escorted only by his ability (which is much advanced, after he was able to be with me, to enjoy the honor of serving Y.R.H. personally, it being now three years ago), he goes, almost like a wanderer, to encounter those opportunities which will present themselves to him to become known, and which are awaited in vain in Rome today. I intend, before he goes off on the way to meet his fortune, that he show himself at the feet of Y.R.H., receive and carry out your high venerated desires, as his and my greatest high Lord, most clement Patron and benefactor. It is glory, honor, and gain, both his and mine, that the World should know us as Y.R.H.'s most humble servants.

This reflection consoles my spirit, and makes me hope for every good outcome for the Pilgrimage of this Son who, since I have recommended him to divine Providence and Protection, as the highest origin of all good, immediately after I offer my most humble supplications to the high, most powerful protection of Y.R.H., to whom I humble him, as I do myself who, with the most profound respect and obedience, I bow, as throughout my life, Y.R.H.'s/most humble, most devoted, and most obliged Servant/Alessandro Scarlatti."[43]

Even in a letter full of his customary deference to the most artistically endowed of all his patrons, Alessandro writes in terms that bring out his whole personality "in the round." There is the *father* with all the responsibilities connected with such a role, in so important a matter/. There is the disappointed *man* who nevertheless does not renounce his own authoritarian stance with regard to his son and suddenly drops his ceremonious tone to declare that he had "detached him by force" from a city unworthy of his talent. From this phrase I detect that his son showed a certain reluctance to leave Naples. It is likely that the other members of the Scarlatti clan, who were intent on enjoying the benefits that the young musicians's ascent made available to them, which were threatened by Alessandro's continued absence, had influenced his state of mind.

The pun on Naples the *place,* which makes *place* for a talent superior to the *place* (the position, in this sense) that it finds in the hierar-

43 Fabbri, *Scarlatti,* 58-59.

chy of values of the Royal Chapel, should not be understood in the sense of casting a slur on a provinciality connected with decentralization, but in the sense of the inadequate recognition of evident merit. We have seen what the situation in Rome was: in speaking of *Music,* "who lives here like a beggar," Alessandro alludes to himself. The "beggary" is the continual search for support and aid to which his own uncertain condition as an "assistant" obliged him.

Et in Arcadia ego ...

But Scarlatti senior had not yet touched the depths of the disappointments that Rome had saved up for him. For that to happen, a deceptive ray of light had to pierce the Sicilian's fundamentally pessimistic horizon.

Alessandro Scarlatti, Pasquini, and Corelli had frequent contacts with the Arcadians through their cardinal patrons (members of Arcadia since 1695) and Maria Casimira (welcomed with the Arcadian name of Amirisca Telea). Della Seta's researches give a more precise outline of their enrollment,[44] which took place in April of 1706 —a notable delay by comparison with the systematic admission of poets in line with the programs of the academy.

Until the publication of Della Seta's essay, the accounts of the enrollment and of the famous poetico-musical meeting that took place in the house of the abate Domenico Riviera were taken from the registers preserved in the "Serbatojo" ("Reservoir," the archive of the Academy) and from the *Arcadia,* a sort-of chronicle-novel by Crescimbeni. Della Seta has revealed certain nuances that induced the Arcadians to distinguish *Alessandro Scarlatti of Palermo* and *Bernardo Pasquino of Pescia* from *Arcangelo Corelli of Fusignano called the Bolognese.* To the first two they assigned the description "Illustrious Master of Music" and to the third "Most famous Master of musical Sinfonie, and of the sound of the violin."

Della Seta's examination of the documents allowed him to substantiate Alessandro's poetic capabilities, already hypothesized by other explorers in the *mare magnum* of the Scarlatti cantatas. To confirm by the words "and is also a practitioner of poetry," which accompany the description of him as a musician, Alessandro produced three sonnets. The first was ceremoniously addressed "To the noble, Famous Assembly of Shepherds of Arcadia; on the occasion of their having given a place, in the same [Arcadia] to Terpander of Palermo Composer of Music." The second was directed to the "Guardian of Arcadia Alfesibeo Cario" (Crescimbeni). The last, *dulcis in fundo,* was dedicated "to his

---

[44] Della Seta, "Arcadia," doc. II, 141-142.

high, amiable Patron and Lord, the Most eminent and Most reverend Prince Signor Cardinal Pietro Ottoboni from whose most beneficent hand" Scarlatti received "the honor, and Diploma of Shepherd of Arcady."[45]

Alessandro had been transformed into Terpandro in homage to the ancient author of *nomoi* for the cithara, the winner of a musical contest celebrated in honor of Carneian Apollo. The pastoral name taken by Corelli was Arcomelo, while that of Pasquini was Protico. It was Ottoboni, Della Seta has finally clarified, who extended the smiling fields of Arcady to music. The fact that the composers admitted were the three musicians closest to Christina of Sweden confirms norms of choice like those that were valid for the poets. (The brothers Benedetto and Alessandro Marcello were enrolled in the Venetian colony "Animosa" as much in their capacity as patricians and amateurs of poetry as in that of musicians.)

We also learn that by 1696 there was a project of founding a "Chorus of Arcadia" composed of "various excellent Virtuosi of Music, and of Instruments" who had asked to "display their Skill" to the shepherds of the academy. To underline the differences between the true shepherds and these potential subordinate associates (not always well-off, as we know), the latter had to be exempt "from all the Collections and burdens to which the other Shepherds are subject" but would remain obligated to other duties, among them "singing compositions by foreign masters." From a contemporary note we learn that the musicians who aspired to be admitted were Corelli (in the capacity of "player," together with his faithful Matteo Fornari and Giovannino Lulier, as well as Bononcini) and "Bernardo Pasquino Maestro di Cappella," together with two "Musici": the castratos Giuseppe Ceccarelli (called "the Orsino," referring to his first post as virtuoso of Cardinal Orsini) and Pasqualino Thiepoli, the famous soprano from Udine, like the others connected with various activities promoted by Cardinal Ottoboni. The name of Alessandro Scarlatti, still resident in Naples, was missing.

When the "Chorus" failed to materialize, in 1706 the three musicians previously named were admitted as full members of their Arcadia, and their number was destined to remain unchanged for a decade. Andrea Adami of Bolsena (the favorite of Ottoboni) would enter Arcadia in 1711 (a year after the death of Pasquini), and Francesco Gasparini, who had left Venice in 1713 to make Città di Castello the base for his journeys to various important centers on the Italian opera-map, would be

[45] Della Seta, "Arcadia," doc. III, 143.

admitted in 1718 (five years after the death of Corelli). Only in 1716 would Gasparini move to Rome, in the service of Prince Ruspoli. The account of a brilliant meeting of the Arcadians that took place in the palace of the abate Domenico Riviera, transformed by the fanciful Crescimbeni into "the Hut of Metaureo," has often been quoted. (It should be noted, however, that it was not an official "ragunanza," which explains the participation of other performers along with the three famous shepherds: thus the projected *coro* was realized as a private entertainment). The chronicle speaks of a "Musical Academy made by the nymphs," and even at the beginning of the account Alessandro Scarlatti seems to hold a position of leadership:

> When Terpandro with his companions had set in order what was needful, Arcomelo began the musical festivity with one of those beautiful sinfonie made in the noble hut of the acclaimed Crateo and later published to the world with such glory for him [...].

(Crateo was Ottoboni, and this time the extravagances of the Arcadians had transformed into a "noble hut" nothing less than Palazzo della Cancelleria.)

> After that, Terpandro took out of his knapsack several canzoni for music, and spoke thus to the group: May God will that the music of these songs bring you the same delight as the verses will bring, whose author is present here and is greatly venerated by me [...].

In fact, the verses were the work of one of the greatest poets of those years, perhaps the best among those who had founded the Academy: Tirsi, alias the lawyer Giovan Battista Zappi of Imola. He was the husband of Aglaura Cifonia, another acclaimed poet of Arcadia (in the outside world Faustina Maratti or Maratta, the daughter of the famous painter Carlo Maratta). After skirmishes of compliments between the poets Tirsi and Terpandro, Protico (Pasquini) sat down at the harpsichord to "give rule and direction" to other "lesser instruments" which accompanied a "most sweet voice" employed in a cantata. Then Scarlatti himself sat down at the instrument to accompany a duet and other instrumental music. Seeing that Tirsi was thoughtful and realizing that he was absorbed in composing verses, Terpandro convinced his friend to recite them and he immediately set them to music. These improvised displays animated by competition were typical of Arcadia: the old ritual of the poetic competition was refined through the union of the arts, and the bystanders poured out their admiration. Crescimbeni informs us of other improvisations of Tirsi and Terpandro, commenting:

In the meantime everyone remained overcome to see how they competed, these two excellent masters, one of poetry and the other of music [...].

The pastoral diversions of Arcadia shortened at least momentarily the social distances between one shepherd and another. Alessandro customarily respected such distances in his relations with personages placed above him on the social pyramid by birth or by acquired advantages that were universally recognized. When he encountered persons who were unqualified in human terms, the observance of the customary rituals must have been particularly difficult for the proud Sicilian, constrained above all by his own permanent state of need. In this sense, his entrance into Arcadia—a select assemblage in which nobility of birth must at least symbolically be coupled with artistic talent—helped to assuage wounds that the musician's self-respect had suffered for many years. The credit goes to Ottoboni; in those years of rather obscure navigating, Alessandro was perhaps too ready to choose the brilliant cardinal as a cynosure.[46] At the same time that Alessandro attended the uncertain ascent of Maria Casimira's comet in the Roman firmament, he maintained a distant relationship with Ferdinando de' Medici (*Spes, ultima Dea*) and he continued to enjoy the ever-discreet favor of Pamphilj.

Ottoboni had shown himself the Christina's genuine heir, offering—as Da Ponte would say—his protection to that same triad of musicians who had enriched the entertainments of the little Swedish court in exile. At the resumption of theatrical activities—always in a subdued key, since to the fear of natural calamities had been added the threats of Mars—his competition with Maria Casimira of Poland appeared to remain within the limits of the most courteous rivalry. Although he had never known Christina personally, the cardinal could measure the abyss that separated the wishful copy from the incomparable original. Some years later, before financial embarassments forced Maria Casimira to take refuge in France, Saint-Simon's *panier* still had its bottom. Ottoboni must have been the first to laugh at the patents of nobility by which the "Polastra" sought to silence her creditors, while the Roman aristocracy turned up their noses.

But before we examine the activities that kept music alive during that long Lent, let us amuse ourselves by considering, as a consequence of the busy increase of sheep-rearing fostered by the Arcadia, the arrival in Rome of two very special examples of the ovine race: a lost sheep and a black sheep.

46 This metaphor, attuned to the period, cynosure—literally "tail of the dog"—was Orsa Minor and the term was employed in the sense of "guide," or "point of reference."

XI

Fugue in two voices with many artifices

The Palermitan upheavals of 1708 gave Francesco Rincon d'Astorga senior one last opportunity to rescue his reputation from the disgrace to which his excesses had led him. At that time Emanuello was far away: in all probability he had secretly fled from Palermo on 21 August 1707. This important detail permits a more precise reconstruction of the wanderings of our noble adventurer. The recent discovery that he filled a post in Palermo between 1705 and 1706 definitely excludes his presence in Rome earlier. There, from 1699 the Duke of Uzeda was Philip V's ambassador to the Holy See and in this new role he continued to protect Sicilian musicians—all the better if they were aristocrats—without giving up other, more doubtful, traditions of hospitality(like those we have been unable to justify in one of his predecessors[1]). Along with our talented son of a good family in momentary difficulties, the duke welcomed a curious adventurer-poet who had fled his native Naples, leaving behind a wife, thirteen children (fifteen, says Scherillo[2]) and deep suspicion of complicity in a fraudulent bankruptcy.

Sebastiano Biancardi, better known as Domenico Lalli, was also prolific as an author of opera libretti and succeeded in making a name for himself during the years in which Apostolo Zeno flourished and Metastasio's career was reaching its apotheosis. Born in 1679 of a rich Neapolitan family and adopted by an elderly gentleman who left him all his goods, Sebastiano was the cashier of the Bank of the Santissima Annunziata when an immense deficit induced him, if we believe his story, to pay the entire debt out of his own money and to abandon wife and children, fleeing to make a new life (and to conceal his own shame, I add; in the light of what follows, I do not much believe in the interested party's protestations of innocence). The Duke of Uzeda must have believed that Sebastiano was not implicated in the deficit. Indifferent to the temptations his collection of treasures presented to a potential thief,

---

[1] Concerning the Marchese del Carpio, ambassador in Rome, see Chapter I.

[2] Michele Scherillo, *L'opera buffa napoletana* (Palermo: Sandron, 1914 [hereafter Scherillo]), 496: he assigns another fifteen to Biancardi's second marriage.

he hired Biancardi at a handsome salary. The poet himself continues the story, which Scherillo[3] could not easily fit into the context of the characters later singled out by Walker[4] and developed by Tiby. In the *Compendio della vita del Signor Bastian Biancardi napoletano* which prefaces Biancardi's *Rime,* printed in Venice in 1732, we read:

> Meanwhile in Rome, Biancardi struck up a pleasant friendship with Sig. D. Emanuele Barone d'Astorga, a distinguished Gentleman from Palermo, who found himself in the court of that ambassador, having fled from his father's house owing to disagreements with him; [he was] unprovided with the needful and trusted to his own skill, since he was a noted composer of music for his own pleasure. Therefore, since Biancardi consulted often with this erudite Gentleman, he began to set to music many of his cantatas and serenades, by which they strengthened between them so firm a bond of confident friendship, that they decided to seek a better fortune by undertaking some more distant journey; for the which, when Biancardi had taken leave of the Sig. Duke of Osseda [Uzeda], he set off with the Sig. Barone d'Astorga and a valet (hired for their service, a Venetian named Agostino Zimbelli) on the way to Genoa. When they had arrived there, they were hindered by the most deplorable calamities: at night they were unexpectedly robbed of their clothes, money, and every other valuable; which made Astorga take the honorable course of composing for the impresario of the Theater of Genoa the music for a certain drama which was to be performed there, for which he received several *dobles* as a gift. This served to set them on their way toward the invincible Venetian Republic, in order to find the thieving servant who they believed was probably headed that way. Since they were ill-attired and not of presentable appearance by reason of the theft, and in order to find the faithless servant with less suspicion, they agreed that one should call himself Domenico Lalli instead of Bastian Biancardi, and the other Giuseppe del Chiaro instead of Barone d'Astorga.

From the first measures of this new fugue we find that we have fallen into a comedy of errors. The wanderings of the two friends carry them around Italy, both urged on by a thirst for adventure born in both from a need to exorcise deep anxieties. It is not necessary to stress the improbability of their pretext: following an unfaithful servant is an illusory objective, and a celebrated page of Casanova shows how unsatisfying and unrewarding the desired result could be. But comparing the

---

[3] Scherillo, 492ff.

[4] Frank Walker, "Astorga and a Neapolitan Librettist," *Monthly Musical Record,* May, 1951.

Mémoires of Casanova with this little tale of a poet intent on justifying some murky episodes in his re-emergence to credibility would be like putting the *Odyssey* alongside the confession of a third-class reformed crook. Let us see how the two friends dealt with the troubles into which they inevitably fell:

> When Domenico Lalli and Giuseppe Del Chiaro had set off toward Milanese territory on their way to Venice and had arrived in Tortona, not having passports, they were arrested and imprisoned for having claimed that they were Romans, since that was the time of some preparations for war between the Emperor and the Pope; but when Lalli had written a most humble letter to the Governor of Milan in that emergency, pointing out to him the theft that they had suffered and the pursuit of the faithless servant that they had undertaken, and explaining who they were, they were soon freed from prison. Deprived of everything because of this last misfortune, they reached Pavia and there embarking on the Po, in a few days they came to Venice; where they flattered themselves that they would find their fugitive servant; but when all their efforts were in vain, constrained by need, they decided on the alternative of seeking service with some German prince, Giuseppe Del Chiaro assuming the character of a *maestro di cappella,* Domenico Lalli that of a *maestro* of letters and player of the archlute. To begin the scheme, since the Baron d'Astorga had had a long correspondence with Signor Apostolo Zeno, the most famous man of letters of our century and now historian and poet of His Imperial Majesty, he arranged with Biancardi to write him [Zeno] as from Palermo a false letter in his name, recommending to him two virtuosi, friends of his, who by means of his valued protection wished to be decently employed in the service of some prince. The idea was happily carried out and in the company of Lalli, Giuseppe Del Chiaro went to the said Signor Zeno showing the said letter about himself; and being kindly welcomed by the cordial politeness of Signor Apostolo, they were quite pleased with his suggestion to take them to the palace of Signor Count Ercolani, at that time Imperial ambassador in Venice, to whom such a commission had been entrusted by a German prince.
>
> When they had set off on the way there, it happened by chance that they heard there was with the said Signor Count Ercolani a Roman gentleman who was their mutual friend; whence in order not to be discovered, they abandoned the undertaking and decided to go off to Mantua with the qualifications they had thought up, one a music-teacher, the other a teacher of letters and the archlute. When they arrived there, always under the same names, they got access to a certain distinguished Gentleman of the House of Gonzaga, a friend

of the Baron d'Astorga, in the same manner as to the said Signor Apostolo Zeno, whence with the same strategem that had introduced them to him, they made themselves known to this man; since the said Gentleman (with all the nobility of Mantua, and especially the ladies) sponsored them, they began with great pleasure and profit to give lessons of music and letters, leading for thirteen months a happy and tranquil life. But when the late Signor Giovanni Paita, famous singer and their most kind friend, arrived there by chance he revealed both of them for what they were; whence blushing at the disclosure they decided it was expedient to return to Venice; and with the good offices of the said Signor Paita they were welcomed in the house of the N. H. Signor Pietro Foscarini of blessed memory, who lived in contrada S. Agnese, where they stayed for thirteen months, loaded with immense favors and infinite kindnesses. In the meantime some of the music of the said Signor Barone d'Astorga had come into the hands of the Most August Emperor now reigning as Charles VI, then Charles III [of Spain]. Since the manner of this composition was pleasing to him, he had him summoned to Barcelona; since it was suitable for Astorga to unmask himself, he left Venice to fulfill the sovereign command. Lalli was left alone without his dear companion; having passed from the house of the Most Excellent Foscarini to that of the N. H. Signor Bernardo Trivisano of blessed memory, he struck up a closer friendship with the most virtuous Signor Zeno, who aided him willingly with endless generosity, whence being directed and instructed in the manner of composing dramas by his wise and sincere affection, in the year 1710 he produced one for the first time, entitled *L'Amor tirannico.*

Before examining all that our Biancardi-Lalli wishes to communicate, I would note that the music of *L'Amor tirannico* was not written by a second-rate composer, but by Francesco Gasparini. This again demonstrates the links between many of the characters in our story.

I consider Lalli's account to be a kind of *commedia dell'arte* scenario, fancifully developed and sprinkled with artificial sweetenings of a reality that remains bitter indeed.

Twice our professor of *belles-lettres* employs "inviarsi" ("to go away") in the sense of "incamminarsi" ("to set out"); more striking than the ambiguity of the term is the unconscious choice of a verb that accentuates the idea of flight. To go *away,* because the ground is always scorching under the feet of these two poor devils tricked out as adventurers; the cheeks of the two companions burn with the blushes provoked by their embarassing unmaskings. Could you imagine Casanova or Cagliostro in place of Lalli and Del Chiaro? Even the choice of the name Del Chiaro, a pseudonym that seems to invoke transparency, makes our strayed Sicilian sheep's attempt look foolishly out of place. Lalli's desire to tamper with the cards already on the table was not matched by an ability to do so with impunity.

Tiby has stressed the emphatic repetition of the number thirteen.[5] I would observe that Biancardi was the offspring of a land dominated by certain good-luck charms. There were thirteen children of his first marriage (and he was to have thirteen more in Venice, if in this case the data correspond to the truth); he passed thirteen months happily and tranquilly in Mantua; he spent thirteen more in the house of the good Pietro Foscarini. The professor of letters would have had difficulty in augmenting his income by teaching mathematics, since in his stories too many things happen in too little time. The data contained in the *Compendio* should be compared with those collected *ab antiquo* by Mazzuchelli and D'Afflitto.[6] We discover that Biancardi was not following only the thieving servant, but indeed the real culprit of the Neapolitan embezzlement; that his first wife was the sister of a bishop and that she must have been dead when the Venetian Barbara Pazini married him to start the second brood of little Lallis.

The dedication of a collection of *Rime* to Cosimo III, which shows that the poet was in Florence in 1708, may be an important fact (see below). Walker and Tiby have already dismantled the chronology suggested by the *Compendio,* although they accept those thirteen Neapolitan children whose existence I could believe only if they had been born in job-lots of three or four each. According to Tiby, the two certain reference-points are the performances of *Dafni* (Genoa, 21 April 1709) and *L'Amor tirannico* (Venice, autumn 1710). Between these dates should be placed a first stay of a few weeks in Venice (and the imprisonment in Tortona) and the two long stays in Mantua and Venice. These would total almost three years, against the eighteen months available. It is reasonable to follow Tiby in shortening of the two stays. All the same I remain doubtful about the dates of Emanuello's departure from Sicily and of his meeting with his kindred spirit in Rome. Despite the improbabilities pointed out by Tiby and Walker, the itinerary of the two companions around Italy remains convincing. Assigning a certain length to the period that Emanuello spent with the Duke of Uzeda, I left open the

---

[5] Tiby, *Astorga,* 103 n.

[6] [?] Mazzuchelli, *Scrittori d'Italia,* quoted by Scherillo, 493 n.; Eustachio D'Afflitto, *Memorie degli scrittori del Regno di Napoli, raccolte e distese da..., domenicano* (Naples: Stamperia Simoniana, 1794), II, 119.

possibility that his removal from Sicily had taken place in the earliest years of the century. The fact that Francesco senior had returned to liberty, recovering his baronial investiture, reinforced this placement of Emanuello's flight from Palermo. However, the appointment of the young aristocrat to the *Tavola nummularia* and the contents of a petition addressed by him to Charles VI in 1712 counsel a return to the hypothesis of preceding biographers, retouched where appropriate.

It is possible that in 1702 Emanuello was in Sicily. In Catania, far from Palermo, he was already flaunting the baronial title he had only obtained in 1714 by a formal investiture. In the *Elenco cronologico dei drammi rappresentati o pubblicati a Catania dal 1700 al 1800* I find the

> *Dialogue on the occasion of the ceremony of enrolling D. Vincenzo Paternò Asmundo in the noble Military Order of the Apostle St. James,* poetry by D. Francesco Maria Landolina, music by D. Eman. Rincon de Astorga, baron of Ogliastro, Printed by Bisagni."[7]

After the youthful exploit of *La moglie nemica* it is significant that the only traces of performances of our hero's music in Sicily—the aforesaid *Dialogo,* the *Ave maris stella* recently discovered by Nicolò Maccavino in the cathedral of Piazza Armerina,[8] another *Dialogo* sung in Syracuse in 1728—refer to localities nearer to his native Augusta than to Palermo.

The libretto of the Catania *Dialogo,* consulted by Policastro in a large private collection now dispersed, conforms to the traditions of the time. The author of the text is the same Landolina who the preceding year had written a "Dialogue in honor of Philip V"[9] set to music by D. Giuseppe Acciarelli, chapel master of the cathedral of Catania. The printer is Bisagni, as for all the other Catanian libretti of the same period. The 1702 *Dialogo* was composed for an occasion suited to the social class of the "baron": the entry of another aristocrat into an order of chivalry. We are in the festive era of Cardinal del Giudice and it does not seem degrading for a baron to put his name to his own participation in an artistic event called on to solemnize the ceremony.

After 1702 the reliable references would have been those discovered by Tiby, if the appointment in Palermo and a Viennese petition had not furnished new perspectives on Astorga's chronology.[10] On 17 April 1712 Don Emanuello requested of Charles VI a pension to indem-

---

[7] Guglielmo Policastro, *Catania nel Settecento,* Turin: SEI, 1950, 373.

[8] Nicolò Maccavino, "Una sconosciuta composizione sacra di Emanuel Rincon barone d'Astorga: *Ave maris stella,"* *Studi musicali* XXVI (1998), 89-122.

[9] Policastro, *Catania nel Settecento,* 373.

[10] Villabianca, *Della Sicilia nobile* (Palermo: Stamperia SS. Apostoli, 1759), III, 186.

nify him for the loss of his possessions in Sicily. He had lost their income when he was obliged to flee from Palermo because the Marchese de los Balbases, the Spanish viceroy,was about to issue a capital proclamation against him for involvement in pro-Imperial conspiracies.

"I exiled myself voluntarily from my fatherland," writes Astorga, where the necessity of adhering, at least in appearance, to the usurped sovereignty of Your Majesty's enemies and of your most august house, caused me such remorse that I decided to free myself of it even at the price of losing everything. That which I resolved with so much zeal, I faithfully carried out on 21 August 1707; when under the pretext of revisiting certain possessions of mine, I left Palermo, and Sicily, abandoning my three fiefs of Ogliastro, Mortilletto, and Milaina, with many other possessions which belonged to me by ancient inheritance of my house; which were worth not less than three thousand dobles of income every year. No sooner had I set foot in a place safe from the violence of the Ministers of that government, than I began to cultivate by letter various affairs intending to promote the acclamation of Your Imperial Majesty's name in that Realm, and whether it was the less cautious behavior of my correspondents, or my own ill fortune, the whole thing was discovered by the vigilance of the Marchese de los Balbases, who presided over that government as Viceroy; so that there followed the publication of a capital decree against my person, confiscation of my goods, destitution of my honors, together with everything which is customarily done against those convicted of the crime of lèse-majesté. In such circumstances I remained for some time in Italy, hoping, by rendering my correspondence more cautious, to be able to bring my desired undertaking to the conclusion of reducing Sicily to the obedience of Your Imperial Majesty. But having experienced that fortune was always contrary to my desire, little by little I was reduced to such poverty by the lack of assistance from my family, that where before I did not wish to bring myself to Your Majesty's feet in Barcelona without having rendered you the signal service which I proposed; afterward I could not bring myself there for simple lack of funds to make the trip. Finally I came in the manner known to Your Majesty; and I left within a few months because of Your Majesty's departure for the army. From then on I have always remained in Vienna; where after the death of the Most Noble Emperor Joseph of glorious memory I have awaited from the arrival of Your Imperial Majesty the only relief for my poverty [...].[11]

[11]Sommer-Mathis, n. 50 of "Nuevos documentos," 59.

We have no certain information before *Dafni,* and we cannot judge the length of the Roman parenthesis. (It could not have been short, if Emanuello had time to form a friendship with Biancardi and to set to music the texts of many cantatas and several serenatas of his: while cantatas could be performed frequently, serenatas were linked to celebrations separated in time.) If we take Biancardi's account as absolute truth (and in this matter he would have had no reason to change the facts), the musician and poet departed from Rome together before the Duke of Uzeda left the city (1709), since the *Compendio* states clearly that Biancardi had resigned from the service of his protector. In 1707 Komarek printed in Rome a collection of *Sonetti in lode dell'Em.mo e Rev.mo principe il sig. Card. Pietro Ottoboni, vice-cancelliere della S. R. Chiesa,* which informs us that Sebastiano was linked to the personage who emerges from every corner of our story.

It is possible that Astorga also benefited from the cardinal's patronage. Volkmann suggested that two large cantatas by Emanuello, accompanied by a large number of instruments comprising an orchestra, were intended for the musical entertainments organized by Ottoboni. On the manuscripts the scholar read "January 1708," later interpreted as "Genoa 1708." This was the source of the seemingly plausible reference to Astorga's presence in Rome that year. Vangelisti printed in Florence other *Rime* of Biancardi, dedicated to Cosimo III, in 1708. (Hoewever, we would have to know the month of publication to date this volume exactly, since the Florentine calendar deceptively began the year *ab Incarnatione,* March 25, and not *a Nativitate,* December 25). If this does not coincide with the chronology proposed in the *Compendio,* at least it makes the unrolling of events was less congested.

The Genoese performance of *Dafni* remains a sure point of reference. Here everything coincides with Biancardi's account and there is no reason to doubt it, since the episodes he confesses are hardly edifying. The contents of the Viennese petition resolve in a positive sense the doubts about Astorga's presence in Barcelona, to which Volkmann dedicated an entire chapter of his essay.[12]

But what was so interesting in Barcelona in 1709? If you remember "the lovely womb of the Royal Bride" and the barren prophecies of fecundity expressed in the prologues of the *Inganni felici,* an historical atlas will show that Spain was divided in two in those years by the question of the Spanish Succession. Philip V was more or less firmly installed in Madrid, while Barcelona harbored the Austrian archduke

---

[12] Volkmann, *Astorga,* I, Chapter IV, 62-78.

who had proclaimed himself king as Charles III. Half a century later, when a son of Philip V ascended the throne of Spain, his adoption of the name Charles III—a disdainful passage of the sponge over a decade of bloody struggles—would occasion many joys to collectors of porcelain but at least as much confusion to indifferent students of history.

Unlike his antagonist, who was bored by an *Adagio* of Corelli, Charles of Habsburg loved music and had not wished the war to deprive him of a pleasure for which a long family tradition made him both qualified and dedicated. After Naples had been taken from the Spaniards without striking a blow, the king had been able to recruit in that musical goldmine whatever he lacked to complete the personnel of a full "Cappella." Prota Giurleo[13] noted that it was the Austrian viceroy, Count Daun (the commander of the well-trained army that chased out the "other" Spaniards), who sent to his ruler the young Giuseppe Porsile (who had recently become known through sacred music and the opera *Il ritorno di Ulisse alla patria)*. He was accompanied by other "Neapolitan Musicians" enticed by good earnings and by the possibility of gaining the favor of the man they now considered their king.

In addition to Porsile, the little group of musicians imported from Naples included a tenor, a bass, and four players of archlute, violin, violoncello, and contrabass; a small number for performing the operatic repertory. However, operas could be imported from Italy already packaged and tested, as with *Dafni*.

At the end of May, when the series of performances in Genoa was finished, the company embarked for Barcelona, where the king was pleased to hear *Dafni* several times. The titlepage of the manuscript score of the first act of the opera[14] informs us that it was a "Pastoral drama with music performed in Barcelona before their Catholic Majesties. The Year 1709 on the [...] of June" and specifies: "Music by the Baron d'Astorga." An *Avviso* from Naples announced on August 13: "Barcelona, 23 July. For the amusement of these Majesties there was repeatedly performed the Pastorale, that was recently done in Genoa titled *La Dafne* [sic], whose sets and music turned out very pleasingly."[15] Distance had transformed the Sicilian shepherd into a nymph.

The monarch's pleasure must have been genuine, since the venturesome baron could later extract a notable pension from him.

---

[13] Ulisse Prota Giurleo, "Giuseppe Porsile e la Real Cappella di Barcellona," *Gazzetta Musicale di Napoli* II, 10, October 1956, 160.
[14] Volkmann, *Astorga*, I, 62-63.
[15] Ibid.

... in Venice, where virtù finds every esteem and favor

Although the Scarlattis came from an area of Franco-Hispanic senti-
ment, after the Neapolitan celebrations in honor of Philip V the Viceroy
Ascalona had not secured for Domenico the advantages that his father
had hoped for. Any possible ill-will on Alessandro's part must have
been relative given his relationship with Ottoboni, who was increasingly interested in absorbing the office of "Protector of France" that
Cardinal Medici was about to renounce along with his cardinalate. Only
later, when he felt betrayed by Ottoboni, did Scarlatti senior pose as a
victim of Spanish tyranny, which would again carry him to the pinnacle
of Neapolitan musical life.

Alessandro's Roman sojourn was the choice that corresponded
most closely to his character, secretly but transparently insecure. In
Rome he could maneuver cleverly; his first relations with Cardinal
Grimani went back to these uncertain years. (We have already seen
Grimani as an agitator of great force; we now discover him as a serious
librettist belonging to a Venetian family that owned a famous theater.)
Alessandro could mark time while awaiting the sensational coup of which
he already dreamed. Embittered by the stagnation of the Roman scene,
disappointed in the hope of permanent attachment to Ferdinando de'
Medici, Scarlatti senior observed Gasparini's move to Venice with an
interested eye. Perhaps sending Domenico to Gasparini was a preliminary attempt to explore territory that was open for conquest. While the
armies of the belligerents were employed in more saguinary deeds,
Alessandro dreamed of the bloodless conquest of an important musical
fortress: Venice, which had been the matrix for so much of the seventeenth-century operatic repertory and continued to exercise all the fascination as a city teeming with musical and theatrical activities.

As I have said, Domenico set out for Venice as a "pilgrimage."
Mario Fabbri[16] has emphasized the religiosity of this term, but if I think
of Ferdinando de' Medici, the recipient of the letter in which it is employed, I can only smile.

I have called Alessandro's analysis of his son prophetic: "an
Eagle, whose wings are grown" implies a judgment of excellence; and
the fact that Scarlatti senior speaks of "grown" and not "barely sprouted"
indicates that he already considered Domenico a mature musician, not
merely a promising apprentice. Evidently, I repeat, he must have known

---

16 Fabbri, *Scarlatti,* 58.

something quite different from the modest pages of vocal music in the surviving manuscripts securely datable to those years. Less convincing, however, is his standing aside in order not "to impede the eagle's flight." In fact, for twelve years more Alessandro would reserve the right/duty to direct that flight through his oppressive and anachronistic exercise of the *patria potestas*.

This would square with the idea of employing Domenico as a scout, of taking advantage of the results obtained by a musician in whom Alessandro placed great trust, before venturing upon the desired conquest himself.

A large subtext hovers over the entire letter: was it so necessary for Domenico to go "almost as a wanderer" as far as Venice? Might not "opportunities [...] to become known" be offered to him in Florence? Domenico's ability was "greatly advanced" in the three years that had passed since Ferdinando had heard him for the first time; let the Grand Prince deign to put him to the test again. In the case of a positive result, Ferdinando could "raise up" the timid pilgrim who had come to cast himself at his feet by giving him adequately remunerated employment.

I find a false note, however, in all of this. Papa Scarlatti could not be unaware that the Grand Prince expected something more than music from Petrillo and Cecchino. At nearly three centuries' distance we know the depraved habits of the last Medici from the indiscretions of the musicians of equivocal qualifications engaged at court. According to the pamphlet already quoted concerning Ferdinando, he would be surpassed in homosexual excesses by his timid younger brother. When he was crowned Grand Duke on the death of Cosimo III, Gian Gastone de' Medici gave himself over to unbridled orgies involving numerous youths hired by a pimp-factotum, but these orgies also included musicians who were already famous or on the way to being so. This entertaining pamphlet explains the Florentine sojourn of *Il Buranello* (Baldassare Galuppi), the future darling of Europe, which was prolonged after the end of his theatrical undertakings:

> Some time ago there came from Venice along with the singer [Antonia] Pellizzari, who came to perform in the theater of Via della Pergola, a very handsome harpsichord player who played in that theater, called Buranello because he was from Burano, an island near Venice; who was said to have a pitiless animal, and for that reason it fitted, as they say, very well in the shop, and was in truth a monstrous thing. The Grand Duke made him stay on for several months after the operas were ended and gave him an endless quantity of money, and he repaid Antonio Cecchini, who

boarded him in his house, generously for the expenses which he submitted, and he recounted to some friends what went on with the Grand Duke and that his colt was always in action [...].[17]

In 1705 the Florentine orgies of Gian Gastone and of his "ruspanti" were still to come. (The term has nothing to do with poultry [*ruspanti*, free-range chickens]; *ruspi* were the coins, the *quattrini* which the Grand Duke distributed to his mercenary soldiers of love.)[18] Even so, neither Cecchino or the Bambagia gave Ferdinando's artistic *entourage* a tone in confirmity with the fulsome professions of austerity and religious piety in his correspondence with Alessandro.

Is it possible that unscrupulous ambition for his career so blunted the wits (or moral sense) of Scarlatti senior, that pious humbug, as to induce him to sacrifice his eaglet/lamb to his patron/wolf? Alessandro's human contradictions remain many. In any case, I note that to the Sicilians, customarily so sensitive in matters of honor, we owe a proverb that will shock many of my readers: "U Re nun fa cuorna!" ("The King does not make horns!").

However imprudent his enterprise was, in undertaking it Alessandro still maintained that he was turning to a patron who was sensitive to the needs of others. Bit by bit, his correspondent the Grand Prince would serve to show how bitterly different the reality was.

On this occasion, Ferdinando displayed his concern by recommending Domenico to a Venetian nobleman of his acquaintance, writing immediately to the father to bear witness to the admiration aroused in him by the young prodigy: "Your son Domenico has in truth such a capital of talent and wit, as to be able to procure his fortune anywhere, but especially in Venice, where *virtù* finds every esteem and favor."

---

17 Ombrosi (?), *Storia,* c. 172. The manuscript transmits the same excerpt, with slight variations, on c. 309 of the old numbering (157 of the new); the most interesting of the variants is the one which begins the story with "Around 1727," instead of "Some time ago," permitting a more precise dating of the episode. Not less revealing is the transformation of the "handsome harpsichord player" into "a most handsome young man who played the harpsichord;" it should be said, however, that the text I have preferred appears competently corrected of errors, since the well-known name is restored, as opposed to "Moranello since he was from Morano an island near Venice." There is no choice between the obscene details: the metaphor of the merciless animal is balanced by the variant "he is said to have been so astonishingly priapic that it was a marvelous thing."

18 The manuscript contains on cc. 182-187a a *List of provisioned employees of the chamber of the R. H. of the Most Serene G. D. Gio. Gastone vulgarly called Ruspanti;* I leave its analysis to experts in economic geography, since the meticolosity of the writer foreshadows Da Ponte's Leporello in cataloguing all that fresh meat which had rushed to Florence from every part of Italy ...

An extraordinary *lapsus* follows: "It was he [Domenico], *in my passage for that city*, who saw me and brought me your amiable letter, which was rightly solicitous for your son's advantages; whence I, who also regard him with great benevolence, have accompanied him with my letter for the noble Sig. Alvise Morosini, and I will be greatly pleased if my good offices bear some fruit [...]."[19]

This could be a Freudian slip. If taken literally it would say that the meeting between Domenico and Ferdinando took place in Venice; that Ferdinando had returned to the goal of his pilgrimages, that sanctuary "where *virtù* finds every esteem and favor." Clearly, his desire for the journey was so strong that the Grand Prince was unaware that he was identifying himself with the young musician who was preparing for it. Fabbri proposed to interpret the phrase in question as "in his passage [from Florence], toward that city."[20] This seems confirmed by the clear dating of the letter ("The 8th of June 1705, from Florence") and finds further confirmation in the recommendation addressed to Morosini, which is again "from Florence" and bears the date of June 6:

> The Young Domenico Scarlatti, Son of Alessandro, famous Composer of Music, following the path of his virtuous Father in that Profession—arousing every great expectation for himself, not only because of the excellent guidance he has had from his Father, but also because of the great capacity of his own spirit—aspires to prove his talent and to find himself an adequate fortune in that City, for which he is setting out, and where ability [virtù] is accustomed always to find every best welcome and favor. Whence I, who desire for him both the one and the other, in the liveliest manner—also for the consolation of his Father, who, with the praiseworthy services that he has many times rendered me, has acquired more than ordinary gratitude and benevolence in my soul—I recommend him, with all affection, to the goodness of Your Lordship, since it appears to me that I could not find for him, under this heaven, either a more kindly, or a more efficacious influence than your Protection, [you] who are led by your noble instinct to favor, with the most helpful influences, persons of talent and of merit.[21]

On June 27 Morosini replied,[22] stating that he was most honored by the attention which Ferdinando had paid him and assuring the prince that he would assist Domenico as far as his own "weakness" per-

---

[19] Fabbri, *Scarlatti*, 59.
[20] Ibid., 122.
[21] Ibid., 60.
[22] Ibid., 611.

mitted, in order to deserve the "revered comands [sic]" of the Grand Prince. Conventional ceremoniousness and attitudes worthy of Pontius Pilate: deaf to the indirect request that Alessandro had addressed to him in the hope of seeing his son hired in Florence, Ferdinando behaved with the cynicism of certain contemporary politicians, real virtuosos of the useless but documented recommendation. With regard to Alessandro his conscience was clear: Domenico had "such a capital of talent and of spirit" that he did not need much help. Thus the Grand Prince could roll a fine stone over the episode and send to Alessandro—only a day after having expressed himself so favorably about his son's talent—a new letter commissioning another opera for Pratolino, without wasting another word on the musical genius who his father had hoped would be employed to direct it from *his* harpsichord.

The noble Morosini probably did what he could to introduce Domenico Scarlatti into one of those worldly gatherings immortalized by the Venetian painters of the eighteenth century, but I do not believe that much effort was necessary to admit him to a musical scene where the support of Gasparini or of Nicolino himself [23] could be worth more than that of a nobleman.

In any case, none of the support that he enjoyed helped Domenico to enter into the intense musical (and non-musical) life of Venice. His fairly prolonged stay in the lagoon city itself has left no important traces. This is surprising if we remember that we are dealing with a young man who, according to the judgment of a passionate partisan of Venice like Ferdinando de' Medici, could count on "the great capacity of his own spirit," or who indeed disposed of a great "capital of talent and spirit."

Spirit, spirit ... But *was* Domenico "spirited"? I believe that he was potentially so, but I fear that he did not always wish to display it. Freud, basing himself on the complex situation of the Jews in the Vienna of the Habsburg twilight, singled out the *Witz,* the witty phrase, as a safety valve for certain frustrations. Although I lack the technical ability to apply Freudian theories to Domenico, I can affirm that the absence of his oppressive father must have encouraged liberating episodes. Alessandro had written the Grand Prince that his son's ability was "much advanced" in the three years that had passed since their first visit, and this was certainly true; but I suppose that this time in Florence the twenty-year-old Domenico could be more naturally himself because he did not

---

23 Grimaldi, not Paris, as has been written more than once. The worst is that the errors of others have led me to make a mistake concerning the interpreters of a Roman performance of *Rosmene* (see *Scarlatti,* ERI, 83.)

have to put up with reproaches or criticisms from a father who was providentially far away.

"Detached by force" from Naples (after having been prematurely flung into an exposed situation there), sent away from Rome, welcomed but not kept on in Florence, the "wandering eagle" was slow to reach the success that had been foretold for him. While waiting, he must have been disturbed by the contrast that his new life-experiences revealed between his father's moral preaching and a daily reality of glaring deviations from the straight and narrow.

The figure of Francesco Gasparini, who was engaged from June 1701 by the deputies of the Ospedale della Pietà as "maestro di choro," acquires notable importance in the musical panorama of early eighteenth-century Venice.[24] His tasks were more extensive than modern terminology would suggest. The "chorus" included not only voices but also the ensemble of voices and instruments; in addition, the maestro had to instruct the girl boarders of the institution in singing, counterpoint, and keyboard instruments. This explains why Gasparini's salary (two hundred ducats a year) was four times that of a younger but quite promising "maestro di violino" named Antonio Vivaldi, hired at the Pietà together with Gasparini, but without the latter's unanimous favorable vote.[25]

The year following his installation, Gasparini entered the Venetian operatic season with a *Tiberio imperatore d'Oriente* at the Teatro Sant'Angelo. It was not a completely happy debut, since there were economic difficulties caused by the ugly mess that Giazotto summarizes in his *Vivaldi*. According to the documents he discovered, four "girl singers who came from Ferrara" sang in the opera, and after having worked for four evenings without receiving the pay agreed upon, they decided to return home but were stopped by four thugs hired by Gasparini and the impresario Santurini. As the hour of the performance approached, the singers resisted as much as they could. Nonetheless, they were carried to the theater by force and with great tumult. This enraged the impresario and composer, who ordered the bravos to reduce those devil-possessed furies to reason. To make a long story short, one of the girls ended up in the water and her body was never found. From the trial that

---

[24] Giancarlo Rostirolla, "Il Periodo veneziano di Francesco Gasparini (con particolare riguardo alla sua attività presso l'Ospedale della Pietà)," in *Francesco Gasparini (1661-1727), Atti del primo Convegno Internazionale,* ed. Fabrizio Della Seta and Franco Piperno (Florence: Olschki, 1981 [hereafter "Francesco Gasparini"]), 85-118, 89

[25] See documents 8, 11, 13, 17, 22 (the only unanimous vote for Vivaldi), 24, Rostirolla, "Francesco Gasparini."

followed it would seem that Gasparini was principally responsible for the violent outcome of the event, but the exalted protection that he enjoyed and the well-rehearsed witnesses so confused matters as to make it seem that the agents employed

> had invited the girls, who were lowborn and disobedient to their contract, to the evening's performance with good manners and courtesy, and that the girls themselves exchanged protest for rebellion; thus there was such an uproar in the neighborhood inhabited by respectable people that they could not take them from there to silence them with great loss to the theater S. Anzolo and to the noble gentlemen and ladies arriving in their gondolas to attend the performance [...].[26]

On the basis of this discovery and a suspicion of insufficient diligence at the Pietà, Giazotto formulates a rather negative judgment on Gasparini.[27] Overlooking his merits as an artist and teacher, he stresses his presumed acquiescence in the bad behavior of "Giovanna, one of his daughters." Giazotto was unaware that the singer in question (Bolognese by birth) was not the daughter of Francesco Gasparini, who in any case had left Venice a couple of years before the lively Giovanna gave the Inquisitors reason for inquiry. Although Giazotto is severe and even unjust, it seems to me that as a human being Gasparini did not correspond exactly to the good-natured man that the Acts of the International Congress that celebrated him in 1978 at Camajore describes.

This bloody episode must have ended Gasparini's connection with the Teatro Sant'Angelo. It would be wrong, however, to think that it harmed a theatrical career that, transferred to the glorious stage of the San Cassiano (the first public theater in the history of opera), would develop triumphantly. Gasparini produced twenty-three operas performed in barely eleven years,[28] in victorious competition with the other musicians active in Venetian theaters: Carlo Francesco Pollarolo and his son Antonio, Marcantonio Ziani, Carlo Pallavicino, Domenico Gabrielli, Giacomo Antonio Perti, Tommaso Albinoni, and Antonio Lotti.

Supported by Gasparini, Domenico Scarlatti must have had the best opportunities to consolidate his own experiences in composing church music as well as in theatrical practice. The female pupils of the Pietà did not limit themselves to making music in the circle of the Ospedale, but were sometimes employed, singly or in small groups, for outside engagements, not without various inconveniences.

---

26 Remo Giazotto, *Antonio Vivaldi* (Turin: ERI, 1973 [hereafter Giazotto, *Vivaldi*]), 48.

27 Ibid., 94-95.

28 See the list in "Francesco Gasparini," 93-94.

Some decades after Gasparini's departure, the Ospedali still enjoyed an exceptional musical reputation, of which we find traces both in
the amusing description of the Président de Brosses, quoted *in extenso*
by Kirkpatrick,[29] and in the passage in the *Confessions* in which Jean-
Jacques declares his own preferences as a listener:

> A music in my opinion much superior to that of the opera the-
> aters, and which has no equal in Italy, nor in the rest of the world, is
> that of the *scuole*. The *scuole* are charitable institutions founded to
> educate young women without means, to whom the Republic then
> assigns a dowry, for marriage or the cloister. Among the talents
> which are cultivated in the girls, music occupies the first place.
> Every Sunday, in the churches of each of these four *scuole,* there
> are heard at vespers motets for full choir and full orchestra, com-
> posed and directed by the greatest Italian masters, performed be-
> hind the grills of the tribune exclusively by girls, the oldest of whom
> is not twenty. I cannot imagine that anything could be as volup-
> tuous and moving as this music: the riches of the art, the exquisite
> taste of the singing, the beauty of the voices, the precision of the
> performance. In these delicious concerts everything combines to
> produce an impression certainly not in conformity with good be-
> havior, but before which the heart of a man is defenseless. Carrio
> and I never missed vespers at the *Mendicanti,* and we were not the
> only ones. The church overflowed with devotees: even the singers
> of the opera came in order to form themselves in real vocal taste,
> basing themselves on these supreme models."[30]

Rousseau then describes the disillusionment that followed the
verification of the physical appearance of the angels to whom these voices
belonged: Sofia was horrible, Cattina cross-eyed, Bettina was disfigured by smallpox! None of the most admired singers was free from
notable physical defects; the only two or three passable ones sang in the
chorus. Despite this visual disappointment, the ear continued to be delighted, and

> the voices succeeded in masking so well the faces of the women to
> whom they belonged, that I persisted in finding them beautiful while
> they were singing, without trusting what my eyes had told me [...].[31]

In the case cited by Rousseau the musicians were only students
in an Ospedale. Casanova's stories extend to nuns the most incredible
licentiousness, encouraged by the constant maskings that so lengthened

---

[29] Kirkpatrick, *Scarlatti,* 24.

[30] Jean-Jacques Rousseau, *Les Confessions* (Paris: Garnier, 1947), II, 122-123.

[31] Ibid., 124.

the famous Carnival. The reality of Venice far exceeded all the occasions of scandal foreseen by papa Scarlatti in his sermons. If elsewhere scandal was characteristically connected with the life of the theater, in Venice the libertinage invaded even ospedali and convents, transforming the very churches into places of unedifying and sometimes sacrilegious encounters, like the episode Giazotto drew from the archives:

> Yesterday evening an official of the Signor Catholic Ambassador was seen to enter the church of Giovanni in Olio in the company of the musician Matteuccio of Naples and those who said that the musician was supposed to sing were not believed and they were seen in a truly scandalous act of love right in front of the high altar [...].[32]

Matteuccio: Matteo Sassano, the capricious musician competed for by kings (Charles II) and emperors (Leopold I and his sons), the arch-interpreter of Alessandro Scarlatti's operas and serenades. He was destined to finish his days gloriously in Naples ("virgin," his death-certificate specifies!) with the title of marquis and great riches, which he astutely promised and then wickedly snatched away from a foolish testament-hunter.[33]

In this Venice swarming with music and other unedifying activities, Domenico Scarlatti would have passed like a ghost[34] if he had not encountered two foreign musicians visiting the city—but we will speak of that later. If Domenico had come to Venice as a scout for his father, he must have sent Alessandro fairly encouraging signals the year after his arrival. Short of money as a result of Roman asceticism and now about to lose the employment that Ferdinando de' Medici had so far renewed for him, Scarlatti senior accepted well in advance[35] an extremely important engagement: that of composing two new operas for the Carnival season of 1707 for the theater belonging to the Grimani and dedicated to San Giovanni Cristosotomo: *Il Mitridate Eupatore* and *Il Trionfo della libertà*. We have already seen Alessandro's about-face in regard to the Franco-Hispanics; it is possible that this was the work of Cardinal Grimani. The relationship that had ripened in Rome between him and

---

32 Giazotto, *Vivaldi, 21*.

33 Ulisse Prota Giurleo, "Matteo Sassano detto 'Matteuccio' (Documenti napoletani)," *Rivista Italiana di Musicologia* I (1966), 97-119, 97.

34 Marc Pincherle, *Vivaldi* (Paris: Plon, n. d. [1955]), 16, lists him among the teachers active in the four "hospices" or "conservatories," but does not specify the source of his information.

35 By 3 July 1706 he could already foresee "being bound for Venice, around next September" (letter to Ferdinando de' Medici, Fabbri, "Scarlatti," 79).

Scarlatti explains the promptness with which the cardinal, when he became Austrian viceroy in Naples, reinstated Alessandro as *maestro* of the Cappella Reale. To find our hero engaged in the Venetian theater of which Grimani was co-proprietor is to catch the uncertain and circumspect man whom I have attempted to describe in the act: to surprise him just at the moment when a mask falls from his face.

This important invasion was aimed at unblocking an absurd situation. Considering the enormous spread of Scarlatti's operatic repertory in Italy it is surprising—and significant—that the public theaters of Venice remained excluded from that diffusion. It was not a question of chance: the composers active in the Venetian theaters had succeeded in erecting a blockade against their feared rival. Now something had changed: Gasparini and Grimani had made possible to import the celebrated musician in person, and the paying public could satisfy its curiosity by hearing two new operas by the composer of whom all Europe was talking. I say the paying public, because prince Gasparo Altieri had privately broken the blockade in 1690, when he presented in his garden —and therefore for a very socially limited public—Alessandro's export opera *par excellence: Gli equivoci nel sembiante,* rebaptized for the occasion as *Gl'amori fortunati negl'equivoci.*

In spite of the guarantees that he had received, Alessandro Scarlatti must soon have realized that he had got himself into serious trouble by this sortie, which now endangered his reputation. Venice must have shown itself immediately hostile to the composer who, even if people no longer spoke of "the borders of Christianity" (his sojourn in Rome had served for something), remained a southerner come to colonize the shores of Adria. The librettist of the two operas was Giacomo Frigimelica Roberti, a severe poet quite distant from the charms of Arcadia. Giazotto discovered that the authorization of the performances bears the date 30 November 1706, but that *Il Mitridate Eupatore* was performed at the end of Carnival in 1707. Someone had spread the word that the Inquisitor General had found in the text things that did not conform to "what belongs to the Catholic religion." These obstacles seem to have been removed by the intervention of the Austrian ambassador Ercolani, but this could only arouse new hostility from the francophiles.

Facing a situation so far from the triumph he had taken for granted, it is understandable that Alessandro Scarlatti became upset and began to commit tactical erors from which his enemies were quick to profit. The documents cited by Giazotto[36] inform us that on the eve-

---

36 Giazotto, *Vivaldi,* 99.

nings of the performance of *Mitridate* or the *Trionfo della libertà* Venice seemed crazed, but such animation was not necessarily positive. On hearing, the two operas were revealed as very knowingly conceived, perhaps too much so. Alessandro ignored the lessons of his long relationship with Ferdinando de' Medici,who was about to return to Perti, after having repeatedly but unsuccessfully asked Alessandro to write "rather easy and noble Music." Instead, Scarlatti had wished to impress the Venetians by operas imbued with all his knowledge of composition. To the two operas he added to this the oratorio *Il Primo omicidio,* planned on similarly severe lines and performed during Lent. Having failed in his artistic strategy, Alessandro had aggravated the situation by allowing himself to be drawn onto the terrain of vulgar gossip by rivals more shrewd than he. Pistocchi's letter to Perti showed us what was concealed behind the Florentine success, but in that case the open protection of the Grand Prince had obliged the jealous Pistocchi to stifle his rage and to keep a tally of the honors and rewards reserved for his rival. Here the situation was very different. If there was a Scarlattian party, as there must have been, its efforts were not enough to outweigh those of the opposite camp.

Not to mince words, it was a fiasco: all the more serious because Alessandro had wagered a great deal—almost everything—on his Venetian card. The more favorable (or less hostile) welcome was reserved for the *Trionfo della libertà,* whose music has not survived. We do know *Il Mitridate Eupatore,* and the profundity and density of its musical fabric show that Alessandro carried to its final consequences the encounter of his own operatic utopia with the environment that, according to him, was the most qualified to welcome his message.

Against Scarlatti, the long satire of Bartolomeo Dotti, that viper disguised as a poet, is a chilling document of Alessandro's human as well as artistic failure. I cannot omit it, since it remains an eloquent documentation of the damage that his own *gaucherie* did to Alessandro Scarlatti:

> Let cancer and rabies attack whoever blasphemes Scarlatti and let him be shut up in a cage where they put the insane.//How can they not say everything good of so learned a man, whose style has been made incorruptible by the drops of Hippocrene?//In esteeming him I agree with the whole world, which declared him a second Orpheus merely on seeing him.//I would be called, and not wrongly, ignorant and malicious if I directed one twisted thought against so virtuous a man.//Be patient, Gasparini, and you, Lotti, and you, Coletti: the quintessence of the most perfect masters has arrived here.//And if you don't believe me, believe him: if you listen to what he says you will hear that his skill is indeed excessive.//In

hearing the whole opera that he has made of Eupator every stone and every beast seems moved and goes off to him.//Evil spirits cannot deny that it is sweet music since it introduces a sweet sleep into the eyes of those who lack it.//My mind, always oppressed by harsh and severe torments, to which rest is hardly ever granted by its thoughts,// Can say better than others the truth about the sweetness of that drama because having heard it, it proclaims: 'I could not keep from sleeping.'//It is ten proof stronger than Tonino's best [wine], to which I know that that of San Fantino is lower by three./ /And thus it occurs that the sleep-inducing effect of the 'sweet melody' operates so that at the end of the opera no one knows what they have heard.//And as happens to the inhabitants of the lands bordering on the Nile, they have lost their hearing from the noise of the cataracts.//It also happens to the public (many people gathered here), that they hear nothing, even if they keep their ears attentive.//

Informed of such things, I acknowledge the merit of him who has now reached the pinnacle of glory by arduous roads.//It only displeases me, that adorned and filled with such an air of virtue, with his natural haughtiness he should despise most those who least merit it.//It is true that he is prudent also in this, if I observe well, that he foresees his imminent cruel and arrogant destiny.//As one who clears away some high plant because it could harm the flowers, thus he turns his ass, his head to anyone who could overshadow him.//Scarlatto [a rough cloak] shelters others from rain and storm; this one prepares wind and hail for the heads of others.//Hail worse than the most frozen snow [slander], which falls on the honor of accredited persons to wound them. //Scarlatto covers the defects of others' clothes, with envy he uncovers only the errors of a learned man.//I wish Scarlatto as rich a mantle as I could, but I would not wish on that account to wear one like that.

This would be worse than the shoddiest wool and in need would not be my shelter, but my hindrance.//Whence I would often be persuaded, and not in jest, either to sell it for nothing or rip it up and put it in the fire.//On the contrary, he is so much the slave of the unruly mob that a buffoon, more than an honest man, seems to be worth more with him.//Night and day his thoughts are turned to San Fantino because, between us, he has superfine taste.//He protects, from what I hear, a wretched young woman, whom he values, horrid case, much more than Diamantina.//But what I call a low and unworthy deed is perhaps one capable of bearing greater praise (to the one who stains himself with such an action)?//Since if Phoebus is accustomed to lighten rough glebes, impure objects, he wishes to render all the other lights as dark as he can.//He behaves in the same manner, the one who peerless among us in composing, puts in the shade with his disdainful judgments those who write with judgment.//

On the contrary, by approving the ignorant he makes them famous, as long as they approve him, and in the number of the many he himself is found.//In order to know who is more worthy than he of being honored, it is he himself who points it out, without wishing, with his pitiless and biting speech.//And without being aware of it he makes himself the author of his own harm just when, perfidious one, he seeks to damage the reputation of others.//Already one hears: 'So-and so is unlearned in the opinion of Scarlatti,' soon they hold him for the most learned and follow him like madmen.// And turning against the evil detractor of others' fame they make him a just example as of one who defames others. Because, if he does not know it, this is a noble country that has no partiality and is courteous to knowledge alone.[37]

Dotti's dishonesty is obvious: it is sufficient to remember the close of his satire, speaking of "courtesy to knowledge." Could Alessandro be butchered as an incompetent? Evidently a weapon had been put in the poet's hand by someone who had been wounded by the undiplomatic guest's imprudent judgments and who turned on him with every kind of accusation. The music of *Mitridate* was soporific; Scarlatti's praise was poured out only on those who could not put him in the shade. In addition there is the protection of the "miserable young woman" who sings in San Fantino: according to Dotti, Scarlatti must have lost his head over the singer. If the imprudent comparison with Diamante Scarbelli, called the Diamantina, does not arise merely from the necessity of finding a rhyme, Scarlatti had let himself be dragged onto particularly treacherous terrain by showing that he preferred an obscure singer employed in a minor theater (San Fantino) to the acclaimed diva who would later sue the Grimani for their disloyal competition with other theaters by lowering the price of admission.[38]

It is obvious that the humidity of the lagoon city encouraged the accumulation of rust: so much the worse for those who exposed a metal that was apparently as solid as iron to the attacks of the atmosphere, without taking due precautions!

Dotti was a good-for-nothing, a vicious slanderer: writing perfidious satires was as necessary to him as breathing. The Venetians fol-

---

[37] Text taken from Andrea Della Corte, *Satire e grotteschi di musiche e di musicisti d'ogni tempo* (Turin: UTET, 1946), 243.
[38] Giazotto, *Vivaldi,* 102.

lowed with justified trepidation the diffusion of the ever-new products of his slimy muse. They sighed with relief every time they learned that they could laugh behind someone else's back, since for the moment they had not been struck by his poisoned arrows. The blackguard knew that he was running real risks since he did not scruple to strike at powerful personages. He came to the end which he deserved and which he had boasted of in his verses, even if—immodestly comparing himself to Horace, Persius, and Juvenal—he hoped to get off as they had, by dying in his bed. In 1713, when an assassin's dagger shut him up forever, another good soul jotted down an epitaph which refers explicitly to his satire against Scarlatti:

> You have spoken evil of everyone, but you have done evil yourself. You spat on the arias of Scarlatti, you pilloried clergy and nuns, you libelled the secrets of families, and now you have paid with justice. Let thanks be rendered to you ...[39]

---

[39] Ibid., 100.

XII

Roseingrave, Handel, and the devil

The blow inflicted on Alessandro by his Venetian adventure must have had a somewhat positive effect on Domenico: perhaps in these very circumstances a healthy doubt about his father's infallibility began to insinuate itself into the young man's mind. Not that the quality of Alessandro's music was in question, but that there was a suspicion that the path to follow was not the one advocated by Alessandro; that his strategy was, at least in certain cases, counterproductive.

The psychological repression that Domenico had undergone continued, however, to have its effect. Lacking the energy necessary for a radical change of attitude, Domenico continued to be the obedient son he had been up until that moment. He was, perhaps, a little tired of playing the part while cultivating the artistic autonomy that sought an outlet in the free exercise of improvisation. It is more than certain that Alessandro insisted that he not abandon the customary patterns (and if not in words, then by his example, in the best repressive Sicilian tradition). His son's psychologically subordinate condition rendered everything easier, making any unorthodox initiative almost impossible for Domenico.

Within the general vagueness of the younger Scarlatti's biography, the years of his sojourn in Venice remain among the most mysterious. Having disproven the hypothesis that would have left Domenico marooned in the lagoon city for many years, I assume that he left it on more than one occasion. I am also certain that he returned to Venice at least once in years that earlier biographers tell us were spent without moving from Rome. From an examination of the new data at our disposal there emerges a much more mobile Domenico.

I would like to deny categorically that the Venetian encounter between Domenico and Roseingrave took place at the beginning of 1709. The information recoverable from the inexhaustible Burney[1] deserves

---

[1] Burney, *General,* II, 702-703.

the credit denied to it by Kirkpatrick,[2] who wished to make the chronology fit with Domenico's arrival in Rome (Lent 1709), a date he mistakenly supposed to be definitive.

Burney collected his description directly from Roseingrave, an Irish musician destined to become the principal herald of "the English Cult of Domenico Scarlatti."[3]

Roseingrave was sent to Italy by the Dean and Chapter of St. Patrick's cathedral in Dublin with a scholarship of ten guineas

> to improve himself in the art of music [...] that hereafter he may be useful and serviceable to the said Cathedral [...].[4]

Thus say the acts of the Chapter in a document that bears the date 14 December 1709 and removes any possibility of a previous encounter between the two musicians. But let us see what Burney has to tell us:

> Being arrived at Venice on his way to Rome, as he himself told me, he was invited, as a stranger and a virtuoso, to an academia [sic] at the house of a nobleman, where, among others, he was requested to sit down at the harpsichord and favour the company with a toccata, as a specimen *della sua virtù*. And, says he, 'finding myself rather better in courage and finger than usual, I exerted myself, my dear friend, and fancied, by the applause I received, that my performance had made some impression on the company.' After a cantata had been sung by a scholar of Fr. Gasparini, who was there to accompany her, a grave young man dressed in black and in a black wig, who had stood in one corner of the room, very quiet and attentive while Roseingrave played, being asked to sit down to the harpsichord, when he began to play Rosy said, he thought ten hundred d—ls had been at the instrument; he never had heard such passages of execution and effect before. The performance so far surpassed his own, and every degree of perfection to which he thought it possible he should ever arrive, that, if he had been in sight of any instrument with which to have done the deed, he should have cut off his own fingers. Upon enquiring the name of this extraordinary performer, he was told that it was Domenico Scarlatti, son of the celebrated Cavalier Alessandro Scarlatti.

---

[2] Kirkpatrick, *Scarlatti,* 30, n. 27.

[3] Other writers have already mentioned the popularity enjoyed by D.S. in eighteenth-century England, employing this phrase taken from the title of an interesting article: Richard Newton, "The English Cult of Domenico Scarlatti," *Music & Letters* XX (1939), 138-156.

[4] *New Grove* 1, v. 16, 195.

Roseingrave declared that he did not touch an instrument himself
for a month; after this rencontre, however, he became very intimate
with the young Scarlatti, followed him to Rome and Naples, and
hardly ever quitted him while he remained in Italy; which was not
until after the peace of Utrecht [...].[5]

Roseingrave's account finally presents us with Domenico in flesh
and blood. However, the figure in black is different indeed from our
image of the young man whom a true connoisseur had already defined
as endowed with "much capability of his own spirit," all the more so in
the context of the Venice. I recall a fine simile of Wilfred Mellers, who
compared François Couperin to one of those isolated figures in certain
pictures of Watteau who stand out from the background of a varicolored
crowd thanks to the dark costume they wear. The painter has employed
this dark spot to obtain a counterpoint of colors, but Mellers assigns a
psychological value to the choice, affirming that the solitary presence is
not intent on arguing the vanity of the celebration, the emptiness of
worldly attitudes, the hypocrisy concealed under the urbanity, but only
wishes to remind us that it is possible to feel solitude even when one is
in pleasant company.[6]

The young man of severe aspect is dressed and bewigged in a
manner to accentuate, by means of all that black, the contrast with the
diabolic-sounding dance that his hands unchain from the harpsichord.
Ten thousand d—ls (British respectability forbade Burney to write out
the word "devils"): a goodly number, if we consider the limited sound of
the harpsichord. The hyperbole tells us that "the ingenious jesting with
art"—thus Domenico will define it in the preface to his *Essercizi*—had
already achieved, in the early Scarlatti, those exciting results that would
give a characteristic weight to the virtuosity activated in the sonatas.

Be that as it may: Domenico wore black and his wig was not
powdered. Was he already the "abbade" Scarlatti of whom on two occasions the chroniclers of Lisbon transmit a hazy image? Casanova shows
us that a Venetian abate could practice the art of arousing the devil in
many ways other than playing the harpsichord, and in Venice more than
elsewhere the "monk" of the proverb ("the habit does not make the
monk") was not bound by his habit. Above all it was easy to turn certain
situations upside down. If a masquerade allowed a nun to violate her
claustration and her vows in order to go off to an amorous rendezvous,

5 Burney, *General*, II, 703-704.

6 Wilfred Mellers, *François Couperin and the French Classical Tradition* (London:
Dobson, n. d. [1950]), 47.

other disguises were also possible, such as the one permitting a spirituso twenty-five-year-old to pretend austerity only to increase the amazement aroused by the revelation of his secret resources.

But I am unable to believe that Domenico was capable of such detached undertakings. I maintain that in that period he still felt strongly the contradiction between Christian morality and the necessity of adapting himself to the general trend of life. This especially concerns the man: in music, his adaptation to the current patterns threatened to overcome his talent. Many years were to pass before Domenico freed himself from the compulsion of copying a schoolroom formula and occasionally losing sight of "profound Understanding" (again the future preface of the *Essercizi)* in order to give more stability to free manifestations of originality, which for the time were confined to his liberating moments of improvisation.

If my hypothesis is correct, dark clothing and severe aspect served him as armor more than disguise: they form the cocoon allowing the chrysalis to await patiently the right conditions suitable for a metamorphosis that is still far off.

Another extremely important encounter is supposed to have taken place in Venice—but before the one we have just narrated, as we are now able to establish incontrovertibly. This time, scenario and characters match our expectations. It is Carnival, and the black of the dominos removes any exceptional character from Domenico's attire, assuming that the young man had already adopted the severe and almost funereal outfit described by Roseingrave. Handel is masked—yes, George Frideric Handel, enticed to Italy by Ferdinando de' Medici, who had succeeded in breaching the Saxon's prejudices against *welsche Kunst.* Handel sat down at the harpsichord to astonish bystanders who were already accustomed to the performances of Domenico Scarlatti. The latter was present at the improvised concert (and thus was not unwilling to mix with a crowd of masked merrymakers) and diagnosed, without a moment of hesitation, that behind that disguise there must lurk "the famous Saxon, or the devil himself."[7]

This time, not a thousand devils but the Devil in person. We know however that Beelzebub was too busy in Venice to allow himself an innocent "break" at the harpsichord. There remained the "famous Saxon," whom Domenico must have encountered previously elsewhere, if he was capable of recognizing *ex ungue leonem.*

[7] John Mainwaring, *Memoirs of the Life of the Late George Frederic Handel* (London, 1760), 51. [hereafter Mainwaring, *Memoirs*]

After observing that the anecdote anticipates an entire series of similar legends concerning Paganini, Liszt, and other virtuosi suspected of diabolic pacts, Kirkpatrick places the Venetian encounter in the winter of 1707-1708, an opinion shared by both Emilia Zanetti and Reinhard Strohm. In fact, the fame of the legendary Saxon could have preceded his arrival in Venice. On 14 January 1707, in Rome, Valesio had noted in his diary:

> There has arrived in this city a Saxon, an excellent harpsichord-player and composer of music, who today displayed his skill at organ-playing in the church of S. Giovanni to the amazement of all.[8]

It is quite unlikely that Domenico left Venice at the beginning of 1707, in the decisive days of his father's difficult debut.The news of the astonishing abilities of the Saxon could have reached him directly from Rome or from Florence, which Handel had already visited twice. Since it was Ferdinando de' Medici who urged him to come to Italy, it is understandable that during his wanderings Handel did not fail to attend the autumn performances at Pratolino. His pilgrimages to Pratolino or to Florence were not limited to a visit to a patron or to restricted listening experiences but furnished the young man with his first opportunity for contacts with important musicians, to be deepened elsewhere. We have seen how patrons were linked to one another by personal relationships that allowed them to exchange news of emerging talents (and in some cases, I suppose, to communicate symptoms of decline). Emilia Zanetti[9] has supposed that Handel's first connection with the most accomplished circle in Rome reflects the protection of Francesco Maria de' Medici. Cosimo III's brother was a powerful Roman cardinal until the genealogical debacle of his family forced him lay aside the purple in the hope of giving the Medici their longed-for heir. His marriage was grotesquely unfruitful and therefore absolutely appropriate to the catastrophic atmosphere in which it took place.

The support that Handel enjoyed in Rome was soon evident. The organ performance already mentioned was not an isolated episode, and soon the Saxon was employed to compose cantatas on texts of Cardinal Pamphilj or even an oratorio on a libretto of Capeci, commissioned by Marchese Ruspoli, another emerging exponent of Roman patronage.

---

8 Valesio, *Diario,* III, 754-755: the doubt, scrupulously raised and happily settled by Ursula Kirkendale, "The Ruspoli Documents on Handel," *Journal of the American Musicological Society* XX (1967), 222-273,224, n. 12, that it could be another "Saxon" is typically "Barbarian" (see Chapter XV).

9 Emilia Zanetti, "Händel in Italia," *L'Approdo musicale* 12 (1960), 3-46, 7.

The discovery that Domenico Scarlatti did not remain in Venice for the entire period preceding his return to Rome—at least the return that we must consider definitive—allows me to suppose that Domenico could have recognized Handel because the famous Roman combat promoted by Ottoboni had already taken place. Mainwaring, the Saxon's first biographer, recounted it thus:

> When he came first into Italy, the masters in greatest esteem were Alessandro Scarlatti, Gasparini, and Lotti. The first of these he became acquainted with at Cardinal Ottoboni's. This Scarlatti, the elder of the two, was the author of the opera *Principessa fedele* which, of its kind, was considered a chef d'oeuvre, a magisterial work. His various cantatas are also greatly appreciated by connoisseurs of music. Here also he became known to Domenico Scarlatti, now living in Spain, and author of the celebrated lessons. As he was an exquisite player on the harpsichord, the Cardinal was resolved to bring him and Handel together for a trial of skill. The issue of the trial on the harpsichord hath been differently reported. It has been said that some gave the preference to Scarlatti. However, when they came to the Organ there was not the least pretence for doubting to which of them it belonged. Scarlatti himself declared the superiority of his antagonist, and owned ingenuously, that till he had heard him upon this instrument, he had no conception of its powers. So greatly was he struck with his peculiar method of playing, that he followed him all over Italy, and was never so happy as when he was with him.

> Handel used often to speak of this person with great satisfaction; and indeed there was reason for it; for besides his great talents as an artist, he had the sweetest temper, and the genteelest behaviour. On the other hand, it was mentioned but lately by the two Plas [the famous Hautbois] who came from Madrid, that, Scarlatti, as oft as he was admired for his great execution, would mention Handel, and cross himself in token of veneration.

> Though no two persons ever arrived at such perfection on their respective instruments, yet it is remarkable that there was a total difference in their manner. The characteristic excellence of Scarlatti seems to have consisted in a certain elegance and delicacy of expression. Handel had an uncommon brillance and command of finger: but what distinguished him from all other players who possessed these same qualities, was that amazing fulness, force, and energy, which he joined with them.

That Handel traveled throughout Italy was well known, but it is surprising to learn that he could be accompanied freely by Domenico

Scarlatti, who the evidence tells us was subject to the imperious demands of his father-puppeteer. Mainwaring's evidence is of great importance because it throws light not only on certain of Domenico's characteristics as a performer (we will return to the younger Scarlatti's "elegance and delicacy of expression"), but also on a lovable human figure in whom "great artistic talents" found an unusual completion in the "sweetest of characters" and the "most courteous manners that one could imagine." It is worth anticipating here a reference to a much later document: the letter (the only one of Domenico known to us) that the aged and ill musician wrote to the Duke of Alba. When we read it, we shall find in his epistolary style, sober in nature and thus far from the repertory of flattering and servile phrases of the period, the best confirmation of the human portrait that Handel's first biographer gives us. From the height of the pedestals on which their own excellence as "virtuosi" placed them, Handel and Scarlatti could recognize the profound affinity of their artistic conceptions. Although the impression that each aroused in the other was notable, given the differences that Mainwaring brings out, it could not translate itself into specific influences. Perhaps it was the very diversity of the artistic itineraries travelled by the two musicians in their maturity that left intact the esteem in which they continued to hold each other even so long after their exciting experiences together. It would be pleasant to believe in the wanderings that, according to Mainwaring, carried Handel and Domenico Scarlatti around Italy. Every trace of a correspondence that would have revealed illuminating details has disappeared, but we know that the nordic Handel limited himself to glorifying the artistic and human qualities of his distant friend, while Scarlatti— as a good southerner— instinctively made the sign of the Cross not only to testify to the supreme valor of his rival, but also perhaps against the possibility that behind the fair appearance of the "famous Saxon" there indeed lurked "the Devil in person"!

If taken literally, Mainwaring's evidence would help us to follow Domenico's movements on the basis of Handel's. Even giving it only relative credibility, it remains likely that Domenico did not remain fixed in Venice for so many years, as the greater part of his biographers would like to consider indisputable.

This idea of a permanent settlement first in Venice and then in Rome is denied by both of the English sources. From 1708 to the beginning of 1710 Mainwaring describes Domenico as following Handel, but that "he was never so happy as when he was in his company" suggests interruptions, even if temporary, of their companionship, which repeats the wanderings of the Lalli-Del Chiaro pair. Domenico must have enjoyed traveling in the company of a musician friend, since after Handel's departure he would permit Roseingrave to follow him "to Rome and to Naples" and not to separate himself "as long as he remained in Italy, until after the peace of Utrecht" in 1713.

But these carefree images draw us away from the human drama that was consuming Alessandro.

... *on the occasions of greatest need* ...

Before following Domenico Scarlatti to Rome it will be necessary to step backward in time to deal with his depressed father, who had taken refuge in Urbino until the wounds inflicted on his pride by his Venetian adventure should heal over. Maintaining his own disastrous habits, Alessandro delayed taking up his duties as coadjutor in Santa Maria Maggiore. As the guest of his son Pietro, he perhaps consoled himself by comparing his own unfortunate greatness with the calm mediocrity of his eldest son, whom the pope's kindness had allowed to settle down in Urbino as *maestro di cappella* of the cathedral. If the Rome of the long Lent had offered Alessandro opportunities for meditation, now the tranquil little Renaissance city must have been favorable to new and not very consoling examinations of conscience—but only if Scarlatti senior were capable of looking reality in the face.

Deaf to the unpropitious signals that he had received from Florence (but had not recognized, or wished to interpret), on 18 April 1707 Alessandro had the particularly unhappy idea of turning to Ferdinando de' Medici—the man whom he continued to consider the patron *par excellence.* If the correspondence of Mozart and Puchberg did not exist, Alessandro's letter would be the most dramatic evidence of a famous musician's state of need. Scarlatti took advantage of the approaching Easter celebrations to begin with profuse protestations of devotion and sighs invoking the Heavens to lavish every good thing on his benefactor. Then he came to the point, with a blunt request for help that only a cynic like the Grand Prince could pretend not to have understood:

> High, Royal and true Lord, I must make clear to you my present condition, which, rendering me free from present service and at my own free will but nonetheless exposed to uncertain human Providence, is insufficient to support the heavy weight of a numerous family which, however adorned with the mantle of virtue, is naked of every succor and pity, since the opportunities to exercise them in their own support are lacking everywhere, either by the fatal constitution of the times, or by my own misfortune (which almost al-

ways is born a twin of the other), or by the composition of my own
particular horoscope [*ascendente*].

For that reason I do not blush, indeed I glory and proclaim myself fortunate in this point and condition, that I throw myself at the
feet of Your Royal Highness, as of my tutelary God and the peren-
nial fountain from whom I have received so many times the precious waters of so many, highest, most clement graces.

I do not dare to ask other than as much as may serve your high
royal commands, and all that the Most High will inspire to such
royal clemency, for the employment of all my weak forces and those
of my children, greater service and glory of Your Royal Highness,
in whom I have such trust as I ought, founded on your high virtues
and most kindly expressions, with which you have ever deigned to
honor me, to return to your royal feet, on the occasions of greatest
need. This present [need] of mine is the greatest that has happened
to me up to this point in my life; perhaps because I hoped too much
in one who never ought to have failed me in a time of need; only
because perhaps he considered me bereft of any other human, let
alone sovereign support, or perhaps withdrawing his right hand, as
an experiment to see what other person there might be on earth
who could sustain more effectually a falling virtue.

I do not go further with this reflection, since the cause is hid
from me; and, while I might assert it, that duty which imposes ven-
eration and respect, which is owed to every greater person
[*maggiore*] imposes an eternal silence [...].[10]

So chilling an appeal would seem made to arouse pity in anyone
who did not have a heart of stone (or of artichoke: in the case of
Ferdinando, the reference to Proust's Charlus is particularly appropriate). If Alessandro suspected that another of his patrons had abandoned
him "in time of need" (perhaps enjoying the spectacle of the ex-protégé
in trouble without doing anything to help him), he had an even more
cruel reply from the Grand Prince whom he had invoked:

I am obliged to you as well for the news that you bring of your
present difficulties, and I pray for you the necessary comfort from
Heaven; not doubting that fortunes appropriate to your merit and to
my desire will not be lacking to your virtue, in the meantime I confirm to you all my special fondness, and I pray God that He fill you
with true consolations.[11]

10 Letter to Ferdinando de' Medici, 18 April 1707, Fabbri, *Scarlatti,* 85-86.
11 Letter of Ferdinando de' Medici, 23 April 1707, Fabbri, *Scarlatti,* 86.

Although Scarlatti could not have known it, turning certain importunate requests over to Divine Providence was an inveterate habit of
Ferdinando, even to the disadvantage of his own mother. When that
foolish woman had tried to induce him to steal some jewels from the
Medici treasury and send them to her to compensate for his father's
miserliness, her son wrote:

> I am saddened that I can do nothing with my august father; I too am
> in a situation so critical that I must make a virtue of necessity, and
> I can only offer my heart [...].[12]

With his customary *gaucherie,* the instinct, fatal and infallible,
that impelled him to importune the wrong person at the wrong moment,
Alessandro believed that he could resolve a painful situation by laying
his troubles at the feet of his correspondent. However, the Grand Prince
did not welcome the prospect of so heavy a burden, especially given the
decline of his enthusiasm for the composer whom in the past he had
seemed to prefer to any other.

Do I need to identify the one "who never ought to have failed
me in a time of need?"

The title of "present Maestro di Cappella of His Eminence the
Signor Cardinal Ottoboni," displayed on the libretti of the operas presented in Venice, was not mere boasting, even if the relationship could
not be defined as "present." The documents published by Hans Joachim
Marx[13] inform us that Alessandro was included among the "Ministers"
of the spendthrift cardinal in the period from April of 1705 to February
of the following year. I do not understand why Marx should consider
the fact that from March 1706 the name of Corelli replaces that of
Alessandro Scarlatti until 1713 (the death-date of the famous violinist)
to be "an evident error of the accountant." Ottoboni had good reason to
be fed up with supporting a musician who was excellent, but whose
sense of duty left much to be desired. The archival documents of the
Basilica Liberiana (Santa Maria Maggiore), published by Vito Raeli,[14]
fully confirm the unedifying professional profile that had already emerged
from Alessandro Scarlatti's failings in Naples.

---

[12] Acton, *Last Medici,* 177-178. The cynical coldness of Ferdinando's character
remains clear, but I repeat that the discoveries of Holmes also assign to Alessandro's
untimely previous efforts an influence on the decisions taken by the Grand Prince in
these difficult circumstances.

[13] Hans Joachim Marx, "Die Musik am Hofe Pietro Kardinal Ottobonis unter
Arcangelo Corelli," *Analecta Musicologica* V (1968), 104-177.

[14] Vito Raeli, *Da C. Cecchelli a R. Lorenzini nella Cappella della Basilica Liberiana*
(Rome: Tipografia Artigianelli, 1920). [hereafter Raeli]

We have already noted that on 31 December 1703 the cardinal's support had produced for Alessandro the appointment of coadjutor to the aged and ill Antonio Foggia. It seems that Scarlatti did not take his new responsibilities too seriously, since the Chapter complained that they had seen him in church only once or twice a year. The matter came to a head on 28 February 1706, when the condition of Foggia's health had become more serious, and the absence of his coadjutor was reflected in the inadequate preparation of the choir. The Chapter applied to Ottoboni to dissuade the absentee from persisting in this reprehensible attitude. He must have given his protégé a real dressing down, perhaps to the point of the break that the financial records of his Computisteria unmistakably document.

I maintain that it was a passing storm: Alessandro's admission into Arcadia, clearly presided over by Ottoboni, follows by barely two months his disappearance from the salary-rolls of the Computisteria. At the time, Scarlatti can not have taken the matter as a tragedy, occupied as he was in cultivating his Florentine hopes (Fabbri has pointed out that the year 1706 marks the greatest intensification of his correspondence with the Grand Prince) and in opening negotiations with Venice. After that disastrous trip it must have been his depression that made him consider a betrayal what had only been the consequence of his foolish behavior. He turned to Ottoboni once again, however, after Ferdinando's disconcerting reply. The cynical prayers of the Grand Prince had at least succeeded in obtaining from Divine Providence the dispatch of poor Foggia to his eternal rest, and consequently the prospect that Alessandro would succeed him immediately as head of the Cappella Liberiana.

The documents published by Raeli reveal the events that led to Alessandro's anything but triumphant *rentrée* to Rome. The minutes of the Chapter meeting of 3 July 1707 inform us that Alessandro, "Urbini degens" ("Sojourning in Urbino"), had been informed of his appointment but that—surprise!—he had requested a postponement "per totos aestivos calores" ("for the entire period of the summer heat").[15] The Chapter, which had clearly been urged by Ottoboni, did not refuse the postponement, but they decided to prepare a detailed summary of the duties connected with the post so that Alessandro "should consider better" the service that he was to provide for the Basilica ("ut novus accedat, sed melius cogitet de servitio Ecclesiae prestando," the minutes state precisely).[16]

15 Ibid., 16.
16 Ibid., 16.

In the following session of 24 July 1707 the musician's formal acceptance must have been read; perhaps news had reached him of the granting of the postponement, which was significantly worked into the following document:

Instructions for the sig.r Maestro di Cappella pro tempore of the Sacrosanct Basilica of Santa Maria Maggiore.

First he must be elected by the Most Illustrious, and Most Reverend Canons gathered in Chapter, unlike the other Singers, and Musicians, for whom it is sufficient that they be admitted to the service of the Basilica by the Most Illustrious Sig.r Canon Prefect of the Music pro tempore.

2° He must live in the House assigned to him by the Most Reverend Chapter close to the Church, to be more diligent in the service, and more convenient for the needs of the Cappella, which can occur unexpectedly.

3° He must depend in everything, and for everything on the Most Illustrious Sig.r Canon Prefect, both for the brevity, and for the length of the music, also in carrying out that which may be ordered from him [the maestro] by him [the prefect], either to reform, or innovate, concerning the same [music].

4° He must be present in Choir, or at the organ, in cassock and cotta, and supervise the modesty, and quiet of the singers, making them render him due respect, which if they fail, he must communicate to the Sig.r Canon Prefect, who will take the appropriate resolutions, either by fining or by chastising, or by dismissing [them], as the cases merit.

5° He must be present in Choir at every function, or Chant, that may require beating time, that is on all Feasts, Sundays, and ferial days at the Sung Mass, at Vespers on festive days, whether they are in composed Music or Gregorian, on the Anniversaries when there is a mass of the Canons, and at other times according to the style, and custom of the Basilica.

6° He must also walk, in cassock and Cotta, in all the Processions whether within, or outside the Basilica, with the Singers or Musicians.

7° He must not take it on himself to receive into service new Singers or dismiss the old ones, since such authority belongs only to the Sig.r Canon Prefect, who in many cases is accustomed to ask for the opinion of the maestro di Cappella as advice, and specially when he wishes to admit some musician to service by means of a competition.

8° He may call the musicians of the Basilica at his pleasure, when he wishes to rehearse some new composition for the Church.

9° For special music, and always when outside Musicians, or Players must be called in, it will depend entirely on the will, and resolution of the Sig.r Canon pro tempore Prefect of the Music, to whom the maestro di Cappella will give a list, or a note of whom he wishes to call, since this, and every other thing is dependent on the office of the aforesaid Sig.r Canon, by whose will whatever concerns the Music of the Basilica of S. Maria Maggiore must be resolved.

10° He must provide for all the music, Cantatas, and other of his office for all the Functions which the Most Reverend Chapter of Santa Maria Maggiore performs, or is to perform, without any recompense for the composition, or the effort or expenses of copying."[17]

There is nothing more to say. Don Geronimo della Marra had worthy successors, and at Santa Maria Maggiore the negligent Alessandro had been given something to think about.

Still more interesting are the minutes of the Chapter meeting of August 14, which was held in the presence of Cardinal Ottoboni. Alessandro had received the document drawn up by the Chapter and declared himself "paratum ad omnia" ("ready for everything"), but asked that he be given the equivalent of his rent in cash, since a friend had offered him the use of a house equally near the Basilica free of charge. The Chapter allowed him not to inhabit their house, but Alessandro himself had to see to renting it and was to receive directly the resultant income. The conclusion of the minutes was particularly important: after declaring that Scarlatti is appointed, it notes that during the delay of his acceptance other illustrious *maestri di cappella* had shown themselves willing to fill the notable position. (This is how I interpret the phrase "plures habuerunt Cappellae Magistros concurrentes officio" which led Raeli to imagine a formal competition: an hypothesis in contrast with the negotiations of a coadjutor who was supported, throughout the ups and downs of their relationship, by the all-powerful Ottoboni).

The list of aspiring musicians comprises the most famous Roman *maestri di cappella*: "Don Ottavio Pitoni, of the Church of S. Apollinare./ Bencino./ Cesarini./ Pompeo Scannaciari [or Camicciari in other documents], of the Church of S. Spirito in Sassia./ Giovanni Pietro Franchi, of the Church of S. Maria dei Monti./ Giuseppe Amadori./

---

[17] Ibid., 16-18.

Tommaso Pierantonio./ Giuseppe Salina of the Cathedral of Palermo./ Giuseppe de' Rossi of the Cathedral of Loreto./ Francesco Gasparini of the Church of the Pietà in Venice./ Francesco Mancini Maestro di Cappella in Naples."

The minutes, signed by *Aloysius de Chierichellis, Canonicus secretarius,* end the list with a menacing "ad memoriam futuram," which seems to me to be directed more to Ottoboni than to Alessandro Scarlatti and closes with an enumeration of the

> Benefits of the Sig.r Maestro di Cappella pro tempore of the Sacrosanct Basilica of Santa Maria Maggiore.
>
> First, twelve scudi a month of fixed salary.
>
> 2° The house marked number 4, which is reckoned at thirty scudi a year in rent.
>
> 3° At the installations of the Most Illustrious Sig.ri the new Canons, a gold scudo.
>
> 4° At the funerals of Canons, or other solemn burials, double the musicians' salary.
>
> 5° At Christmas his percentage of several Anniversaries, and Masses [...]."[18]

We may combine these interesting notices with a meteorological deduction: the *aestivi calores* of the year must have lasted longer than usual, since Alessandro began to receive his salary only from the month of December!

In Rome, Alessandro found life as usual.[19] Carnival was officially prohibited except for the customary infractions: on the part of Ottoboni (cantatas performed every Wednesday at the Cancelleria, "with the attendance of many ladies, cardinals, and much nobility" in a "most beautiful theater"); on the part of the Duke of Carbognano; and of Maria Casimira (an improvised French comedy, performed by her gentlemen).

On February 23 Cardinal Grimani obtained from Barcelona the appointment as viceroy of Naples that had been denied him by Vienna. Twenty days later he returned for an audience with the pope, after a long absence: he had to negotiate the passage of the "German knights" from Rome and from the Papal States.

---

[18] Ibid., 21.

[19] Information from Valesio, *Diario* V; I give only the more important references, noting the dates in the text.

In Lent, the performance of oratorios continued as usual. An up-
and-coming patrician had entered the lists of patronage: Marchese Ruspoli
immediately caught a papal scolding for including a female singer among
the performers of the oratorio he sponsored. He quickly regained the pope's
favor (and the title of Prince of Cerveteri) by offering to arm a regiment of
five hundred men (and asking the rank of colonel for his young son).

There was indeed need of armed men. On leaving Rome,
Grimani had exploded a real bomb: Austria occupied the territories of
Comacchio, which had been declared an imperial fief by the Diet of
Ratisbon, although she declared herself ready to restore them "when it
could be shown that they legally belonged to the Church." It was out-
and-out war, in which the Ruspoli regiment had a great deal of work to
do, but not much luck doing it.

The return of her younger children ruined Maria Casimira's relations with the pope and the Curia. First the queen was "displeased"
that the cardinals of recent nomination denied her recognition (if he had
known, Saint-Simon would have rejoiced), then Valesio reported the
rumor that she was "worried about the income of money that she had in
France" and was therefore ready to move to Lyon. Finally, certain searches
and arrests in the immediate vicinity of her mini-palace offended the
susceptibilities of the hotheaded Alexander Sobieski, who ordered his
"Spahis" to disperse the policemen with thrashings. The public forces
returned with an incredible deployment of troops. Unable to risk an encounter, the queen's servants assumed a menacing attitude,

> appearing at the windows with firearms, and it was impossible to
> hold back prince Alexander [...] who wished to jump out with his
> weapons and with his armed retainers [...].[20]

Ten days later, ten members of Maria Casimira's household were
sentenced to banishment for life. At the same time, the queen compromised a possible settlement by making it a point of honor to include the
banished persons in her own suite on every official sortie, very much in
the style of Christina. On July 30 posters put up everywhere in Rome
advised that merchants and other creditors were invited to present their
accounts at Palazzo Zuccari, since the queen had decided to leave Rome.
It required Ottoboni, as usual, to reach a settlement: the papal pardon
was granted to the servants so that everything should be in order for the
customary celebration of the liberation of Vienna. Thus on 12 September 1708 the public that crowded into the little church of the monastery

20 Valesio, *Diario,* 115.

of Palazzo Zuccari could hear *La Vittoria della Fede* (poetry by Capeci, music by Alessandro Scarlatti).

I maintain that the agreement with the pope was part of a tacit permission to activate the little theater that Maria Casimira had constructed in Palazzo Zuccari. The French nuns had not "found Italian damsels who wished to enter their monastery," and they had returned to France.

On December 17 Valesio reports:

> This queen of Poland has begun the performance of an opera in her beautiful and small theater in the casino that she inhabits at Trinità de' Monti, which is the [casino] of the Zuccari."

A contradiction only in appearance: the theater is *beautiful* precisely because it is *small;* soon another Sicilian, Juvarra, will arrive to enhance its possibilities, creating seeming grandeur by his miracles of perspective. The opera was *Il figlio delle Selve,* an old text of Capeci "newly corrected and changed in several places,"[21] with new music by Alessandro Scarlatti.

At the beginning of November our incorrigible nuisance asked the Chapter of the Basilica for four months' leave of absence, declaring candidly that he wished to go to Naples to compose and direct "commedie."[22] In the discussion that greeted the request it was once again apparent that, even after all the promises that had preceded his installation, Alessandro did not excel for zeal and assiduousness in their service. It would have been particularly absurd to release him just as the most important religious festivities were approaching.[23]

It is interesting to read in the minutes of the meeting that Scarlatti offered an unspecified son (Domenico?)[24] as his substitute for the months of his absence. When the secret vote had been taken, the permission was denied. Scarlatti must have importuned his cardinal protector, since the latter charged the prefect of the singers to communicate to the Chapter that the cardinal himself "strongly desired"[25] that the leave be granted, although at a time and under conditions that were considered convenient.

---

[21] See Alberto Cametti, "Carlo Sigismondo Capeci (1652-1728), Alessandro e Domenico Scarlatti e la Regina di Polonia in Roma," *Musica d'Oggi* XIII (1931) [hereafter Cametti, "Capeci,"], 55-64, 58.

[22] Raeli, 22-23.

[23] Since Easter 1709 fell on March 31, Alessandro's absence for four months (December-March), would have included not only Christmas, but Holy Week and Easter as well.

[24] See Eleonora Simi Bonini, "L'attività degli Scarlatti nella Cappella della Basilica Liberiana," *Händel e gli Scarlatti a Roma* (Florence: Olschki, 1987), 154-172, 155-156.

[25] Raeli, 23.

The granting of a week during the next Lent has the flavor of an impatient concession by comparison with the initial request (although the Chapter was lavish with obsequious expressions to Ottoboni). They decided however to retain a month of Scarlatti's salary as a pledge, to be restored to him only on his punctual return. In the face of such a manifestation of distrust—well merited, after all—Alessandro decided to settle himself definitively on the shores of Naples. With all due respect to my censorious reader, Malcolm Boyd, the delusions that Alessandro had suffered, human insatisfaction, and weariness made him desire, at the age of forty-eight, a tranquil old age.

... made to return here to the service of this royal Chapel by His Eminence...

In Rome, where he was the moving force in all the attempts to drive the Franco-Hispanics out of Naples, Vincenzo Grimani had been able to gain a good knowledge of Alessandro Scarlatti, his music, and his human tribulations. The Venetian origin Ottoboni and Grimani had in common had allowed their personal relationship to survive in spite of their adherence to opposing political factions. This culminated in the anomaly of Ottoboni, now openly Franco-Hispanic and intriguing to be named "protector of France" welcoming Grimani, the leader of the Austrian party, after a long journey, with a "splendid dinner with entertainment of exquisite instrumental music " on 11 July 1706) .

The international congress that the Academy of Santa Cecilia dedicated to "Händel and the Scarlattis in Rome" produced a definitive re-evaluation of the length and purpose of the Saxon's sojourn in Naples. Ursula Kirkendale's analysis of the documents in the Ruspoli archive has already revealed that Handel did not remain in Naples until the wedding of the Duke of Alvito, described in such a lively manner by Newman Flower in *George Frideric Handel* (1923). We now know that only with great difficulty could the serenata *Aci, Galatea, e Polifemo* have served as an epithalamium,[26] the purpose to which preceding Handel historiography believed that it had been destined.

While waiting for the permission that would be denied him and while *Il figlio delle selve* was going onstage in Maria Casimira's "most beautiful and small theater," Alessandro must have reached an agreement with Cardinal Grimani. On 1 October 1708 he addressed to Grimani

---

26 Cfr. Antonello Furnari, "I rapporti tra Händel e i duchi d'Alvito, *Händel e gli Scarlatti a Roma* (Florence: Olschki, 1987), 73-78, 75.

the petition that Corticelli and Maione discovered along with other important Scarlatti documents in the Archivio di Stato of Naples:[27]

> Alessandro Scarlatti, Your Eminence's most humble Servant,
> devotedly explains to you, how for the space of twenty Years he
> had the honor of serving with all due attention as Maestro of the
> Royal Chapel of Naples, with the result of meeting with the general
> satisfaction of everyone; but by the deceits of his perverse Destiny
> it was necessary for him to betake himself to Rome with all his
> unmarried daughters, with a permission for two Months, from the
> Duke of Ascalona; After which, he attempted by means of the most
> important personages, to obtain an extension of four Months, which
> was denied him; for which it was necessary (without reflecting on
> the considerable loss of fifty-four ducats a month which your Ser-
> vant, and his son Domenico, had as Salary) to remain absent from a
> place, returning to which put his life, and the honor of his House, in
> danger, since God has willed that every worldly Treasure be ne-
> glected in favor of the latter. For every reason let the circumstances
> of the Plots woven against him, by the arrogance of the Minister of
> a Foreign power, be kept silent, whence the absence which arises
> from so legitimate a Cause is not only excused, but forgiven by all
> the laws, which likewise do not wish, that the detestation of others'
> crimes rebound to the harm of the Innocent. For that reason your
> Servant permits himself to implore, from Your Eminence's most
> high Clemency, and equity the favor of being restored to the said
> position, offering to pray the divine Majesty for your glorification.
> Your Eminence's Most Humble Servant, Alessandro Scarlatti.

Given the precedents one can only laugh at a justification that
implicates the attempts of an arrogant "Minister of a Foreign power" on
the customary mantle of virtue of Alessandro's daughters, whose strict
safeguard kept them from marrying. Grimani swallowed the contents of
the petition whole and decreed thus:

> Considering that Alessandro Scarlatti has served twenty years as
> maestro of the Royal Chapel with full approval, and without reason
> the post was taken from him, since he was obliged unjustly to give
> it up, it is our will to return him to the said employment with the
> salary and benefits pertaining to it, the present Maestro di Cappella
> Francesco Mancini remaining to substitute for him in his absences
> and infirmities with the post of First Organist with the salary and
> benefits which pertain to it.[28]

[27] Francesco Corticelli and Paologiovanni Maione, *Musica e istituzioni musicali a
Napoli durante il viceregno austriaco (1707-1734)* (Naples: Luciano, 1993),
Appendix I, letter n. 1.

[28] Ibid.

When I recounted the episode without knowing of the petition, I had limited myself to seeing in the recovery of a musician of Scarlatti's stature a *felix culpa* on the part of the despotic Grimani. A newcomer to the Neapolitan scene, the cardinal could pretend to be unaware of Alessandro's infractions and the reprimands that contradict the "full approval" asserted and accepted. Grimani could believe that Alessandro had acquiesced in his resignation, as he claimed, a move that I have considered motivated instead by a desire to make room for Domenico. Alessandro Scarlatti had learned at least one thing from his troubled life as an absenteeist. In this sense I interpret the fact that in the appointment of Mancini (and in his later promotion to the post of Vice Maestro), absences of the *maestro di cappella* are referred to as something agreed upon in advance, if only tacitly. Judging from the musical sector, faithfulness to the Imperial cause was ill-rewarded. Francesco Mancini, the acknowledged leader of the austrophile musicians, must have thought so when he had the unpleasant surprise of finding himself demoted to first organist, owing to an "act of justice" that "restored" to Alessandro Scarlatti the direction of the Royal Chapel.

Cotticelli and Maione have revealed that the unexpected death of the cardinal created new problems for the improvident Alessandro, who had employed his authority to "detach," in his customary manner, his son Pietro from his position in Urbino without waiting for the formalization of the post of organist of the Royal Chapel that constituted part of his agreements with Grimani.

Whether the persecution by a powerful libertine was true or merely a pretext, the reference recalls the scandalous episode that had stained his Neapolitan debut in 1683. Given their father's concern for their honor, the nieces of Alessandro's sister, the notorious "la Scarlati" did not take lovers, but indeed remained "spinsters." The documents published by Holmes have clarified the motivations and the manner of Alessandro's flight from Naples in 1704. His foolish appeal for earnings to satisfy the needs of his numerous family amounted to an attempt to impose Domenico on the Neapolitans so that Alessandro could pursue his Florentine mirage. When his attempt regarding the "Eaglet" had failed, he detached Domenico "by force" from Naples. Four years later, the city that had not deserved Domenico's talent suddenly appeared worthy to compensate his father for his wrongs (probably imaginary) through the unbiased cardinal whom we have seen engaged in still less commendable undertakings.

Even the libretto of the opera with which Scarlatti senior presented himself anew to the Neapolitans—*Il Teodosio*—is attributed to the cardinal. This hypothesis, supported by a tradition reported by Bonlini in confused and contradictory terms, is based on its attribution, repeated by Sonneck, to a "noble pen" that had left the libretto incomplete "since it had flown off to heaven." I agree with Strohm when he writes that

> the new viceroy certainly did not have spare time to think about operatic projects let alone draw up a libretto,[29]

He is speaking of the *Agrippina* of Handel destined for Venice, but this holds even more so for *Il Teodosio,* a text which any theatrical poetaster could have fished out of oblivion to fit up for new needs. In any case, this identification with the "noble pen" is ridiculous: Grimani was not yet ready to "fly off to heaven" since he attended the performance of *Teodosio* in person. This is established by the *Avvisi,* which do not mention any relationship between the viceroy and the libretto.[30]

Along with Alessandro Scarlatti, the cardinal had brought to Naples a slanderer of our musician: the Bolognese count Francesco Maria Zambeccari, whom we met in Rome in Valesio's diary. He was enrolled in Grimani's household as a turbulent and not always irreproachable "riding master."[31]

The younger son of a Bolognese noble family, Zambeccari had arrived in Rome in 1700 dressed as an abate, with the intention of studying law and the French language. He was too young to obtain a canonicate, and he ended his difficulties by an opportunistic decision.The enterprising young man quickly abandoned his ecclesiastical prospects for the shining possibility of becoming Cardinal Grimani's riding master.

The situation was the rosiest that a younger son could hope for. Zambeccari was not the customary ne'er-do-well and must have had his own fortune, since he could write to his brother:

> I command three horses and more than fifteen persons like an absolute ruler, without rendering any account. In Rome, I do not know what more I could desire, having a house for nothing, having servants for nothing, having a carriage not only for myself, but also to lend to anyone I want; commanding without subjection, and doing all this with someone else's money, I certainly do not know what else I could desire and I believe that I shall have much occasion to be envied by everyone.

> But to dress myself as a layman it is necessary for you to send me a lot of money. I do not want you to send me your own, not

---

[29] Strohm, 169.
[30] Prota Giurleo, "Breve Storia," 86.
[31] Valesio (*Diario* II, 633-634) describes one of his bloody exploits.

even half a *quattrino*; but I intend and wish that you dispose freely
of mine, for which I give you full permission.[32]

On 22 November 1702 Grimani gave him the appointment but
without a salary, and at the beginning of the following year the cardinal's
departure for Vienna left his riding master in difficulties, with ever more
insistent rumors of dismantling the stables and selling the horses. Worst
of all, the ex-abate had gotten into trouble by killing a lackey of the
Spanish ambassador in a nocturnal brawl. Zambeccari wrote to Bologna, however, that he was being slandered by persons jealous of his
privileged status. In every case, he had succeeded in standing up to
everyone "beginning from the first gentleman down to the last scullion."
A fine type, there is nothing more to say, with a great will to live well by
profiting from circumstances. No matter how indulgent and generous
Grimani was, he must have had reason for discontent, at least from time
to time, if the "signor contino" found himself the precursor of Figaro
and Leporello in a letter of 27 April 1707:

> Last summer when I was working as Maestro di Camera, as sec-
> retary of the embassy, and as everything else, then I could do no
> wrong, now I am the dummy, and as a reward for my efforts I re-
> ceive nothing but grunts; and seeing that I please so little, indeed
> not at all, I am absolutely fed up, and who knows whether one day
> I will not dump their service, [...] in short serving a certain kind of
> people whom nothing pleases is a dog's life, and I don't know if I
> can endure it [...].

He endured it, naturally, since the ten *scudi* that he now received
from the cardinal added to the thirty that arrived from home every month
assured more than adequate pocket money for the restless gentleman,
who in the meantime had been promoted to Master of the Horse. The
rumors of his private undertakings and his position at the court of the
hated Grimani rendered the young count *persona non grata* to the pope
and the Curia. The cardinal's appointment to Naples resolved things for
the best, but not for Alessandro Scarlatti.

When it came to theatrical matters, Grimani gave fully to his
protégé the trust that he only doled out to him in affairs of other importance. It is likely, however, that the viceroy employed his Master of the
Horse as a sort of man-of-all-work, without paying too much attention
to Zambeccari's slashingly severe critical judgments.

---

[32] I take the biographical data from an article by Ludovico Frati, "Un'Impresario
teatrale del Settecento e la sua biblioteca," *Rivista Musicale Italiana* XVI (1911), 65-
84. [hereafter Frati].

Francesco Maria had the use of a box in all the theaters of Naples, and he participated in the organization of theatrical life, of seeking and engaging singers; but I maintain that his interference must have ended along with the Serino administration. A letter of 16 April 1709 informs us that things were changing in the management of the theaters:

> Concerning those Gratianis who are mixing themselves up in the opera now, I tell you: know that Contarini has the theater, but does not appear, using Scarlatti, the one who did the last opera that did not please at all, as a front man; whence we will always have the boredom of hearing him. He is a great man, and although he is so good, he succeeds badly because his compositions are extremely difficult and are things for a private room, which do not succeed in the theater, *in primis* those who understand counterpoint will esteem them; but in a theater audience of a thousand persons, there are not twenty who understand [counterpoint], and the others get bored from not hearing theatrical and lively things. Then, since it is such difficult stuff, the singer must stay alert not to make a mistake, but he does not have the liberty to gesture in his own way and tires himself too much; whence everywhere his style for the theater has not pleased, since you need lively things and dance rhythms, as they have in Venice. But to return to Contarini, what is more knavish, they have taken the theater away from that poor bugger Nicola Serino who paid everyone punctually and who had the lease for five years, a thing detested by everyone.[33]

The letter raises a curtain on the intrigues of the theater and confirms Alessandro Scarlatti's extremely odd position in the operatic panorama of the period. We know that from the time of his first experiences in Naples he was active as an impresario in certain emergencies, by engaging an entire company from Rome (the letters reported by Holmes[34] confirm similar activities). We may observe, however, that he was personally too circumspect to come out into the open. Usually, there was his shameless brother-in-law Pagano to sign dedications, contracts, and serve as a figurehead. Zambeccari's comment about the abstruse refinements that rendered the operas of the greatest composer of the time boring and unacceptable to the general public fits perfectly with Alessandro's Florentine and Venetian experiences. Zambeccari might have been prejudiced, and his factiousness certainly arose from his partisanship for the good Serino against the "Gratianis," but in his simplistic, "although he is so good, he succeeds badly" I read the human and artistic tragedy of Alessandro Scarlatti.

[33] Frati, 69.
[34] Holmes, "Lettere," 369-378.

It is difficult to guess the preferences of the Bolognese patrician. Having praised "lively things" and "dance rhythms," he fires point-blank at the most important Neapolitan novelty of those years: comic opera.

Another of the letters published by Ludovico Frati informs us that at least one opera—the *Astarte* of Zeno and Pariati, with music by Luca Antonio Predieri (Bolognese, it goes without saying)—"succeeds excellently, with good dances and everything handsome." It is a pity that

> these Neapolitans, who all have the worst taste, don't go to it, and instead fill the theater of the Florentines, where they are performing an indecency, unworthy of being seen, in Neapolitan dialect.[35]

... a graceful and most pleasing comedy in music ...

Although it may seem unlikely, Neapolitan opera buffa, born as an emanation of middle-class taste, did not take its first steps on the mismatched boards of some little popular theater. Like Scarlatti's children, it was held at the baptismal font by aristocrats with high-sounding names, although the first documented performance of *Cilla* (27 December 1707, in the house of the Prince of Chiusano) was preceded, more than a year before, by a performance whose site is today impossible to determine. In any case, Piovano,[36] Sartori,[37] and Prota Giurleo[38] have corrected the information furnished by Scherillo, establishing that *La Cilla* was performed in the presence of the viceroy to celebrate the return of Tiberio Carafa from Barcelona, where the Habsburg Charles III had made him a grandee of Spain to reward him for his participation in the so-called conspiracy of Macchia. The performance must have been a success, since the prince opened the rooms of his palace for a repeat. Nor were the authors of *Cilla* rude plebeians: they were two lawyers, and a connection with the forensic and notarial classes continued to mark the first flowering of this happy genre.

This was not a mushroom that had sprung up unexpectedly: dialect elements were circulating in the comic scenes of serious opera and even in some cantatas or oratorios. The diagnosis that the shift of power to Austria allowed possibilities for a new genre that would have been incompatible with Spanish *gravitas* is simplistic. We need only remember the mixture of tragic and grotesque characterizing the great classics of the Spanish theater, Calderón first of all. It was their closed mental-

---

35 Frati, 71.

36 Francesco Piovano, "Baldassare Galuppi: Note bio-bibliografiche," *Rivista Musicale Italiana* XIII (1906), 676-726; XIV (1907), 333-365; XV (1908), 233-274.

37Sartori, "Gli Scarlatti a Napoli,"*Rivista Musicale italiana* XLVI (1942), 374-390, 380.

38 Prota Giurleo, "Breve Storia," 82.

ity, their fear of lowering themselves, that kept artists of discrimination from embracing a genre that could be considered buffoonish and low.

Alessandro Scarlatti was the most circumspect of all. Claudio Sartori unmasked his timid and modest approach to the new genre that musicians pretended to despise, as if it were "the daughter of the bondwoman."[39] Almost all the Scarlattis had been sent out as scouts by their cautious "capo." Tommaso had transferred the role of buffo tenor, already characteristic of Venetian opera composers, to the new genre. Francesco, back from Palermo, appeared in *Petracchio scremmetore,*[40] performed in 1711 at Aversa. Nicola Pagano maneuvered adroitly between his regular tasks as contrabassist and occasional ones as impresario. It is inconceivable that the puppeteer of the clan kept himself aloof from these goings-on. Alessandro's cautious attitude was that of a musician who had seen his rosiest hopes go up in smoke and who therefore did not wish to compromise the decorum and relative tranquillity that he had finally achieved. Sartori recognized two arias from Alessandro's *Inganni felici* that had been transferred to *Petracchio,* and I have suggested that the clan also drew on the comic scenes that its most illustrious representative had composed to insert into his operas or those of others.[41]

In one case, the severe *paterfamilias* dropped his mask by signing a *cantata in lingua napoletana* that is a real working model for comic opera, unless it is a fragment of a still-unidentified "chelleta" or "sketch."

The incredible text[41] offers a veritable thicket of trivial commonplaces and obscene double meanings. The garments of Arcadia have been thrown into the nettles, the Tirsi and Clori of hundreds of cantatas have put on the sock and buskin of comedy to transform themselves into Cicco and Zeza, and the sigh of the abandoned young shepherd gives way to the colorful invective of the plebeian going to the dogs.

Cupid is the target of a whole mudslide of insults, then the desperate Cicco compares his past well-bring with today's misfortunes. His attempt to recover the love of Zeza, literally strewn with obscene allusions, is unsuccessful; she disdainfully dismisses Cicco:

> Sse brache salàte,/non voglio pezzentune nnamorate./Non saie, facce de squessa,/Ca n'è pe tutte lo magnare allessa?

> ("These filthy old trousers!/ I don't want lovesick beggars/ Don't you know, ugly face,/That not everyone can eat bollito?")

[39] Sartori, "Gli Scarlatti," 390.
[40] Ibid., 389.
[41] *Scarlatti,* ERI, 211.
[42] Reproduced in *Scarlatti,* ERI, 212-213.

I have asked myself what could have impelled Alessandro to betray hundreds of delicate Arcadian yearnings at a single stroke. If it was not the high command of a viceroy or of a Maddaloni that led him to such profanation, it must have been the idea of astonishing the friends who sat around his harpsichord, never supposing that they would hear Tommaso (the cantata is for tenor) employed in this astonishing vocal "skit" whose use of dialect and unexpected vulgarity link it unquestionably with the buffo genre.

Did Zambeccari ever hear the cantata? In any case he revealed his hatred of this type of dialect muse when he even changed his opinion about Serino as soon as he had realized that the impresario, in order to keep up with the times, was disposed to include in his repertory "knaveries and indecencies of operas" or "knaveries in the Neapolitan language."[43]

Cardinal Grimani was able to enjoy the musical results of the act of "justice" that had restored Alessandro Scarlatti to Naples for little more than a year: at the end of September of 1710 he departed for the other world. Count Carlo Borromeo, who succeeded him in the post of viceroy of Naples, kept Zambeccari on in his service, but the latter did not earn enough to balance the difference between his own income and the high cost of living in Naples. In those conditions, opera became a kind of vice for the penniless count. The possibility of attending any performance whatever without paying was a decorous way of solving the problem of too much free time. For a moment Zambeccari even toyed with the mad proposal of becoming an impresario. Fortunately for him, his wise older brother turned a deaf ear, or the list of the martyrs of the Teatro San Bartolomeo—whether they had failed for the love of the art or of the artistes—would have been enriched by yet another name.

Instead, the young count showed that he was fairly prudent by setting up as a protector of "virtuose" without pushing the game too far for fear of finding himself ensnared in situations his poverty would not have allowed him to confront boldly. There remains a real monument to his fervent attachment to the theater: the collection of opera libretti, scores, and letters wisely donated to the Institute of Sciences in Bologna, that offers today's scholars texts and documents that probably would not have been preserved if they had remained in private hands.

Having paid this homage to the only wise moment in a wild life, I return to my Scarlattis and to their compatriot whom we have left between Genoa and Barcelona.

---

43 Frati, 71.

XIII

Bloodless disputes of courteous patrons, against the background of a war which only indirectly besieges Rome

The son whom Alessandro Scarlatti had shaped as a stopgap for the demanding canons of Santa Maria Maggiore found a better placement for his talents with Maria Casimira, to whom the adjustment of her affairs in Poland and the death of her dissolute father had restored resources and credit. Before leaving Rome, the elder Scarlatti had already benefitted from the ex-queen's revived patronage.[1] Now Domenico took up the post of *maestro di cappella* that had reawakened in his father the dream of returning to the days of Christina.

Desirous of multiplying his oppportunities for artistic enjoyment, Ottoboni encouraged the undertakings connected with the little theater in Palazzo Zuccari by every means, generously allowing artists whom he maintained in his own service to collaborate in the performances organized by the queen.

First among these artists was another Sicilian: Filippo Juvarra, a priest from Messina who had landed in Rome with a letter of recommendation from a noble nun. His astonishing natural talent would refine itself through the important artistic experiences he assimilated under the guidance of Carlo Fontana. According to an anonymous eighteenth-century biographer,[2] Juvarra had designed scenes for Ottoboni's theater in the Cancelleria at the request of a compatriot who had then shown them to the cardinal as his own work (see Fig.7 on p. 219). Discovering

---

[1] We have already noted that in 1708 Alessandro wrote for Maria Casimira of Poland the oratorio *La Vittoria della Fede* (which must have been performed on September 12 in the course of the "special celebration in the little church" of the monastery of Palazzo Zuccari, according to Valesio, *Diario* IV, 153) and *Il figlio delle selve* (perhaps the opera performed December 17 "in the beautiful and small theater in her casino [...] at Trinità dei Monti, which belongs to the Zuccari," but most certainly on 17 January 1709, since on this date Valesio writes: "The queen of Poland is putting on Capece's old play titled *Il figlio delle selve* set to music in the little theater of her palace at Trinità dei Monti."

[2] See Mercedes Viale Ferrero, *Filippo Juvarra scenografo e architetto teatrale* (Turin: Fratelli Pozzo, n. d. [1970] [hereafter Viale Ferrero]).

the deception, Ottoboni quickly secured Don Filippo's services permanently, naming him his chaplain and entrusting important tasks to him. Mercedes Viale Ferrero, the distinguished scholar of this architectural genius, has seen in this episode a sort of opera plot, rendered probable by the atmosphere of Ottoboni's court, which was populated by artists but also infested with parasites.

In Carnival of 1709 the severity of the prohibitions had been relaxed despite the increase of tension with the Franco-Hispanic faction. The news spread that Frederick IV of Denmark, tired of political intrigues and wars, had come to Italy to distract himself and thought of pushing on as far as Florence and Rome after the traditional visit to Venice.[3] By receiving a Protestant king with splendor, the pope perhaps was thinking of the political implications such as conversion that the Danish sovereign had not foreseen. In any case, Ottoboni and the Barberini were ready to sacrifice part of their magnificent furnishings so that the glorious Palazzo Riario on the Lungara might recover the splendors of Christina's times.

Maria Casimira did not wish to do less and had "her little theater embellished," Valesio informs us, in order to entertain the royal guest fittingly. For the entire month of March efforts to make a good impression multiplied. Even the miserly Don Livio Odescalchi participated in furnishing Palazzo Riario with his own furniture, which had once belonged to the queen of Sweden. Just as the Romans were crowding to visit the palace now restored to its ancient splendors, an icy shower for everyone descended from Florence:

> [T]he king of Denmark had resolved not to come on to Rome and [...] had decided to send, as he did, one of the gentlemen of his chamber to thank His Holiness for the demonstrations made for his reception. It is believed that the said king had decided, at the persuasion of his court preacher and his counselors, to avoid his people's suspicion that he was about to embrace the catholic religion, to which he seems greatly inclined.[4]

But now the enchantment was broken, and finally the public theater would have picked up momentum if diplomatic impediments had not intervened. The Prince of Avellino, named ambassador by Charles III, and the Duke of Uzeda, ambassador of Philip V, both claimed the box reserved for Spain. For the moment, it was deemed prudent to suspend activities (leaving the manager of the Teatro Capranica in difficul-

---

[3] Valesio, *Diario,* IV, 241.

[4] Ibid., 242.

Plate 7

Filippo Juvarra: Set for Alessandro Scarlatti's Ciro *(Rome, Teatro Ottoboni, 1712) (Turin, Biblioteca nazionale)*

ties). The high aristocracy could choose either the *Costantino Pio* of Pollaroli, performed with great splendor at the Cancelleria, or the repeats of Alessandro Scarlatti's *Figlio delle selve,* which Maria Casimira was putting on at Palazzo Zuccari, or a pastorale performed in the theater of the Contestabile Colonna.

Beginning with that Lent, Domenico Scarlatti's relationship with Maria Casimira was regularized. As far as we know, it began with *La conversione di Clodoveo Re di Francia,* an oratorio on a text of Capeci. From that date, the queen's secretary furnished the young *maestro di cappella* with at least one opera libretto a year (two in 1713, when they wished to balance *Ifigenia in Aulide* with an *Ifigenia in Tauride).* Ottoboni's generosity allowed some of these productions to be enriched by the collaboration of Juvarra, whose fame had now crossed the Alps thanks to the engravings printed in opera librettos.

These successes had a sensational effect in Vienna, where Joseph I, for example, who

very much enjoyed theatrical works, had written to the most eminent Cardinal Albani that he order a group of scenes from Don

Filippo Juvarra since those that he had made for the most eminent
Ottoboni pleased him so greatly [...].[5]

So many thorny diplomatic problems to overcome: Caesar wishes
to employ an artist in the service of the cardinal protector of France.
The difficulty would have been insurmountable if Ottoboni had not been
at the center of things with his impartiality (and perhaps his negotiations
with the Austrians for the recovery of the incomes of certain abbeys that he
possessed in the kingdom of Naples and in the state of Milan ...).[6]

Cardinal Albani's zeal impelled him to obtain for the emperor
one of the most luxurious of surviving opera manuscripts, the fruit of a
collaboration among three of the most important musicians of the period (Carlo Francesco Cesarini, Antonio Caldara, and Alessandro
Scarlatti), each employed to composean act of *Giunio Bruto o vero La
Caduta dei Tarquini*. The opera, on an appropriately Roman subject, is
copied in splendid calligraphy in a volume whose rich titlepage, decorated initials for every scene, and sixteen scenographic designs[7] should
have brought Caesar the most effective evidence of Juvarra's lively desire for a permanent engagement in Vienna.

Unfortunately Joseph I never saw *Giunio Bruto* performed. Probably he never received the beautiful manuscript today preserved in the
National Library of Vienna: as I have already noted, on 17 April 1711 Joseph I departed this world. These were ugly times for pleasure-loving patrons: for several years Ferdinando de' Medici, stricken by violent attacks
of epilepsy, had been heading for the horrifying end to which his squalid
triumph over the pathetic refusals of the Venetian lady had doomed him.

At this point I had inserted "a striking testimony" to the "painful physical deterioration of the Grand Prince:"the text of Francesco
Mannucci's "memoria."[8] However, the pitiless researches of Juliane
Riepe, Carlo Vitali, and Antonello Furnari have now revealed it to be the
product of the disastrous imagination of Mario Fabbri.[9] I have already
clarified in my preface the reasons hat led me to renounce these evoca-
tions of the "Musicians and Virtuosi who had been in the service of His
Highness" and the picturesque touches that, against the pathetic back-

5 Viale Ferrero, 28.

6 Valesio, *Diario*, IV, 244.

7 See the reproductions of the splendid designs in Viale Ferrero, 163-187.

8 Mario Fabbri, "Nuova luce sull'attività fiorentina di Giacomo Antonio Perti,
   Bartolomeo Cristofori e Giorgio F. Haendel," *Chigiana* XXI (1963), 145-149.

9 "Il Pianto di Maria (HWV 234): Rezeption, Ueberlieferung und
musikwissenschaftliche Fiktion," *Göttinger Händel-Beiträge*, 1993, 270-296 (with
bibliography on 303-307).

ground of Ferdinando de' Medici's decline, described "the Saxon Hendle" as a barefaced thief of other composers' music. I must also give up the nickname— "Minichino"—applied to Domenico Scarlatti, clearly a figment of our prankster's imagination, since no historical source confirms it.

A barony that kills music

The contents of the petition that has recently come to light make it clear that Astorga arrived in Vienna before Joseph I died and that he had to await the return of Charles VI before obtaining from the imperial exchequer a gratuity for the losses he had suffered in Sicily through his faithfulness to the Imperial cause.

The death of Joseph I had given an unexpected twist to the situation in Spain. After many tergiversations (owing in part to the loyal proposal of not abandoning his faithful Catalans to the revenge of Philip V), Charles of Habsburg had decided to hurry to Vienna to become Charles VI and to exchange a royal for an imperial crown. At first, his dear wife remained in Barcelona to act as regent; it was immediately clear, however, that the balance of European politics would not tolerate a return to the multinational empire of Charles V. Negotiations were immediately set in motion (or rather unblocked, since the Sun King had already begun to make contact with the Anglo-Dutch in an attempt to refute the reputation of war-mongering all Europe attributed to him— and to catch his breath after his bloody and exhausting wars). The negotiations culminated in the Peace of Utrecht, which finally reunited the two Spains and gave Victor Amadeus of Savoy the title of king, "glorious ... not imaginary, as that of Cyprus," Muratori says, "but substantial with the dominion of an Island most fortunate on several counts, and the greatest in the Mediterranean:"[10] Sicily.

In the midst of such political upheavals, we would expect to find Astorga more than ever in favor in Vienna. Instead, he had once again gotten into trouble. For a certain kind of individual an increase in income is harmful, since it impels him to exaggerate his optimism and he soon finds himself once again in debt. While waiting for his pension, paid irregularly and ferociously scythed by taxes even heavier than those which afflict us today, Astorga had to obtain loans from his friends in order to survive without compromising his dignity as an L. B. (free baron, which appears in the Viennese documents). The decree with which Charles VI granted the pension is dated 12 June 1712 and the payment

[10] Muratori, *Annali,* XVI, 131.

of the first trimester took place punctually on September 12. However, in April of 1713 it was necessary for the emperor to order that Astorga's arrears be paid by the Bohemian Deputation.[11] Discounting rich revenues from Sicily of which Astorga could not dispose even later, Volkmann imagines a situation of relative discomfort, caused by the delays of the imperial finances. In reality, Don Emanuello had returned to the privations of his former condition as an adventurer, now unable even to conceal his own poverty under the cast-off skin of the discredited "del Chiaro."

On 9 May 1712 *D. Antonius Caldara Magister Capellae Augustissimi Imperatoris* had his daughter *Sophia Jacobina Maria* baptized in the cathedral of Saint Stephen. The godparents were the ambassador and ambassadress of Holland, represented by a certain Maria Susanna Gessingerin and by the *Most Illustrious D. Emanuel L. B. Astorga.*[12] "Prings," writes the cathedral scribe, uncertain of the Dutch pronunciation. The family name was Bruynings, and we find the ambassador mentioned in a document of quite another kind at the beginning of 1714. It shows him as the baron's *Creditor* (together with a Count Gambalonga, Gaudenz Zanoli, and Jacob Antoni Badia) for a total of 1,480 florins and requesting payment from the imperial treasury, which, in turn, was in debt to Astorga for new installments of his pension.[13]

Other information shows that our Sicilian was linked with the rich and powerful Althanns. Volkmann has described the romantic marriage of Count Althann, who had gone to Spain as a gentleman of the archduke, with Marianna Pignatelli, a noble pupil in the convent in Barcelona that had offered shelter to Charles and his suite from the bombardment of the French fleet.[14] The manuscript of a cantata by Astorga is dated "Znaim 1713" and reveals the hiding-place of the beleaguered musician, who was perhaps a guest in his friends' castle.

Since the situation in Vienna continued to be hopeless, in the spring of 1714 Astorga once again chose flight as a remedy for financial embarassment. However, excellent reasons now impelled him in a specific direction: to Palermo, where after the death of his elder brother his aged father had also died.

---

[12] Volkmann, *Astorga,* I, 79.

[11] Volkmann, *Astorga,* II, 134.

[13] Volkmann, *Astorga,* II, 134-135.

[14] Volkmann, *Astorga,* I, 85. Marianna Pignatelli was the future muse (and perhaps morganatic wife) of Pietro Metastasio.

Perhaps Astorga's disappearance, which covered his shame as a pursued debtor, delayed the mournful news that opened new prospects for him. The laws of Sicily demanded that the succession to a title and its goods be claimed within six months of the previous holder's death. If the legitimate successor failed to present himself, the treasury confiscated both fief and title. While Don Emanuello remained a fugitive, his mother and his sister Tommasa (the failed victims of the *ictus carrabinae,* you may recall) went to great trouble to block the treasury from appropriating the barony.[15] A closer reading of the notarial acts already studied by Tiby reveals that our noble scatterbrain was already in Palermo on 14 September 1714,[16] intent on taking the fief away from his mother. She, at least in appearance, had been obliged to contest it with her daughter, who had been invested with the fief on October 23. Since for many years Donna Tommasa had found refuge from the unhappiness of the world in a convent, it is clear that the whole barrage of lawsuits was a charade. In the last act the widowed baroness even claimed to have consulted "her lawyers and soliciters" before recognizing her son's right to inherit his father's fief, which in any case was entailed.[17]

When he had taken possession of his wealth, the new baron allowed himself the luxury of recognizing that the claims of his sister the nun were well founded. She wanted a sort of mortgage on the income from the fief of Ogliastro (mostly ceded in leases to an army of direct cultivators) in order to guarantee the "dotes de paraggio" assigned to her by her father in the contract of her monacation. Don Emanuello declared that he wished to satisfy these claims "amicabiliter et absque iudiciali strepitu" ("amicably and without judicial clamor") and bound himself to pay her forty-six *onze,* eighteen *tarì,* eight *grana* and one *picciolo*[18] every year. In an act drawn up a month later he demonstrated his gratitude for an allowance of three hundred *onze* made by the poor nun to show him "amorem" and "benevolentiam."[19]

---

[15] Tiby, *Astorga,* 106.

[16] This appears without doubt from the act of 14 September 1714 (notary Antonino Fazio, now in the Archivio di Stato, Palermo—*Notai defunti);* Tiby (106) read it incorrectly and thought that it had been promulgated by the dowager baroness "foreseeing the imminent return of her son."

[17] The observation of legal customs intended to complicate the most calm and instinctive decisions of all of the contracting parties induces the mother to keep silent about the response of the lawyers whom she says that she consulted and to declare that she decided on her renunciation in favor of her son "nolens contra ipsum judicium ingredi" ("not wishing to enter into judgment against him").

[18] Act of the same date, which follows the first in the protocols of the same notary.

[19] Act of 8 October, by the same notary.

Victor Amadeus of Savoy had come to Palermo to be crowned, but the Sicilians soon understood that once again they were to obey an absentee king. Before returning to his beloved Turin the king had spent four months in Messina. On August 29 he embarked on the vessel that would take him away from Sicily forever. During his short visit to Palermo, at the same time that Don Emanuello was regularizing his family affairs with the notary, the king had slept on board ship, so that no one could consider his return permanent. If the new baron wished to kiss the king's hand, he would have had to line up with the nobles and functionaries who thronged to render homage to the king before his departure. Count Maffei stayed on in Sicily as viceroy; from him Astorga would obtain the remission of the late fee for the delay in his investiture and, later, his appointment as senator.

Although the Sicilians reacted badly to the austerity that blighted their social life with the arrival of the Piedmontese, the king's presence brought about a few novelties in the musical life in the island's principal cities. For the ceremony of his coronation the *maestri di cappella* of the Senate and the cathedral had to give way to Andrea Fioré because His Majesty had wanted the musical ceremony to be entrusted to the maestro who had accompanied him from Turin.[20]

Perhaps a great violinist had also come to Palermo in the king's suite. Listening to Antonio Lolli seventy-six years later, the Marchese of Villabianca—a fertile ruminator of family memories, expecially if they brought luster to his house—would abandon his usual lack of interest in music to recall

> the times in which there flourished the great violinist Lorenzo Somis
> Ardì of the city of Turin with whom there often played together in
> musical events my Father the late virtuoso Benedetto Emmanuele
> *olim* marquis of Villabianca of happy memory who was very skilled
> and distinguished himself among the nobles of Palermo with that
> rare and difficult instrument, the Archlute. The prints of the com-
> positions for violin of the said Somis Ardì were then circulating,
> made under the patronage of the late great Federico Napoli prince
> of Resuttano to whom they were dedicated, being printed in Rome
> in 1722 by Angelo Antonio della Cerra.[21]

The violin of Somis beside the antiquated archlute of a nobleman: an adequate image for the encounter between Piedmont and Sicily.

---

[20] Antonio Mongitore, *Diario palermitano,* 178.

[21] Francesco Maria Emanuele e Vanni, marchese di Villabianca, *Diario palermitano,* XVI, 277, ms. in the Biblioteca Comunale, Palermo.

Villabianca senior certainly did not feel demeaned by playing beside an esteemed musician. Astorga was quite different from him; barely restored to respectability, he felt himself reborn as the young aristocrat who a few years earlier had been thanked for having "revenged the most exalted delight from the vileness of low class earnings." Hence he was reluctant to display himself in his native land as a working professional musician. The baron's silence is yet more surprising owing to his rapid accession to important public duties, and to the decisive stimulus that he imparted to cultural activities, not limited to the area of music.

I discovered Astorga among the founders of the Academy of Good Taste, a "colony" of the Roman Arcadia without doubt, the most important literary society in Palermo. I can also attribute to his efforts at least two undertakings that had positive results on the musical activities of the city. To these years belongs the development of the professional instruction that transformed the Casa degli Spersi, an orphanage dedicated to the Buon Pastore, into a real musical institute. And in these years Palermo may have imported a real musical genius, one who had come to the land of his ancestors perhaps to exorcise the profound conditioning that continued to impede his free flights of fantasy.

Aurea mediocritas romana

As I have already noted, Alessandro's maneuver to ease his son's Roman career did not apparently succeed. Domenico's tasks as *maestro di cappella* of the queen of Poland must have been few indeed: to set to music Capeci's texts for the serenatas celebrating the liberation of Vienna or for the annual opera in the "domestic theater of the queen" (as the title pages of the libretti printed for those occasions designate the hall of Palazzo Zuccari). On a special occasion, the Arcadia played host to the repeat of *Tolomeo et Alessandro o vero la Corona disprezzata,* an opera whose complicated historical-allegorical subject exalted the disinterest of Maria Casimira's younger sons in a throne from which the numerous reasons already examined excluded them. As Kirkpatrick revealed,[22] the volume that the Arcadians printed as a souvenir of the event[23] gushes with verses celebrating Maria Casimira, Prince Alexander Sobieski, the

---

[22] Kirkpatrick, *Scarlatti,* 52.

[23] RIME / DI DIVERSI AUTORI / PER LO NOBILISSIMO DRAMMA / DEL TOLOMEO, E ALESSANDRO / *Rappresentato del Teatro Domestico della Sacra /* Real Maestà / DI MARIA CASIMIRA / REGINA DI POLONIA, / DEDICATE / ALLA MAESTÀ SUA / IN ROMA per Antonio de' Rossi alla Piazza di Ceri. 1711 (dedication dated 1 April).

librettist Capeci, the singers Paola Alari and Maria Giusti and the other performers of the opera, but they pass over in silence Domenico Scarlatti, who had written the music for it and who must have directed the performance from the harpsichord. No one thought of admitting Alessandro's son into the Academy which five years earlier had transformed his father into Terpandro Politeo, or of paying Domenico's music even the conventional tribute of praise that was being lavished in every other direction.

The ex-eaglet had little reason to be pleased with his own successes, even if his post was prestigious, and more important ones in the Vatican would follow. Within himself, Domenico must have mulled over his dissatisfaction at having achieved the brilliant career that his father had prophesied only at the level of dull routine .

Maria Casimira was back in financial difficulties, which now forced her to reimburse her landlord and other creditors with aristocratic titles and patents of nobility. In the meantime, Domenico had been able to profit from the opportunities opening up in the Cappella Giulia after the death of the aged Lorenzani. In November 1713 Tommaso Bai, dean of the singers, was named to the vacant post of *maestro di cappella,* and the post of assistant was assigned to Scarlatti junior. (As in his father's case at Santa Maria Maggiore, this would allow him to succeed Bai after his death, which took place at the end of December of 1714.)[24]

It was lucky for Domenico that this new path had opened: in June of 1714 Maria Casimira left Rome forever.

Not even decrepit age (both his own and that of the ex-queen who had begged him to let her return to France) had softened the Sun King. Since the vengeful monarch still harbored all his resentment "dans l'esprit et dans le coeur," Maria Casimira could only select one of the decaying royal castles of the Loire and hang on there in privation for the year of life which remained to her. If he had not allowed the hoped-for *tabouret* to the *maréchale* of former years, now he did not want the ex-queen underfoot. He permitted her to return to her original state as "sujette," but on condition that she stay away from Versailles and Paris.[25]

Probably Domenico functioned as maestro of the Cappella Giulia even before Bai's death. This explains the promptness with which, only two days after his predecessor's demise, a pastoral cantata by Domenico could be performed at the Apostolic Palace during the same Christmas ceremonies that on previous occasions had seen the birth of the most celebrated of Corelli's concerti and other vocal compositions by father Alessandro.

24 The appointment, quoted by Kirkpatrick, *Scarlatti,* 332, is dated 22 December.
25 Saint-Simon, *Mémoires,* X, 248.

As Kirkpatrick noted,[26] the new *maestro di cappella's* activity must not have been too different from that described by Andrea Adami of Bolsena in his *Osservazioni per ben regolare il coro dei cantori della Cappella Pontificia,* published in 1711 under the customary patronage of Ottoboni, with engravings by Juvarra and others.

A manuscript once in the possession of Dr. Burney[27] testifies to an extraordinary friendship between Alessandro Scarlatti and Adami: a collection of thirty-six cantatas, for the most part autograph, composed between 5 October 1704 and 24 September 1705. A communication by Strohm to the conference in Rome corrected certain inaccuracies that have rebounded from one account to another for two centuries, because Burney had read in the handsome manuscript a sort of musical equivalent of Cicero's *Tusculan Disputations* (or a precursor of Paolo Rolli's *Tudertine).* The connection with Tivoli is completely mistaken. Some of the datings in the manuscript refer to Albano (Cardinal Pamphilj's summer residence, Strohm notes), but on this occasion (unlike his visit to the Grand Prince)Alessandro Scarlatti is innocent of being an importunate and suffocating parasite. The collection is a sort of conventional correspondence among friends, linked to festive anniversaries and other obligatory greetings, such as "good holidays," "happy new year," "for a happy Epiphany" (thus I interpret what Strohm reads as "For the Pasqua of Epiphany," since the cantata is dated January 4), and "good Lent." The titling of a little set of three cantatas is particularly curious: "A happy trip and a swift return," "Welcome," and "The Cart [Baroccio] to S. D. Andrea Adami." If we remember the references to the postillion that in the very same years the young Bach dropped into his *Capriccio sopra la lontananza del fratello dilettissimo,* it seems to me that a famous Beethoven sonata might find in this music its almost exactly centenary predecessor.

Adami was indeed dear to Cardinal Ottoboni, who found himself obliged more than once to swallow bitter pills for his sake. In April of 1706 the cardinal had wished to confer on his protégé a vacant canonicate in San Lorenzo in Damaso, but the other canons opposed the appointment of the "castrato singer and his favorite," objecting that since in the past "that Chapter [had been] full of men who were notable for learning or for nobility, when he wished to number Bolsena also among them, they had unanimously resolved no longer to appear in choir."[28]

---

[26] Kirkpatrick, *Scarlatti,* 58.

[27] Burney, *General,* II, 629.

[28] Valesio, *Diario,* III, 582.

Having swallowed the affront, Ottoboni countered. Valesio tells us that having conferred a vacant benefice in Santa Maria Maggiore "on that capon [...] the son of a peasant," the cardinal succeeded in having the Venetian Republic name Bolsena, "his family and descendants," Venetian citizens of the first class.[29] Not everyone would concern himself with the descendants of a castrato!

In May of 1709 Ottoboni suffered further affronts from Ferdinando de' Medici when he went to Florence to discuss with Cardinal Francesco Maria the possibility of taking over his protectorate of the crowns of France and Spain. As part of his suite, in addition to the Marchese De Cupis Ornani, he brought "the cavaliere Sciarp who formerly had a hairdresser's shop opposite the palace of the Gaetani, and Lorenzino who was formerly his lackey now maestro di casa, and Bolsena, an old castrato singer now his confidant." On Ottoboni's return to Rome, it was known that he had been well received by the Grand Duke, to whom he had brought as a gift "a thorn of the Redeemer in a golden reliquary of exceptional work," but that he had

> encountered there some unpleasantnesses by having brought with him among his gentlemen Bolsena, a castrato singer, as majordomo (and when the Grand Prince invited him to sing, he gave him six flasks of wine, treating him as an ordinary castrato) and the cavaliere Sciarp, formerly a hairdresser on the Corso and, wishing to send him on a mission to the Grand Prince, the latter was unwilling to admit them: indeed from the first evening he made him eat in the mess with the *aiutanti di camera*. [30]

Even in his miserable condition, Ferdinando preserved his haughtily punctilious character intact—and he knew a good deal more than Ottoboni about glorifying his *castroni*-factotums. Having recorded this Florentine encounter between the two patrons in whom Alessandro Scarlatti had placed his hopes, let us return to his puppet-games in Rome.

In the ever-torturous activity of his last period in Naples, papa Scarlatti never broke off his relationships with Rome, with its patrons, with its theaters. Even at the height of his new achievements, Domenico remained under his father's thumb, and he must have had to follow his advice blindly. When Domenico had completed his "domestic" theatrical experience in Maria Casimira's shadow, he returned to the public theater with an *Ambleto*. The music has not survived, but the text could be a watered-down version of Zeno and Pariati's *Ambleto,* which

[29] Ibid., 582.
[30] Valesio, *Diario,* IV, 288.

Gasparini had already performed at the San Cassiano, in the same year that Alessandro's wounded pride carried his eaglet off to Venice.

A gap in Valesio's diaries does not help us to verify Kirkpatrick's hypothesis[31] that the failed performance of the *Maestro di musica* was the result of the censor's intervention. This intermezzo by Girolamo Gigli, better known as *La Dirindina,* was set to music by Domenico Scarlatti. It has survived to claim the lion's share of the tributes that certain Italian musical institutions offered to the composer on his tercentenary, ignoring the more characteristic products of his theatrical muse. The subject does not seem scabrous enough to incur the anger of the Roman censorship. It consists of the usual satire on the "routine" of the period, with a music lesson, a decrepit teacher jealous of an unpromising female student, and a broad-minded castrato. The fulminations of the censor were aimed rather at the author of the text, the same Girolamo Gigli who had already become famous in Siena and Florence with more incisive satires against bigots and the Inquisition. Whatever the reason, in the "Hall of the Sig.ri Capranica" two *Intermedj pastorali* were inserted in place of the *Maestro di musica.* The libretto informs us that they were entrusted to singers employed in the *Ambleto,* a castrato and a bass. The traditional "couple" of the intermezzi must have been adapted to Roman usage, which continued to exclude women from the public stage.

But what was not performed in Rome perhaps had oppportunities for vindication elsewhere. In the same year we find a libretto of *Dirindina* (printed in Lucca as a "second edition," which suggests a first Roman printing) provided with a final note which indirectly confirms that "sweetest of characters" and those "most polite manners imaginable" attributed to Domenico by Handel's first biographer:

> The excellent music of this little farce is by Sig. Domenico Scarlatti, who will willingly make it available to everyone.[32]

What a philosopher, our Domenico! Don't give yourselves too much trouble, you pirates who appropriate scores without giving credit: "Pulsate et aperietur vobis!" Although *Ambleto* did not forestall his father's return, other tasks remained for the *maestro* of the most prestigious church of all Christianity. Domenico certainly must have been

---

[31] Kirkpatrick, *Scarlatti,* 63-64. In publishing the critical edition of the two intermezzi (Milano: Ricordi, 1985), Francesco Degrada reprinted a letter from Gigli in Rome to Anton Francesco Marmi in which the story is given of the plot woven by the musicians who were ridiculed (supported in their intrigues by so important a busybody as Cecchino de Castris).

[32] Kirkpatrick, *Scarlatti,* 417.

capable of rivalling Adami (who had been established at the head of the
Cappella Pontificia), Pompeo Cannicciari (who succeeded Alessandro
at the Liberiana), and the musicians who directed the other important
cappelle of Rome. Domenico's surviving church music is in no way
compatible with the future author of the *Sonate*. Deeper scholarly study
of his vocal productions is still in progress, but one work stands out
from the emerging sampling: the extraordinary *Stabat Mater*. Domenico
composed the work for ten voices without adopting the traditional division into a double chorus of five parts each. Rather he indulged his whims
by contrapuntal interweavings that assure the piece a special place in the
whole panorama of eighteenth-century choral music. Here the eaglet
flies to the dizzying heights that his father's pride had predicted. The use
of the minor mode achieves an harmonic color that, even if characteristic of Naples, has nothing in common with languid "sicilianas"
but goes back to the bold solutions of an anti-conformist prince whose
madrigals pleased Christina of Sweden "more than any other composition". . .

In the modern edition of this work, Jürgen Jürgens hesitates between attributing its genesis to Venice or to the period that its author
spent in the Cappella Giulia. It is strange that no one has suggested that
it might be a later work. If I were to do so I would contradict what I am
about to write about a process of artistic maturing that only later would
embark on a path far from the sound-world of the *Stabat*. Datings based
on stylistic considerations can sometimes be contradicted by documentary discoveries that disperse, by means a single sheet of paper, the volumes of painstaking erudition that the scholarship— and the lack of
imagination— of the experts have been able to jumble together about a
given work. In the case of the *Stabat* the data at our disposal are not of
much help. If we wish to connect the work with the Cappella Giulia, the
personnel of the singers was augmented by two sopranos in the last years
that Domenico directed it, but the preceding group already contained
the four "canti" necessary for performing this lovely score one to a part.
Domenico's *Stabat* remains rooted in a past divergent from the other
"Neapolitan" line: the one that, taking off from papa Alessandro's *in-
cunabulum,* the *Stabat* for two voices, violins and continuo, set off toward the Pergolesian sunset. It passes, however, through the intermedi-
ate stage of another *Stabat* in C minor (the tonality, the same as that of
Domenico's highly dissimilar work, is mentioned out of mere curiosity), a solitary monument among the vocal productions of another of our
southern musicians: the Baron of Astorga, as Don Emanuello boastfully
succeeded in being called.

Although I have just pointed out how diverse were the treatments that the two musicians gavethe same text, Domenico Scarlatti and Astorga had several reasons for mutual understanding. Astorga, I have sought to remind us, should be considered a member of the Scarlatti clan. There is the tradition that he was probably Francesco's pupil; there are the many possible encounters between the adventurous and wandering baron and the two principal musicians of the Scarlatti family; there is the flagrant derivation of the baron's cantatas from Alessandro's (already pointed out by their contemporaries); there is the possibility that in the years that he spent in Rome with the Duke of Uzeda, Don Emanuello could often have approached the father (for his advice) and the son (to profit by the company that Handel and Roseingrave so appreciated); there is the possibility—or the virtual certainty—that the maskings in Venice offered the shady Astorga the most suitable of hiding places. I like to imagine that Astorga was present when Domenico recognized Handel: we would thus have another reason for finding a reference to Emanuello's trip to England that my discoveries in Palermo could restore to the old chronology proposed by Hawkins.[33] But all this aside, the little baron and Domenico had a more specific reason for affinity. If they compared their experiences as adolescents and as human beings, both had to deal with fathers who were hindrances in varying degrees and in any case oppressive.

Thinking of all this, I cannot believe that I am too far from the truth when I imagine that from Palermo where the egregious baron began to get bored there arrived "signals" that the celebrated and respected maestro of the Cappella Giulia would not have left unanswered.

---

[33] John Hawkins, *General History of the Science and Practice of Music* (London, 1776), V, 212. The chronology of the first part of Astorga's biography is falsified by the idea that he was already in Vienna at the beginning of the century, "greatly favoured by the emperor Leopold." Hawkins is aware of the baron's Sicilian origins, but does not know of his return to his native land and has him going to Spain, and says that he was ennobled in unspecified circumstances. He even states that he does not know Astorga's family name. The following biographical passage, closer to the English sojourn, acquires new credibility: "He was at Lisbon some time, and after that at Leghorn, where being exceedingly caressed by the English merchants there, he was induced to visit England, and passed a winter or two in London, from whence he went to Bohemia; and at Breslaw, in the year 1726, composed a pastoral intitled *Daphne,* which was performed there with great applause."

The repeat of the opera already performed in Genoa and Barcelona (perhaps the baron passed off the music of *Dafni:* here again we find the confusion with Daphne) sets us back on the tracks of Volkmann's biography.

XIV

... et petisse, ut vellet, ipsum emancipare et a Patria potestate, et paternis nexibus liberare ...

A catalogue of musical activities in Palermo, which I had arranged in advance to clarify the activities of the musicians who interest us, shows that 1716 was a year of absolute poverty in artistic events. The baron must have been greatly bored. It would almost seem as if he had vanished if he had not later been appointed Senator of Palermo (1 May 1717-30 April 1718), a post awarded only to subjects participating fully in the socio-political life of the Città Felicissima. Tiby[1] maintained that Astorga might have been traveling. Thinking of poor Maria Casimira's yearnings to display herself as a queen to those who had known her as a "petite particulière," I can imagine that a similar impulse might have induced Don Emanuello to return as a legally recognized feudal lord among those who had dealt with an imaginary baron. Possibly Rome attracted the traveler more than Naples, which was full of Austrians who might know the mortifying reasons for his flight from Vienna. And in his new role as behind-the-scenes protector of art, Astorga might have traveled in search of singers for the Teatro Santa Cecilia.

As soon as Victor Amadeus had left, the puritanical gloom of the Piedmontese weighed down on Palermo, reducing festivities and spectacles to austere dimensions far from the ingrained habits that had only been heightened during the Franco-Hispanic era. In any case the Sicilians had few reasons to feel content. Alberoni's Spain wanted to recover by force a kingdom that the Savoyards could not defend, while on the eastern front the appetites of the Austrians encamped in Calabria were whetted by the sight of the coast of Sicily. The situation of Astorga, in favor with the Savoyards, could have changed under the other two claimants. The Spaniards of Philip V might not have forgotten his pro-Imperial plot and certainly did not view favorably the merits he had acquired in Barcelona. The Austrians of Charles VI were possibly informed about his flight from Vienna.

---

[1] Tiby, *Astorga,* 106-107.

However, it does not seem that these risks worried the ex-adventurer who had now achieved baronial respectability. If it is true that in 1716 he pushed on to Rome (although he could have attained similar results by a letter), I am tempted to attribute to him an important role in the unforeseeable metamorphosis of Domenico Scarlatti to which the following document testifies:

Emancipation for Domenico Scarlatti

On the twenty-eighth day of the month of January of the X. Indiction 1717. Naples—Signor *Alessandro Scarlatti* the son of the late . . . well known to me presented himself personally before us asserting, and affirming, that Signor *Domenico Scarlatti* his son had repeatedly insisted also by means of letters written in due form, requesting that he wished to be emancipated from the Patria potestas, and freed from his paternal bonds, and that recognizing that these requests were just and reasonable, and he was ["not" inserted in the text, either by error or by ellipsis] willing to oblige and to satisfy him. Not being presently able to come to the City of Rome, where his said son resides, he decided[2] to appoint the undersigned as his Procurator with the faculties set forth here, in order to carry out these things voluntarily in our presence by every best way etc. has made, and constituted as his Procurator etc.[3] Signor Raimondo Scarlatti, another of his sons living in the said City of Rome absent but as if he were present so that he may appear personally in the name[4] of the said Signor Constituent [i.e., Alessandro] all the times that it may be necessary before whatsoever general and competent judge, and before the same he may emancipate according to the customs his aforesaid son Domenico from the authority and the fatherly power and free him and unbind him completely from the paternal bonds which tie him to the same Signor Constituent in such manner that, following the said Contract of emancipation of the said Signor Domenico his son, he may leave his former condition and be *homo sui juris,* obtaining in his own person all the rights and the goods and the things that he now has and in future will have and that he have power, administration, and usufruct and the dominion over his heirs and successors whatsoever, that he have full, free, and general faculty, authority, and power to do in general and in particular everything which an *homo sui juris* can do and that in the future he be capable of contracting and terminating business, making testaments, gifts among the living and by death, to buy and

[2] Typographical error ("decrecisse") in Prota Giurleo.
[3] Prota Giurleo's "per" arises from a mistaken resolution of the abbreviation for "etc."
[4] Although the "m" of "nominem" is omitted, "ad" takes the accusative.

sell, alienate, agree and settle, and he may bind himself and his
own heirs, their goods and rights, in favor of any Persons whatsoever, as also to pledge a guarantee, and to carry out anywhere the
other licit and honest acts, contracts, and terminations that an *homo
sui juris* can perform and to dispose and have[5] [juridical] capacity
[*Iudicio*] in court and out, as well as in cases and affairs of whatever sort in every best manner etc.[;] and that there must be transmitted and conceded to the said Signor Domenico his son who is to
be emancipated all the express faculties and authorities together
with all the other said necessary and opportune things etc.[;] and on
the basis of all these premises and in every single one of them to
ask, beg, and obtain from the said or from other Judges[6] to inter-
pose the Judicial Authority formally; and that it should be requested
and obtained that concerning the preceding one or more instrument
or instruments be made, registered, and notarized by any public
notaries that through the said Procurator may oblige the Constituent himself and his heirs to the observance and the inviolable fulfillment of what has preceded and has been promised and any right
whatsoever in the most ample and legally most severe form and R.
C. A. doing other things that previously were necessary and appropriate and that the Constituent himself would and could do if he
were personally present, even if they were such as to demand a
more detailed mandate of proxy, with respect to the one expressed
to those present ...

Giving, and conceding etc. promising etc. to have ratified, and
consequently has sworn etc. in Witness of which matter etc.

In the presence of the Notary Judge Jacopo Gerace of Naples
regio ad contractus, the Magnificent Alessandro Binni, Doctor of
Both Laws, and Filippo Genovese of Naples, witnesses etc.[7]

I was bewildered by the muddled notarial "latinorum" of the document, and on a second reading certain portions of the transcription seemed
suspect. Those ridiculous dots of omission replacing the baptismal name
of Alessandro's deceased father suggested the hypothesis that Prota
Giurleo was dealing with a rough draft and not the final notarial act.
However, after consulting the original document I have learned that in
eighteenth-century Naples a notary could permit himself liberties that

---

5 "valet," *recte* "valeat."

6 Prota Giurleo misread this as "Indice" et "Indiciariam."

7 Archivio Notarile di Napoli, Prot. Notaio Giovanni Tufarelli, Rep. 45, anno 1717, ff.
45-46. Transcribed with some errors in Prota Giurleo, *Palermitano,* 34-36; for the
Latin text see the Appendix.

today would get a lawyer into serious legal troubles costing him his license. By declaring that at the drawing up of the act there was actually present an Alessandro Scarlatti incapable of furnishing his father's first name, the notary Giovanni Tufarelli is caught red-handed in tampering with a public document.

I feared that the disasters of World War II or subsequent earthquakes would prohibit a verification that, instead, I was able to complete after some false starts. The xerox of a document written out in beautiful calligraphy—which I give in a corrected transcription (see Appendix)—clarifies some of my doubts and has permits the correction of some of Prota Giurleo's mistakes A few of these slips—a meaningless "decrecisse," the missing "n" of "constituit"—are clearly typographical errors. The worthy pioneer of Scarlatti research did not have the aid of the photocopies that today allow us to check and re-check our texts without leaving our desks. The one thing of which he is guilty is the misreading of an abbreviation that inverts the real situation: only by substituting "etc." for the "per" transcribed by Prota Giurleo is it possible to restore to Raimondo Scarlatti the role of procurator assigned to him by his father.

It remains to interpret the absurd "non dignetur" that appears clearly in the original document, which the eminent latinist Prof. Marco Grondona suggests represents another bit of sloppiness by the scribe. We need only read "non *indignetur*" ("that he *not* disdain") to restore logical coherence to the text. If the document had been drawn up by Alessandro himself, Freud would have provided a clear justification for that negation. It is simpler to imagine a number of distractions for the scribe and his employer—not to mention a present/absent Alessandro, the other notary Gerace and the witnesses, at least one of whom was familiar with Latin, since he described himself as "Doctor of Both Laws" (i.e., Canon and Civil). This *locus desperatus* of the text has determined the unfavorable emphasis that all Alessandro's biographers—I more than the others—have placed on the father sullenly reluctant to sacrifice his own anachronistic rights as a *paterfamilias*. Evaluating this new information, I maintain that even if certain appearances had to be saved with regard to his other children, papa Scarlatti had understood that at least on this occasion Domenico had to be satisfied. The scenario of insistences and denials in the document emphasises the disagreements between the two parties, the same type of scenario encountered in the acts drawn up by the Astorgas in those years. If Domenico did indeed send "letters written in due form" to his father, reading the two pieces of his writing (the preface to the *Essercizi* and his urbane letter to the Duke of Huescar) that have come down to us leaves a keen regret for the loss of Domenico's "epistolae.".

Misled by the current interpretation, I had always considered the state of subordination in which Alessandro Scarlatti kept his "eaglet" as the consequence of obscure misdeeds (ruinous losses at gambling?) committed by Domenico in his youth. I maintained that in expending all his authority to save his son from some difficulty, Alessandro had assumed an iron control over Domenico's actions. The truth is much less fanciful. I owe to Prof. Bernardo Albanese and to Dr. Roberto Berna, whom I thank, the solution of the problem that the emancipation of a celebrated man of thirty-one poses to someone like me, who lacks an extensive familiarity with the legal code.

The situation of *filius familias* [son of a household], of *homo non sui juris* [a man not independent] —of a person therefore deprived of juridical capability—was a perfectly normal one in the eighteenth century. A law derived from the Code of Justinian stipulated that, in the absence of an explicit renunciation, the *patria potestas* expired only on the death of the father. Even if we discount the repeated insistences that the document implies, Domenico had good reasons to request something that did not arouse his father's enthusiasm. Although less haughty than I had depicted him, Alessandro still remains the man who boasted of having manipulated his brilliant son like a puppet, "detaching him by force" from Naples and then "sending him away from Rome." The authoritarian attitude of his Sicilian mentality was supported by the legal situation that I have described.

Now that Domenico was an independent *homo sui juris,* he did nothing different. He was no longer obliged to give Alessandro an account of his earnings and expenses, but we would be wrong to believe that his new status also carried with it artistic independence: as Kirkpatrick wrote,[8] the younger Scarlatti had to wait a long time for that. In order to check on the new behavior of his liberated slave, a few months after having swallowed the bitter juridical pill Alessandro took one of his customary leaves of absence to go off to Rome where his *Telemaco* was to be staged at the Teatro Capranica, in competition with *Berenice, regina d'Egitto,* an opera that Domenico had composed in collaboration with Porpora for the same theater.

It has been widely assumed that Domenico's new status was related to the trip to England that he announced by leaving his prestigious post at the Cappella Giulia in 1719.[9] My discoveries in Palermo

---

[8] Kirkpatrick, *Scarlatti,* 65.

[9] Ibid. He quotes the Diari (3 Sept. 1719) of the Cappella Giulia in the Archivio Capitolare di San Pietro: complete text of the annotation on 333-44.

gave a different geographical and human destination to his flight from Rome, but a Spanish document published by Kirkpatrick suggested that Domenico's desire for independence might have more plausible justifications.

The *Historia de familia y mi ultima voluntad* written around 1912 by Carlos Scarlatti—a direct descendant of Domenico who drew his information not only from documents but also from the oral tradition of the family—attributed to our musician a marriage disapproved of by his father:

> His marriage caused displeasure to his father, who was a famous musician and lived in Florence, capital of the Grand Duchy of Tuscany, the source of his possessions and title of Baron, with the honors and coronet of a Duke. Until a few years ago his palace in Florence still existed, with his arms over the door, but the Italian government disputed it along with its dependencies [en sus dependencias]. He was born in Naples and his wife D.a Catalina Gentili Rossetti [was born] in Rome (second marriage) [...].[10]

Kirkpatrick dismissed the information the manuscript furnishes about Domenico as "very inaccurate." In the light of other discoveries of mine I was not prepared to discard all that Carlos Scarlatti tells us, the more so since Alessandro could be identified as the "músico celebre," capable of "disgusto" in the face of a marriage of which he disapproved. The description of the Florentine sojourn was less persuasive, even if the title of baron was one of the gifts that the "most fortunate abate [Pompeo] Scarlatti" had bestowed on the members of his family, according to Valesio.[11] One might suppose that the lapse of time and Carlos' desire to transfer the coat of arms to his own ancestors had led him to muddle up his parade of coronets and palaces. The information concerning the disputed marriage seemed to be factual, since it was confirmed by the "segundas nupcias" in parentheses beside the note of what all previous biographers had considered to be Domenico's first marriage.

My hypothesis turned out to be incorrect, although Kirkpatrick was mistaken in discrediting the picturesque *Historia* completely. Alessandro was not the only "músico celebre" in the Scarlatti family. Quite unexpectedly we find a Domenico Scarlatti intent on unloading on an eighteen-year-old son—called Alexandro, as it happens—the same kind of coercion he had suffered from his own father! Documentation discovered in Spain confirms that there was a contested marriage, but the father little disposed to indulge the desires of his son was actually

[10] Kirkpatrick, *Scarlatti,* 359.
[11] Valesio, *Diario* II, 695-696.

the sixty-eight-year-old Domenico, so obstinate in his opposition as to force Alexandro into a rash "matrimonio segreto."[12]

But I do not wish to anticipate the narration of events that belong in the twilight phase of Domenico Scarlatti's human experience. Le us return to the Palermitan adventures of the Baron of Astorga, who was now preparing to bid farewell to bachelorhood.

Don Emanuello owed a great deal to his mother, to the generous sister who had given a part of her income to him, and even to the memory of the blustering old baron who had left him a title and a fief. He had a dynastic duty to carry out, and the choice of a bride—a girl of barely fifteen, the daughter of a baron from Augusta—shows how much influence the members of the family must have had in so important a decision. Emanuela Guzzardi e Nicolaci, daughter of the Baron of San Giorgio, had a dowry of 2,800 *onze*, of which 1,800 were in money and 1,000 in jewels, furnishings, and furniture. In the marriage acts the bridegroom promised to

> receive the said lady as his bride and to treat her well and consider her his dear and beloved wife and to betroth her and espouse her under the benediction of the church which must follow the Lord permitting in the month of October p.v. [*proximi venturi*=of the next] 1717 and to administer well and preserve the said dowry and dower objects and in case of restitution *seu* separation of the present marriage and in any other case of restitution *statim et incute integre et indiminute* [immediately and entire and undiminished] and without any diminution to the said bride."[13]

Tiby could not find the marriage act, but it must have taken place on the date stipulated, because on October 14 the first installment of the dowry was paid punctually. In normal times the ceremony would have had a particularly solemn character, for in that year Don Emanuello held the office of Senator of Palermo. But the happy event took place in a larger context where everything that added solemnity to religious rites had harsh consequences for the priests involved, because of the papal interdict following the so-called "Liparian controversy."[14] This turned into a fierce controversy opposing the rights and attitudes of the crown

12 Beryl Kenyon de Pascual, "Domenico Scarlatti and his Son Alexandro's Inheritance," in *Music & Letters* 69 (1988), 23-29.

13 Tiby, *Astorga,* 107.

14 Cf. the exhaustive account in chapter IV ("L'amara cioccolata di monsignor Riggio") of *Sicilia ed Europa dal 1700 al 1735* by Luigi Riccobene (Palermo: Sellerio, n. d. [1976]). From that distant episode Leonardo Sciascia drew the inspiration for his *Recitazione della controversia*

of Sicily (upheld more proudly than over in the Savoyard era, with the increased persecution of priests loyal to the papal directives) to the reactionary immobility of certain elements in the Sicilian clergy. The clergy were inhumanly encouraged to resist the state by a pope more disposed to fulminate excommunications than to heal a schism that continued to have sad consequences in divided loyalties. At the time that the baron held office, the persecution of priests who absented themselves from official ceremonies in which those who had been excommuncated participated reached its height. Not a day passed but some of these martyrs of the faith were sent into exile by stern Savoyard officials who found in the policeman Matteo Lo Vecchio a zealous instrument for their persecutions. As often happens, however, the law was not the same for everyone. Canon Mongitore, for example, was too universally respected for the governors to risk a confrontation. When the persecution came too close to Mongitore, Lo Vecchio, who directed the harassment of the ecclesiastics, informed him that he would not be bothered if he gave up his post of confessor in ordinary to the monastery of Santa Elisabetta (which required him to take part in processions) and retired to the country.

Mongitore, to whom we owe among other things the *reportage* revealing the violent excesses of Astorga senior, had remained loyal to Rome, but he certainly had no vocation for martyrdom. Past the age of fifty, the inconveniences of an exile that would have separated him from his books and notebooks must have made him very uneasy. He took Lo Vecchio's hint by taking to the *maquis* in a country retreat of his at the foot of Monte Caputo, not far from Palermo. There he received the startling news that the Senate of his city had named him its *secretario*. When he was sounded out in advance, Mongitore

> resolutely answered that he did not wish to accept such an honor, since he did not wish to be thrust into new occasions where he would be obliged to take part in processions and to be present in chapel services with the senate. Without further notice, the Senate made their decision: they sent him the news at Caputo. He returned to Palermo, and since he did not wish on any account to accept, he was assured by D. Emmanuele Rincon d'Astorga baron of Ogliastro, senator, in the name of the senate, that he would not be bothered, or constrained to go to chapel services and processions; since before the election his reluctances had been considered, to which he added his entreaties, as did also the *praetor*. With this condition he accepted the honor offered to him and took possession of the office."[15]

---

[15] Antonio Mongitore, *Diario palermitano;* see Di Marzo, *Biblioteca Storica e Letteraria di Sicilia,* VIII, 276-277.

Honors awarded to a worthy individual often offend the unworthy: so it was in this case. Some runner-up for the post informed the viceroy. Count Maffei, whom the *praetor* failled to placate, was enraged and threatened to exile the trembling canon within two hours if he did not participate in the solemn procession that was part of the festivities of Santa Rosalia. After many negotiations, Mongitore was able to avoid the viceroy's anger by renouncing this inconvenient dignity.

Although processions and religious solemnities remained exposed to such serious inconveniences and hindrances, musical life continued to find its most natural outlet in the theater despite the dangers of war. The *Bibliografia Siciliana* of Giuseppe Mira furnishes the titles of some texts for music from this period, 1717-1718, attributed to an obscure Giuseppe de Pasquale. They merit a few lines of comment:

—La pazienza in cimento, ovvero il santo Eustachio, opera sacra in -4o. Palermo, 1717./—Il Totila in Roma, dialogo, in -4o. Palermo 1717./—Il Sebeucio, dialogo, in -4o. Palermo 1717./—La Perfidia punita, dialogo, in -4o. Palermo 1718.[16]

The alternative title confirms that *La pazienza in cimento* might have been a "dialogue," the designation that the libretti of the period gave to compositions performed with music in Sicilian churches, halfway between the cantata and the oratorio. But the phrase "sacred opera" leaves open the possibility that it is an opera on a sacred subject staged during Lent at the Teatro Santa Cecilia. *Il Totila in Roma* and *Il Seleuco,* two operas presented in the same years in other Italian theaters, are operas, not "dialogues."[17] Despite the seriousness of a local situation further aggravated by the arrival of the Spaniards and the threats of the Austrians, the inhabitants of Palermo could not give up their operatic spectacles.

On 1 July 1718 the Palermitans crowded their celebrated promenade on the seashore, their curiosity aroused by an extraordinary sight: the bay was full of sailing ships headed toward the east. It was the Spanish fleet, which Victor Amadeus had written to Maffei to welcome in a friendly manner, even to furnishing provisions and refreshments in order to facilitate their undertaking against the Austrians in Naples.

The reconquest of the kingdom of Naples was certainly one of Alberoni's objectives. However, he had sent off those five hundred sail-

---

16 Giuseppe Mira, *Bibliografia Siciliana,* (Palermo: Gaudiano, 1881), II, 189.
17 Although Mira clearly had fairly precise topographic references, I do not believe that his information is first hand, as witness the alteration of *Seleuco* to *Sebeucio* and the designation "dialogue" added to two obvious operas (or two prologues added to operas with these titles). Only the recovery of the libretti could furnish other details.

ing ships from Barcelona with sealed orders for the Marquis of Lede, commander of the fleet and of the formidable army which it transported. Only in Sardinia, where the marquis was authorized to open the packet, did he learn the goal of so powerful a warlike expedition: Sicily was to be retaken.

After the disembarkation of the troops had revealed the error of those who believed the fleet was friendly, the aristocrats of Palermo were able to convince Maffei to locate his attempted resistance far from the capital of the island: Palermo must not be damaged by the bombardments. The Piedmontese certainly had not made themselves loved, and the increase of financial pressure willed by their king had prompted the Sicilians to create the anagram *Victorius Amadeus=Cor eius est avidum*. The negotiations with the captain general of Philip V's army were quick and easy. The Marquis of Lede welcomed the ambassadors of the Senate with great courtesy, and the agreement that was drawn up showed that the city was ready to receive the victor as its new viceroy.

Except for the cannonades of Castello a Mare, where a Piemontese garrison had barricaded itself, Palermo virtually changed masters without being aware of it. Even the siege was merely a matter of form, since everyone had agreed to spare the city and its citizens. On July 13 the Piedmontese finally hoisted a white flag, barely in time to keep their cannonades from mixing with the fireworks for the traditional celebrations of Santa Rosalia, which the Marquis of Lede could see comfortably from the Royal Palace. Instead of the procession, blocked by a torrential rain, the viceroy transformed his visit to the Palace of the Senate into a sort of musical entertainment, listening to the musicians together with the assembled nobility.

Palermo had become Spanish again. In this situation, Astorga could not profit from his own musical abilities: the circumstances obliged him to remain a baron.

The Marquis of Lede may not have known about Don Emanuello's Austro-Catalan past (although it is more likely that he did not pay much attention to it), since the latter remained afloat in the public life of Spanish Palermo. From 1718 to 1720 the baron was named hospitaller of San Bartolomeo degli Incurabili. In the same years, his attempt to discharge his dynastic duties brought into the world two useless baby girls: Maria Giovanna (born 24 February 1719) and Giovanna Anna Maria (born 20 August 1720).

In the meantime the war had arrived at the gates of Palermo. Having taken possession of the northeast zone of Sicily, the Austrians pressed on with their victorious armies, but on 2 May 1720, after a bloody combat, news arrived of the Peace of the Hague, which assigned the island to the Empire. The Marquis of Lede received orders to turn affairs over to Count di Mercy, commander of the attacking army, until an Austrian viceroy could arrive to rule Sicily in the name of Charles VI. The people of Palermo, who had been present at the preparations for the battle invoking the protection of heaven on the arms of Spain from the walls of the city, wept at the news. With all the limitations that history has pitilessly exposed, the government of Spain remained the one most acceptable to the Sicilians.

It is understandable that such sad events had negative effects on theatrical activities. Perhaps the Palermitans did without operatic spectacles in 1719. Misled by an incorrect reference, I maintained that in that same year an unusual prosperity had allowed the Unione di Santa Cecilia to finance and execute the sumptuous stucco decorations conceived by Giacomo Serpotta for an oratory that the Musici had previously employed temporarily, "Santa Maria di Tutte le Grazie sotto titolo del Ponticello" (Saint Mary of All the Graces under the title of the Little Bridge). For these years it is right to restore the monument—and the credit for its splendid decorations—to the Compagnia of S. Maria delle Grazie.

The recovery of a pamphlet[18] cited incorrectly by Carandente[19] has re-established a "truth" which counterposes the glorious magnificence of that monument against the squalor of the times. The pamphlet, *Le Meraviglie in prospetto,* which describes Serpotta's artistic program, makes no mention of the Unione di Santa Cecilia and ascribes the occasion entirely to the Compagnia di S. Maria:

> *Dialogue in five voices and several instruments to be sung in the Venerable Company of St. Mary of all the Graces ... for the Solemnity of the Perpetual 40. Hours With a short synopsis of the Concepts of the stories set up in the said Temple ... Set in Music by Padre Gio: Gaetano Perez of the Third Order of St. Francis. In Palermo ... 1719.*

18 *Le Meraviglie in prospetto. Dialogo á cinque voci e più stromenti da cantarsi nella venerabile Compagnia di S. Maria di tutte le Grazie sotto titolo del Ponticello per la Sollennità delle 40. Ore Circolari Con un breve argomento dell'idea delle storie in detto Tempio inalzate. Posto in note del Padre Gio: Gaetano Perez del Terz'Ordine di S. Francesco. In Palermo Nella regia Stamperia d'Antonio Epiro,* 1719, attached by Mongitore to his ms. which treats *Chiese di Compagnie,* now in the Biblioteca Comunale of Palermo (Qq E9, ff. 155-156).

19 Giovanni Carandente, *Giacomo Serpotta (*Turin: ERI, n. d. [1966]), 78 and n. 142 (101).

Without the documentation of the payments to the artisans, published by Meli[20] and repeated by Garstang in his detailed study of
Serpotta,[21] I would have asssumed that one of the customary typographical errors had misdated the libretto: Mongitore, who carefully included
in his *Diario* any notice of religious celebrations, does not mention the
solemn ceremony that the pamphlet commemorates. Although he discusses at length the Company to whom the credit of the restoration and
of the adornments is really due,[22] he ignores this prominent artistic initiative which the printed account states was concluded by the sodality in
the same year that the learned canon gave his volume to the printer.

Now that we have ascertained that the Musici—aside from the
few involved in the performance of the dialogue by Perez—did not participate in the solemn ceremony, the hypothesis that it was sponsored by
Astorga, now in favor in Palermo, also collapses.

Let us return to Rome, where finally Domenico Scarlatti is taking advantage of the emancipation he extorted from his father. A brief
note by the *puntatore* Francesco Colignani (from a *Diario* in the archive
of the Cappella Giulia of San Pietro in Vaticano) informs us that on 3
September 1718:

> Since the sig. Scarlatti Maestro di Cappella of S. Pietro has left for
> England, sig. Ottavio Pitoni, who was at S. Giovanni in Laterano,
> has been made maestro.[23]

Domenico could have been attracted to London in those years
for many reasons. We have already seen that in 1719 Francesco, the ill-
fated "brother to the famous Allessandro Scarlatti," was active in the
English capital; Handel was in favor in London; since 1713 the faithful
Roseingrave, back in his native land, had been laying the foundations
for what would be called "the English cult of Domenico Scarlatti," which
from the beginning had its center in London.

Kirkpatrick recognized that Domenico's presence in Lisbon on
various occasions did not contradict the possibility that on 30 May 1720
the composer was in London when the curtain rose on *Narciso* "in the
royal Theater of the Haymarket." However, he nevertheless cast serious

---

[20] Filippo Meli, *Giacomo Serpotta* (Palermo, 1934), 37-38.

[21] Donald Garstang, *Giacomo Serpotta and the Stuccatori of Palermo 1560-1790*
(London: Zwemmer, 1984) 265-267. Garstang states that "Of all the destroyed
decorations by Serpotta, this was the most important. . ."

[22] Antonio Mongitore, *Palermo divoto*, I, 352-360.

[23] Quoted in Giuseppe Baini, *Memorie storico-critiche della vita e delle opere di
Giovanni Pierluigi da Palestrina* (Rome, 1828) II, 280, n. 623.

doubt on the journey.[24]   Jane Clark,[25] on the other hand, gave full credit to the notice in the Vatican *Diario*. She justified Scarlatti's absence from the premiere of his opera (which was directed by Roseingrave, who had provided the customary changes and additions)[26] by Domenico's desire not to compete with Handel, whose *Radamisto* was to be performed the same season.   Boyd[27] described as "highly conjectural" both the musician's presence in London and his sudden departure. Learning of my Palermitan discoveries, he formulated a yet more picturesque hypothesis: ruined by his notorious weakness for gambling, Domenico might have followed a suggestion by his uncle Francesco, who indicated Palermo as a hiding-place with opportunities for work and one where his creditors could not reach him.

A document discovered and recently published by Edward Corp[28] offers new support for the hypothesis of Domenico's planned move to England. The Continental wanderings of James Stuart, Catholic claimant to the British throne in exile, greatly influenced his changing musical tastes. Corp documents the passage of Stuart, the so-called "Chevalier Saint Georges," from his initial enjoyment of French music to the "full immersion" in the Italian style in which he took every possible opportunity to satisfy the passion for opera nurtured by his long stays in Italy.[29]

The diary of David Nairne,[30] secretary of the unsuccessful Pretender, furnishes further details, the most interesting of which confirms Domenico's vocal capabilities previously known only from the discoveries in Lisbon. The stay in Rome to which the diary refers lasted from 22 May to 17 July 1717.[31] Nairne lists a series of visits to churches for sumptuous religious celebrations enriched by appropriate music during those eight weeks. Cardinals Pamphilj and Ottoboni competed as usual, organizing entertainments of the highest level, but it was Princess Teresa

---

[24] Kirkpatrick, *Scarlatti,* 66.

[25] Jane Clark, "His own worst enemy," *Early Music* IV (1976), 532-547.

[26] Burney, *General,* II, 703.

[27] Boyd, *Scarlatti,* 30.

[28] Edward Corp, "Music at the Stuart Court at Urbino, 1717-1718," *Music & Letters* 81 (2000), 351-363, 355.

[29] Ibid., 366. In a letter of 28 December 1717 the Duke of Mar speaks explicitly of a "conversion to Italian music."

[30] *Journal du séjour de S.M.B. à Rome*, Oxford, Bodleian Library, MS. 208, fols.338-356.

[31] During a later and longer stay in the Eternal City, the Pretender gave a flamboyant

Albani, niece of Clement XI, who offered the rarest discovery to James Stuart. In her palace on 3 June 1717 "Mr. Scarlatti le jeune, grand musicien, joua du clavessin et chanta" ("the younger M. Scarlatti, great musician, played the harpsichord and sang").

Without consulting Italian sources that took the success of the expedition to Scotland almost for granted, Corp considered the possibility that Domenico Scarlatti had been called to direct the opera theater of London in the case of a Jacobite restoration. Underestimating an important detail, he missed the solution of the enigma posed by the *Diario Colignani*. I have a new hypothesis, strengthened by the pope's support that was intended to transform the "Chevalier Saint Georges" into James III. In Rome the invasion of Protestant England was felt to be a sort of crusade destined to succeed by divine protection. Only the prudence of a wise cardinal had induced the pope to wait until the armada was firmly installed in Scotland before transforming his announced support into potentially ruinous financing. As in an epic poem, it was Neptune who upset all the predictions. A lethal storm scattered the Spanish fleet, forcing it to turn back and abandon the enterprise.

Perhaps the same lack of reflection that had led the Scarlattis to so many hasty decisions impelled Domenico to leave the Cappella Giulia before being sure of his new situation in England. His destination provides an additional indication. The diary does not mention London and we should remember that the projected invasion was to start in Scotland. According to the Vatican diary, Domenico had already "left for England." He was reached on his journey with the news of the naval disaster. It is not difficult to imagine him mortified by the setback: at least as discouraged as Alessandro must have been, when his abandonment of the Neapolitan treadmill had not resulted in the hoped-for employment in Florence, or the unlucky Pietro, when death had prevented Cardinal Grimani from keeping his promise to enroll him in the Royal Chapel of Naples. In such uncertainty, before the possibility of Lisbon appeared, an employment in Palermo might have materialized. Such employment would have been subsequently respected by João V, satisfied by his brilliant raids on the musical chapels of Rome.

I am resigned to the censure of critics who resist the hypothesis that Domenico was active in the musical life of Palermo. I merely re-

---

boost to the activity of the opera theaters, his name appearing on most dedications of printed libretti. In the meantime, he had married Princess Clementina Sobieski, whom we last saw as a little girl reclining on a cushion at the feet of Maria Casimira, her grandmother, in the two ceremonial *mises-en-scène* presented by the ex-queen of Poland.

state the facts and quote the documents that I have discovered, without concealing my own doubts about such casual mobility in a man of the eighteenth century whom various documents show as frail and sickly.

The first mention of a "Dominicus Scarlatti"—enrolled in the Unione di Santa Cecilia in Palermo and therefore a musician—indicates his presence on 16 April 1720. This was an important meeting during which the superior, the two associates, and fifty-eight other musicians "uti major pars confratrum illius venerabilis Unionis" ("as the majority of the members of that venerable Union") modified the provisions of a statute that had proven to be entirely inadequate.[32]

Was this the Domenico that we know?

Portuguese glories of a delayed Ulysses

Before the discoveries of Professor Doederer[33] enriched the history of Domenico Scarlatti's activity in Portugal with new and reliable data, Domenico's journey to London and his visits in Palermo offered the biographer only a few reference-points in the "black hole" between his departure from Rome and his appearances in Lisbon. Now all the material must be re-examined on a different basis, but I believe—as I have written in the preface to this volume—that this new information only modifies in certain details the biographical span that I have hypothesized.

Doederer's discoveries might have validated the visit to London in 1720, which, however, does not fit with the Jacobite hypothesis that I find convincing. In any case, one must give weight to an important circumstance that biographers have undervalued. The date recorded by Colignani in the Vatican *Diario* refers to the appointment of a successor and is therefore only a *terminus post quem* with respect to Domenico's departure. He had ample time to undertake the journey that should have carried him across the Channel, to interrupt it, and to change destination.

On 12 September 1719 the Lisbon Nunciature recorded the great preparations for the "Musicians, who are momentarily awaited here from

---

32 Acts of the notary Gioacchino Miraglia on the same date, Palermo, Archivio di Stato—Notai defunti.

33 The detailed examination of forty-one volumes of *relazioni* sent to Rome from the Nunciature in Lisbon furnished material for two important contributions: Gerhard Doederer, "Aspectos novos em torno da estadia de Domenico Scarlatti na corte de D. João V (1719-1727)," preface to *Libro di Tocate Per Cembalo di Domenico Scarlatti* (Lisbon, 1991 [hereafter Doederer 1991]); Gerhard Doederer and Cremilde Rosado Fernandes, "A Música da Sociedade Joanina nos relatórios da nunciatúra apostólica em Lisboa (1706-1750), in *Revista Portuguesa de Musicologia* III (1993), 69-146. [hereafter Doederer 1993]

Rome, nationals as well as those of the Cappella Pontificia, and others." João V had furnished

> with his customary royal generosity [...] a large house near the Church of Loreto, in which they will be maintained for a month at the King's expense, after which they must see to maintaining themselves with their assigned salaries.[34]

The first nine musicians, who arrived by sea on September 14, fulfilled a vow to St. Philip Neri a week later, singing a solemn mass in the Patriarchal Basilica. Participating in the performance—at the King's expense, naturally—was "a fine Chorus according to the custom of Italy." The chorus received great approval, except from "the other musicians of the Country," who vented their "customary jealousy by reason of their tenacious attachment to their own things." Gratified by the large public attendance, João V distributed a thousand *scudi* to the Italian musicians. He also threatened severe punishments when he was informed that the curiosity aroused by the castrati—a novelty on the Portuguese scene— was followed by scorn, fomented by the slighted "national Musicians."[35]

It is significant that the king derived his greatest satisfaction from the "performances in plainchant in the manner of the Cappella Pontificia." In these, passages performed in Gregorian (sung by Portuguese musicians who had been sent to Rome to familiarize themselves with this special style) alternated with polyphony sung by the Italians.

João V may have had his heart set on transplanting Roman practice to the sacred music performed in Lisbon. However, his royal bride—the daughter of Leopold I of Austria, a musician endowed with a deep humanistic culture—had found a providential ally in Don Antonio (the king's brother who would discover in Domenico an extraordinary teacher) for promoting secular musical performances.[36] We should not be surprised, therefore, at the casual versatility of those Italian musicians. Having aided João V in immersing himself in the sonorities of the Roman liturgy,

> the same night [they] diverted Their Majesties with lovely cantatas, accompanied by various Instruments, to the great pleasure of the Royal House, and especially Her Majesty the queen, who understands and composes in music perfectly.[37]

[34] Archivio Segreto Vaticano, Segreteria di Stato-Portugallo [hereafter ASV-Port.], vol. 75, f. 209.

[35] ASV-Port., vol. 75, f. 215.

[36] Cfr. Doederer 1993, 76.

[37] ASV-Port., vol. 75, f. 215.

At the end of September the "musicians of the Cappella Pontificia" received the pay established by the King: sixty *scudi* for each of them, "from the first day that they were engaged." The same pay was credited to the others, but it was later reduced to fifty *scudi* a month. The poison of their Portuguese colleagues was ineffective. The musicians were welcomed everywhere and worked their way into Lisbon life (a few days after their arrival, they went to applaud two aristocrats who took part in a bullfight). They drew further earnings from occasional services that D. João made possible by consenting to additional activities.[38]

But the days passed, and the most eagerly awaited musician still delayed his arrival in Lisbon. The papal Nuncio dictated to his secretary:

> The Maestro di cappella Scarlatti, and the musicians Mossi [Roman tenor], and Floriano [castrato *discantista*], who still have not arrived, are anxiously awaited by the King.[39]

On October 22, the King's birthday, three of the Italian musicians sang in the Queen's apartments

> a beautiful serenata [...] the same one, that the Marquês d'Abrantes had had sung in Rome.[40]

This is a valuable bit of information. The unnamed composer of the music is Domenico Scarlatti, who had written it five years before, in his post as "maestro di cappella of his excellency," to celebrate the birth of the future king, José I. The fact that an *Applauso genetliaco* could be transformed into a *Triunfos de Ulysses & Glorias de Portugal* says a lot about the recycling possible with serenatas. Boyd rightly considered the involvement of Ulysses and Circe as "nothing more than a long and elaborate diversion,"[41] but Scarlatti had been farsighted in setting a text that could be adapted without difficulty to celebrate either the birthday of an infant in swaddling clothes or that of a sovereign. The serenade, whose music has been lost, must have been selected in order to prepare the terrain for the Portuguese glories of Domenico/Ulysses, at that point still a wanderer.

But now there has come onstage—on tiptoe— one of the builders of the musical bridge between Rome and Portugal: the Marquês de Fontes, newly created Marquês d'Abrantes. So discreet an entry is

---

38 ASV-Port., vol. 75, fols. 225-226.

39 ASV-Port., vol. 75, fol. 226.

40 ASV-Port., vol. 75, fol. 241v. D. Rodrigo Annes de Sà, Almeida, and Menezes, Marchese de Fontes, ambassador extraordinary of João V to the papal court, was named Marchese of Abrantes after his return to his country.

41 Boyd, *Scarlatti,* 107.

scarcely appropriate for the personage who amazed Rome with the splendor of the carriages he commissioned for his installation (which later would be used by the queen in Lisbon). But the real manipulator who contrived to transfer the best musicians of the Cappella Giulia to Lisbon was D. Andrea Mello de Castro, Fontes' predecessor. Mello had remained in Rome for the entire period of Fontes' special embassy, at the end of which he returned to the title and functions of Portuguese Ambassador.

Around 20 November 1719 Mossi and Floriano arrived in Lisbon, "His Majesty awaiting with impatience the arrival of Signor Scarlatti, who is to be the Head, and director of all his music at the Patriarchal Basilica."[42]

The King's anxiety had turned to impatience. Before Corp's article suggested the considerations already mentioned I wondered if Alessandro had not inspired in his son a similar delay, by traveling overland, in taking up an employment that was much more remunerative and satisfying than his father's. Now, in the light of the "Jacobite" hypothesis, the risks of the state of war, and the hurricanes that had lashed the Spanish fleet would have weighed against a sea voyage. Domenico was after all a nephew of that Francesco Scarlatti who the Viennese documents inform us miraculously escaped shipwreck in his flight from Sicily.

Finally, at the beginning of December the Nuncio communicated:

> On the 29th of last month there arrived happily at this Court Signor Scarlatti, travelling by Post, and he has already had the honor of making Their Majesties hear his virtù."

We would expect to find this "virtù" embodied in a spectacular performance at the keyboard, but the account does not mention this. Instead, it presents us with a sort of comedy of misdirection, with Domenico in a surprisingly unaccustomed role as the object of "a most singular honor" on the part of the queen. Not at all intimidated by a direct confrontation with the greatest harpsichordist of all time, Maria Anna of Portugal "wished to accompany him at the Harpsichord while he sang."[43]

The documentation by Doederer does not only establish the arrival date of the "anxiously" awaited Scarlatti. Nothing that we knew even recently could have led us to imagine the vocal performances by Domenico that Corp's discovery now shows were anticipated two years

---

[42] ASV-Port., vol. 75, fol. 262.
[43] ASV-Port., vol. 75, fol. 272.

earlier in Rome. These gleams of light make us lament that such information emerging from the darkness of centuries is not more detailed. Nonethess, Domenico Scarlatti's performing venues no longer appear a luxurious sepulcher to which he was condemned by his function as mentor to a princess of genius—the *maestro di cappella* transformed into a master of refined private ceremonies by his years in Spain. In Rome there had been no queen disposed to play the harpsichord to accompany our versatile musician, and Scarlatti had to do it himself. Perhaps in Lisbon a pinch of courtly astuteness induced Domenico to profit by the honor that the queen reserved for him, and to limit his debut to an area that left the thousand devils who had astonished Roseingrave in their infernal home. This is pure fantasy on my part: the displays of virtuosity had only been postponed, but this putative choice coincides fully with the episodes of modest "understatement" that punctuate the biography of our musician.

　　　Successive *relazioni* confirm that Scarlatti immediately had a new task: that of refining the musical talent of the Infante D. Antonio, the King's brother. We also learn that previously "Scarlattino, most singular Professor of music recently arrived here"[44] had taken lodgings, together with other musicians, in the large house put at their disposal by the King, but then he and Mossi had been granted the privilege of separate houses "and the convenience of coaches," as well as the gift of "a Jewel of about four hundred *scudi*."[45]

　　　I am unsure about the significance of the diminutive: was Domenico called "Scarlattino" because he was spindly or short? Or was he compared unfavorably with papa-Scarlattone (big Scarlatti) even in Portugal? João V would never have fed Domenico's inferiority complex. As Kirkpatrick pointed out, for a king who had obtained permission from the pope to celebrate mass, it must have been extremely important to have the ex-director of the Cappella Giulia in his own service.[46] Was it so important as to allow Domenico to leave Lisbon— perhaps once a year?—in the periods least marked by solemn ceremonies and by the festivities that required the most sumptuous court celebrations?

　　　The reports of the nuncio and the *Gazeta de Lisboa* contain no further news concerning Domenico Scarlatti until 24 June 1720. The possibility of a first journey would fit here. So soon after Domenico's arrival in Lisbon it could be justified only by the king's consent, as well

---

[44] ASV-Port., vol.75, fol. 278v.
[45] ASV-Port., vol. 75, fol. 300.
[46] Kirkpatrick, *Scarlatti*, 68.

as by the court mourning (and consequent restriction of musical perfor-mances) to which the *relazioni* of the Nunciature repeatedly refer.[47]

The data discovered by Doederer show that I was certainly in error when I maintained that our hero had gone to Palermo from Rome before coming to harbor in Lisbon. Neither date is incompatible with those in the *relazioni* of the Nunciature or in the *Gazeta de Lisboa* mark-ing the presence in Portugal of the musician whom the king had been so anxious to secure. The first mention finds "Dominicus" in Palermo on 16 April 1720, involved in voting for the change in the statutes of the organization, together with another fifty-eight musicians "uti major pars confratrum illius venerabilis Unionis." The date does not contradict the attendance registered in the Vatican Archive or the notices that subse-quently appeared in the *Gazeta de Lisboa*.[48]

In maintaining the possibility of Domenico's long sojourn in the land of his ancestors, I supposed that the indication of the *Diario* of San Pietro was deliberately misleading. There were logical reasons for such an interpretation. First of all, the intention might have been to disguise a departure in a direction unpleasing to the papal Curia. Sicily was certainly such a direction while the "Liparitan controversy" was raging. Portugal could have been another. Although the king pharaonically sank the gold from Brazil into acquiring indulgences and ecclesiastical privileges, he also used it to hire away the Papal Chapel's most famous musicians by offering salaries that were more than competitive. How-ever, the Vatican documents betray no hostility toward the fugitives. Perhaps the operation was even carried out with the connivance of the Roman Curia, wishing to heal dissensions arising from the notorious question of the Chinese rites—the concessions to local customs that the Jesuits deemed necessary for the conversion of China to Christianity.

The Curia, troubled by such concessions, called for the restora-tion of orthodoxy. However, their rigor could not meet favor with a na-tion like Portugal, whose commerical activities in the Far East were be-ing actively developed. Although the break between the Curia and Por-tugal turned out to be inevitable, for the moment the Church attempted to satisfy the pious spendthrift ruler, when possible. The artistic drain from San Pietro at least transferred to Portugal "the manner of the Cappella Pontificia," satisfying João V's ardent desire.[49]   The priest-

---

[47]ASV-Port., vol. 75, f. 374.

[48] Atti del notaio Gioacchino Miraglia, 16 April 1720 and 9 December 1722, Archivio di Stato di Palermo-Notai defunti.

[49] ASV-Port., vol. 74, f. 440, and vol. 75, ff. 4-5, f. 209v, f. 215r-v.

king did not want open rebellion against Rome; in such a context his ostentatious desire for ritual orthodoxy seems significant, since the economic interests in play were minor when compared with those theatened by eventual Chinese reprisals against Christian merchants.

The two Domenicos?

This looks like the title of an opera buffa, but it is only an hypothesis that I wish to consider before someone else seizes on it: an homage to Kirkpatrick, who amused himself by imagining that the Scarlatti sonatas were composed by Maria Barbara.

To play the devil's advocate, I must admit the possible existence of *two* musicians of the same name, but so unusual a circumstance would probably have leaped to the eyes of their contemporaries or of the first biographers of the Scarlattis. Although duplication of names would have been easy in such a numerous family, we know of only one other Domenico, the son of Alessandro's not exactly brilliant firstborn. On the death of Pietro, 22 February 1750, the aforesaid Domenico and his siblings Alessandro and Anna turned to Charles III of Spain, on the basis of their father's forty years' service as organist of the Royal Chapel in Naples and to the brilliant merits of their grandfather ("in the same Chapel in the post of First Maestro") and of their uncle ("Maestro of their Royal Majesties of Spain") to request— unsuccessfully—that the vacant post be conferred on Alessandro, the only one of them "who is employed in the same profession as his Father."[50]

If a different Domenico from the one we know was present in Palermo, he was not descended from the Scarlatas of Trapani. On the other hand, the professional fortunes of João V's new *maestro di cappella* and of the Baron d'Astorga were so interwoven in the third decade of the century as to undermine any hypothesis that denies the presence of the *real* Scarlatti in Palermo, where Astorga was chafing at the limitations imposed on him by a miserable and tiresome respectability. (The fortunes of the two would remain linked, since a document to which we will soon refer shows their relationship reflected in the contiguity of their works in a rich musical library). I had supposed (and continue to believe) that to the baron went the credit of having attracted his friend to the land of his ancestors. I maintained that their double transmigration to Lisbon began in 1721, with Astorga sent as a scout by a Domenico

---

50 Naples, Archivio di Stato, *Esped. dell'Ecclesiastico Fasc. 144, aprile 1750,* in Prota Giurleo, "Palermitano," 28-29.

who needed—or simply wanted   to delay his own installation. Knowing now that it was Scarlatti who arrived first in Lisbon in November
1719, I find it more logical than ever to attribute to Domenico the final
impulse for Astorga's transfer to a sumptuous capital, where he would
be welcomed at Court as a baron, without having to renounce his status
as a musician.

  The new Portuguese data shattered my hypothesis of an extended
stay in Palermo by Domenico. There also falls the possibility that it was
he who prepared and directed from the harpsichord the performance of
his father's *Scipione nelle Spagne,* whose librettto I had the good fortune to discover in a private colection.[51] The impresario's dedication
establishes that the music is by the "most noble swan of the Oreto."
Restraining the amusement aroused by the vision of a white bird bogged
down in the muddy little river on the edge of Palermo, we realize that
once again a libretto printed in Alessandro's birthplace succeeds in sup-
pressing the name of the great deserter. The pamphlet does not furnish
indications of the date of performance and a typographical error dates
the libretto as 1731. A contemporary correction in ink, "1721," re-es-
tablishes the correct date, confirmed by two further bits of information.

  First of all, in 1731 the theaters of Palermo were closed. After
the 1726 earthquake "they observed a rigorous silence for the course of
five or ten years."[52] In the second place, like the preface to the libretto
of *Ginevra Principessa di Scozia,* the dedication of *Scipione nelle Spagne*
is signed by "Simone Bellucci Impresario."[53] This suggests that the two
operas formed part of the same theatrical season, despite their placement in successive years. The impresario maintained the custom of dedicating the first opera of a season to the viceroy and one of the subsequent ones to the vicereine (or her daughter or daughter-in-law).

  Scipione nelle Spagne is dedicated to "D. Maria Francesca de
Moncajo [...] Principessa Pignatelli." I been unable to determine this
lady's relationship with the viceroy, Nicolò Pignatelli. If she is the

---

[51] *Scipione nelle Spagne / Drama per musica da rappresentarsi nel Teatro di Santa
Cecilia, consagrato alla grandezza della Signora D. Maria Francesca de Moncajo,
Blanes y Centellas, Aragon, Palafox, y Ventimilla Principessa Pignatelli.*

[52] Francesco Maria Emanuele e Vanni, Marchese di Villabianca, *De Teatri antichi e
moderni della Città di Palermo,* in *Opusculi palermitani,* XII no. 5, 4 (ms. in
Palermo, Biblioteca Comunale).

[53] Roberto Pagano, private collection. Unlike *Scipione nelle Spagne,* the libretto
furnishes the date of the first performance (17 November 1720) of the opera, as well
as the list of the performers; in this case as well the author of the music is not named.

vicereine, Bellucci had little time to render this homage. On March 31 she left Palermo

> after having had serious displeasures with her husband the viceroy, to the point where it was bruited about the city that she wished to poison the said viceroy."[54]

My exploration of notarial acts has revealed that Bellucci was not the typical impresario "in dire straits." He was involved in ventures as far from theatrical activity as armaments, the rentals of boats and ships, the acquisition of the monopoly on tobacco, the most varied commercial relations with centers all over Sicily (Cefalù, Licata, Caronia), the advance purchase of the production of wooded or tilled land, the renting of a fief, the transport and sale of grain, and the transport of charcoal (in one case for the vicereine).

Bellucci was not the usual scrounger, perpetually in debt and intent on begging concessions from the powerful. If it was Astorga who chose him, he chose well indeed. The names of the singers in the libretto of *Ginevra* (Giovanni Ghiringhelli, Margarita Salvagnini, Domenico Egitij [sic], Giovanna Scalfi, Antonio Baldi, Giovanna Puzzi, Pietro Ricci, with Marianna Monti and Giacomo Ambrosio in the comic parts) show that no expenses were spared. Among the artists named, two stand out: Domenico Gizzi (the title of Virtuoso of the Royal Chapel of Naples, printed on the libretto, confirms that it is the celebrated soprano, about to abandon the stage to become a highly appreciated singing teacher); and Marianna Monti (although not the more celebrated singer of the same name, it is the "buffa" who had made her debut at the age of barely thirteen in Naples in 1717). Giovanni Ghiringhelli and Antonio Baldi were also already known to the Palermitans, having sung on previous occasions. The reference to the name-days of the august monarchs Charles and Elizabeth reveals that the opera was performed somewhat in advance of the "first movements of the Carnival rejoicing" to which the dedication to the Viceroy Monteleone refers. The name-days were celebrated on November 4 and 19, when the *Ceremoniale of the Signori Viceroys* specifies that "in the evening in the Gallery there was Music, as customary." This suggests that the performances later transferred to the public stage of the Santa Cecilia theater originated in the palace. The opera was evidently repeated from Naples, where it had been performed on January 20 of the same year with music by Domenico Sarro, the composer who sixteen years earlier had shared with Domenico

---

[54] Antonio Mongitore, *Diario palermitano, cit.,* at the date.

Scarlatti the duty of writing music for other serenatas commissioned by a Sicilian aristocrat.

So far the investigation of the documents for those years has revealed no information concerning Domenico Scarlatti other than his membership in the Unione dei Musici confirmed on the two occasions already cited. A *Dominicus Scarlatti* appeared later in Palermo, where on 10 March 1730 he received some jewels from an Anna Bianciardi, undertaking to return them to Antonio Ranieri, who claimed them after the annulment of his marriage to Bianciardi. Although it is not specified in this case that "Domincus" was a musician, it is possible that it was our hero, since Anna could be a daughter or a sister of Sebastiano Bianciardi. A slender corroboration also comes from Lisbon: in December 1720 a Luis Blancardi, priest, was enrolled, along with Domenico Scarlatti, in the Brotherhood of Santa Cecilia.[55] (I present such information suggesting tenuous connections only so that it may be investigated by others.)

Domenico's affiliation with the Lisbon brotherhood has been seen as inconsistent with a possible trip to Palermo. For musicians even transitorially active in the latter city, membership in the Union of Santa Cecilia was obligatory, imposed by number XV of the *Capitoli* approved by the Viceroy Conte di Santo Stefano in 1679.[56] If the Lisbon Domenico came to Palermo to stage an opera by his father or by himself, he must have joined the Union. It would also be unthinkable for him not to be enrolled in the Lisbon Irmandade, given the role that he played in those years in the musical life of the Portuguese capital.

Not all the members participated diligently in its meetings. This is clear from the "uti major pars confratrum" of the document already quoted, and this explains why some of the singers employed in the performance of *Ginevra di Scozia* do not figure in the notarial document that attests to the presence of the mysterious Scarlatti in Palermo. The list of musicians does include Giovanni Ghiringhelli. Although he was a Roman by birth, he held so prestigious a place in the musical life of his adopted city that he could rise to the office of counselor [*congiunto*] of the Union in 1722, the year in which we find "Dominicus Scarlatti" again associated with the Union. Astorga's relationship with the Musici can be documented through Ghiringhelli, but the relevant documents discovered by Anna Tedesco, who kindly pointed them out to me, throw a surprising light on this relationship.

---

[55] Annotation by the Treasurer of the Irmandade, facsimile in Pl. X -XI of Doederer 1991.

[56] Reproduced in Roberto Pagano, "Le origini," 545-563.

On 24 November 1720 Ghiringhelli appeared before the notary Miraglia to receive from the impresario Bellucci sixty *onze* toward the amount due him

> for performing in this present carnival as a character in the said theater in all those operas that the said Bellucci will perform in the said carnival of the present year 1720 and 1721.[57]

Ghiringhelli did not require this sum for his personal necessities: the Baron d'Astorga was present, ready to pocket it to round out a previous debt to the amount of one hundred *onze*. He acknowledged its receipt and in a notarial act executed immediately after the first one promised to repay it all.[58] Anyone who expected to find Don Emanuello shining with the merits of patronage will be disappointed; in fact, the income of his fiefs was not sufficient to guarantee the baron the life-style to which his rank as an aristocrat obliged him.

The transfer of Sicily into Austrian dominion had not benefited the baron. The viceroy to whom Bellucci dedicated *Ginevra Principessa di Scozia* was Nicolò Pignatelli e Aragona, Duke of Monteleone and Terranova. He was a relative of that Marianna Pignatelli Countess of Althann who must have been perfectly familiar with the contretemps that had obliged Astorga to disappear, to escape—*entweichen*, "abscond," the Austrian documents say mercilessly—from Vienna.

Perhaps the political favor Don Emanuello had enjoyed in Palermo up to that moment was abandoning him, but one thing is certain: the adventurer who slumbered within the baron was beginning to strain at the leash, barely tolerating his position as an impoverished nobleman frustrated in his creativity as a musician. Finally a summons from afar opened new and distant prospects for Astorga, ones so attractive as to impel him to something very much like a flight with no thought of return. His wife's new pregnancy availed nothing: Don Emanuello was called away by affairs so pressing as to remove his curiosity to know whether at least his genealogical debts would be paid.

On 18 March 1721 the baron declared before a notary that he had to leave as soon as possible, "quam primum," to go outside the kingdom, called there by "aliquibus eius ingentissimis negotiis et causis quas hic exprimere minime potest" ("certain most pressing business and matters of his which he cannot explain here").[59] All this mystery sounds like a spy story, but this would contradict the exceptional length of the

[57] Act of the notary Gioacchino Miraglia.
[58] Ibid.
[59] Tiby, *Astorga,* 108.

"quam primum:" almost five months, spent in drawing up notarial documents. The baron restored to his wife her household furniture and dowry in exchange for the sum of two hundred *onze*. He also ceded to her the income of his fiefs, although he reserved for himself the heavy life-interest of 286 *onze* a year. Tiby commented:

> But what were the important affairs that called our musician out of the Kingdom is nowhere stated, not even distantly.[60]

Now, however, we know where the restless baron was in such a hurry to transfer himself.

If the 1755 earthquake had not destroyed the Portuguese royal archives, we might know exactly the nature and the length of the engagements that kept not only Domenico Scarlatti but also the Baron of Astorga in Lisbon, where the latter composed, performed, and had printed a series of his works. The documentation published by Doederer furnishes reliable and precious points of reference. In an attempt to reconstruct a scenario destined to remain incomplete, let us turn to the data of "Scarlattino's" activities in Lisbon.

Even if we learn that the air of Portugal was not healthy for Domenico, for the moment it seems that the milieu indeed encouraged facets of his artistic talent hidden during his Italian years. We have seen Domenico transform himself into a singer in order to be accompanied by a queen: now we see him as a poet:

> The night of the 26th of the past [month] Her Majesty ordered that there be sung in her Apartments a beautiful cantata in honor of the glorious Saint Anne, whose name her Majesty the Queen bears. The function was performed in the fourth inner apartment of the King, and the composition was by Sig.r Domenico Scarlatti, the words as well as the music, being sung by three sopranos and a Tenor, all Italians, and by the best of the Patriarchal Church.[61]

The manuscripts of two cantatas by Don Emanuello, now preserved in the library of the Royal College of Music in London, are dated "Lisbon 1721" and "Lisbon 1722."[62] In the same years the *Gazeta de Lisboa* records the performances of serenades by Astorga: *Aci e Galatea,* 27 December 1721, for one of the king's name-days (uncertain in his devotion between John the Baptist and John the Evangelist, João celebrated his *onomastico* on both June 24 and December 27). *Il sacrificio*

---

[60] Ibid.

[61] ASV.-Port., vol. 75, f. 425.

[62] *The New Grove,* I, 633.

di Diana was performed for the queen's name-day (26 July 1722). In the first case the *Gazeta* calls the serenata, "em que harmoniosamente se representou a Fabula de Acis & Galatea" ("in which the fable of Acis and Galatea is harmoniously represented), "amiravel" and specifies that the work, "discreta & elegantemente composta pelo Baraõ de Astorga," (dicreetly and elegant composed by the Baron of Astorga")was "executada com muyta destreza" ("performed with great skill").[63] Of the second it speaks of "uma Serenada, composta pelo Baraõ de Astorga, Cavalheiro Siciliano, que se acha no presente nesta Corte" ("a Serenade, composed by the Baron of Astorga, Sicilian Knight, who is presently in this Court").[64]

The data gathered by Doderer and those from the Sartori catalogue[65] reflect only a part of the flowering of serenate and intermezzi that occupied Domenico Scarlatti and Astorga in courteous competition at the court of João V. The inventory of the collection of manuscripts left to Farinelli by queen Maria Barbara that the great singer brought with him to Bologna when he was obliged to leave Spain, discovered and published by Sandro Cappelletto,[66] lists fifty-six serenades as collected in the same cupboard (*papelera*). Fifteen of these are by "Sig.r Domenico Scarlatti" and five by the "Baron d'Astorga."[67] If these are arranged like the parallel listing of operas, whose titles are given in chronological order, the concentration of the *serenate* of Scarlatti and Astorga at the beginning of the catalogue suggests that they were composed in the years that the two musicians were active in a Lisbon. During those years, João V's bigotry kept opera, which he considered sinful, far distant. This dating is confirmed by the fact that in the catalogue Astorga is always given the title of baron, while the Sig.r Scarlatti cannot yet display his title of *cavaliere* since the honor was bestowed on him by the king of Portugal only in 1738. The catalogue is evidently derived from the title pages of the manuscripts (unfortunately, the scribe specified the number of singers employed to perform them rather than indicating the titles of the *serenate*). It could be objected that the greater

63 *Gazeta de Lisboa*, 1. I. 1722.

64 *Gazeta de Lisboa*, 30. VII. 1722; I am indebted to Prof. Doederer for the identification of the second title.

65 Claudio Sartori, *I libretti italiani a stampa dalle origini al 1800*, Indici I (Cuneo, 1993), 70.

66 Sandro Cappelletto, *La voce perduta - Vita di Farinelli evirato cantore* (Torino: EDT, 1995), 209-221 .

67Ibid., 215-216.

part of the *Sonate per cembalo* (collected in volumes which can easily be identified as those now in the Biblioteca Marciana in Venice and the Conservatory in Parma, both compiled after Domenico's admission to the Order of Santiago) are catalogued simply as "by Scarlati," "of Scarlati," and "of Señor Scarlati." However, here the scribe simply followed the title pages of the manuscripts, in which the title of "cavaliere" appears only in the two volumes (the *Essercizi* and the first volume of the Venetian series) dated closest to the granting of the title.

The favor enjoyed by Astorga, the "Cavalheiro Siciliano," in Lisbon is reflected in an unusual collection of cantatas, published in the Portuguese capital in 1726 with a double poetic text, Italian and Spanish. In the preface to the volume the baron discusses the stylistic differences between Spanish and Italian vocal chamber music and declares that he has attempted a synthesis of the two genres, thanks to that

> inclination, which from my earliest years led me to learn this science for my delight and the interest which by the prompting of nature I take in both nations: recognizing as my Fatherland not only Italy, where I was born, but Spain, where my ancestors were born.

Four years later, when it is likely that Astorga had left Portugal, his cantatas were still performed every evening by two exceptional interpreters: the Spanish infanta Maria Anna Victoria and her mother-in-law, the same queen Marianna who eleven years before had accompanied Domenico Scarlatti on the harpsichord. In a letter written in disastrous French, the infanta tells her mother, Elisabetta Farnese:

> Toute les apresdiner la rayne touche le clavesin et je chante les cantatas dubaron Dastorga ("Every day after dinner the queen plays the harpsichord and I sing the cantatas of Baron Astorga").[68]

After other wanderings that are difficult to reconstruct with certainty, Astorga finally found in Spain an appropriate equilibrium between his own position at the upper-middle level of the social pyramid and the semiprofessional practice of composition. The researches of Juan José Carreras[69] have restored credibility to some of the data in the biographical notice that Zoppelli edited a few years after the baron's death. It said that Astorga was named by king Fernando "to the governorship of a distinguished Piazza, where he died with the highest honor

---

[68]Annibale Cetrangolo, *Esordi del melodramma in Spagna,* 28, quoted by Juan José Carreras, "Tra la Sicilia e la penisola iberica: il barone d'Astorga alla corte di Filippo V di Spagna," *Avidi lumi* V (Palermo, 2002), 59-69, 63 [hereafter Carreras, "Astorga"].

and glory."[70] This should be clarified, since the office—"correxidor," Carreras specifies—was not military but administrative. If it is true that in 1739 and 1744 important occasional compositions were commissioned and paid for, Astorga could accumulate five of these administrative sinecures without interference with the practice of musical composition. Carreras has established that in 1744 a serenata was commissioned from Astorga, "correxidor que ha sido de Mancha Real."[71] This resolves the confusion of names with a Baron Emanual Osorio de Astorga, who filled public offices at Madrid in the 1740s.[72] The existence of two Barons of Astorga increases the comedy of errors that our protagnists have created.Carreras pointed out that the favor enjoyed by our Astorga in the Spain of Fernando VI provides yet another confirmation of his relationship with Domenico Scarlatti, the king's favorite. In Palermo Astorga's abandoned wife was forced by her debts to sell the fiefs that justified her husband's title. But in his carefree "happy ending" in the land of his ancestors Astorga did not lose his boastful ways, continuing to call himself "barone" and burying forever his inconvenient family name (in Spanish, "rincon" means "street corner," "nook," or even "hideout").

Heic situs est eques Alexander Scarlactus ... musices instaurator maximus

The Siculo-Lusitanian vicissitudes of Domenico Scarlatti and the baron Astorga have distracted us from the pathetic decline of another of our protagonists. In the superb harbor of Naples, the immense vessel of Alessandro Scarlatti's glory had come to anchor at last. When the polemics had ceased (the grumbles of a Zambeccari are not worth serious consideration), there remained the wonder that so great a musician could still increase the large catalogue of his works. We left Alessandro coming to grips with the thorny problem posed by the nascent opera buffa: was it prudent for so famous a musician to display himself in a change of direction that all right-thinking people must consider risky? Adapting himself to the taste of the Neapolitans by enriching austere melodramas with comic elements was one thing. It would be something else again to abandon oneself completely to the temptations of a coarse vernacular. The solution of the dilemma had been worthy of

[69] Carreras, *Astorga*, 56-67.

[70] Francesco Tommaso Zoppelli, quoted in Volkmann, *Astorga*, I, 134.

[71] Carreras, *Astorga*, 63.

[72] Volkmann, *Astorga*, II, 150.

him; he had remained behind the scenes while the low artisans of his clan came out into the open. Finally he too emerged from his cautious reserve, but only to compose the music for that *Trionfo dell'onore* that Francesco Antonio Tullio (the best of the dialect librettists, already known as Colantuono Feralentisco and perhaps the author of the text of *La Cilla)* had been persuaded to write "in the Tuscan idiom." Forgetting the twenty-year-old Alessandro's Roman beginnings with the romantic comedy *Gli eqivoci*, his biographers have continued to see the *Trionfo dell'onore* as the master's first approach to the comic genre.

The Teatro dei Fiorentini must have had serious reasons for giving up the dialect tradition and taking the great leap into Tuscan speech. The impresario had turned to the public, declaring:

> The comedies of the little theater of the Florentines appear in another guise this year. They have passed from the Neapolitan speech to the Tuscan, not with heroic and regal Plays, but with domestic and familiar happenings, in which between the serious and the comic characters, we hope, that their seriousness and their wit will be equally pleasing.[73]

It is likely that the choice was dictated by the impresario's wish to ingratiate himself with an Austrian viceroy innocent of the picturesque Neapolitan dialect; in any case the choice must have been pleasing to Scarlatti.

The eighteenth-century historian Napoli-Signorelli had praised Tullio's *Le Fenziune abbentorate,* "a bourgeois play expressed with truth and energy and with the grace proper to the local dialect, despite the continuous rhyme which he adopts."[74] He reacted negatively to the linguistic crossover in the *Gemini amore*, judging that "The Author deprived himself of his strongest weapons, that is of the grace of his native language, which he possessed to a marvel."[75] A partisan judgment, since the text of *Il trionfo dell'onore* shows that Colantuono was capable of transferring to the "Tuscan speech" all the casual grace for which Napoli-Signorelli gave him credit in his use of dialect.

The diffusion of Spanish theater in southern Italy supports the hypothesis that Tullio's text was derived from the subject of the *Burlador di Sevilla,* the famous comedy of Tirso de Molina. However, the derivation was not direct and may have been influenced by the *commedia*

[73] Preface to the libretto of *Il gemino amore,* Naples, 1718.
[74] Pietro Napoli-Signorelli, *Vicende della coltura nelle Due Sicilie* (Naples, 1786), V, 441.
[75] Ibid.

dell'arte scenarios derived from the same plot. The custom of sweetening plays by means of a happy ending justifies both the repentance and the survival of Don Juan, and the untying of all the sentimental knots capable of impeding the quadruple wedding which at the end of the comedy leaves the public pleased and edified at the end of the comedy.

The *Trionfo dell'onore* dates from 1718. Three years earlier Alessandro Scarlatti had already composed his one hundredth opera, *Il Tigrane*. How much Baroque eagerness to astonish there is in this Leporellian catalogue, which evidently adds to his original operas the reworkings of operas by others and perhaps the *serenate*, if not also the oratorios. The author of the libretto is another old acquaintance: Domenico Lalli, the ex-crony of Astorga. *Il Tigrane* must have been epoch-making if Napoli-Signorelli[76] could still cite it seventy-one years later as an example of an heroic drama with two comic personages. We are present at the perfecting of the formula of Neapolitan opera, which in the *opere serie* of Alessandro Scarlatti had achieved the embodiment of its essential characteristics.

In the same year as *Tigrane* Alessandro set his hand to a sensational change of direction. The success of the Corelli's posthumous *Concerti grossi* induced Alessandro to venture upon *12 Sinfonie di concerto grosso*, followed by a series of six *Concerti* conceived for a similar instrumental ensemble. The manuscripts of several of the *Toccate* for harpsichord or organ bear dates indicating that they were also composed in the last years of the musician's life. In the case of a manuscript preserved in the Biblioteca del Conservatorio in Palermo the date 1729 must refer to the copying, unless it is a copyist's error (1729 instead of 1723). 1723 is clearly indicated in the so-called Higgs manuscript at the head of the famous "Toccata per cembalo d'ottava stesa." The *7 Sonate* for flute and strings bear the date of 1725 and were, perhaps, composed for Quantz, who had succeeeded in overcoming certain prejudices of the aged musician.[77]

Why so unexpected an interest in instrumental music? Perhaps Alessandro felt that this was the direction in which the most brilliant of his sons would emancipate himself in terms more meaningful than those enumerated in the legal document. The *Toccate* for harpsichord, espe-

---

76 Napoli-Signorelli, *Vicende,* V, 438.

77 Charles Burney, *The Present State of Music in Germany, The Netherlands and United Provinces* (London: Becket and Co., 1773), II, 183-184. [hereafter Burney, *Germany*]

cially, have survived in many manuscripts, one of which seems to have been edited for publication (as does the source that transmits the *Sinfonie di concerto grosso*).[78] Since after his father's death Domenico would wait for thirteen years before publishing the *Sonate* which perhaps were already astonishing his listeners, Alessandro's late initiative may have been dictated once again by his frenzied desire for preeminence, to prove his own supremacy over a docile subject ...

I draw a parallel between the attitude which induced Alessandro to astonish his listeners by his obscene cantata in Neapolitan dialect and that of Giuseppe Verdi. Verdi (also in Naples) played on his friends the "April fool's" joke of performing his Quartet in E minor, a work inspired more by a desire to show that he could write one than by a sudden passion for a genre that he detested.[79] Alessandro's *Concerti* and *Sinfonie di concerto grosso* were born of the same spirit of rivalry. I have already noted that Scarlatti senior judged that the works that had brought Corelli enormous celebrity were not very interesting. I would like to point out that the instrumental compositions of the mature Scarlatti represent perhaps a step backward by comparison with the formal perfection of Corelli's works, but they transfer to instrumental music at least a part of the harmonic refinement displayed by Alessandro in his vocal music. The most important of the *Toccate* contains an *Adagio* that offers us the instrumental equivalent of recitative and the fanciful harmonic modulations worthy of the unconventional harmonies of a Gesualdo di Venosa, a model that is always invoked.[78]

Together with these tail-lashings of a proud protagonist intent on defending the supremacy that had induced him to tread the path of the *inhuman* in his exchange of cantatas with Gasparini, there are second thoughts about sacred music. The *Messa dedicata a S. Cecilia,* composed in 1720 for Cardinal Acquaviva, shows a breadth of novelty in the emancipation of voices and instruments from old formulas. Beside this work, which Dent[81] considered a precursor of the masses of Bach, Haydn, and Mozart, there are other sacred pieces in which, according to Hasse and Jomelli,[82] Alessandro left his most lasting impression on the field of church music, still today inadequately explored.

---

[78] Claudio Sartori, *Alessandro Scarlatti, Primo e secondo libro di Toccate,* Appendix, *I Classici Musicali Italian* (Milan: Ricordi, 1943), 142.

[79] *Scarlatti* ERI, 214.

[80] *Toccata VII,* ed. cit.; *Adagio,*77; see Alessandro's letter to Ferdinando de'Medici of 28 August 1706.

[81]Dent, *Scarlatti,* 181.

[82] Burney, *Germany*, I, 348 n.

Hasse: another "Saxon" who had come from his distant homeland to bask in the sun of Italy and to seek stimulation in the transparent
vocality of Italian melody. Burney tells us about him:

> On his arrival in Naples, he was thought a very good player on the
> harpsichord. He studied first a little while under Porpora, as I had
> been before told by Barbella; but Hasse denied that it was Porpora
> who introduced him to old Scarlatti. He says, that the first time
> Scarlatti saw him, he luckily conceived for him such an affection,
> that he ever after treated him with the kindness of a father.[83]

Authoritarian with Domenico, but ready to open himself to a
young foreigner "with the kindness of a father" from their first meeting:
in this evident contradiction lies one of the secret pangs that must have
gnawed Alessandro in his old age. We may be certain that his benevolence toward the young Saxon was effective from the story of the descent of another great German into Italy: Johann Joachim Quantz.

> In 1725, he went to Naples, where he met with his countryman
> Hasse, then studying under Ales. Scarlatti [...] Quantz intreated
> Hasse to introduce him to his master, Scarlatti, to which he readily
> consented; but upon mentioning him to the old composer, he said:
> 'My son, you know I hate wind instruments, they are never in tune.'
> However, Hasse did not cease importuning him, till he had obtained
> the permission he required.

> In the visit he made to Scarlatti, M. Quantz says, that he had an
> opportunity of hearing him play on the harpsichord, which he did
> in a very learned manner; but he observes, that his abilities on that
> instrument were not equal to those of his son.[84]

From Marpurg[85] we learn that Alessandro accompanied a "solo"
of the young flutist and that the latter had "the good fortune to earn his
fondness," so much as to induce the musician to compose for him "a pair of
soli for flute" (these could be the Sonate already mentioned, dated 1725).

Evidence showing that Domenico was present in Italy in 1724
and 1725 goes back to the two sources cited by Burney. On the basis of
these data doubts have been raised about an uninterrupted stay at the
Portuguese court. Now, the documented passages of Scarlatti junior
through Paris confirm my hypothesis about the generous concession of

---

82 Burney, *Germany*, I, 348 n.

83 Ibid., 343-344.

84 Ibid, II, 183-184.

85 Friedrich Wilhelm Marpurg, *Historisch-kritische Beiträge zue Aufnahme der Music*
(Berlin, 1744-1745), I, 197-250.

annual holidays. This perhaps allowed "Dominicus" his Sicilian excursions in 1720 and 1722, but certainly permitted "Scarlattino" to be admired by Quantz in Rome in 1724 and to take a pathetic leave of his father. In 1725 Alessandro was not healthy and flourishing as João Pedro d'Alvarenga supposes,[86] but up to his neck in troubles.

Before knowing the contents of the excruciating petitions that document a series of misfortunes and the hopeless poverty in which the imperial bureaucrats and administrators forced Alessandro Scarlatti to die,[87] I had spoken of an "air of general consensus" in which "there died in Naples one of the great incomprehensibles of all music history."[88] Even after learning the chilling finale to Alessandro's story I do not wish to retract anything, quoting a series of testimonies that confirmed—and continue to confirm—the contrast between glory and need that marked Alessandro Scarlatti's entire life.

The influence that he exercised on the young musicians of Naples did not extend to personal instruction, except Carlo Cotumacci. We know that "by reason of his advanced age, and his indispositions" Alessandro could lend his services as maestro of the Royal chapel only rarely,[89] but in his last years he was revered by all, like a god. Except for the irregularity of his payments, the Austrian viceroys honored their signed agreements (and presumably those that were tacitly understood as well). When the Maestro asked permission to travel to Rome "to compose two operas for the Teatro Capranica" and for "assistance in maintaining his numerous family" he was granted four months of leave, during which the entire amount of his salary was paid to his family in Naples.[90]

The high esteem enjoyed by Scarlatti is shown in this passage from the curious *Memorie* of Bonifacio Petrone, called the abate Pecorone:

> [...] a few months later it happened that they had to fill one of the two places for bass voice in the Royal Chapel, and I abstained from competing because of the *hominem* that I did not *habebam* to propose me, or rather to recommend me to His Excellency. Because up to that point I had clear experience that without support

---

[86] João Pedro d'Alvarenga, "Domenico Scarlatti, 1719-1729: o período portuguès" in *Revista Portuguesa de Musicologia* 7-8 (1997-1998), 111 [hereafter d'Alvarenga, "Scarlatti"].

[87] Cotticelli and Maione, *Musica e istituzioni musicali a Napoli,* 22.

[88] Pagano 1985, 369.

[89] Cotticelli and Maione, op. cit., 21.

[90] Ibid., App. I, Letter 13, f. 1534, 16X. 1719.

and help it is difficult for a person to achieve what he desires, even
if adorned with whatsoever merit, or virtue. While I was about to
forget about it, good friends, among them Sig. Domenico Gizzio, a
man who was greatly commendable both for his soprano singing
and for the endowments of his soul, Sig. Domenico Floro of equal
virtù, a contralto singer, and Hebdomadary of the Cathedral of this
City, and Sig. Giuseppe de Bottis, famous Maestro di Cappella while
we were singing in several Choirs of Music for the Feast of the
glorious St. Francis of Paola in his own church near the royal Palace, which for many years has been solemnized by the charity and
piety of the most excellent House of Bisignano at its own expense
out of pure devotion; finally, in addition the strong pressure of the
Sig. Marchese Matteo Sassano, commonly called Matteucci, a very
famous soprano singer, exhorted me to apply to the Sig. Viceroy
himself and also to mention it with Sig. Cavaliere Alessandro
Scarlatti, the first Maestro di Cappella of the Royal Palace, the
Orpheus of Music, and the most learned man in counterpoint, that
has ever been seen in our days, as is known to those who know
these things, and is made manifest by his many works. Then the
most courteous Sig. Cavaliere assured me of his efforts, adding to
me: 'Go this very hour to the Signora Vicereine, on my behalf;
present your Memoriale to her: tell her that you are the bass who sang
the Prophecy for solo voice in the Palace on Christmas eve [...].'

The sequel to the story recounts the warm welcome given the
petition and the petitioner, who clearly had found in Alessandro the *hom-
inem* most suited to the circumstances. It is to be noted that even
Matteuccio—at the time a star, and risen to the title of marquis—regarded the intervention of Alessandro as more efficacious. Then the
abate concludes:

I also went to thank the Sig. Cavalier Scarlatti: who after a few
months, to my sorrow, passed to a better life, and the most virtuous
Sig. Domenico Sarro was elected to the post of first Maestro di
Cappella of the Palace to my great content: men well known in this
City and elsewhere.[91]

The strongly positive judgment of Alessandro's sacred music
was cited by Burney from Jommelli, who was barely eleven at the time
of the patriarch's death (he had landed in Naples from his native Aversa
in 1725). The young musicians of the new generations studied Scarlatti's
works with interest, and their preference for his sacred music speaks

---

91 Bonifacio Petrone, *Memorie dell'Abate Bonifacio Pecorone della Città di
Saponara* (Naples, 1729), 76ff.

volumes. We have already seen the decline of Scarlatti's popularity as an opera composer. Despite the activity of some musicians of the following generation, the chamber cantata would also practically have died with him if Scarlattino had not continued in his father's tradition to adorn the refined private entertainments of the Princes of the Asturias. Malcolm Boyd suggested that these cantatas of Domenico's mature years were intended for Farinelli, but now we know that they could have been performed by the composer himself.

Burney and other eighteenth-century historians had already indicated Astorga as a proselyte of Alessandro Scarlatti, one of the last champions of the chamber cantata. The restless baron rushed around Europe carrying a large number of cantatas. A colorful passage of Hawkins describes him as absorbed in singing them, accompanying himself on the harpsichord (Domenico Scarlatti was not the only *cantautore*), bent over in an uncomfortable position owing to his myopia. It is noteworthy that it was an aristocrat who contributed, through these pilgrimages, to the survival of the most aristocratic musical genre of the period. It would be a mistake, however, to suppose that the performance of cantatas took place only in the salons of noble palaces. The biographical notice dedicated by De Dominici to the painter Francesco Solimena suggested that Alessandro Scarlatti's old age at home was serenely musical:

> Being a lover of music, in the evening he [Solimena] was accustomed to go to the house of the cavaliere Alessandro Scarlatti, a marvelous musician, and of whom few equals will come into the world, for composing operas with the greatest expression and melody, which ravished hearts while arousing the passions. At Scarlatti's house they were entertained by hearing the singing of Flaminia, the daughter of that great virtuoso, who sang divinely, and her friendship was so cordial that he wished to make her portrait together with that of her father Scarlatti; but he made one showing her wrapped in a dressing-gown, in such a pose, and so well painted, that it was the object of the praise of all, and I was present once when it was greatly praised by certain virtuosi from beyond the Alps, who could not stop looking at it . . . [92]

Solimena's fine portrait best transmits the features of the mature but not decrepit Alessandro Scarlatti. It is now in Madrid, in the private collection of the Dukes of Alba (See Fig. 3, p.27).

The documents recently discovered show that in his old age Alessandro Scarlatti tried to attend to his duties as *maestro di cappella*

---

[92] Bernardo De Dominici, *Vite de' Pittori, Scultori ed Architetti Napoletani* (Naples, 1742-1744), IV, 471.

with a scrupulosity that redeems his earlier absenteeism. However, they also throw a chilling light on the composer's last year, for by September 1724 he was described as infirm, rarely able to perform.

On 15 June 1723 the *Avvisi di Napoli* published for the last time a report of the performance of a composition by Alessandro Scarlatti:

> Sunday evening in Palazzo Stigliano at the Toledo they sang an excellent serenata intitled *Erminia,* for four voices, set to music by the never sufficiently praised Cav. Alessandro Scarlatti, of whom it truly can be said, that as much as he increases in age, so much the more does he acquire new sublime ideas in his Compositions, and it was sung by the first four Virtuosi who can be found in this City, that is Carlo Broschi, called *Farinelli,* soprano, who with great applause performed the part of *Erminia;* as likewise Andrea Pacini, Contralto, the part of *Tancredi;* Annibale Pio Fabri, Tenor, the part of *Polidoro,* and D. Antonio Manna, Basso, who performed the part of *Pastore;* and H. E. the Viceroy came to hear it privately, and showed himself especially pleased.[93]

The viceroy who went privately to applaud the serenata was Cardinal Althann, linked by family ties both to Pignatelli di Monteleone, whom we last saw as viceroy in Sicily, and to Astorga's Viennese protectors. Widowed by Count Althann, in Vienna Marianna Pignatelli would become the muse of Pietro Metastasio. It only remains to add to these names that of Farinelli, the applauded protagonist of the serenata, to recognize the passage from the era of Alessandro Scarlatti to that of his Neapolitan successors. With Vienna as a jumping-off place, these were destined to spread the success of Italian opera all over Europe.

On another occasion I already raised the question whether the text of the *Erminia* might be numbered among the first nuptial odes of Metastasio's muse.[94] It is interesting to imagine that Metastasio received a kind of investiture from the most celebrated Neapolitan opera composer of the moment, making him the symbol of the successful theatrical genre that Alessandro Scarlatti had brought to its definitive codification. There is another remote possibility of linking Alessandro Scarlatti's name with another Metastasian text of different importance. Let us recall a mysterious Roman performance of *Didone abbandonata* whose music certain literary sources attribute to Alessandro or Domenico Scarlatti and which they place in 1724 (immediately after the Neapolitan "prima," staged in Carnival of that year at the Teatro San Bartolomeo with music by Domenico Sarro).[95]

---

[93] Quoted by Prota Giurleo, "Breve Storia," 94.

[94] *Scarlatti,* ERI, 232.

[95] Cf. Kirkpatrick, *Scarlatti,* 427.

I have not discovered the origin of the attribution to Scarlatti, but seems confirmed by a third performance of the opera in the same year at the Teatro Santa Cecilia of Palermo. For a beginning opera librettist, we can say that the fine weather was already visible in the early morning![96] Sorge had already pointed out certain reworkings of the original text: the prudent (and economically wise) substitution of Jove for Neptune in the original spectacular Neapolitan finale; and a new comic couple, Melissa-Lucilla, in place of Dorina and Nibbio in the original version. The libretto names neither the poet nor the composer. Sarro was well known in Palermo. In 1704 he shared with the nineteen-year-old Domenico Scarlatti the task of composing serenades for the Prince of Villafranca. All the evidence suggests that he composed the *Ginevra Principessa di Scozia* performed at the Teatro Santa Cecilia in 1720. However, we should not overlook the possibility that the "Dominicus Scarlatti" present in Palermo in April of that year was in some way involved in the performance. It is possible that also in the case of *Didone* the musical arrangement was his. His intervention in the score might have been justified by the cool reception given to Sarro's music as opposed to the success of the libretto.[97]

Scarlattians of sure faith, such as the veteran Lauro, were employed to sing the Palermo *Didone*. Giovanni Rapaccioli, who had been the pupil of Gasparini, was sent in 1702 to Naples by Violante of Bavaria to study singing with Alessandro Scarlatti himself.[98]

I have conjured up this improbable attribution to Alessandro only because I wished to see the farewell to the stage of a glorious representative of the past coincide with the launching of a new and no less important protagonist. The Scarlatti who put his hand to the lightning reworking of the *Didone* (I am increasingly skeptical about the possibility of a completely new musical version), given the performances in Rome and Palermo, was almost certainly Domenico. As far as we know, it was a farewell to the operatic stage for him as well, a final and pathetic homage to his father's wishes.

The precarious financial stability of the Scarlatti family had been put in crisis by Alessandro's old age and the illness that rendered additonal

[96] The Palermitan libretto from which Sorge gathered his information (Sorge, *Teatri*, 226) long remained untraceable because it was miscatalogued in the Biblioteca Comunale of Palermo. The credit for its recent identification goes to Consuelo Giglio.

[97] Saverio Mattei, *Elogio del Jommelli* (in the Neapolitan edition of Metastasio's *Poesie*, v. XIII, lvii-lxi), quoted in Benedetto Croce, *I Teatri di Napoli—Secolo XV-XVIII* (Naples, 1968), I, 244.

[98] Personal communication from Franco Piperno; Holmes, "Lettere inedite," 375.

earnings impossible. An excruciating malady of the "Flaminia who sang divinely" was added to the chronic delays of the Austrian finance office to devastate Alessandro's farewell to life.

On 12 October 1725—ten days before his death—Alessandro Scarlatti sent the viceroy a petition, whose contents reveal the discouragement that guided his pen in describing a state of poverty that swept away any reticence:

> Most Eminent and Most Reverend Prince, and Lord/ The poor and most wretched Cavaliere Alessandro Scarlatti returns to the feet of the High Pity and Sublime Justice of Your Eminence with the deepest humility, obedience, and submission to Your Eminence's greatness, describing to you, that for the extreme excess of his innumerable misfortunes, for which he finds himself in such extreme need of his daily bread, that he is beginning to beg assistance from private alms; it happens that he can still see no result from the Sovereign Most Righteous Order of Your Celestial Justice and Piety, given to the Commissioner of the Aggiunta of Tobacco in the previous Memorial, which your supplicant placed at the Feet of Your Eminence, with these precise words: Dese la orden para que se le deviere; y para que en lo sucessivo se la satisfagan sus mesadas con la puntualidad, que hasta a qui en 3 de Octobre 1725. Newly supplicating Your Eminence's Heroic Piety and your Most Holy Justice to succor this poor man languishing even for bread, with which for five years with this provision he has sustained himself and his family; bread given him by the Most Clement Beneficence of the Most August Sovereign, which has never failed him until not only two months had passed, when it should have been given him, July and August, but now it is near on two other months which end the last day of the current October, so that four months' salary should be consigned up to that day. Bewildered, and beaten down, your supplicant is at the end of his strength (to whom has happened the misfortune of the loss of his daughter, who had six continuous months of hopeless and very expensive illness, the Lord having deigned to call her to Heaven), throwing himself at the Feet of the Exalted Throne of the Justice, and Pity of Your Eminence, he begs You to give him aid, Justice, Pity, and Compassion, with that great Charity which serves in your Heroic Heart and as that true, Great Lord, which the Divine Majesty of God has deigned to create You, in Grace, and Justice, like God.

The words of the viceroy in Spanish show that a preceding petition had already been ineffective, although he had arranged to grant what it requested.

The researches of Prota Giurleo[99] established that Alessandro Scarlatti died on 22 October 1725. The death certificate in the archive of the Neapolitan parish of Santa Maria Avvocata says that he was buried in Monte Santo. On 30 October a brief obituary was published in one of the customary *Avvisi:*

> Last week the famous Alessandro Scarlatti gave up his Soul to the Lord; Music owes him much for the many works with which he has enriched it.

The funerary tablet set into the pavement of the Chapel of Santa Cecilia, in which Alessandro—a member of the Ceto dei Musici of Napoli since 1693—was buried is said to have been dictated by the somewhat dubious compassion of Pietro Ottoboni:[100]

> HEIC SITUS EST/EQUES ALEXANDER SCARLACTUS/VIR MODERATIONE BENEFICENTIA/PIETATE INSIGNIS/ MUSICES INSTAURATOR MAXIMUS/ QUI SOLIDIS VETERUM NUMERIS/NOVA AC MIRA SUAVITATE MOLLITIS/ ANTIQUITATI GLORIAM POSTERITATI/ IMITANDI SPEM ADEMIT/ OPTIMATIBUS REGIBUSQUE/ APPRIME CARUS/TANDEM ANNOS NATUM LXVI EXTINXIT/ SUMMO CUM ITALIAE DOLORE/IX KAL. NO-VEMBER MDCCXXV/MORS MODIS FLECTA NESCIA.

> HERE LIES ALESSANDRO SCARLATTI, KNIGHT, A MAN DISTINGUISHED FOR MODERATION, BENEFICENCE, AND PIETY, THE GREATEST OF ALL RESTORERS OF MUSIC, WHO, HAVING SOFTENED THE SOLID MEASURES OF THE ANCIENTS WITH A NEW AND WONDERFUL SWEETNESS, DEPRIVED ANTIQUITY OF GLORY AND POSTERITY OF THE HOPE OF IMITATION. DEAR ABOVE ALL TO NOBLES AND KINGS, HE DIED IN THE SIXTY-SIXTH YEAR OF HIS AGE ON 22 OCTOBER 1725 TO ITALY'S UTMOST GRIEF. DEATH KNOWS NO MODE OF APPEASEMENT.

The final desperate appeal of the dying man obtained the payment of two of the four months in arrears: a few days after the death of the "poor and most wretched Cavaliere" his "most wretched widow" returned to entreat the viceroy:

---

[99] Ulisse Prota Giurleo, "I Congiunti di Alessandro Scarlatti," *Celebrazione del Terzo Centenario della Nascita di Alessandro Scarlatti* (RAI, Radiotelevisione italiana, Naples, 1960), 57.

[100] Dent, *Scarlatti,* 193; translation based on Kirkpatrick, *Scarlatti,* 75.

Antonia Scarlatti wife of the late Cavaliere Alessandro Scarlatti, Your Eminence's most humble servant, and a Most wretched widow, weighed down by her family, in supplication explains to Your Eminence, that, as the last two Months' salary (minus eight days) of her late husband for the sum of 94 ducats should be paid, simply to feed her, with her poor family (in addition to being loaded with debts), she begs the High Clemency and Inborn Goodness of Your Eminence for this in Visceribus Christi, that you be willing to command that it be paid, and she will not fail, wretchedly from her side, and from her family, to pray God for the Health of Your Eminence: That in addition to its being just she will receive it as a Grace from God.[101]

101 Cotticelli and Maione, op. cit., 22.

XV

Music, the solace of illustrious Souls ...

The sad documents that have come to light in Naples show how mistaken João Pedro D'Alvarenga[1] was in maintaining that Domenico's farewell visit to his father, attested by the oldest sources, is unsubstantiated.

Alessandro's death left the ex-eaglet (now forty) with new doubts, new responsibilities: in certain cases, an oppressive father furnishes his children with the best of alibis . . .

Now his choices were no longer directed, except by the assimilation of certain artistic and moral teachings (almost all of the latter negative ones). His artistic inheritance is beyond discussion: despite the differences in their most typical productions, father and son could identify the forms best suited to their artistic imaginations, and they moved with an incredible variety of approaches within the golden cages created by their own rigid sense of self-discipline.

As the orphan of a much-admired father, Domenico would have had abundant reasons for spending the rest of his life in the warped psychological condition of too many child prodigies. I am not thinking of an "Amadeus" before the fact: even in the years in which his father's moral and psychic pressure weighed most heavily on him, Domenico appeared to his contemporaries to be something more than Peter Shaffer's merry simpleton (let the appreciation of Ferdinando de' Medici stand for all of them). It is true, however, that the music he improvised or wrote down did not seriously threaten his proud and haughty father's need for primacy.

Perhaps it is appropriate to recall Mainwaring's portrait of Domenico, with that "sweetest of characters" and those "most polite manners that one could imagine" joined to the talents of an artist. I believe that this human mildness could only favor the calm and yet fertile assimilation that Domenico had to undergo in view of the important changes lying before him. At the beginning of this new phase of his life, he could not know that the gods would give him much more than he could ask.

---

[1] Alvarenga, "Scarlatti," 111

In leaving for Portugal, Domenico must not have nurtured too many regrets. He left behind an Italy linked with his previous condition of human and artistic subordination. Long gone were the times of happy wandering of which the biographers of Handel and Roseingrave have given us a glimpse. These artistic companionships had always been carried out with young foreign musicians, under the banner of a mutual curiosity not limited to the area of music. Perhaps Domenico had an inborn thirst for knowledge that influenced his decision to move abroad.

The Lisbon that offered itself to him was the great Atlantic city that Kirkpatrick described as surprisingly akin to Naples and capable of reawakening "eastern strains" and those "Saracen traces" that formed part of Domenico's Sicilian background.[2] João V, wealthy beyond measure and as much a lover of luxury as only a king enriched by the gold of Brazil could be, "combined the splendid sensuality of an oriental sultan with the ostentatious devotion of a Roman prelate." As Kirkpatrick noted, Frederick the Great wrote savagely about him and his strange mania for religious ceremonies, in the spirit of Voltaire:

> Having obtained permission from the Pope to found a Patriarchate and another which authorized him to say mass, he practically became a consecrated priest. Religious functions were his diversions, his constructions were convents, his armies were formed by monks, and nuns were his lovers [...].[3]

If the predilections of Scarlatti's patron were potentially limited to religious functions, Domenico must have made considerable use of the experience which he had acquired at St. Peter's. In addition to music expressly composed for these sumptuous ceremonies, he could rework pieces already performed in Rome, adapting them to the personnel of the Portuguese Royal Chapel. The membership of the Chapel is described in Johann Gottfried Walther's *Catalogue of the most important instrumentalists:*

> *Scarlatti*, maestro di cappella, Roman./Giuseppe *Antoni,* vice maestro di cappella, Portuguese./*Pietro Giorgio Avondano,* first violin, Genoese./*Antonio Baghetti,* first violin, Roman./*Alessandro Baghetti,* second violin, Roman./Giovanni Pietro, second violin, Portuguese, but of German parents./*Tommaso,* third violin, Florentine./ *Latur,* fourth violin and second oboe, French./*Veith,* fourth violin and first oboe, Bohemian./*Ventur,* viola, Catalan./*Antoni,* viola,

---

2 Kirkpatrick, *Scarlatti,* 67.
3 *Oeuvres de Frédéric le Grand,* Berlin, 1844-1857, II, 13, quoted by Kirkpatrick, *Scarlatti,* 68.

Catalan./Ludewig, bassoon, Bohemian./Juan, violoncello, Catalan./ Laurenti, violoncello, Florentine./Paolo, contra-violino, Roman./ Antonio Giuseppe, organ, Portuguese./Floriani, discantist, Roman castrato./Mossi, tenor, Roman.

In this cappella there must have been already in the past as many instrumentalists. The number of the singers, for the greatest part Italian, is estimated at between thirty and forty persons.[4]

Although Alvarenga[5] tries to minimize Domenico's duties in Lisbon, our composer had not taken a step backwards by leaving St. Peter's: the new means at his disposal might well have stimulated his creative fancy. This was perhaps the case with the Te Deum "elegantly set to music and distributed among various choirs of musicians by the famous Domingo Scarlatti" performed on 31 December 1721 in the church of San Rocco.[6] However, this may have been a piece already composed in Rome, now adapted to the possibilities of the Royal chapel.

The colorful imagerie that characterizes Sacheverell Sitwell's little book, A Background for Domenico Scarlatti,[7] even offers the reader a description of a cruel auto-da-fé. Unfortunately, the author refers only in passing to a magnificent harpsichord lacquered in red belonging to João V, who had given it to one of his mistresses—a nun, as was to be expected—in the Cistercian convent of Odivelas near Lisbon.[8] As if the object of his gossip were not the greatest harpsichordist who ever lived, the author prefers to give the horrifying details of the auto-da-fé and neglects to describe the harpsichord he saw in London, before 1935, or to clarify why he maintains that it was built around 1720 and therefore might have been played by Scarlatti. The rich decoration of the harpsichord would reflect its royal proprietor's desire for splendor, but Sitwell is silent about the organological details that would confirm the dating and tell us more about the instruments that Domenico found in Portugal. The terrible earthquake of 1755 and unpardonable human carelessness did not spare even one of the harpsichords used by Domenico and his pupil the queen in Portugal and in Spain.

In Portugal Scarlatti found not only religious ceremonies and harpsichords that today would turn the head of an antique dealer, he also

---

[4] Walther, Lexikon, 489.

[5] Op. cit., passim, but especially 118ff.

[6] Gazeta de Lisboa, 1 January 1722, quoted in Kirkpatrick, Scarlatti, 69, n. 11.

[7] Sacheverell Sitwell, A Background for Domenico Scarlatti (London: Faber and Faber, 1935).

[8] Ibid., 62.

had the pleasure of discovering the talent of two royal children entrusted to his care as a musical pedagogue. In addition, he had an encounter—which has been considered influential—with a young Portuguese musician, José Antonio Carlos de Seixas. Seixas certainly deserved Domenico's appreciation, since he is cited as Domenico's vicemaestro and organist in Walther's census of the Portuguese Royal Chapel: "Giuseppe (José) Antoni" and "Antonio Giuseppe" are the same person.

The young Portuguese whom Scarlatti assisted as best he could—we shall soon see why—was born 11 June 1704 at Coimbra, where Francisco Vaz, his father, was organist of the cathedral. The reason José Antonio Carlos Vaz adopted the patronymic Seixas, the family name of a personage who will immediately arouse our interest, has not been ascertained. In those days, however, a certain number of young musicians showed their gratitude to generous patrons or worthy teachers by taking their names, without the benefit of legal adoption. José Antonio must have enjoyed powerful patronage if in February of 1718—at the age of less than fourteen—he was able to succeed his father as organist of the cathedral of Coimbra. Two years later, when he had moved to Lisbon, he was appointed organist and later vice-maestro of the Royal Chapel.[9]

The Infante Don Antonio, the brother of the king, who had entrusted his musical training to Scarlatti, was an important patron of Seixas. The Infante's name appears on the titlepage of a collection of sonatas by Ludovico Giustini of Pistoia (Florence, 1732, perhaps reprinted in Amsterdam in 1737), the first printed work bearing a specific designation for the "Harpsichord with piano and forte called commonly with little hammers."

This *Opera Prima* of Giustini was dedicated to Don Antonio by a certain Don Giovanni de Seixas. Robert Stevenson[10] identifies Seixas as João de Seyxas da Fonseca, a rich Brazilian prelate, named Bishop of Arcopolis a year after the publication of the *Sonate*. Cardinal Guadagni, a nephew of Clement XII, presided at his consecration, and Stevenson believes that "[Seyxas'] interest in art and music had endeared him to Pope Clement XII as well as to his nephew, who was a lover of the art."[11]

The dedication of the volume to Don Antonio di Braganza is written in Italian, despite being addressed by a Brazilian to a Portuguese

[9] Cf. Carlos de Seixas, *25 Sonatas para instrumentos de tecla,* Estudio de Macario Santiago Kastner, Introduçao, VII (Lisbon, Fundaçao Calouste Gulbenkian, 1980.)

[10] Robert Stevenson, "Some Portuguese Sources for early Brazilian Music History," *Yearbook, Inter-American Institute for Musical Research* IV (1968), 1-437.

[11] Ibid., 5, n. 11.

royal prince. Defoliated of its fawning decorations, it provides some useful information:

> Royal Highness / I present with the most devoted respect to Your Royal Highness these sonatas which I have already heard with particular satisfaction during my stay in Italy and [which are] judged by the Connoisseurs of that Profession to be of great good taste [...]. I hope that Y. R. H., who is not only capable of rendering so sure a judgment of this sweet and delightful science, as of all the other ones, but to the greatest amazement of those who have the honor of hearing you, even knows how to exercise it perfectly, will not disdain to bestow one of your beneficent glances on these Pages in those hours, in which you are accustomed to give your sublime thoughts some relief and repose [...]."

Seyxas had heard the sonatas in Italy, where the experts appreciated them. By having them printed to offer to the prince, the Brazilian did not rely only on his patron's favorable opinion, but also on the delight that Don Antonio would be able to draw from them in those hours of relaxation he spent playing. From all this there emerges clearly the indication of a certain technical prowess on the part of the dedicatee, but also the proof that the Infante possessed and employed the instrument for which the sonatas had been conceived.

Comparing this information with what I have already written about Domenico Scarlatti and the earliest fortepianos seems to confirm the hypothesis of Kirkpatrick,[12] who suggested that certain rather easy sonatas that the Scarlatti manuscripts transmit in a characteristic grouping, were created for the new instrument.

I would also like to stress an unmistakable connection between Domenico Scarlatti, Portugal, and Tuscany: a strange relationship, delineated through a number of details. In 1714 the Portuguese ambassador to the Holy See had printed in Lucca the libretto of the *Applauso genetliaco* to be sung in Rome with music by Domenico. A year later, also in Lucca, the "second edition" and the "third edition" of the libretto of *La Dirindina* were printed. Since precisely during these years Domenico Scarlatti went from the service of Maria Casimira to that of the Portuguese ambassador, there may have been some secret reason that made Lucca a suitable alternative place for printing texts such as *La Dirindina,* which would have been much more easily printed in Rome but which could not circulate freely there. Giustini's sonatas, instead, were printed in Florence, and the Portuguese or Spanish importations

---

[12] Kirkpatrick, *Scarlatti,* 184.

originating in the Tuscan capital were not limited to printed material. In each of the principal Spanish royal residences Scarlatti, his royal pupil, and her husband—not to mention Farinelli—had at their disposal a "clavicordio de Piano echo en Florencia"("a Piano harpsichord made in Florence").[13] The ancestor of the modern pianoforte, then, was not excluded from the sound world of the great musician whose final artistic development would mature in the Iberian peninsula. For the moment it is sufficient to point out this circumstance, in my opinion an important one.

The Infante Don Antonio did not limit his xenophilic preferences to instruments. Kirkpatrick quotes Mazza's *Diccionario biografico de músicos portugueses* to inform us that

> Guided as he was by the mistaken conviction that, whatever they did, the Portuguese would never succeed in equalling the foreigners, the Most Serene Infante D. Antonio asked the great Escarlate, in that period at Lisbon, to give some lessons to Seixas, and he sent [Seixas] to him. It was enough for Scarlatti to see Seixas put his hands on the keyboard to recognize (so to speak) the giant from his finger and to tell him:—It is you who can give lessons to *me*. — Then, encountering Don Antonio, Scarlatti said to him:—Your Highness ordered me to examine him. But I must tell you that this is one of the best musicians that I have ever heard—.[14]

What could he have found in the young Portuguese that was so astonishing to the man who had measured himself against Handel, the performer who had mortified and bewitched Roseingrave?

Certainly there is a dose of exaggerated local pride in the story. The sincere appreciation recounted by Mazza could be well-founded only if we knew with certainty the dates of specific sonatas by Seixas. In any case, Domenico's judgment seems to concern Seixas' technical ability as a performer. As far as composition is concerned, the musical content of the eighty sonatas of Seixas does not justify the hypothesis that the Portuguese composer exercised a decisive influence on characteristically Scarlattian choices.

Comparing the surviving sonatas by Seixas with the considerably better-known masterworks of Scarlatti, Kirkpatrick reached the conclusion that "Seixas remains a provincial composer." He does recognize that "some developments in form in the pieces of Seixas seem to anticipate those of Scarlatti," solomonically proposing a mutual influ-

---

13 *Inventario degli strumenti della regina Maria Barbara*, in Kirkpatrick, *Scarlatti*, 361.
14 José Mazza, *Diccionario biografico de músicos portugueses* (Lisbon, 1944-1945), 32.

ence between the two musicians.[15] Kirkpatrick reminds us several times that it is likely that many of the sonatas in which Domenico Scarlatti demonstrates the fullness of his singularly late maturity were composed after the death of Seixas in 1742. Mazza's account thus regains a certain credibility. He has taken advantage of the unprejudiced attitude of the musician who in Ottoboni's competition had recognized Handel's superiority at the organ and who now acknowledged the talent of the young and obscure Portuguese submitted for his evaluation as a master.

If the unpretentious pupil of Alessandro and Gasparini had been quick to recognize that the organ style of Handel opened previously unimagined horizons to him (horizons subsequently lost from sight, judging from Domenico's surviving organ compositions), now the successful musician recognized the young man's mastery. However, I do not think that Seixas' shadow is projected on Scarlatti's entire corpus. The "Iberian characteristics" cited by Kirkpatrick[16] are only marginally relevant. It is enough to draw attention to certain analogies (such as following the principal section of a sonata with a tiny *Minuet)* to establish an affinity of formal choices, but the insidious hypothesis of "influence" must be founded on a precise dating of the materials to be compared.

At the beginning of Domenico's residence in Portugal, the other royal pupil who had been entrusted to the great master's care was still a little girl. Kirkpatrick[17] justified Maria Barbara's talent on genetic grounds. She was a great-granddaughter of João IV of Portugal, a good composer, an impassioned bibliophile, and an erudite polemicist impelled to write the almost obligatory *Defensa de la música moderna.* On her mother's side, she was the granddaughter of Leopold I of Austria, another crowned musician, the author of genuinely praiseworthy operas.

In 1738, offering to João V the first printed edition of his *Essercizi* (see Fig. 8 on p. 280), Domenico inserted into the verbal delirium of a conventionally Baroque dedication certain expressions that point up the difference that must have existed between the king's "Royal Brother the Infante Don Antonio" and "your deservedly most fortunate Daughter the Princess of the Asturias." All the contemporary testimonies agree in drawing a pleasing portrait of this ugly, brilliant princess, and it must have been an incomparable experience for Domenico Scarlatti to set up his own *Gradus* to the *Parnassum* of perfection by serving as a mentor to so gifted a pupil.

---

[15] Kirkpatrick, *Scarlatti,* 73.
[16] Ibid.
[17] Ibid., 72.

Fig. 8 After Jacopo Amigoni: Titlepage of Domenico Scarlatti, Essercizi
(Washington: Library of Congress)

We know little about the music Domenico composed during his
Portuguese years. If we are to take literally that part of the dedication to
João V that says that the *Essercizi* were composed under his "most high
auspices" and "in the service" of Maria Barbara and of the Infante Don
Antonio, we need only compare these pages of anti-conventional genius
with the cautious orthodoxy of Domenico's *Tocata 10* to measure the strides
Scarlatti had made in this first phase of his evolution. *Tocata
10* is a sort of second-class Handel suite in embryo. It has a lively "Fuga"
that contains the work's only anticipations of Scarlattian *Spielfreude*.[18] This
is contradicted by a flat opening *Allegro* halfway between Venetian *rou-*

---

18 Literally "joy in playing": Kirkpatrick felicitously employed this German expression, weighted with an untranslatable ambiguity.

tine and an homage to papa Alessandro. There are also two dances—a Giga and a Minuetto—that must have given little pleasure to his exceptional pupil, if it is true that she had rhythm in her blood.

I have mentioned the *Tocata 10* because before Gerhard Doederer discovered the important *Libro di Tocate per cembalo* (certainly compiled after 1738, the date the title of "Cavaliero" was granted, a date that figures on the titlepage of the collection),[19] it was the only harpsichord composition by Domenico Scarlatti transmitted in a Portuguese manuscript. The resemblance to minor Handel suggests, however, that the *Tocata-Suite* might go back to the *Wanderjahre,* to the exchange of experiences between the two young men who had remained friends despite the cock-fight between Domenico and "the famous Saxon"organized by Ottoboni at the Cancelleria. This idea is prompted by a strange manuscript in Bologna, in which fugues and sonatas by Domenico are associated with fugues that Handel later included in his large *Suites.* What leads me to call the Bologna manuscript "strange"? Its florid titlepage, which after speaking of "Two diverse Works/The first by Sig.r Domenico Scarlati,/ and the second by Sig.r Federico Handel," offers us, at the foot of the page, a minuscule indication of ownership that is a real gem: "For the Study of Francesco Gasparini."

Although this discussion of sources does not form part of the general plan of this work, I could not omit this detail in order to share the complex problems facing anyone who ventures into the labyrinth of conjectural datings.

The first problem is the identification of the owner: is it Gasparini, the celebrated teacher? If so, we must consider the possibility that the two "fuguers"went to consult the oracle: thus I interpret the phrase "for the Study" of an old and revered master. However, the death of Gasparini (22 March 1727) limits the dating of the pieces contained in the manuscript. The works by Scarlatti include the notorious *Cat's Fugue* (K. 30), a group of sonatas homogeneously placed in the Kirkpatrick catalogue (K. 148-150, 155, 158), and two other apparently later sonatas (K. 426, 430) that not even my bias against rash stylistic analysis can convince me are located correctly in the Venice and Parma manuscripts and in the Kirkpatrick catalogue (above all, the famous *Tempo di Ballo,* K. 430). K. 426, although finally employed in the manuscripts as the first element of a pair completed by the famous K. 427, is extremely close to other early *Andantes* in the first volumes of the Venice series.

---

[19] Doederer, *Tocate.*

But even if the *Essercizi* (or part of them) had already been composed in Portugal, only Domenico Scarlatti's later Spanish experience would
permit him to detach himself finally from vocal *routine* to which his duties
as court *maestro di cappella* obliged him. The eagle had to free himself of
such heavy ballast in order to soar off on the incomparable flight whose
results might have left papa Alessandro surprised, but not displeased.

Ma in Ispagna ...

On the throne of Spain there sat—against his will—that same Philip V
whom we last saw intent on waging war with Charles III after having
mortified Corelli in Naples.

    With the death of Maria Luisa of Savoy, the wife who bore two
future kings of Spain, Philip had fallen more than ever under the influence of Anne La Trémoille, widow of prince Orsini, the powerful
camarera mayor whom Louis XIV had imposed on his grandson. The
rumors that the marriage of the young and weak king with the ancient
noblewoman was imminent were quickly denied. Madame des Ursins
(as the princess called herself, combining her French origin with a bad
translation of her Italian title) was too intelligent not to realize the im-
possibility of binding to herself by means of the bedchamber a young
ruler whose insatiable sensuality bordered on erotomania. The problem
was well known to the *camarera,* who in Maria Luisa's last days had
been obliged to take on the delicate task of asking Philip V to spare his
dying wife, who was covered with sores, the macabre evidence of his attachment dictated by a permanent state of erotic excitement.

    Ministering to the needs of a satyr who was both a king and a
bigot constituted a real political problem. The situation left scope for
the initatives of Giulio Alberoni, the astute Italian abate destined to flame
like a bloody meteor across the history of Spain and of Europe. His debut
was worthy of his capacities for intrigue. When he had insinuated himself
into Mme. des Ursins' good graces, Alberoni told her about a simple little
princess, brought up in the ducal palace of Parma, who only knew how to
do a bit of sewing ... At the same time the abate succeeded in dazzling
the king with the prospect of ending his long abstinence by marrying "a
plump Lombard woman, kneaded up with butter and parmesan [...]."[20]

    Alberoni later declared that the only things needed to dominate
Philip V completely were "a prie-dieu and a woman's thighs."[21] The abate

20 Docteur Cabanès, *Le Mal Héréditaire* (Deuxième série), *Les Bourbons d'Espagne*
(Paris, n. d. [1927]) [hereafter Cabanès], 122.
21 Kirkpatrick, *Scarlatti,* 84: he explains that he found the Italian phrase in D. A. Bal-

did not consider himself enough of a churchman to manage the prayer-desk in person, but his extraordinary subtlety worked out on the pun on "thighs" ("coscie") and "conscience" ("coscienza") possible in Italian.

Presented in a light that was so favorable to the king's needs and to Mme. des Ursins' requirements, Elisabetta Farnese was chosen as the wife of Philip V. Alberoni taught Elisabetta well. When the *camarera mayor* received the young queen, with some reproach for delaying on her trip, Elisabetta had her arrested and immediately exiled her to France, not even giving her time to change out of her low-cut court dress. Alberoni had assured royal approval for the whole operation, reminding Philip of Mme. des Ursins' interference in his semi-necrophiliac practices.

The prince of Monaco, who had the opportunity of observing the young queen when he entertained her for several days on her slow journey from Parma to Spain, had already undermined the myth of the simple little girl. He enumerated artistic and venatorial capabilities in the princess that went far beyond the semidomestic dimension craftily pointed out by Alberoni, culminating in an observation that interests us more closely:

> She loves music passionately, knows it wonderfully, accompanies perfectly on the harpsichord, but sings little because, according to what she did me the honor of confiding to me, her voice was too weak [...].[22]

The meeting of the spouses was completely appropriate: a mass, so that the sacramental rite could complete the marriage already celebrated by proxy; then off to bed for several hours, leaving the nuptial chamber only to attend midnight mass.

Saint-Simon observed that the queen found herself both jailor and prisoner, but it was Alberoni who kept the key of the prison in his pocket ... [23] Even in the first phase of her marriage, Elisabetta was accused of arousing her already boiling spouse to the point of paroxysm by a diet based on spices, ragouts, meat, and Alicante wine, assuring her complete domination by the shrewd administration of caresses and refusals.

Several years later, when Alberoni's intrigues as unofficial first minister of Spain had earned him the hostility of all Europe, he suffered the fate he had once prepared for Mme. des Ursins. His revenge for his exile consisted of recounting the backstage gossip of alcove and prayer-

---

lesteros, *Historia de España* (Barcelona, 1914-1941), VI, 524; and in C. P. Duclos, *Mémoires* (Paris, 1791), II, 64.

[22] Letter of 19 October to Torcy, quoted by Cabanès, 130.

[23] Saint-Simon, *Mémoires,* XII, 317-318.

stool, the means by which he had been able to impose himself on Spain and on the world. To rescue the image of the princess whom he had brought to the throne, Alberoni (who in the meantime had been raised to the purple in spite of the opposition of Cardinal del Giudice) attributed to Philip V full responsibility for dragging the queen into his bestial lasciviousness. He revealed that the king's abrupt transition from erotic stimulation to fear of heavenly punishment catapulted him into the disturbed mental condition that would soon become obvious to everyone.

In 1721 Saint-Simon[24] arrived at the court as French ambassador extraordinary charged with concluding a double marriage, one of those multiple knots designed to assure the durability of political alliances but often belied by the inexorable course of history. An infanta of Spain, still a child, was promised as a wife to Louis XV and moved to France to be prepared for her role as queen, while Louise-Elisabeth de Montpensier, daughter of Louis XIV's brother, the Duke of Orléans, married Philip V's first son, Luis, heir to the throne. When Saint-Simon was received at court, he could not recognize in the emaciated human wreck on the throne the handsome Duke of Anjou whom the Sun King had theatrically presented to his courtiers on the death of Charles II by announcing in the style of Tacitus: "The king of Spain!" "A portrait by Mignard repainted by Zurbarán" was Saint-Simon's acute comment.

Only three years later Philip V's mental deterioration was so advanced as to prevent the ambitious Elisabetta from opposing his abdication, and on 10 January 1724 the king signed the solemn act which unloaded the cares of state onto the fragile shoulders of his son Luis. The ex-king retired into a convent with his wife and a modest suite, with the intention of "meriting a more lasting kingdom in heaven." The example of the great emperor Charles V had suggested such a remedy for earthly ills, but Cabanès (author of the colorful monograph dedicated to the mental disasters of the kings of Spain, from which I have drawn a large part of the information contained in this chapter) rightly points out that Philip V was only a pale imitation of his great predecessor.[25]

The behavior of the young French princess who had ascended the throne left much to be desired; it appears that the young king also left something to be desired in the fulfillment of his marital duties. When the extravagances of the new queen had passed every limit, Philip V, consulted in his refuge, decided that Louise-Elisabeth should be shut up in the royal palace in Madrid to do penance. After a few weeks, how-

---

[24] See the long account in vols. XVI-XVII of the *Mémoires*.
[25] Cabanès, 148.

ever, the capricious little queen promised to reform herself and the youthful menage was re-established.

But only for a short time: on August 31 a violent attack of smallpox carried Luis I off, leaving the Spanish with the embarassment of yet another widowed queen (the severe and composed widow of Charles II was still alive). Louise-Elisabeth was quickly sent back to her native country with an entourage worthy of Spanish magnificence, but the irregularity with which her income was paid reflected the dislike in which the shrewish princess was held.

The unhappy experience of a kingdom entrusted to an immature king obliged Philip V, urged on by Elisabetta, to renounce his pious retirement in order to take up again the reins of goverment, although he reserved the right to abdicate again when his second son Fernando had come of age.

Philip had heirs by both his wives, but even a young king could be a cause of concern when the direct succession was not assured, as occurred in France after the illness that had endangered the life of Louis XV. Given her youth, the Infanta of Spain—the royal fiancée imported by Saint-Simon—could offer no immediate solution to the thorny problem of an heir. For reasons of state it was decided to restore the young girl to her parents. When the Spanish ambassador in Paris was informed of the dismaying news, he declared that "all the blood of his compatriots would not suffice to wash away the offence that France had given his king." He received the reply that "all the tears of the French could not erase the sorrow that they felt at being obliged to such a grave decision."[26]

After explosions of rage proportionate to the seriousness of the situation, the crisis was overcome. Philip answered Elisabetta, who demanded the expulsion of all the French from Spain, with unusually humorous good sense: he ordered all his baggage to be prepared, since his birth obliged him to set an example and be the first to respect so severe an order ...

In reality the problems at the Spanish court were quite different: the king's old illness was reappearing in worrying forms. This time, having gotten herself onto the Council of the Crown together with the Prince of the Asturias (the future Fernando VI, son of the king's first marriage), Elisabetta did not let her husband out of her sight for a minute, fearful that he would sign a new act of abdication. When this did in fact happen in June of 1728, the president of the Council of Castile, who should have published the king's decree, delayed completing the for-

[26] Ibid., 216.

malities until the queen and the French ambassador could persuade the sick man to rescind his decision. From then on, Philip V no longer had pen or ink at his disposal: only burnt-out candle wicks dissolved in water and little rolls of paper, on which he could amuse himself by drawing ...

Even the pleasures of the bedchamber had lost interest for the king, and through the Prince of the Asturias he tormented Elisabetta, the jailer whom he had come to hate since her "coscie" no longer interested him. Fernando was the heir to the throne, and his father reserved for him his gleams of affectionate humor, arousing the jealousy of his ambitious consort. Nonetheless, she was obliged to pretend affection for the detested stepson who—for the moment—barred the way to the throne of her own son Charles. Elisabetta Farnese and her husband were unaware that Fernando would be incapable of assuring the hoped-for heirs to the crown of Spain in the direct male line.

In the meantime reasons of state made it opportune to bury old disagreements and to consolidate the links between Spain and Portugal by means of a double marriage. The heir to the Spanish throne took as his wife the Infanta Maria Barbara; the future José of Portugal wedded Maria Ana Victoria, the rejected queen of France. His doctor, his confessor, and his tutor had expressed doubts that the Prince of the Asturias was mature enough for a regular married life.[27] Although the marriage was solemnized at Lisbon on 11 January 1728 where the future Fernando VI was represented by his father-in-law, the actual wedding was not celebrated until 19 January 1729.

Music had its part in the sumptuous festivities in Lisbon, but no document certifies that Domenico Scarlatti was physically present at the performance of the *Festeggio armonico,* an epithalamium for the "royal marriage of the most high and most mighty most serene lords D. Ferdinando of Spain prince of Asturias and D. Maria Infanta of Portugal" and sung on January 11 and 12, 1729 on both occasions "in a kind of theater, constructed for this purpose" in the Paço da Ribeira.[28]

Alvarenga believes that Scarlatti remained in Rome, taken up with preparations for his own marriage. He finds a confirmation of the musician's absence from Lisbon in the fact that, contrary to every local custom, on the libretto printed for the occasion Scarlatti's name appears

---

[27] Pedro Voltes, *La vida y la época de Fernando VI* (Madrid: Planeta, 1996), 49.

[28] The serenata, performed 11 January in the king's apartment, was repeated the following day in the queen's. News of it is found in the *relazione* of the Nuncio and in the *Gazeta de Lisboa Occidental* of 15 January 1728, which gives the detail about the construction of the theater.

with the title of "Royal composer" and not "Maestro di Cappella of the King."[29] This detail would suggest a special commission and does not imply that Domenico had again taken up his previous post. It seems certain that Scarlatti also was not present at the complicated ceremony in which the crowns of Spain and Portugal exchanged heirs to the throne and Infantas. In a late account of the event only the name of Francisco Antonio de Almeida, organist of the Patriarchal Basilica, is mentioned.[30]

The participation of Philip V and João V had created thorny problems of etiquette, diplomatically overcome by their masters of ceremonies, who devised a brilliantly eccentric solution: on a river between the two kingdoms there was built a sumptuous pavilion allowing the two monarchs to participate in the ceremony without crossing the border, and therefore without compromising their respective prerogatives.

Fernando was sixteen years old and his bride seventeen. It seems that at first the young prince could not hide his disappointment (see Fig.9 on p. 288). The English ambassador, who was in a position to gather every detail of the ceremony, wrote:

> I could not but observe, that the princess's figure, notwithstanding a profusion of gold and diamonds, really shocked the prince. He looked as if he thought he had been imposed upon. Her large mouth, thick lips, high cheek-bones and small eyes afforded him no agreeable prospect [...].[31]

But Maria Barbara had other attractions, and the union of the two, sterile and incomplete from a physical point of view, was exemplary in terms of affection, mutual esteem, and absolute identity of tastes.

Some years after the marriage their failure to produce the desired offspring aroused the general suspicion that all was not well in that *ménage*. The series of children Elisabetta Farnese had brought into the world, a primary consequence of her exaggerated conjugal duties, eliminated any risks for the succession, but international diplomacy wanted to know the facts. The French archives reveal what nourished Philip V's depression but secretly delighted Elisabetta.

In a dispatch of 19 January 1739, which I must quote in French in order not to compromise the play of *double-entendre*, La Marck wrote to the minister Amelot, concerning Fernando:

[29] Alvarenga, 113-114.

[30] Ibid.

[31] Quoted in William Coxe, *Memoirs of the Kings of Spain of the House of Bourbon,* 2nd ed.(London, 1815), III, 231-233.

Fig. 9 Nicolaus Valleta: *Maria Barbara de Braganza*
from G. B. Martini, Storia della Musica
(Biblioteca Apostolica Vaticana)

Quoique, par sa grande jeunesse, il se trouve en lui les mouvements nécessaires pour contenter une femme, cependant il lui manquait *naturellement* ce qu'on ôte par artifice en Italie à ceux qu'on veut faire entrer dans la musique, en sorte que ce prince avait beaucoup de feux, mais qui ne produisaient aucunes flammes, ni aucunes suites propres à la génération.[32]

(Although by reason of his great youth, he finds in himself those movements necessary to satisfy a woman, nonetheless he lacks *by nature* what one removes by artifice in Italy from those whom one wishes to make enter [the profession of] music, so that this prince had many fires, but they produced no flames, nor any results proper to procreation.)

If I understand correctly, there was enough mechanical capacity, aided by the "flames," to satisfy his wife, but no descendants; I am not certain that I have interpreted adequately the metaphor of "flames." Maria Barbara, however, had very different reasons for satisfaction: it must have been particularly pleasing for an unprepossessing woman to exercise an enormous influence over her husband, which no one could say resembled the influence that had enslaved Philip to Elisabetta.

Amid so many affinities of taste, music was the couple's special meeting ground: they gorged themselves on it in the privacy of their apartments while the court followed the inverted schedules and rhythms imposed by the madness of Philip V. When we recall that Domenico Scarlatti taught music not only to the Princess but also to the Prince of the Asturias, we see how great a part he played in these entertainments.

This new employment removed Domenico from the usual chronicles of the period. Sometimes the *Gaceta de Madrid* reported vaguely "el festejo de una primorosa Música de vozes, y instromentos" ("the entertainment of an exquisite Music for voices and instruments") that the "Princesa" held in her apartment,[33] without ever mentioning the name of the musician who must have been the protagonist of those and other more intimate evenings. A thick curtain of discretion surrounds this period of Domenico's activity. He must have been intent on cultivating the talent of his splendid pupil by initiating her into the "more intimate knowledge" and "more recondite artifices" of music, as Padre Martini put it.[34] He also initiated the mild Fernando into the joys of paw-

---

[32] Quoted by Cabanès, 244.

[33] Kirkpatrick, *Scarlatti*, 87; he quotes numbers 21, 49, and 52 of 1729.

[34] Giambattista Martini, *Storia della Musica* (Bologna: Dalla Volpe, 1757) I, VII (dedication to the "Sacra Real Maestà MARIA BARBARA infanta di Portogallo, regina delle Spagne ec. ec. ec.)

ing away at the keyboard, performing simpler pieces or accompanying singers and instrumentalists willing, like courtiers, to pardon him
for being out of time or for the incorrect choice of some chord.

In spite of her documented taste for music, Elisabetta Farnese
was excluded from these concerts for several reasons. In addition to her
jealousy of the Princes of the Asturias, she could not lose sight of her
husband even for an instant, and he was too little given to music to be
attracted to those refined gatherings. Paradoxically, the heirs to the throne
owed to an initiative of the queen the addition of a major protagonist of
European musical life to their entertainments: the great castrato Farinelli.

In the distant days of the physical and mental decline of Charles
II, the singing of Matteuccio (the musician who made love to an officer
in a church in Venice) had shaken the insane monarch out of his lethargy. Facing a repetition of this tragic situation, the older courtiers must
have recalled the ancient miracle and perhaps demanded a similar therapy.

Probably no one knew that in his youth Philip V had displayed
intense boredom listening to an adagio of Corelli; the fact remains that his
condition was so desperate that the queen resorted to this last-ditch attempt.

Her choice fell on Carlo Broschi called Farinelli, the most acclaimed singer of the period (see Fig. 10 on facing page). Spanish diplo-
mats reached him in England where he was enjoying a triumph and promised him double his fabulous earnings merely to have him in Spain. We
read of this important installation in Giovenale Sacchi's biography:

> Farinelli found himself in London in 1737, the thirty-second year
> of his age, he was at the height of his fame. That was the last year,
> that he was heard on the Stage, because from then on he employed
> his voice, and his whole life in the service of the Kings of Spain in
> order to soothe their soul from the cares of the kingdom, or better
> the weight of mortality, which tires, and oppresses Kings, no less
> than private persons. He was called to this office through the doing
> of Queen Elisabetta heir not only of the State of Parma, but also of
> the protection, and benignity, which the Dukes of Parma her elders
> had had for him in his first youth. She thought of substituting this
> expedient for the hunt, for which King Felipe Fifth was no longer
> sufficiently strong [...]. On the journey he sang for the King in
> Paris, where according to what Riccoboni narrates, he ravished all
> his hearers. The French at that period detested Italian music, but on
> that occasion they had occasion to doubt, that they were deceived.
> He arrived in Madrid on the day of S. Gaetano [Thiene: August 7],
> to whom he had a special devotion, and in his first trials so pleased

Fig. 10 Pier Leone Ghezzi: Farinelli in a Female Role
(The Pierpont Morgan Library)

the King, that he decided to keep him constantly near him, whence he established for each year a salary corresponding to that which would have been given him in London for six months by means of a royal decree, that declares him a member of his household, and a servant independent of any Tribunal, except only of his Royal Person, and of the Queen, adding to the said salary a house, and a carriage from the royal stables with the king's livery, and carriages for his entourage [...].

It seemed that the King could not live a day without him, which should not be attributed to his singing, but rather, or at least much more to his excellent manners. He spoke Italian and French notably well; in a short time he accustomed himself to Castilian; he also had a bit of German, and English. He was most polite, and very prudent, but at the same time open-hearted and frank; by which virtue the King was greatly pleased. And certainly Kings must feel more than others the pleasure of friendly conversation without pretence and artfulness when they find it in someone, and according to their rank they can allow it, since it is very rare that they find such a one [from whom] they do not have to fear deceit, or who should not seem to offend their dignity, and sovereign will in some manner. The sweetness of such conversation was increased by the remembrance of the cities, and of the things of Italy, where the King had been for some time. Every day as soon as he awoke he said: Let Farinelli be informed, that this evening we await him at the customary hour. Farinelli presented himself a bit before midnight, and was never dismissed, but at daybreak, that is about four hours later and he then retired to his apartment; for he had an apartment at Court, although he also had another house. Every evening he sang three or four arias; and, it seems barely believable to say, always the same ones. Two were by Signor Hasse: *Pallido il sole: E pur* [recte: *Per*]*questo dolce amplesso.* The third was a minuet, which he was accustomed to vary at his pleasure; the fourth an imitation of the nightingale, I do not know by which Poet, nor who set it to music. Of what arias could it ever be said, that they were more fortunate than these? And if by chance (that all the same was very rare) the others were omitted, the aria of the nightingale was never omitted. Farinelli was nonetheless dispensed from such conversation, and service, every time that his most pious Prince approached the Holy Sacraments, because he employed the preceding evening in preparation. Farinelli knew the sincere affection that the King bore to him, and reciprocated it fully, because he loved him as much as one most tender friend could love another. He strove to keep him happy, in which he had great ability with his discourse, although he himself was of melancholy temperament; and as he sometimes found himself indisposed, he courageously conquered himself, and never allowed the King to want for his service [...].[35]

This is an extraordinarily saccharine version of the real facts. Farinelli's continued loyalty to his royal benefactors prevented him from telling the truth about the ritual that for long years had transformed him into a kind of Scheherazade in reverse. He was constrained to repeat himself—consoling himself with the improvised variations on the unidentified minuet—every evening to renew the myths of Orpheus, Linus, and Amphion, in order to drag out of his lethargy a sick man who, when young and healthy, had experienced the opposite effect from his contact with music of exceptional quality.

Among other things, this extremely discreet account shows us a Philip V more or less master of himself. However, other sources make it clear that by Farinelli's arrival on 7 August 1737 the king had lain in bed for many months, never allowing anyone to attend to his personal cleanliness, change his sheets, or renew his linen.

His melancholy no longer consisted of the passing crises which in his youth had troubled the king's Italian journey. Now dark fears paralyzed his every effort, and not even Alberoni's old expedients succeeded in dragging Philip out of a lethargy that combined terror and a desire for death. The "thighs of a woman" ... these erotic fantasies must have been far distant from that living corpse, deaf to earthly entreaties and terrified by the mysteries of the Great Beyond. There still remained the "prayer-stool," but it seemed impossible that the king could emerge far enough out of his depression to kneel there.

A harpsichord was placed in a room of the royal apartment, at some distance from the sordid pallet. The queen ordered the doors to be opened, and the sublime song of the famous castrato poured out to the ears of the king. In the face of so special an entreaty, the madman shook off his torpor, moved by curiosity to know whose voice had dared to snatch a dead man back from Hades.

Farinelli approached the bed to complete his marvelous exorcism. Having promised his savior to grant any request that he might make, Philip suffered a new shock: instead of claiming riches and honors, the great singer begged him courteously to transform the stinking human larva vegetating in his bed back into a king of Spain, willing to return to the tasks of government.

---

[35] *Vita del cavaliere Carlo Broschi scritta da Giovenale Sacchi...* (Venice: Coleti, 1784) [hereafter Sacchi, *Broschi*], 17-20.

Philip could not go back on his promise, but Farinelli would have every reason to regret the miracle that he had worked: for many years the king had been accustomed to a reversal of timetables, which even Sacchi's prettified account does not conceal. Imposed on the whole court, this schedule tested the resistence of dignitaries who were no longer young. When Philip V asked the great singer to renew his spell in the middle of the night, his insistence displayed all the characteristics of psychotic infantile regression, including both the necessity of frenzied repetition as well as the grotesque need to imitate his model. (In the critical phase of his illness the king competed with Farinelli, attempting to emit lacerating high notes that were strangled in his throat.) Along with a splendid career—his return to the stage was unthinkable—Farinelli had renounced his endless repertory. The insane king only wished to re-hear the pieces that had become his talismans. When the howls of the madman drowned out the enchanted song of the pathetic nightingale, Farinelli must have clearly realized the abyss into which he had plunged.

The power that the singer acquired at court has virtually no parallel in history. Before the generous and disinterested instrument of her ambitions, Elisabetta Farnese was disarmed. The musician administered his influence over the king scrupulously and was never willing to draw illicit profits from his exceptional privileges. The numerous attempts to corrupt him by Spanish aristocrats and representatives of the principal European powers failed. Returning a coffer filled with gold to the nobleman who had delivered it, Farinelli said that he had no need of money and added proudly that he was certain that in case of need the king would not leave him in difficulties. There was a spirit of sacrifice in his renunciation of artistic success, but also loyal gratitude to the monarchs who offered him a new prestige that completed the unanimous recognition of his merits and compensated him for certain joys from which his emasculated condition excluded him.

Metastasio's correspondence reflects the affectionate relationship that linked the poet and Farinelli (whom he always called his "Twin" in memory of the debut in Naples that joined them in success from 1722 on). A letter of 1751 in which the poet rejoices in the news from the new Spanish plenipotentiary at the court of Vienna is particularly significant:

> I questioned him a great deal about you, for whom I am solicitous, as everyone is for the things which are dearest, and I was highly consoled by his answers. He assured me that the prosperous circumstances in which you find yourself have not changed your sweet, even character one bit. A rock (according to both ancient and modern examples) most difficult to avoid: and much more

among the favors, than among the persecutions of fortune. He assured me that in so enviable a state you have no enemies. To achieve that I can imagine how wise, how disinterested, and how kindly your conduct must be. I rejoice with you in this inestimable capital that is yours, and not the property of fortune; and I rejoice with myself that I have known and loved you, before you had given such shining proofs of being lovable to this degree.[36]

A portrait of Farinelli as an artist would be incomplete without his encounter with the emperor Charles VI, an encounter that was decisive for his maturing as an interpreter. Since Kirkpatrick quoted Burney's account, I turn to Sacchi to relate the episode:

When he [the emperor] had therefore heard Farinello several times, and accompanied him himself at the harpsichord, he condescended to speak with familiarly about art, and with that kindness, which was incomparable in him, he said to him:

"All the components in you are admirable. When you sing you neither move, nor stand as others do. You surpass the slowest in slowness, and the swiftest in velocity. All other things in you surpass expectation. This was the sure way of arousing wonder, of making yourself famous. Now would be the time for you to think of pleasing better by employing the gifts with which nature has most liberally enriched you. To that end it is appropriate, that your steps be those of a man, not of a giant. Choose a more simple and even method, and you will ravish hearts." [37]

The strange coincidences of history: the man who cured Philip V being instructed in the art of capturing hearts by Philip's bitterest enemy. We should note, however, to note that in order for his therapy to succeed Farinelli had to emphasize his capacities as an astonishing vocal wizard, rather than the expressive components of his singing.

When his vocal servitude did not keep him busy with the sick king, the great singer took part in the quite different musical entertainments that were held in the apartments of the Prince or the Princess of the Asturias. An English traveler transmits an extraordinary testimony of Farinelli's astonishing firmness with the queen to whom he owed his present fortune:

---

[36] *Raccolta di lettere scientifiche, familiari, e giocose dell'abate Pietro Metastasio Romano*, 1st ed. (Rome: Gioacchino Puccinelli, n. d.) [hereafter Metastasio, *Raccolta*], IV, 131.

[37] Sacchi, *Broschi,* 28.

While the late king Ferdinand was Prince of Asturias, upon some umbrage, she [Elisabetta, jealous as we have seen of the musical pleasures from which she was excluded] sent a message to Farinelli never to go and sing or play any more in the Prince's or Princess's apartment. For the late Queen Barbara was not only very fond of, but an excellent judge of musick. But Farinelli's answer does immortal honour to that musician. 'Go,' says he, 'and tell the Queen, that I owe the greatest obligations to the Prince and Princess of Asturias, and unless I receive such an order from her Majesty's own mouth, or the King's I will never obey it.'[38]

Elisabetta's resentment is more than understandable. In the padded atmosphere of those princely chambers the miracles of Scarlatti's art were combined with hearing a mythical singer whom the general public could no longer applaud, and whom the queen herself was obliged to hear under the twisted circumstances we have described.

From the great deal that there is to say about Farinelli's Spanish sojourn I would like to extract an observation from Burney describing Domenico Alberti's passage to Spain:

[...] an illustrious amateur from Venice, he has a good right to be included here as a dramatic composer and as an exquisite player on the harpsichord, and the author of elegant and pleasing pieces for that instrument. He was a pupil of Biffi and Lotti and went to Spain as page to the Venetian ambassador at that court. His manner of singing aroused the wonder of Farinelli himself, who declared that he was right to be happy that Alberti was not a professional, 'since,' he added, 'I would have had in him too formidable a rival with whom to compete.' Alberti later went to Rome, where he continued to cultivate singing and performance on the harpsichord. In 1737 he set to music *Endimione,* written by Metastasio; and, some time later, *Galatea* by the same lyric poet. In Venice I procured various compositions of Alberti, little known in England and rare everywhere, and I consider them the most exquisite of the period in which they were composed.[39]

The expressions he used to describe a dilettante endowed with great qualities should be taken with a grain of salt: a certain dose of conventional courtesy inevitably plays a part in their formulation. Alberti made a name for himself as an elegant harpsichordist more than as a singer. His name remains linked to the adoption, if not indeed the in-

---

[38] Edward Clarke, *Letters Concerning the Spanish Nation, Written at Madrid during the Years 1760 and 1761* (London, 1763), 329.
[39] Burney, *General,* II, 910.

vention, of the Alberti bass, the accompaniment-formula that dissolves the harmonic blocks of chord texture into horizontal arpeggios. Burney's information makes a meeting between Farinelli and Alberti absolutely unlikely, at least in Spain. The singer arrived in Madrid on 7 August 1737, when Alberti had already moved on to Rome and then to Venice (where on September 24 of that year a "Company of Merchants" performed his serenata for four voices *Endimione,* in a private house).

If Alberti encountered a famous musician in Spain, it could be none other than Domenico Scarlatti (and the ceremonious praise much resembles his previous comments about Handel and Seixas). Domenico's vocal performance, discovered by Doederer, could give new credibility to Burney's version but I prefer to transfer the encounter to the keyboard. Scarlatti certainly knew Alberti's harpsichord works, since he later reproached Alberti and other modern composers for not having exploited the technical possibilities of the harpsichord to their fullest extent.[40] I find indirect evidence of a contact between Alberti and Scarlatti in a manuscript collection of twenty-four Scarlatti sonatas (all datable in a manner compatible with the hypothesis I am formulating), possibly copied by Albertti and now preserved in the Fitzwilliam Museum in Cambridge. The titlepage of the collection states that it is a *Libro de Sonatas de Clave Para el. ex.mo S.or Eñbaxator de Benecia de D.n Domingo Scarlati.*

The manuscript in question is the only source transmitting two sonatas which Sheveloff considers spurious, K. 145 and 146.[41] Tracing this possible link with Alberti could furnish additional information, but especially in the second of these (the famous K. 146 with the chains of written-out appoggiaturas alternating between the two hands) I find very little of the "Albertine" (but indeed equally little of the "Scarlattian," since a similar design does not recur in other Scarlatti sonatas). Without much conviction, I might recall a brilliant *tour de force* of speculation by Kirkpatrick to discover in these pages the exploit of an exceptional pupil, forbidden by her rank to sign the products of her own talent ...

We have arrived at the *Barbarian* hypothesis, maintained with elegant self-irony by Kirkpatrick in a little-known publication: "Who Wrote the Scarlatti Sonatas?" and eloquently subtitled "A Study in Reverse Scholarship."[42] This short essay develops a thesis analogous to the one attributing at least a part of the works of Shakespeare to Bacon.

---

[40] Burney, *Germany,* I, 249.

[41] Sheveloff, II, 450-453 (sonatas K. 145 and 146).

[42] Ralph Kirkpatrick, "Who Wrote the Scarlatti Sonatas: A Study in Reverse Scholarship," *Notes* XXVI (1971), 5-15.

According to this theory, there is no hard evidence that Domenico Scarlatti was the real author of the sonatas; the authentic testimonies of his skill as a player are very few, and almost all of them were given decades after the actual experience of hearing him. Why not view Scarlatti as the complacent lender of his name to the efforts of his exceptional pupil, disqualified by her dignity as a princess, and later a queen, from signing her sonatas?

This in an exercise in speculation, an astute and humorous send-up of the rigorously positivistic attitudes dear to Kirkpatrick himself. The impulse for such a brilliant set of variations arose in the context of a dinner in Rome. It is necessary to have known Kirkpatrick at table—and here I render affectionate homage to the memory of that unforgettable man—to understand how far a convivial moment could stimulate his dialectical capabilities. We need only quote the conclusion of this extraordinary essay:

> It is not necessary to say that I do not believe a single word of the *Barbarian* hypothesis, but since it is based on the very same type of arguments employed in my *Domenico Scarlatti* I prefer to formulate it myself now with a certain dose of frivolity, rather than have someone else advance it with absolute seriousness.[43]

... filium bonae memoriae equitis Alexandri

Once again I have digressed from my historico-biographical objective, but it was tempting to project the shadow of the *Barbarian* hypothesis (in which I scarcely believe) onto the two doubtful sonatas in the manuscript compiled for the Venetian ambassador. The attention devoted to monarchs and ministers has also led me away from the vicissitudes of Domenico.

We must return to Portugal in 1728. According to Walther's catalogue, in that year Scarlatti was installed at the head of musical life in Lisbon, but Doederer's discoveries shatter the categorical time-references given by the German lexicographer. Probably Alvarenga is right when he maintains that the changes in Scarlatti during his period in Rome,[44] may be logically attributed to the removal of his father's crushing influence.

We now know that recurrent physical indispositions had convinced Domenico to return to Rome for his health. His case was not a

---

[43]Ibid., 15.
[44]Alvarenga, op. cit., 113.

new one, and an evocative page of Kirkpatrick offers the reader a catalogue of foreigners who were victims of a sort of Iberian curse:

> [...] Spain has always had a pronounced effect on foreigners; it both fascinates and unsettles them. On those who visit, it makes an unforgettable impression, and on those who go there to live, it works a drastic and sometimes catastrophic change. For some it is a stimulant; for others it is utter destruction. We shall shortly see to what extent the Versailles-bred Felipe V was destroyed by his adopted country. Someone has remarked on the curious dissolution of all the French diplomats who crossed the Pyrenees in his reign; Juvarra and Tiepolo died in Spain, perhaps not quite accidentally. There the painter Mengs was attacked by 'marasmus.' There the aging Casanova had the bitterest and most sombre experiences of his adventurous career."[45]

Unaware of later discoveries, Kirkpatrick pointed out that Scarlatti's youth was passed in a country dominated by Spain, and that as a youth he came in contact with the middle-eastern traditions of the Saracens that in Sicily and in the Neapolitan provinces had almost erased those of Magna Grecia. These, he maintained, protected Domenico from the explosive mixture of Moorish sensuality and the idolatrous bigotry of the Counter-Reformation. Now we know that this was not the case.

By 5 December 1719, a few days after the long-awaited arrival of the new "Head and Director of all the music of the Patriarchal Basilica," the papal Nuncio sent to Rome a *relazione* in which we find Domenico described as "Scarlattino most extraordinary Professor of music."[46] I had imagined that the diminutive applied to his slight physique, without excluding the idea that even in Lisbon "Scarlattino" could be dogged by the comparison with "papa-Scarlattone." Now I understand that the first hypothesis was correct, absurd as it may appear to anyone who rejects the idea that the volcano of vitality and musical invention so many of his sonatas offer was housed in a slender little body.

The *relazioni* of the Nuncio continued to communicate to Rome evidence of Domenico's presence and activity in Lisbon, which Gerhard Doederer and Cremilde Rosado Fernandes transcribed in detail in an appendix to their important article of 1993. João Pedro d'Alvarenga collated this information with extracts from the *Gazeta de Lisboa Occidental,* offering the reader a chronological table showing those lacunae that Doederer explained by Scarlatti's activity in the musical *routine* of

---

[45] Kirkpatrick, *Scarlatti,* 81.
[46] ASV-Portogallo, vol. 75, f. 278v.

Lisbon. Now, after the discovery of Domenico's passages through Paris, such lacunae should be reread as documenting the breaks in his stay in the Portuguese capital. Alvarenga has attempted this, but his results are not always convincing. He considered that Paris was a stopping-point on one or two pilgrimages to the operatic Promised Land of London later than the supposed visit in 1719.

It was difficult for me to believe that Domenico's participation in the musical activities of the English capital had remained unknown to a researcher with the resources of Burney, who was extremely interested in collecting any news concerning Scarlatti. However, the date of Domenico's first trip to Paris, May of 1724, restores credibility to the hypothesis advanced in an earlier edition of Grove concerning the benefit concert in the course of which an unspecified "Signor Scarlatti" performed on March 20 in the Hickford Room.

The indentification as "most likely Domenico" was refuted by Frank Walker,[47] who quotes four extracts from the *Daily Courant* which he discovered in the periodicals collected by Burney. The first two extracts are the well-known ones advertising the performances of *"Signor Francisco Scarlatti, Brother to the famous Alessandro Scarlatti"* scheduled for 1 May 1719 and 1 September 1720. The third extract announces for 28 May 1721 the performance of a *Serenata* composed by the Cavaliere Alessandro Scarlatti and sung by the castrato Senesino, the women Durastanti, Robinson, and Salvai, and the bass Boschi.

The fourth announcement is worth transcribing in its entirety, since the London dates fit perfectly with the first of Domenico's trips to Paris and make it possible that the London notices refer to him:

> This is to give notice, that the Consort of Musick at Mr. Hickford's Great Room in James-Street, near the Hay-market, for the benefit of Signor Scarlatti, which was to be perform'd on Monday next, the 16th Instant [March 1724], is put off till Friday following, the 20th. There will be performed a Pastoral Cantata for two voices, accompanied by all Sorts of instruments, composed by himself on that Occasion. To begin at Seven a-Clock. The Tickets given out for Monday will be taken on Friday. Tickets may be had at the Place of Performance, at 5 S. each.

Domenico's public professional employment in Paris, discovered in a letter of D. Luis da Cunha, Portuguese ambassador to France , could fit in time and place into a stopover there during a journey to or from

---

47 Frank Walker, "Some Notes on the Scarlattis," *Music Review* XII (1951), 185 ff.

London.[48] On that occasion Scarlatti gathered "much esteem and ap-plause" not only "for his great ability," but also for a "disinterest" par-ticularly appreciated in an artist disposed to give away his "virtù." This attitude was particularly pleasing in a city of whose stinginess the young Mozart would complain a half century later.

Domenico would soon repent his generosity. The ambassador's correspondence shows that Scarlatti was up to his neck in troubles, obliged to delay his departure for Lisbon by a week. According to our musician, the refusal of a letter of credit had left him penniless. The disgrace that would have been reflected on João V induced Don Luis to advance Domenico 2500 *cruzados*, to be counted against his succeeding salary-payments. The ambassador swallowed whole "Scarlattino's" ver-sion of the facts, but it seems more likely that the incident was the result of the ruinous vice of gambling, to which Domenico owed the financial diffi-culties of an otherwise fortunate maturity.

The long absence from Lisbon that Alvarenga proposes for the period from 1722 to the end of 1725 seems implausible. On 27 Decem-ber 1725 the feast of St. John the Evangelist was celebrated in the queen's apartments with a *Pastorale* that the Nuncio's *relazione* says was "com-posed by the S.re Abb[at]e Scarlatti, who had all the applause for it."

Thus the "abate" surfaces yet again. Kirkpatrick had already suggested that between 1721 and 1722 Domenico had contracted some ecclesiastical obligation, observing however that the reporters of the *Gazeta* might have been misled by the somber manner of dressing de-scribed by Roseingrave.[49] The reporters were not mistaken: it is un-thinkable to regard as an error such a reference in a document sent to the Curia Romana by a scribe who in the previous *relazioni* had consistently referred to "Sig.r Scarlatti." Since the title of abate recurs only in docu-ments related from a brief phase of Domenico's stay in Portugal, it may reflect the bestowal of some ecclesiastical benefice at the special re-quest of João V.

Information is lacking for 1726, and Alvarenga attributes this silence to Domenico's unstable health. This is confirmed by a request for information coming from Paris, where in 1727 the news had spread of Scarlatti's illness. A *relazione* of the Nunciature, dated 28 January 1727, reports:

---

[48]Communication of Marie-Thérèse Mandroux-França to Manuel Carlos de Brito, quoted in Alvarenga, "Scarlatti," 98 and n., 110, 112.

[49] Kirkpatrick, *Scarlatti,* 77.

[...] Sunday after dinner il Sig.r Domenico Scarlatti m[aest]ro
di Cappella of the King left here for Rome to restablish himself in
Health with the benefit of that air, since he has found there the
method of recovering from his indispositions, His Majesty for the
esteem he bears the Virtù of his subject having dispensed a thousand *scudi* for the trip."[50]

The Roman air must indeed have allowed Domenico to
"restablish himself in Health," since a year after leaving Lisbon his existence took a remarkable turn.

On May 15 the parish priest of the church of San Pancrazio
joined in matrimony

> Dominum Domenicum Scarlatti filium bonae memoriae equitis
> Alexandri romanum de Parochia Sanctae Mariae in Monterone et
> Dominam Mariam Catarinam Gentili filiam Domini Francisci
> Mariae Gentili Puellam romanam de mea Parochia [...].[51]

> (Don Domenico Scarlatti son of Alessandro Scarlatti, knight, of
> happy memory, Roman of the parish of Santa Maria in Monterone,
> and Donna Maria Caterina Gentili daughter of Don Francesco Maria
> Gentili, a Roman Girl, of my parish.)

Since Domenico Scarlatti was given as "Roman," researches in
the parish documents of Santa Maria in Monterone might tell us more
about his return to Italy. It is more likely that he connected himself with
his previous sojourn in order to avoid the delays involved in searching
for documents concerning his residence in Naples, Palermo, and Lisbon.

Kirkpatrick pointed out a strange coincidence: the Roman bride
whom Domenico had chosen was almost the same age as Maria Barbara.[52] The relationship between the Infanta of Portugal and her extraordinary musical mentor might lead us to imagine sentimental ro-
mances worthy of the age of troubadours and châtelaines. Even the severe Kirkpatrick, who generally based himself rigorously on the documents, fell into this temptation, at least by implication. However, it
would be rash to imagine the transference of an impossible passion to an
accessible surrogate. Domenico must have learned all too well from his
father and from all his previous experiences that in everyday life certain
barriers of caste remained insurmountable: when their overthrow was
possible, it remained limited to the area of art.

---

[50] ASV-Portugallo, v. 84, f. 32

[51] Archivio Vaticano, Vicariato di Roma, Santa Maria in Pubicolis, Liber Matri-
moniorum 1679-1757, fol. 70v (Kirkpatrick, *Scarlatti*, 334-335).

[52] Kirkpatrick, *Scarlatti*, 79.

The fascination exercised over the teacher by his young pupil was quite different. With the death of Alessandro, certain of his prohibitions and repressions had lost their force, and the best antidote to those poisons had come from the girl of genius predestined to a throne. While she freed Domenico from the obligations of a musical *routine* mixed with paternal teachings, Maria Barbara also impelled him toward life by showing him—exemplified by her willingness to join her own destiny with that of an unknown prince—that a family could be a fount of affection and not necessarily a source of torments.

Although it is sad to point it out, I repeat that only after his father's death had Domenico been able to realize himself. In this sense, his years in Portugal were a sort of meditative parenthesis, a prelude to the decisive changes of direction, both human and artistic, that allowed a man past forty to embark at last on the road from which circumstances had previously kept him far distant.

Alessandro was only thirty-five at the birth of the last of the ten shoots sent by Providence to form his crown of thorns. I have already advanced the hypothesis that most of his paternal sermonizing stressed the necessity of avoiding the responsibilities and weights of an ungainly family burden. To lighten it in some way was one of Alessandro's constant preoccupations: this is confirmed by the important new information which has emerged from the researches of William Holmes.[53] He has exploded, at least in part, the myth of a Flaminia Scarlatti whose divine talent as a singer was reserved for her father's guests (so as not to risk the inevitable stains on the "mantle of virtue" connected with the public operatic stage). In the presence of sufficiently rich and powerful patrons, Alessandro was quite disposed to lay aside his strictness. In addition, the Albizzi letters have revealed a surprising indiscretion in Alessandro's trip to Florence in 1702. To Ferdinando de' Medici's surprise, Alessandro arrived pell-mell (and without any warning) with *all* his family! In the face of such an intrusion, I should soften some of my judgments on the Grand Prince. His reserve in the face of supplications and requests acquires new significance, and the silence into which in 1706 Ferdinando dropped the offer of a new visit from this importunate supplicant is fully justified.

But let us return to Domenico, to Maria Barbara, and to their respective marriages. The conviction with which the younger Scarlatti, finally born into life, threw himself into his role as a husband and father

---

[53] Holmes, "Lettere."

convinces me how beneficent had been the influence of the pupil I consider had induced the mature master to discover a human dimension that
had long been sacrificed. The positive quality of such an influence will
emerge still more clearly when it is extended to the realms of art.

Maria Caterina Gentili, the "puella romana," belonged to a family in easy circumstances who lived in Palazzo Costaguti.[54] She followed her husband to Portugal and later to Spain. There the court was
obliged to move among the various royal residences according to a calendar Kirkpatrick reconstructed on the basis of notices in the *Gaceta de
Madrid*. For this reason the first two children born to the Scarlattis saw
the light of day in Seville, while the other three were born in Madrid. It
is possible that between Juan Antonio and Ferdinando Scarlatti (baptized on 9 March 1731) there was another son who died in childhood (a
Portuguese document of 27 December 1729 speaks of the "Múzico
Escarlate com a molher fermosa e dous filhos"—("The Musician Scarlatti
with a beautiful wife and two sons").[55]

Except for these notices of the movements of the court, we have
little information about the family nucleus during their first years in Spain.
Without Kirkpatrick's extraordinary discoveries, we would know little
about Domenico, about his two wives (Maria Caterina was a victim of
the southern superstition that the May bride is doomed to die), and his
children.(Kirkpatrick was put in contact with Domenico's descendants,
who preserved a certain number of family documents otherwise lost in
the secrecy of archives, by absent-mindedly looking up "Scarlatti" in
the Madrid telephone book.)

In these Spanish events I see an attempt to accomplish a singular identification with Alessandro (better late than never). Adding to the
six children of Domenico's first marriage the four who were born later
we reach the number of ten, thus achieving parity for the nuclear families of father and son. Before joining a more important battle with
Alessandro's ghost on the field of art, Domenico needed to feel himself
his father's equal in life. In this sense, perhaps the fact that everyone
continued to consider him "filium bonae memoriae equitis Alexandri"
had a certain weight. It needed a knighthood to play out this game also
to a draw, and with the tense relationship between Maria Barbara and
Elisabetta there was little hope of obtaining it in Spain.

---

54 Kirkpatrick, *Scarlatti,* 359, quotes a Roman parish certificate of 1819, which
shows that the Gentili family lived in the palace of Marchese Costaguti, "nobly, and
with splendor, employing servants, a cook, and maids."
55 Kirkpatrick, *Scarlatti,* 338

Kirkpatrick supposed that it was Maria Darbara who asked her father to comply with her faithful music master's desire. It seems probable that things occurred exactly as the American scholar reconstructed them with the aid of important documentation preserved by the members of the Scarlatti family.[56] There is only one detail to add, which until now has escaped all Scarlatti's biographers: in the same year 1738 João V also conferred the same honor on Seixas.[57] To facilitate Domenico's admission into the order of Saint James (Santiago, in Portuguese), the king excused him from the usual year's novitiate so that the solemn ceremony of his initiation could take place on 21 April 1738 in the convent of San Antonio de los Capuchinos de el Prado; on May 15 of the same year he was inscribed in the Portuguese archives of the order.

The gratitude for grace received was expressed in the dedication of the *Essercizi* (the first printed volume of Domenico Scarlatti's *Sonate,* as far as we know):[58]

TO THE SACRED ROYAL MAJESTY OF JOÃO. THE JUST KING OF PORTUGAL, OF THE ALGARVE, OF BRAZIL &c. &c. &. his most humble servant Domenico Scarlatti / SIRE / The magnanimity of YOUR MAJESTY in your works of Virtue, of Generosity toward others, your Knowledge of the Sciences and of the Arts, your Magnificence in rewarding them, are known excellences of your great Soul. Your greater Humility tries in vain to conceal them: the Tongues of the World echo them, present History recounts them, the future will admire them, and will be in doubt whether to call you either most Powerful Sovereign of Kingdoms, or affectionate Father of his Peoples. But these are only a few numbered Parts of that whole which, like a new shining Star, draws to You all the knowing eyes of the Universe. Their acclamation names you THE JUST. A title which contains all the other glorious Names, since all the Works of Beneficence, to a true Understanding, are nothing other than Acts of Justice to one's own Character and to others. Now who of the least of your Servants can ascribe to vanity [the act of] making oneself known as such? Music, the solace of illustrious Souls, gave me that enviable Fate: and rendered me happy in pleasing the fine Taste of YOUR MAJESTY, and teaching it to Your Royal Progeny who Knowingly and masterfully possess it. Gratitude joined to the sweet pleasure of so honest a boast, wills that I leave public Attestation with my publications. Do not disdain, MOST CLEMENT KING; this casual Tribute of an obedient

---

[56] Kirkpatrick, *Scarlatti,* 101-103; documents 336-338.
[57] Klaus F. Heimes, "Seixas, (José Antonio) Carlos de, *New Grove 2,* XXIII, 52.
[58] But see below, n. 59.

Servant: they are Compositions born under the high Auspices of
YOUR MAJESTY in the service of your deservedly most fortunate
Daughter THE PRINCESS OF THE ASTURIAS, and of your most
worthy Royal Brother the Infante DON ANTONIO. But what expression of Gratitude shall I find for the immortal Honor bestowed
on me by your Royal Command to follow this incomparable Princess? The Glory of her Perfections of Royal Lineage and of Sovereign Upbringing, redounds all to the Great MONARCH HER FA-
THER: but his humble Servant shares in that of the Mastery of
Singing, of Playing, and of Composition, with which She, surprising the marveled Knowledge of the most excellent Professionals;
makes the Delights of Princes and of Monarchs.

Who wrote the Scarlatti dedication? seems to be the question,
since we have only to turn the page to find a brief notice that completely
matches the human qualities praised by Mainwaring and is far indeed
from the delirium of Baroque adulation which we have just read:

Reader, /Do not expect, whether you be Amateur or Professional,
profound Understanding in these Compositions, but rather the ingenious jesting of Art, to train you in Assurance on the Harpsichord. Neither Views of Interest, nor Aims of Ambition, but Obedience moved me to publish them. Perhaps they will seem pleasing to you, and more willingly then will I obey other Commands to
please you in an easier and more varied style. Therefore show yourself more human, than critical; and thus you will increase your own
Delights. To inform you of the disposition of the hands, be aware
that the Right is indicated by the *D,* and the Left by the *M:* Live
happy.

The collection regaled the harpsichordists of Europe with material on which legend must already have been at work. Farinelli assured
Burney that Scarlatti had composed the first two volumes of "lessons"
for Maria Barbara, "his pupil in Portugal and in Spain," (contradicting
Alvarenga's assertion that she sudied with him only in Spain). Farinelli's
reference to the dedication of an unspecified Venetian edition to the Princess of the Asturias might suggest a reprint of the *Essercizi,* or an inaccurate remembrance on the part of the aged singer. In any case, the fact
that the dedicatee was not referred to as a queen assigns the volume to a
date before 10 October 1746.[59] W. C. Smith[60] discovered that on 3 February 1739 Adamo Scola, "Musick Master in Vine Street, near Swallow
Street, Piccadilly, over against the Brewhouse" advertised in *The Country*

---

[59] Burney, *France,* 203.
[60] Quoted in Kirkpatrick, *Scarlatti,* 402.

Journal the possibility of acquiring from him the *"Essercizi per Gravicembalo.* Being 30 Sonatas for the Harpsichord, in 110 large folio pages, finely engraved in big notes, from the originals of Domenico Scarlatti [...]."

According to Smith, without doubt the collection was printed in London, the city where Scola, Fortier (the engraver of the musical text), and Amiconi (designer of the frontispiece)were living in 1739. Since the place of printing is not mentioned in the beautiful and strange volume (in exceptionally large format, as if it had been printed so as to be used by near-sighted readers), I do not feel that I should discredit the evidence of Burney, an Englishman, who mentions Venice. In any case, something had already been stirring for a while, on a European scale, for the publication of Scarlatti's sonatas.

The researches of Cecil Hopkinson,[61] perhaps too quickly discounted by Kirkpatrick (who was not disposed to change an opinion he had once formed), revealed that in Paris Charles Nicholas le Clerc had obtained a royal privilege for the printing of *Les Pièces de Clavecin de M. Scarlati* from 22 August 1737, and that others followed on November 27 of 1738 (*Les premiers, 2e et 3e Livres de Scarlati pour le Clavecin*), 12 January 1751 (*Oeuvres de Musique Instrumentale de Scharlatti*), and 21 August 1765 (*Musique de Scarlatti*).

The first Boivin and Le Clerc edition (around 1742, but marked "Opera Prima") appears to be based on the London edition that Roseingrave, wounded in his prestige as high priest of the "English Cult of Domenico Scarlatti," rushed into print after the appearance of the *Essercizi*. Roseingrave's license to print is dated 31 January 1739, and thus his intention to forestall Scola is evident; but one detail of the titlepage of this edition, in French (*XLII Suites de Pièces pour le Clavecin. En deux volumes. Composés par Domenico Scarlatti*) made me suspect some connection with Paris. Later I realized that the misleading element arises from the fact that Benjamin Cooke, Roseingrave's publisher, used a plate almost identical to the one used some twenty years earlier for Handel's *Suites de Pièces pour Clavecin,* subjecting it to unfortunate manipulations.

The formula employed for the title of the collection is clumsily inappropriate, since the ridiculous "XLII" placed in front of "Suites" promises almost four times the number of pieces actually printed. It would have been necessary to substitute "Sonates" for "Suites de Pièces,"

---

[61] Cecil Hopkinson, "Eighteenth-Century Editions of the Keyboard Compositions of Domenico Scarlatti (1685-1757)," Edinburgh Bibliographical Society, *Transactions,* III/1 (1948-1949), 44-71.

as was done with the "Domenico Scarlatti" in place of "G. F. Handel."
In the *N. B.*that follows Roseingrave in person declares:

> I think the following Pieces for their Delicacy of Stile, and Mas-
> terly Composition, worthy the Attention of the Curious, Which I
> have Carefully revised & corrected from the Errors of the Press.

At the end of the title page we read

> This work contains 14 pieces more than any other Edition hitherto
> extant. 12 of which, are by this Author. ye other 2 is over & above
> ye N.o propos'd.

By Handel's time, the French title page plate was conceived for possible
re-use in continental reprints of the collection (Le Cene in Amsterdam,
Le Clerc le cadet in Paris). The same should be assumed for Roseingrave.

With all respect to the latter, the edition of the *Essercizi* is certainly the one officially authorized by Domenico—as witness the dedication to the king, the rejection of "Visions of Interest" and "Aims of
Ambition," the reference to an act of obedience. The fact that other
undertakings had been stirring previously (the *Essercizi* cannot have been
released for printing before 21 April 1738, the date the knighthood of
Santiago was conferred on Domenico) cannot undermine the official
character of the edition. Roseingrave's edition has been accurately called
"pirated" by Sheveloff,[62] who attributes the addition of the other twelve
sonatas (which almost certainly go back to the years of happy wandering in Italy) to a spirit of rivalry.

The existence of other editions printed before the *Essercizi* is
verified in the conclusion of Scola's advertisement:

> Watch out for incorrect printed editions, a scandal in this great na-
> tion, and made in a manner that its basic principles of liberty and
> safeguarding the rights of property may not be offended by low worms
> who gnaw the fruit of the ingenious labor and of the outlay of others.

Much—too much—success, if we consider that only one act of
"obedience" had set off all this pandemonium. It had been Maria Barbara, proud of the marvels which were bursting into bloom around her,
who insisted that "amateurs" and "professionals" should take notice of
them. Almost certainly it had been Farinelli (just arrived from London
and presumably already in communication with Amiconi, the designer
of the handsome frontispiece of the *Essercizi,* whom he would later bring
to Spain) who established the contacts necessary for carrying out the
edition.

---

62 Sheveloff, "Re-Evaluation," 198.

The address to the reader leaves open the possibility that approval, conventionally and ceremoniously not considered automatic, would induce the musician to obey "more willingly ... other Commands" to please the readers themselves "in an easier and more varied style." But these commands never came; or if they did, they arrived too late for the *Essercizi* to have, during the lifetimes of Maria Barbara and Domenico, its sequel in an abundant group of ten splendidly engraved volumes that would have immediately insured the dissemination of Scarlatti's harpsichord works. And all this not because the readers had shown themselves critical, or more than human, but because of circumstances we shall seek to reconstruct and to document.

Barely a year after she had given her consent to the admission of her husband into the Order of Saint James and six months after bringing a last daughter into the world, Maria Caterina Gentili died in Aranjuez and was buried in the church of the Buona Speranza in Ocaña.

The "puella romana" who had given Domenico all the joys of a family left few traces in this world. The mutual testament registered by the couple in 1735 (which could have furnished us with more detailed biographical information) has disappeared, and a fine portrait that formed a pendant to the one of Domenico rediscovered in Portugal in 1956 is also lost: we know little indeed of the poor dead woman. Her children were entrusted to her mother, Margherita Gentili, who had moved to Spain and remained on the best terms with Domenico and with the family that he was quick to reconstitute. If we remember that Scarlatti was fifty-four years old when he was widowed and that his mother-in-law assisted him in raising his children, we may believe that his experience of marriage had been indeed positive. A short time after Maria Caterina's death Domenico remarried, to Anastasia Maxarti Ximenes, a native of Cádiz, by whom he would have four more children between 1743 and 1749.

There would be little to say about these biographical events were it not for a rather surprising coincidence. Although his last marriage allowed Domenico to fight his demographic competition with his father to a draw, the sonatas or their sketches (the fruits of a different kind of fertility) threatened to remain in the limbo of the unborn.

Even if it is difficult to accept fully the thesis that at least 408 of the 555 sonatas were composed between 1752 and 1757,[63] few of those surviving in sources datable before 1752 were written while Alessandro was still alive. This is the moment to summarize the history of the sources

[63] Kirkpatrick, *Scarlatti,* 144. In order not to venture into the discussion of the individual sonatas discovered after 1953, I abide by the numbering of the old catalogue.

that are still considered primary. In addition to the *Essercizi* and other more or less pirated eightenth-century editions, there exists a double series of manuscripts that were certainly conceived and organized by the desire—it is difficult to establish whether by Scarlatti, Maria Barbara, or even Farinelli—to assure for the entire corpus a certain internal systematization. This is characterized by progressive stylistic changes that eventually result in grouping the sonatas into pairs or triptychs defined by a common tonic. Kirkpatrick has listed a minimum of 194 pairs and four triptychs. So high a percentage shows clearly that the organization of the material transmitted by the sources was intentional. To attribute so striking a phenomenon to the copyist of the unnumbered volume dated 1749 or to the other patient toiler who, between 1752 and 1757, copied the thirteen numbered volumes of the series today preserved in the Biblioteca Marciana of Venice and the fifteen that ended up in the Conservatory of Parma is to disregard the capabilities for interference by an author whose mature biography provides unmistakeable evidence of vitality.

The pairwise organization makes its first appearance in the second of the numbered volumes in Venice (the first, dated 1742 and copied by another scribe, contains six possible pairings, albeit rather forced—twelve sonatas of the sixty-one that the manuscript transmits). Sheveloff, from whom I take this enumeration, also notes that it might be possible to point out two pairs in the *Essercizi* (9-10 and 13-14),[64] but then he speculates about how many pairs one could obtain by giving the collection an ordering different from that of the print.[65] Here I cannot follow him, since the official character of the edition indicates that the choices were willed by its author.

On the basis of the dating of the two Venetian volumes, it appears that the pairwise organization, which Scarlatti had already tried out from time to time at the beginning of the 1740s, became part of his mind-set after 1742—perhaps as a result of the custom of composing and publishing sonatas in two or more movements, increasingly frequent with the harpsichordists of the Italian school. Since the two Venetian volumes of 1742 and 1749 were quite clearly intended to provide a home for material going back to the first phase of Domenico's harpsichord works, we might attribute a certain role in Domenico's slowly ripening change of orientation to his encounter with Alberti, a proponent of the two-movement organization.

---

[64] Sheveloff, 311.
[65] Ibid., 317-318.

I attach a certain imortance to the difference between the retro-spective contents of the volumes of 1742 and 1749 and those of the successive Venetian volumes, since Domenico's children by Anastasia Maxarti Ximenes were born precisely between those two dates. It is attractive to think that the conclusion of the demographic competition with his father coincides with this balance-sheet of domenico's earlier sonata production. In the following phase of the combat, limited to the terrain of the art of composition, Domenico would gather more signifi-cant laurels only after outliving Alessandro.

But before we consider this musical apotheosis it is necessary to record certain events that tore the Princes of the Asturias from their gilded Eden. They were thrust onto a throne which terrified Fernando and one that Maria Barbara, childless and therefore deeply anxious at the pros-pect of outliving her husband and being left in the power of Elisabetta Farnese and her children, had never desired.

XVI

I believe that the waters of the Manzanares must be the waves of Lethe ...
(Metastasio to Farinelli, 24 May 1749)

In his last years Philip V was frequently shaken by uncontrollable fits of weeping; he let his fingernails grow like an animal so that could scratch himself and then claim that someone had wounded him in his sleep or say that scorpions around his bed had bitten him ...

His musical therapy grew ever less effective, but Farinelli continued stoically to suffer by devoting himself to the king who, close to death, ignored the advice of his doctors. He had succeeded in gaining back some weight but seemed to have become smaller. There were rays of lucidity when the sick man followed the thread of conversations, aided by his own prodigious memory. His recollections interwove themselves with Farinelli's stories, but above everything else his nostalgia for his native land prevailed, often mixed with regret for the pleasures of the chase. A French ambassador wrote on 20 April 1746:

> There is not a single hunt in which he has taken part in the Forest of Fontainebleau, which the king does not remember with absolute precision.[1]

On July 9 of that year an apoplectic stroke relieved this human shell of its long sufferings. Fernando was king; Elisabetta Farnese, treated at first with great generosity by her stepson, was finally obliged to conceal her thirst for intrigue in a convent.

The new king was a Spaniard born in Spain, which prompted the English to apply to Portugal to transmit new peace offers based on the weakening of the French hegemony at the court of Madrid. French diplomacy thereupon multiplied its offers of friendship, which were, in any case, advantageous to Spain, always in need of support for its end-

[1] Quoted by Cabanès, 235.

less disagreements with the Empire. Vienna's renunciation of any claim on Naples and the Peace of Aquisgrana restored a certain tranquillity to Europe, and the eldest son of Charles III, king of Naples and Fernando's half-brother, was solemnly declared Infante of Spain. This was not an empty title; although for different reasons, Fernando, like Farinelli was incapable of producing an heir.

However, the apparent tranquillity of the Spanish court was burdened by the spectre of hereditary taints. A French source of the period reveals that Fernando,

> this sweet, calm, and apparently insensitive prince, sometimes emerged from his lethargic state in fits of fury, and it was dangerous to give him the opportunity; he had much of the character of his father, whose states of exaltation were not far from madness.[2]

And Baron Gleichen, in his *Souvenirs:*

> Fernando VI had inherited from his father the illness of the god of gardens [Pan] and his insane fear of attempts on his life. This double susceptibility, moral and physical, rendered him even more the slave of queen Barbara of Portugal, his wife, than Philip V was of his own wife.[3]

That Fernando was "governed despotically" by Maria Barbara is confirmed by François-Joachim de Pierre, Cardinal de Bernis, the former French ambassador in Madrid. He adds that the queen was aware that she could

> preserve a certain authority only by maintaining peace in the country; she was too intelligent, indeed, not to understand that, if the monarchy should come out of its inertia to go into war, she would be constrained to concede the direction of the state to hands more able than hers and more expert in the art of governing. As for the king, he was an honest prince, but little enlightened, who maintained that he had reason to complain of us because of the treaty of Aquisgrana. Proud of belonging to the House of France, but Spanish within, he loved peace and hid from annoyances.[4]

Without music, the life of Fernando and Maria Barbara would not have been so happy. The queen shared certain of her husband's phobias, and after having dominated Spain she did not wish to be left in the uncomfortable situation of a widow without children and therefore

[2] C. P. Duclos, *Morceaux Historiques* (Paris: Belin, 1882), III, 419.
[3] Charles-Henri baron de Gleichen, *Souvenirs* (Paris: Téchener, 1868), 138.
[4] François-Joachim de Pierre, cardinal de Bernis, *Mémoires,* Italian translation by Laura Guarino (Milan: Feltrinelli, 1984), 142.

deprived of effective support. She hoped to die before her husband, as in fact happened; in the meantime she founded a rich convent, reserving for herself an apartment for pious retreats or possible longer sojourns.

Hearing the news of attempts on the lives of the kings of France and Portugal, Fernando was seized absolute terror: after a long silence he succeeded only in exclaiming in Italian: "Daggers here, pistols there: and me in the middle. Woe is me!" and plunged under the queen's bed, from which he was extracted with difficulty.[5]

Farinelli, more in favor than ever, multiplied the efforts of his fantasy in order to offer his protectors the gift of an oblivion composed of music and grandiose spectacles. Historians have called the period of Fernando and Maria Barbara "the reign of the melomanes," but behind its gilded façade Spain still lived out its problems as a great power exposed more than any other to the consequences of bad government.

In Giovenale Sacchi's biography of Farinelli we read a rose-colored catalogue of the royal pleasures:

> When Fernando succeeded Philip, [Farinelli] had greater ease in displaying his talent, and his effectiveness in operating. Fernando not only had a good ear for music, but also precise judgment, having had an excellent Teacher[:] Domenico Scarlatti. Under [Scarlatti's] diligence his wife Barbara had profited greatly; in fact, she was not only of most refined taste, but also fastidious, and not at all easy to please. Broschi was given the task of finding diversions appropriate to the peaceful spirit of the King. Thus various novelties originated. Opera was not customary in the Madrid theater except on very rare, and very unusual occasions. The country contented itself with spoken comedies. Then Operas began to become popular, and Broschi had charge of everything, although he never sang in them. The Tagus, which runs near the Royal Villa of Aranjuez and gives it a most pleasing prospect with its width, was not navigable there, and in addition the swampy shore hindered passage, and with its exhalations rendered the air unhealthy. Broschi proposed that it be filled in, that the land be reclaimed, and that the bed of the river be cleaned: at the same time he had five magnificent and well-adorned boats built, so that the Royal Personages and the Court could disport themselves at their will, either sailing up and down those waters, or strolling on the shore. The most expert pilots and sailors of the royal navy were called here from Cartagena, and a splendid arsenal was built to house the sailors and shelter the boats, and a Chapel, which was blessed by Monsignor Migazzi, now cardinal, and then Nuncio of the Empress Teresa at the Court of Spain.

[5]Cabanès, 246.

When these arrangements had been made, from year to year he continued to think up celebrations which could most amuse the King. Broschi was indeed most adept when he ran a Theater, since in addition to his perfect knowledge of music, he was also learned in painting; and he exercised himself by drawing a bit with the pen. He was prolific in invention; and he himself thought up the machines to produce thunder, lightning, rain, hail; and the famous machine-designer *Giacomo Bonavera* of Bologna was trained under his direction, and with his insights. He was also very solicitous for his piety, and his religion, that nothing should be allowed in the Theater, that could offend morals. According to his orders no one, even from the highest classes, was allowed to approach the rooms where the actors dressed. He wanted the women's dresses to be decently long; and even outside the Theater he himself watched over the conduct of the Singers, male and female. Ballets were completely excluded, as being the least ingenious part of the performance, and at the same time the most arousing to the senses. But the acts were separated by brief comic scenes. The dances were added later after his departure, when the Theater became commercial, because previously it was maintained at the expense of the King alone, and only the Officials appointed to the service of the King, and of the Royal Family, foreign Ministers, and the most distinguished personages were admitted, and a few others by favor. If the Theater can be innocent, it was so then under that wise management. But without doubt in no other [theater] could one better enjoy the sweetness of the singing; because there one never heard the noise, which today is frequent in other [theaters], and which perhaps is a part of their liveliness, but is also a vulgar thing, and indeed contrary to the purpose of theatrical performances, whether serious or comic, and especially of serious ones. There everyone listened in perfect silence; with barely a low whisper to support the applause of the King, and of the Queen, when they bestowed it on one of the actors.

In [Farinelli's] casino near Bologna among the other pictures are seen certain paintings, where the scenes of *Niteti,* and of *Didone,* and of *Armida* are depicted by Francesco Battagliuoli. This last Opera, which was performed on the occasion of the marriage of the Prince of Savoy with the Infanta Donna Maria Antonia, is the only one which was not by Metastasio. In these pictures everyone admires the magnificence of those scenes. The four views of the Royal Villa at Aranjuez are by the hand of the same Painter, and in one of these is depicted an illumination of the garden which was made to appear unexpectedly on the 30. of May of 1751, celebrating the name-day of Saint Ferdinand. This new idea was conceived and carried out in three quarters of an hour, while the King was sitting in the little Theater listening to a serenata. Opening the windows of the room on the grounds that the air inside was too heated, with pleasant surprise they showed him the festivity of those lights, like an artificial dawn rising. In all the pictures which I have mentioned, the painted figures, which are numerous, represent the real persons either of the spectators, or of the actors dressed according to the actual costume of each one. Perhaps some will also wish to see the form of the five boats, which served for the delightful voyages of the King. These can be seen drawn and colored in a large manuscript volume, nobly bound in morocco, which Broschi brought with him from Spain, having left two other copies, one with the King, the other with the director of the Theater. These ships are different one from the other in form, but all are splendid, and ornamented, and they all had certain devices, by which they raised from the hold tables loaded with refreshments, and stands with musical scores and the appropriate instruments, where others might wish to sing, or play, which cannot be seen in the drawings. In the same book is noted when and how often those ships set out; the names of the Ladies, and of the great Lords, who accompanied the Royal Personages on each one; the rules, which were established for directing the pilots, and for the greater security of the navigation. All the Dramas performed are also noted; the Actors who performed; the salaries of each one; the other expenses, and also the gifts, which were distributed on special occasions, because in that book there is an ordered and diligent memorial of every thing.[6]

This long quotation seems appropriate since it is the testimony of Farinelli's contemporary , who was able to take advantage of the latter's stories, to consult documents, and see objects that have since been lost. Reading Sacchi's prose we can plunge into the stream of oblivion the great magician prepared for his sovereigns. The closed private entertainments in the royal apartments had given place to more spectacular *féeries*. (A ritual that offered Fernando VI *only* the singing of Farinelli, or the sonatas of Scarlatti, would have been uncomfortably similar to the exorcism for the ills of Philip V.)

In this situation, inadequately illuminated by preceding biographers and somewhat neglected even by Kirkpatrick, Domenico Scarlatti's exit from the stage complies with a courtly ritual that sacrifices certain superiorities to opportunism having little to do with the values (aesthetic, in this case) in play.

---

[6] Sacchi, *Broschi,* 20-24.

We do not know whether most of the sonatas were already composed by 1752, when an extraordinary amanuensis was engaged—apparently by the royal couple or by Farinelli—to copy the two series of volumes that transmit the best of Domenico Scarlatti's output. If these pieces were a product of the royal gatherings, their composition must predate this theatrical activity, and the datings (1752-1757) on the codices represent those of copying rather than those of composition. Before reconstructing the itineraries of Scarlatti and of the scribe who most certainly worked under his personal direction, let us gather some useful details from the famous letter addressed in 1752 by Domenico to the king's majordomo, Don Fernando de Silva y Alverez de Toledo, Duke of Huescar and later Duke of Alba (see Fig. 11). The duke had asked Domenico to score up a composition in praise of his ancestor, the oppressor of Flanders.

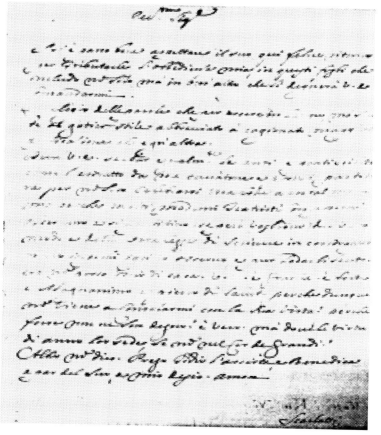

Fig. 11 Domenico Scarlatti: autograph letter to the Duke of Huescar
(Madrid, Museo Alba)

As I have already noted, the style of this prose, ceremonious but dignified and not at all servile, confirms the favorable portrait of Domenico that all the documents at our disposal allow us to reconstruct:

Most Excellent Lord

It seemed to me well to await your happy return to offer you my obedience not only in these sheets of paper which I include, but in any other things that Your Lordship will deign to command me.

The placement of the words, since they are in Latin, but written in the abbreviated Gothic style, has taken more effort than anything else.

Your Excellency must all the same preserve the individual parts, as well as the extract that I have taken out separately in score, not only to celebrate the praise of such merit, but so that many modern theatrical composers may observe and profit (if, however, they wish to) by the real manner and the real rule of writing in counterpoint, which I observe in few today, although I hear them praised.

I cannot leave my house. Your Lordship is great, is strong, is Magnanimous, and full of health, therefore why do you not come to console me with the sight of you? perhaps because I am not worthy of it? it is true. But where do the virtues have their seat, if not in the heart of the Great?

I say nothing more. I pray God that He assist and Bless you equally with Your, and my desire.

Amen

Scarlatti.[7]

Domenico cannot leave his house. Before recent discoveries offered us the new image of a sickly Scarlatti it was a tempting to imagine a segregation imposed by the Queen to guarantee Domenico's commitment to editing the final version of the corpus of sonatas. Tradition has transmitted the charming legend that the twenty-eight volumes today distributed between two important libraries were born of a picturesque exchange. The sums necessary for the payment of his heavy debts would be handed out to the unfortunate gambler in return for his undertaking to give final form to the products of an exceptional talent—products that up to that point had remained in the form of sketches or transient improvisations.

A curious *malade,* our Domenico. When he was over forty, it had been necessary for him to seek in Italy the cure for the ills afflicting him in Lisbon. We now know that the discomforts of long and tedious

---

7 The letter is reproduced in Kirkpatrick, *Scarlatti,* pl. 39.

journeys did not trouble this hypochondriac, wishing to exorcise his malaises and ailments by embarking on excursions prudently avoided by his contemporaries in good health.

The vice of gambling has something of the absurd in Scarlatti. A poor man sees in a lucky win the prospect of freeing himself from need, from dependence on circumstances. This motive might have justified Domenico's gambling in the years before his emancipation from the *patria potestas*. But it is impossible to understand why, when he had become one of the few musicians whose success guaranteed him earnings far beyond his necessities, he should get himself into such difficulties.

It seems to me that his drive to maintain disorder in his life is explained by a state of permanent discontent, growing from the relationship with a father to whom life had given more valid reasons for dissatisfaction. Even Domenico's disdain for "modern theatrical composers" recalls Alessandro. Fortunate circumstances had freed Domenico from the obligation of following his father's course in the field of opera but now, when no one asked him to compose an opera any longer, the praise reserved for third-class musicians wounded the pride of the master who took refuge in contrapuntal science to display his own superiority. This all would still be understandable if we did not know that a few years later Domenico would boast of having broken all the rules consolidated by tradition, but without offending the ear.

"The sweetest of characters" praised by Handel's biographer concealed a difficult man, one more than ever tried by the confrontation with the ghost of his father: "the genteelest behaviour," evident in Domenico's letter to the Duke of Huescar, was perhaps the mask with which Scarlatti succeeded in concealing his own contradictions.

The brilliant operatic activity carried out by Farinelli had endangered the musical gatherings Maria Barbara and Ferdinando had enjoyed as Princes of the Asturias. The threat of madness also weighed on the new king, and it seemed a good idea to keep him far from rituals recalling the still-recent past. The intimate musical gatherings at the highest level where the sonorous enchantments of Scarlatti's art as a harpsichord player blossomed were thus marginalized if not altogether suppressed.

Maria Barbara's support was no longer based on artistic solidarity but became an act of charity to aid Domenico in the consequences of his extravagances. The relationship was no longer what it had been, and one of the customary diplomatic dispatches shows that by 1746 someone else had observed this:

Here the only Italians who merit attention are two musicians, a harpsichord player called *Scarlati* and a singer who is called *Farinello*. I believe that I have already told you on some occasion that the first was the protégé of the Prince of the Asturias, and the second of the Princess. After the change (that is, after the ascent of the couple to the throne of Spain), this latter has overtaken his colleague.[8]

Even before 1746, Domenico seemed to be protected by Fernando rather than by his own pupil. The Prince of the Asturias lived with an awareness of his own limited capabilities. To someone who praised him for his ability as a marksman, he replied, "It would be extraordinary if I could not do *one* thing well." Having been brought to a sufficient level of competence to take turns at the harpsichord with players of real skill must have provided a solid foundation for the gratitude which the prince felt for his teacher.

We find a trace of Domenico's vagaries in a story recounted by Farinelli to Burney:

> this original composer and great performer, like many men of genius and talents, was so inattentive to common concerns, and so addicted to play, that he was frequently distressed in his circumstances, and as often extricated by the bounty of his royal mistress; who, as Farinelli assured me, not only often paid his debts, but, at his intercession, continued a pension of four thousand crowns to his widow and three daughters, who were left destitute at his decease.[9]

Sacchi adds in his his account of Farinelli:

> He not only helped his friends, while they were alive, but also their families after their death. Thus he did with the painter Amigoni, and with Domenico Scarlatti, the first of whom did not live long enough to make the fortune of his family, and the second had miserably dissipated the fruits of his ability and the gifts of royal munificence in gambling.[10]

But other troubles also afflicted Domenico in those years. Although Kirkpatrick found in Domenico's testament and in the division of the inheritance of two of his children elements that contradict the thesis of his poverty, the documents published by Beryl Kenyon de Pascual reveal an unmistakable disorder in his administration of the family patrimony.

[8] Paris, Archives of the Ministry of Foreign Affairs, Quay d'Orsay, 491, fol. 46: Kirkpatrick (*Scarlatti,* 109), translated from the original.

[9] Burney, *Memoirs of the Life and Writings of the Abate Metastasio* (London, 1796), II, 205-206.

[10] Sacchi, *Broschi,* 29-30.

I have already noted that Domenico's tenacious opposition led his son Alexandro to the rash act of a full-scale secret marriage, celebrated in Madrid on 23 August 1752.[11]

Born three years before her lover, Maria del Pilar Perez had not been picked up on the street, since her father exercised the honorable profession of municipal notary. Apparently it was Alexandro's youth that aroused his father's understandable unease, but new documents have caused Kenyon de Pascual to suspect something unpleasant behind the scenes, connected with the financial difficulties our musician experienced because of his disastrous passion for gambling.

The newlyweds had little time to enjoy their contested union: the unhappy rebel died before the birth of his only son, another Alexandro. Left a widow, Maria del Pilar had the right to the restitution of her dowry, but the patrimony of the deceased Alexandro was not sufficient to satisfy her legitimate claim. Another document discovered by Kenyon de Pascual shows Domenico's resistence to Maria's request that he meet his son's debt with the "Lexittima Materna" (estimated at a sum which was close to half his annual earnings). Taking advantage of his privilege as a "criado de S.M. la reyna,"("servant of H.M. the queen") on 8 November 1754 the aged musician turned to a special tribunal—the Bureo de Casa Real—to threaten his daughter-in-law and her father with an action for slander if they continued to declare that Domenico had not paid his children their part of Caterina Gentili's inheritance.

Kenyon de Pascual supposed[12] that Maria del Pilar's claims were not unfounded and that the nearly seventy-year-old Domenico threatened an accusation of slander only because a failure to react to the Perez family's defamation would have seemed a tacit admission of guilt and would have damaged his reputation.

The Spanish musicologist writes, however, that

> it is hard to believe that Scarlatti would deliberately withold his son's inheritance from his daughter-in-law or try to cheat his son's young pregnant widow—even if some personal antagonism were involved—unless it were a case of *force majeure,* [13]

and she suggests two possible solutions:

1) Domenico's notorious financial instability hindered him from meeting the debt, if such existed.

---

[11] See the registration of the respective "belacion" (solemn celebration of the legitimation of the union) published as Appendix 2 in Kenyon de Pascual, "Scarlatti," 27.

[12] Kenyon de Pascual, "Scarlatti," 25.

[13] Ibid., 26.

2) Alexandro had in fact received his legitimate share, concealing it from his wife.

The incomplete documentation does not inform us whether the
affair ended with a compromise. What is certain is that the unfortunate
Alexandro had inherited from his famous grandfather the tendency toward early marriage, and from his father the tendency to economic disorder, if it is true that after a year of marriage his widow's dowry had
virtually gone up in smoke.

Compositions born ... *in the service of the deservedly most fortunate ...* PRINCESS OF THE ASTURIAS

The citation of certain historical texts has provided the worst possible portrait of Maria Barbara. Justice and gallantry now command us to reverse the medal to show some of the merits that impressed her contemporaries.

Do you remember the English ambassador who, full of gossipy
zeal, had rushed to inform his court of the young bridegroom's disappointment at his first meeting with the infanta? It was not long before
Sir Benjamin Keene had ceased to catalogue Maria Barbara's physical
defects, won over by her spirit and fascinated by her artistic talents. He
now declared that if fate had not willed that she be born at the foot of a
throne her fortune would have been assured by her exceptional musical
capabilities and her passion for the dance.

It was not an impulse of flattery, therefore, that impelled
Domenico to declare to king João V that he could not find words to
express his gratitude for being commanded to follow that "incomparable Princess," whose "Mastery in singing, in playing, and in composition" did great honor to her devoted teacher by delighting princes and
monarchs and "surprising the amazed knowledge of the most excellent
Professionals." Almost twenty years later, the financial encouragement
of Maria Barbara, apparently solicited by Farinelli, allowed Padre Martini to begin the publication of his *Storia della Musica* (that monument
of erudition whose rare folio edition is decorated with an engraving depicting Maria Barbara at her best). The Bolognese patriarch acknowledged that his generous protectress had learned "from the Cavalier
Domenico Scarlatti the most intimate knowledge and the most hidden
artifices"[14] of the musical art.

---

14 Martini, *Storia della Musica,* I, vii.

Let us dismiss immediately the temptation to fall into the *Barbarian* hypothesis, and limit ourselves to seeking the reflection of so intelligent a musician in the sonatas that were "born in her service."

The disappearance of the autographs of the sonatas or the sketches that very probably existed for them removes the possibility of reconstructing in detail the didactic relationship in which Maria Barbara must have been quick to assimilate the musical secrets her teacher of genius was happy to confide to her. In this case as well, Domenico received a reward for his own sacrifices while he was still alive: an exceptional pupil gave him the joy of seeing the admiration "of the most excellent Professionals" reflected on himself. If we consider that Scarlatti was the greatest harpsichordist who ever lived, we might liken his retirement from the world to the situation that ended Farinelli's public career. However, the circumstances of a singer cannot be compared with the much more limited possibilities of a harpsichordist in an epoch which, although it practiced contests such as the Roman one between Handel and Scarlatti, had yet to invent the travelling virtuoso. In any case, in the last phase of his life Domenico was able to achieve human and artistic goals that had been denied to his father.

As I have already noted, the two Venetian volumes bearing dates preceding those of the numbered series transmit materials out of a more or less distant past, and this is especially evident in the first of the volumes, dated 1742. In that year Fernando and Maria Barbara were still living in their discreet retirement. If the legend of bartering the *Sonate* for the sums necessary to extricate our unfortunate gambler from his difficulties is true, the diversity of the contents suggests their origin in a collection of sketches and old manuscripts, for which Domenico could now find a definitive expression. If the later sonatas (those included in the series of numbered volumes) had already been composed, at least in part, the criteria for selection were fairly precise. It seems that certain problems of chronological arrangement were kept in mind, and this is confirmed by the homogeneity of the contents that follow in the numbered series. (This homogeneity is occasionally contradicted by the insertion of difficult sonatas in volumes of more elementary content, or of some filler taken from the reserves to even up the numbers in a systematization that the adoption of pairwise organization and the desire to conform to the model of the *Essercizi* sometimes renders problematic.) The chronological arrangement is also confirmed by the differences between the volume of 1742 and that of 1749, such as the disappearance of pieces for violin or other melody instrument and basso continuo, and a more systematic use of pairwise arrangement. In the parallel series of volumes, today housed in the library of the Parma Conservatory, we find evidence that this difference in content was perceived even then.

In the Venetian series the two volumes of earlier dating are accompanied by thirteen other volumes, numbered progressively from I to XIII. Except for X (containing thirty-four sonatas), all the volumes repeat the basic formula of the *Essercizi* with thirty sonatas, now for the most part organized in pairs or triptychs. The new volumes bear datings between 1752 and 1757 and were compiled by someone Sheveloff has called "the main scribe,"[15] a well-merited designation since we owe to this patient Stakhanovist of music paper not only the thirteen Venetian volumes but also the parallel series in Parma. The Parma set contains all the "mature" sonatas of the numbered Venetian volumes as well as a selection (according to criteria of quality which I share, except for the single case that would sacrifice a sonata of genius, K. 45) of pieces extracted from the volumes of 1742 and 1749, and eighteen sonatas excluded from the Venetian series. Sheveloff supposed that the double series of manuscripts had been compiled so that the queen could have "her" sonatas at her disposal in each of the principal residences of the court, Madrid and Aranjuez (according to this theory, the autographs, now lost, would have remained at the Escorial).[16] However, since the Venice volumes are bound in red morocco and bear the engraved arms of Spain and Portugal (see Fig.12 on facing page), I would attribute the commission of the plainly-bound parallel series in Parma to Domenico's other patron saint. Not knowing that within a few years he was destined to inherit all of Maria Barbara's music and several of her instruments, Farinelli perhaps requested a copy of the sonatas for himself (in exchange for the gifts with which he aided his friend in difficulty?). This hypothesis, supported by the absence of the royal arms on the bindings of the Parma volumes, better justifies the exclusion of youthful sonatas that a musician of Farinelli's level had every right to consider of little interest and far from the perfection of the others.

But a picture of the milieu in which the Scarlatti sonatas assumed their final form would not be complete without reference to two Spanish musicians linked with Domenico: Sebastian Albero and Antonio Soler.

Of the first we know little. His name figures as "Alvero" in a manuscript of *Obras para clavicordio* (in Spanish *clavicordio* means "harpsichord" rather than "clavichord").[17] The volume, which presents

---

[15] Sheveloff, "Re-Evaluation," 20.

[16] Ibid., 247.

[17] Quoted by Ioseph Puig Subira, *Historia de la Música Española e Hispano ameri-*

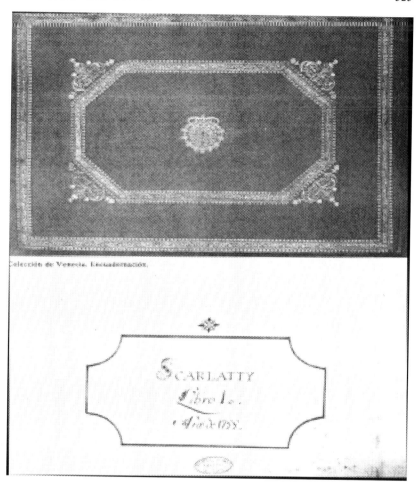

*Fig. 12 Binding of the Venice manuscripts, showing the arms of
Spain and Portugal*

thirty *Sonatas para clavicordio* by Albero, was boldly included by his
royal protectors with the Scarlatti volumes in Venice (with which it shares
its format and internal ordering, as well as the handsome binding with
the arms of Spain and Portugal); it transmits the image of a pale imitator
of Domenico Scarlatti. Born in 1722, Albero died in 1756; we know
that in 1748, when he was named organist of the Royal Chapel in Madrid,
he entered Domenico Scarlatti's orbit,[18] and the relations between the

cana (Barcelona: Salvt, 1953), 465-466.

[18] Linton Powell, "Albero [Alvero] y Añaños, Sebastián Ramón de," *New Grove 2*,
I, 297-298.

two musicians are also documented by a manuscript which Dr. Worgan acquired in Spain, today in the British Library. On the title page one can make out the faint inscription, "de D. Sebastian Albero organista principal de la Real Capilla de su majestad," perhaps erased before the forty-two sonatas were sold to the English collector. The contents of the volume (which coincide in part with the volume collected "para el Eñbaxator de Benecia" that I have ascribed to Alberti) show Albero's familiarity with sonatas of Scarlatti's first period, including the most difficult ones (K. 119, 120, 140, 141). This is surprising, if we consider the dim reflection of such boldness that his own sonatas transmit. That Albero died a year before Domenico Scarlatti has a certain importance.

There is greater substance in the relationship between the old and illustrious music-master of the king and queen and a young monk whom Domenico encountered in the last years of his life. The Catalan Antonio Soler was born in 1729. At the age of barely six he had entered the choir school of the monastery of Montserrat and had been able to profit from the teaching of José Elías. He progressed rapidly, being named in 1750 *maestro de capilla* at Lérida. When Fr. Sebastian de Victoria asked whether he knew any young organist wishing to become a monk in the convent of the Escorial, Soler declared that he was personally interested in the great step and in willingly renounce the world to retire into the convent. In 1752 he was ordained subdeacon and joined the Hierosolymite community of the Escorial, where his final profession took place a year later. The records of the monastery mention his mastery of Latin, his abilities as organist and composer, his irreproachable conduct, and his untiring application to music. Only two years after his profession the monks of the Escorial assigned a pension to Soler's aged father in recognition of Fra Antonio's merits. In 1757 Soler succeeded Gabriel de Moratilla as chapel-master of the Escorial.[19]

Throughout their reign, Fernando VI and Maria Barbara and their entourage spent every autumn at the Escorial. This gave Soler the opportunity of contact with Joseph de Nebra and Domenico Scarlatti, musicians obliged to follow the king and queen in their peregrinations among the royal residences. We know that Soler was the pupil of these two, and it has been reasonably supposed that in winter he remained in contact with them, moving to the house of his Order in Madrid.

Soler attained a certain notoriety through the publication of *La Llave de la Modulacíon* (Madrid, 1762), a theoretical work of such un-

---

[19] Higini Anglès, *Introduccíò i estudi bibliografic,* Antonio Soler, *Sis Quintets* (Barcelona: Institut d'estudis catalans, 1933), v-xi.

prejudiced progressive tendencies as to provoke polemics leading to pamphlets in refutation and rebuttal. Such polemics induced Soler to seek the authoritative support of Padre Martini in order to satisfy his fellow monks, who had willingly borne the expenses of printing the *Llave*.

The letters Soler wrote to the Bolognese patriarch between 1765 and 1772[20] provide useful information for reconstructing certain aspects of his personality and of his relationship with Domenico Scarlatti.

The qualification of "scholar of S.r Scarlatti, of whom Your Reverence speaks with great esteem in the Prologue of your work"[21] is Soler's best credential for introducing himself. He also refers to the dedication of the *Storia della Musica* to Maria Barbara. Since Padre Martini's letters have not been preserved, we lack the inevitable reply that, even in terms of conventional courtesy, could have shown what image the prophet of Bologna had formed of Domenico Scarlatti apart from his merits as a teacher.

Particularly interesting is Soler's declared intention to write "a treatise, divided into five or six volumes on ancient Ecclesiastical Music, [that is] innocent, clear, and devout, and which does not at all resemble that for the Theater."[22] Here Domenico's censure of the "modern theatrical composers" intersects with Padre Martini's reprimand of Pergolesi for having employed "the very same delicate and graceful expressions" in "expressing farcical and ridiculous meanings, like those of the *Serva Padrona,*" as in depicting "pious, devout, and moving sentiments" in the *Stabat Mater.*[23]

Until Padre Soler's notable output of sacred music is adequately explored,[24] we must look to his harpsichord works for traces of instruction by Domenico Scarlatti: not in terms of style but rather in the treatment of the instrument and in the mixture of learned music (tending toward the "galant") with popular ideas. We must not forget that most of Soler's sonatas were probably written after Scarlatti's death and were conceived for the demands and tastes of a new princely pupil, the Infante Don Gabriel. This young prince renewed the enthusiastic devotion of Fernando and Maria Barbara to music after the advent of Charles III, his father, had reversed the trend.

---

[20] Published by Macario Santiago Kastner, "Algunas cartas del P. Antonio Soler dirigidas al P. Giambattista Martini," *Annuario Musical* 12 (1957), 235-241.

[21] Letter of 27 June 1765 to Padre Martini, in Kastner, "Algunas Cartas," 237.

[22] Letter of 2 July 1766 to Padre Martini, in Kastner,"Algunas Cartas," 237.

[23] Giambattista Martini, *Esemplare o sia Saggio fondamentale pratico di contrappunto sopra il canto fermo* (Bologna: Della Volpe, n. d. (1774-1775)), viii (Preface).

[24] See the catalogue of the sources in the Appendix to Anglès, *Introducció*, xliii-lxix.

I suspect that the relationship between Scarlatti and Soler was cemented above all by a very special familiarity, born of a task completely consonant with the monk's well-known tirelessness and compatible with the time-span of his apprenticeship with Domenico: the copying of the sonatas.

In Chapter X of the *Llave de la Modulación* Soler opposes the adoption of the double-sharp sign (which he calls *cruz*) and justifies this by reference to ancient theory based on the division of the whole tone into nine commas. Despite this justification, he is really supporting a practical convenience dictated by the use of enharmonic pitches [e.g.F sharp = G flat], related to the various types of tempered tuning:

> I confess to having used this cross, (without any more reason than that of having seen it) in several sonatas of Don Domingo Scarlati,as well as in the Psalm *Dixit Dominus*, at the verse *Juravit Dominus*, and in the Psalm *Lauda Jerusalem*, at the verse *Quis sustinebit*? I confess my misdeed that the blame be not given to him who does not deserve it; and thus I say that it should not be taken as an example, because it is not good, as has already been proved; and if such a sign be encountered in the Works of Scarlati, do not take it for his notation but mine."[25]

At this point we know that Soler copied "algunas Sonatas de Don Domingo Scarlati" and at least two psalms by the same author that have not survived. The monk's scruple tells us something of great importance. Evidently the copyist received from Scarlatti (or employed himself) a sort of shorthand abbreviation of the texts, something leaving him some slight margin for initiative. The employment of tablature notation, for example, which does not allow certain distinctions in chromatic spellings, could explain the situation. In any case, Soler is at pains to repeat that the blame for those miserable double sharps should be attributed to him and not to Scarlatti, who never wrote them.

I had already written all of this when Frederick Hammond reviewed certain didactic customs of the past to enumerate some possible solutions to the search for the presumed "lost autographs."[26] He begins by pointing out the custom of having students do composition exercises by developing sketches jotted down by their teachers employing various types of musical shorthand. It is likely that Scarlatti employed shortcuts

---

[25] Antonio Soler, *Llave de la Modulación,* 115.

[26] Frederick Hammond, "Domenico Scarlatti: A la recherche des autographes perdus," *Fiori musicologici—Studi in onore di Luigi Ferdinando Tagliavini nella ricorrenza del suo LXX compleanno* (Bologna: Pátron, 2001), 275-295.

of this type to deliver to his scribe indications that served a copyist of the necessary level of competence as sketches of the sonatas to be copied. Hammond quotes various types of musical shorthand (his conjectural reconstruction of the sketch of several measures of the sonata K. 535 is particularly effective), and he supposes that the use of figured bass could contribute to the realization of the sketches. The omission of parts of measures, evident in the comparison of corresponding passages in the two halves of K. 535, reveals some errors in the development of the final version. The most obvious mistakes were corrected by means of written indications, and in the case of the sonata K. 294 in the Parma manuscript the scribe was obliged to glue a patch of blank paper over the measures incorrectly transcribed. The reduced dimensions of the sonata in question allowed him to adopt such an expedient and still distribute the musical text on the customary four pages.

Certain examples suggest to Hammond that errors in the text depend on the failure to observe indications Scarlatti must have given verbally to his scribe. In substance, the hypothesis that seems most likely to him is that the "lost autographs" never existed, and that the sketches were destroyed one by one as the sonatas were lined up in the Queen's series.

Allow me, however, to define another hypothesis: a live dictation of the text, with Scarlatti at the harpsichord and the scribe busily making notes while the swift fingers of the maestro unreeled the skein of a sonata. I have already supposed the employment of a system of tablature in which the sign corresponds to a key on the keyboard but does not express the harmonic definition of the context (e.g. F#G♭). The analogy between certain apparent heterodoxies in some of the sonatas, and certain examples quoted in the *Llave de la modulacion* reinforces the identification of Soler as the "main scribe." It should be noted however that against this identification there is the fact that the "cruz" is not employed in the thirteen volumes of Venice or the fifteen of Parma. In these texts, which were executed in order to transmit a definitive version of the sonatas, a double accidental is indicated by putting a second accidental, in addition to the one indicated in the key-signature, in front of the note affected. Nonetheless, I maintain that Soler may have been the recipient of the dictation and the compiler of a gigantic commonplace book from which the two series of volumes were extracted.[27] In this preliminary phase the monk could employ the "cruz," latter excluded from the Venice and Parma manuscripts. Such an hypothesis should

---

27 This was the system employed by Bernardo Pasquini.

however be carefully verified, and I promise to do so in the essay I wish to dedicate to Domenico Scarlatti's relationship with the keyboard.

On 14 February 1772, Lord Fitzwilliam, the noted English collector, ventured as far as the Escorial in search of manuscripts and other rarities. From Padre Soler he had twenty-seven sonatas of Soler's own composition and two volumes of Scarlatti sonatas, ascribable to clearly-differentiated compositional periods of the master. In one of his replies to Don Antonio Roel del Rio,[28] who had attacked the *Llave,* Soler cited "the thirteen harpsichord books of Scarlatti" as instrumental music that refutes the assertion that modulation was only suited to vocal music. This proved to Kirkpatrick that our monk was referring with perfect familarity to the series of volumes executed for Maria Barbara.[29] The relationship between Scarlatti and Soler coincided exactly with the years in which the manuscripts were copied. It is possible that Domenico's student drew on that source for copies of sonatas that interested him. In this case he could have written the Spanish parts of the composite volume he gave to the English collector in 1772. (Sheveloff distinguishes them from others more hurriedly executed, which he doubtfully attributes to Fitzwilliam himself.)[30]

Kirkpatrick mentions the hypothesis that the "main scribe" was Soler,[31] but without much enthusiasm. When I tried to engage him on this topic, he ignored my urging, perhaps regretful that he had not investigated more deeply in this direction.

The development of certain arguments has led me to discuss Soler's correspondence with Padre Martini and the visit of an English lord to the Catalan monk in 1772 at the Escorial. It is perhaps more to the point to consider an earlier journey, one that brought to Spain an agreeable cosmopolitan with a great belly: M. L'Augier. His encounter with Domenico Scarlatti brings us a truly illuminating account, collected as usual by Dr. Burney.

L'Augier must have been sent to Farinelli by Metastasio, who in a letter following his friend's return from Spain again writes his "incomparable Twin" to assure him of his success with his guest and adds:

> He often visits me, and brings the immeasurable mass of his rotund person to the third story, where I reside, with the lightness of the

---

[28] Antonio Soler, *Satisfacción a los Reparos precisos echos por Don Antonio Roel del Rio a la Llave de la Modulación,* quoted by Anglès, *Introducciò.*

[29] Kirkpatrick, *Scarlatti,* 123-124.

[30] Sheveloff, 93-94.

[31] Kirkpatrick, *Op. cit.,* 140.

most slim dancer. I shall for your sake embrace as much as pos
sible of his majestic circumference.[32]

Burney also refers to L'Augier's "uncommon corpulency" to
point out that this handicap did not prevent the doctor from having "a
most active and cultivated mind."[33] Then he adds:

His house is the rendezvous of the first people of Vienna, both for
rank and genius; and his conversation is as entertaining, as his knowledge is extensive and profound. Among his other acquirements he
has arrived at great skill in music, has a most refined and distinguishing taste, and has heard *national melody* in all parts of the
world with philosophical ears.

He has been in France, Spain, Portugal, Italy, and Constantinople,
and is, in short, a living history of modern music. In Spain he was
intimately acquainted with Domenico Scarlatti, who, at seventy-
three, composed for him a great number of harpsichord lessons
which he now possesses, and of which he favored me with copies.
The book in which they are transcribed, contains forty-two pieces,
among which are several slow movements, and of all these, I, who
have been a collector of Scarlatti's compositions all my life, had
never seen more than three or four. They were composed in 1756,
when Scarlatti was too fat to cross his hands as he used to do, so
that they are not so difficult, as his more juvenile works, which
were made for his scholar and patroness, the late queen of Spain,
when princess of Asturias.

Scarlatti frequently told M. L'Augier that he was sensible he
had broke through all the rules of composition in his lessons; but
asked if his deviations from these rules offended the ear? and being
answered in the negative, he said, that he thought there was scarce
any other rule, worth the attention of a man of genius, than that of
not displeasing the only sense of which music is the object. [origi-
nal note: Scarlatti was the first who dared to give way to fancy in
his compositions, by breaking through the contracted prohibitions
of rules drawn from dull compositions produced in the infancy of
the art, and which seemed calculated merely to keep it still in that
state. Before his time, the *eye* was made the sovereign judge of
music, but Scarlatti swore allegiance only to the *ear.*]

There are many pages in Scarlatti's pieces, in which he imitated
the melody of tunes sung by carriers, muleteers, and common people.
He used to say that the music of Alberti, and of several other mod-

ern composers, did not in the execution want a harpsichord, as it might be equally well, or perhaps, better expressed by any other instrument; but as nature had given him ten fingers, and his instrument had employment for them all, he saw no reason why he should not use them."[34]

Alberti is the only composer named, even if others (perhaps Galuppi or Giuseppe Paganelli—the latter was in Madrid in the year of L'Augier's visit, as master of chamber music to the king) are included in the same negative judgment. The integral use of all ten fingers: the study of Domenico Scarlatti's harpsichord music has revealed that its keyboard technique is based on intensifying the possibilities offered by the most rational relationship between the fingers as the agents and the keyboard as the means. Such a consideration might appear simplistic if the comparison of Domenico Scarlatti's repertory of formulas with that of his contemporaries did not reveal that his declaration to M. L'Augier was founded on objective reality.

I like to find in this declaration a sort of musical application of the New Testament parable of the talents, which must have been Domenico's daily bread in the educational sermons that his father did not spare him. Having said that, the "ten fingers" are employed with the most acute sense of space in deployments that tread paths so unconventional with respect to eighteenth-century routine as to be precursors of Liszt and Chopin in the perfect adequacy of the agents set in motion (the fingers) with respect to the means required.

In general I consider it incorrect, as well as distasteful, to sing the praises of artists whom one loves by transforming their work into a magic telescope capable of showing us the future. In the case of Domenico Scarlatti, however, his contribution to the full utilization of the hand and of the keyboard is justified by the "splendid isolation" of his experience in a fertile artistic independence, far indeed from the paths of routine.

Naturally, I am thinking only of the roots of certain mechanical problems common to Liszt and Chopin in referring to those two champions of Romantic keyboard playing. The technique brought into play by Scarlatti remains as suitable to the Florentine instruments with hammers as to the harpsichord, but it is far indeed from certain later modes of approach to the keyboard dictated by the mechanical and sonorous possibilities of Romantic pianism. In certain cases the problem of the full utilization of the hand/agent is confronted by Scarlatti with so care-

34 Burney, *Germany,* I, 247-249.

ful a search for the most effective results and with such a variety of means as to make me reject the idea that these are occasional productions. But a deeper discussion of the results of my research in this area goes beyond the outline of a historico-biographical volume and could only bore non-professional readers, for whom however I was obliged to point out a specific problem.[35]

Kirkpatrick has highlighted the weak points in the account of L'Augier-Burney.[36] Scarlatti did not live to the age of seventy-three; hand-crossings are still present in the sonatas copied in 1756-1757, although they are rarer than in the sonatas presumably contemporary with the *Essercizi* in the Venetian volume of 1749. In addition, there is the problem of corpulency, which Kirkpatrick considers is more applicable to Maria Barbara or to L'Augier himself than to Scarlatti. This, however, is based on the supposed depiction of Domenico Scarlatti included in the large engraving of Flipart (taken from the portrait of Fernando, Maria Barbara, and their court done by Amiconi in 1752) rather than on his portrait in oils by Domingo Antonio de Velasco (see Fig. 13 on p. 334 and cover), which re-emerged in Portugal three years after the publication of Kirkpatrick's essay and had been the source of a fine lithograph by Alfred Lemoine.[37]

As Kirkpatrick observed in the German edition of his book,[38] the oval format chosen by Lemoine for the series of portraits he drew "from old engravings" shows only Domenico's head and shoulders and therefore does not solve the problem of his corpulence. The Velasco portrait, instead, gives evidence of an *embonpoint* already ascribable to the years of his marriage with Maria Caterina Gentili, the more evident if we imagine "Scarlattino" as a person of short stature.

Although I have considered the hypothesis that the thirteen volumes were copied for Maria Barbara in the years that saw the decline of

---

[35] The first results of a research which I have not yet completed are set forth in my essay "Piena utilizzazione delle dieci dita: una singolare applicazione della parabola dei talenti," *Domenico Scarlatti e il suo tempo* (Siena, 1985), 81-107 (*Chigiana, nuova serie*).

[36] Kirkpatrick, *Scarlatti,* 170.

[37] Amédée Méreaux, *Les clavecinistes 1637 à 1790* (Paris, 1867), 58. Lemoine's lithograph in turn inspired an ignoble Neapolitan dauber to produce the "portrait" in oils of which the Naples Conservatory is mistakenly proud. In 1958—nineteen years after the Velasco portrait had been rediscovered—the ERI committed the gaffe of chosing the Neapolitan *croûte* for the cover of the Italian version of Kirkpatrick's book, assuring an inappropriate diffusion of a real iconographic massacre.

[38] Ralph Kirkpatrick, *Domenico Scarlatti. Leben und Werk* (Munich: Verlag Heinrich Ellermann, 1972), I, 134.

Fig. 13 Antonio de Velasco: Portrait of Domenico Scarlatti
(Istituiçao José Relvas, Alpiarça, Portugal)

the gatherings that had served as the cradle for so many Scarlatti sonatas, L'Augier's evidence links the queen more than ever with the whole span of Domenico's sonata production. There are more elementary sonatas (intended for the first efforts of his pupil,[39] of her uncle or of the Prince of the Asturias, who was already king when the sonatas of the first Venetian volume were recopied). There are sonatas characterized by a "flamboyant" virtuosity (to employ Kirkpatrick's accurate term) and produced for the abilities of the pupil who surprised "the marvelled Knowledge of the most excellent Professionals." There are the sonatas that accompany Maria Barbara in a maturity in which her increasing weight perhaps corresponded physically to the refinement of a taste which all agree was exceptional from the beginning.

Remember the evidence of Sacchi, who attributes to Fernando "a good ear" and "exact judgment," owing to the teaching of an "excellent Master" like Domenico Scarlatti, from whom "his wife Barbara had profited greatly." Farinelli's biographer specifies that "she was not only of the finest taste, but also fastidious, and it was not indeed easy to satisfy her." I find another testimony to this feminine and royal impatience in the same source.

Speaking of the instruments and the musical library that Maria Barbara left to Farinelli, Sacchi declares:

> The harpsichords are much more worthy of esteem, both for their perfection, and for the novelty of their construction. The one with little hammers is the work of the Florentine Ferrini, the pupil of Bortolo of Padua, the first inventor of the *piano, e forte;* the other is quilled, but it forms different registers [*ordini*] of tones with various mechanisms. This is a new invention, party by Farinelli himself and partly by Diego Fernandez, who with this work drew himself out of the obscurity and poverty in which he lived neglected. Speaking casually with Farinelli, the Queen said that she would love to have a harpsichord with more different tones, and asked him if he had seen any. He answered no. When he had left the Queen without saying anything further he consulted Fernandez, whose ingenuity he knew, and when they had designed the work together and had executed it, he had the Queen find it unexpectedly in her rooms. Such was the custom of Farinello, who having understood the desire, endeavored to carry it out without promising anything beforehand. Sig. Paolo Morellati of Vicenza, who was

---

[39] No one has paid sufficient attention to the passage in Burney, *France* (203) which makes a precise reference to the "first two books of pieces" and speaks of a "first Venetian edition" dedicated to Maria Barbara, which might not coincide with the *Essercizi,* as I have already observed.

very learned in Music and in the mechanical arts, made many examinations of the said two harpsichords, and after he had diligently
taken their measurements, worked on his own ones. This latter
built the first of his harpsichords on the commission, and at the
expense of Farinello himself, who then made a gift of it to the present
Duke of Parma, Infante of Spain."[40]

The disappearance of the instruments and the dispersal of the
library that the enlightened and generous Farinelli had wished to entail
forever in order to perpetuate his gratitude to his sovereigns is one of the
greatest disasters of Scarlatti studies. If the great singer's testamentary
dispositions had been carried out, we would know with absolute accu-
racy the best instruments on which Scarlatti's sonatas were performed
and the music Domenico and his royal pupils knew and executed. Before Sandro Cappelletto had the good fortune to discover the important
codicil to Farinelli's will to which I have already referred, we had only
fragmentary information. Sometimes this was full of gaps because it
came from inadequately informed witnesses. In other cases it was short
on detail, since it was provided by persons who treated matters that were
obvious to them but which the loss of traditions and customs of a past
era renders obscure or undecipherable for us.

Now we have a detailed description of the characteristics that
made the harpsichord built by Domenico Fernandez on Farinelli's instructions a sensational forerunner of the *Grand Pleyel* dear to Wanda
Landowska. Probably the instrument Farinelli gave to the queen (which
he later inherited from her) is the notorious "Cembalo espresso"
(="espressivo"?) for which Scarlatti wrote the sonatas K. 356-357, laid
out on four staves instead of two and included in the Parma manuscripts
but not the Venice set.

The inventory attached to Farinelli's will finally clarifies what
and how many were the "various mechanisms" ("diversi ingegni") capable of forming "different registers of tones" ("differenti ordini di voci")
in the instrument Sacchi had vaguely described. The document confirms that the harpsichord was "the invention of the sr. Testator" (i.e.
Farinelli) and was built in Madrid by Don Diego Fernandez. It then
furnishes interesting details: "it plays the pianos and the fortes with quill,"
it has a "long octave" [i.e., a full chromatic octave in the bass] and "three
types of strings, copper, iron, and gut, which sound all together, separately, and mixed, according to the formula of its various Registers which
is given here."

[40] Sacchi, *Broschi,* 47-48.

Already interesting, this becomes thrilling when we find hidden in the stand that holds up the instrument, under the ends of the keyboard, "the springs moved by the Coils, which themselves are hidden under the Pedal, the said Coils are moved by ten buttons, according to the Register you wish to play. There are also two movable knobs of Lead, if you wish to keep one or two Buttons pressed down, when the Feet are not sufficient." The registers, counted from left to right, are:

First button: Full register [i.e. the entire keyboard], *Ottavina.*

Second button: *Archlute*, full register.

Third button: Half [divided] register of Harp in the left hand with gut strings.

Fourth button: Half register of *Ottavina* in the left hand.

Fifth button: *Archlute* and *Ottavina*, full Register.

Sixth button: *Harp* and *Harpsichord,* full Register.

Seventh button: *Harpsichord* in the guise of *Flute*, full Register.

Eighth button: Half register of *Ottavina* in the right hand.

Ninth button: Half register of *Harp* with gut strings in the right hand.

Tenth button: Full register of *Harp* with gut strings.[41]

So profoundly revolutionary an instrument was the offspring of the capricious discontent of a queen and of the brilliant intuitions of a talented courtier, realized by a great artisan. If this is in fact the harpsichord that all those stops finally rendered "expressive," the devoted Scarlatti could not fail to celebrate the novelty with the diptych that we know. But then he returned to composing for *his* instrument, a one-manual harpsichord with only two registers but an ever more extended range (see Fig. 14 on p. 338) whose standard sound realized the artist's fantasy with an ascetism of means but also with the variety of approaches that assured the exceptional vitality for the sonatas.[42]

Having already raised the question of the instruments, I would like to repeat what I wrote about Cristofori (the Bortolo of Padua who was Ferrini's teacher) and of the experiences that had left an impression on the young Domenico. I will not cite the problems of sonority connected with certain limitations of plucked instruments. Builders and performers strove to overcome these by the adoption of interpretive conventions, or by means of mechanical devices able to multiply the "di-

[41] Sandro Cappelletto, *La voce perduta: Vita di Farinelli evirato cantore* (Turin: EDT, 1995), 209.

[42] Some sonatas require a five-octave range, F-f or G-g, obtainable only on the queen's one-manual Spanish harpsichords (see Kirkpatrick, 179).

Fig. 14 Spanish harpsichord ca. 1720
(Collection of Rafael Puyana, Paris)

sounds [*voci*]" (the use of a number of registers praised in special instruments like the "most fine harpsichord with seven registers" which
Valesio tells us on 13 January 1703 was sent as a gift by Ferdinando de'
Medici to the Marchesa Isabella Ruspoli) or finally by exploring the
new paths opened by the "little hammers" of Cristofori and Ferrini.

I have recorded the relationship between the first sonatas published for the new instrument and Scarlatti's pupil Don Antonio, the
Infante of Portugal. Kirkpatrick had already noted the presence of
"clavicordios de piano echos de Florencia" in all the seats of the Spanish
court, permanent alternatives for those who were not content with the
"clavicordios de pluma." There exists, I know, the problem of a pair of
Florentine instruments transformed into harpsichords. Sheveloff[43] solved
it by imagining a greater ease of maintenance for instruments moved
about a country where roads were difficult and where they built (and
therefore would be able to repair) harpsichords, but not fortepianos. In

---

[43] Sheveloff, 357.

any case, it does not seem to me that this fact can be interpreted as an unequivocal denial of the hammered instrument; such a possibility is contradicted by the presence of *clavicordios de piano* at Buen Retiro, Aranjuez, and the Escorial, documented by the inventory included in Maria Barbara's testament.

The instruments of Cristofori and Ferrini had potentially resolved the problem of "enfler et diminuer les sons" in the sense of *crescendo* and *diminuendo* or variety of attack, but not in the sense of sustained sound; but they were still fairly rudimentary instruments. That "art infini soutenu par le goût" Couperin hoped would emancipate the harpsichord from the static sonority to which it seemed condemned was still required. But Couperin's harpsichord music was rooted in lute tradition, and it would be a blasphemy to remove it from the plucked strings of the harpsichord. Domenico Scarlatti, instead, found himself composing idealized music even if it was sometimes full of earthy references such as the songs of mulateers, of porters, of the common people. These suggestions seem to have grown out of a polite connivance between teacher and pupil (do not forget Maria Barbara's passion for the dance, attested by the English ambassador), carried out in opposition to courtly music. When a decidedly popular reference, certainly pleasing to the royal pupil and her meek husband, detaches itself without warning from the Apollonian frame of a piece in which the themes seem suggested by the virtuosic play of the fingers (and therefore "learnèd"), the Scarlatti sonata becomes a Trojan horse, a sound-bridge between the world of the muleteers, porters, and common people, and certain musically heterodox tastes of a pair of rulers and their elite.

Other more distant suggestions were added to those close in time and space: The melodies of the bagpipe players of southern Italy, for example, emerging from the memory of a composer who perhaps had enjoyed inserting them into pastoral cantatas composed for the Apostolic Palace in Rome or for the Portuguese court.

These eruptions of other worlds into the Scarlatti microcosm also raise problems of sonority connected with one or another instrumental medium. The need to give adequate breath to the musical phrases becomes overwhelming in *cantabile* pages related, at least ideally, to vocal music. It would be a mistake to think, however, that in the so-called "brilliant sonatas" similar problems can be overcome by a glittering façade.

Those who wish to waste their time attempting to establish a chronology for the sonatas should abandon the results of bargain-basement scholarship. They should consider instead the progressive refinement of means in the stylistic arch clearly displayed by the succession of the Venice volumes, which Kirkpatrick has pointed out with great critical lucidity: the reservoir of the youthful sonatas culminating in the *Essercizi;* and then the great monument patiently organized by an author who in the "splendid isolation" of his glorious maturity brought a long *recherche* to its conclusion. For Domenico Scarlatti it was not a question of finding the *temps,* more or less *perdu.* Even in the worst of cases it was necessary only to take up the threads of a long creative activity. In doing so, he pursued the individuation of an ideal sound, following it into the realms of fantasy but realizing it with an ascetic essentiality of means in performance. Leaving to Maria Barbara's feminine impatience, to her "fussy" taste, the search for an ideal harpsichord "with many different tones," Domenico continued, like Faust, to follow his own ideal without losing sight of the importance of persevering in his attempt. To give way to the capricious variety that the queen was seeking would have been to miss his objective. Certain interpreters today, even famous ones, do not realize this when they deck out the Apollonian forms of a Scarlatti sonata in the costume of Harlequin.

When he promised his benevolent readers a sequel to the *Essercizi,* Domenico believed that he should employ a "more easy and varied style." Kirkpatrick has reasonably seen in the thirteen Venetian volumes the sequel to the *Essercizi.* If their style is not always "easy," the composer's variety of approaches remains astonishing. To achieve this variety with the uniform means at his disposal was an artistically courageous decision, one directed as much towards the future as to the present. The relative plasticity of the sound of the *clavicordios de piano,* the seeming richness of the complicated instruments desired by Maria Barbara and Farinelli, the sonorous (and therefore pliable) simplicity of the Spanish harpsichords suitable for the last sonatas: these were the means Domenico Scarlatti had at his disposal when, from time to time, he had to adapt to one or the other of those instruments the "happy freaks" of his style already pointed out by Burney.[44]

For their very perfection, which is intrinsically musical, the sonatas are the fruit of a permanent rebellion against every limitation. It is as if Domenico had delivered to his copyist—and to posterity—a series of "works in progress:" pulsating testimonies of an ideal artistic experience, directed towards the future but stylistically well rooted in the present.

Today the harpsichord or the fortepiano (not to mention the modern piano and even the synthesizer) can do justice to the music of

---

[44] Burney, *General,* II, 706.

Scarlatti, if they are entrusted to interpreters who know everything that is stylistically legitimate in it, but who employ this baggage only to extract from it what is appropriate, without forcing of any kind. I am not exhorting performers to the ascetic "faithfulness" to mummified texts that today infects the musical investors who proclaim themselves most "committed" to the concert struggle. There is no need to invoke the legions of devils who terrified poor Roseingrave to show that in every Scarlatti sonata, even the sweetest and most dreamy, there is a breath of life rendering it inappropriate to certain bureaucrats of interpretation.

A performance aspiring to a scholarly seal of approval certainly must not betray the spirit of the sublime music a genius of the keyboard wrote for exceptional listeners but conceived for himself first, and perhaps after that for the incomparable pupil who was capable of following him in his flights. My hypothesis that at the end of Domenico's life the refined entertainments in the queen's apartments grew rarer suggests that in the final phase of his maturity Scarlatti considered himself, above all. What I have said in opposition to the pedants should now be repeated for certain musical acrobats, disposed to demand from the harpsichord (or the pianoforte) something alien to the technical and phonic possibilities of Scarlatti's instruments. In the learned city he inhabited, the most famous of these champions was nicknamed "Twinkle Toes." The nickname suggests the tireless fussing with changes of harpsichord registration possible only with pedals. Domenico Scarlatti could employ this only in the "cembalo espresso" that I tend to identify with the instrument conceived by Farinelli and Diego Fernandez. In any case, even the mechanism described cannot achieve the sound-kaleidoscope dear to the followers of Twinkle Toes, which therefore should be considered foreign to the style of the sonatas.

The texts of Scarlatti's sonatas are sometimes interrupted by grand pauses. The informed interpreter makes these fermatas coincide with changes of registration that in the majority of cases Scarlatti had to execute by hand and that neither can nor should occur while the "ten fingers" are employed elsewhere. For this and for other reasons, Domenico Scarlatti's music should be performed on *his* harpsichord. Anyone who wishes to play the sonatas adequately cannot ignore the wonderful pages that Kirkpatrick devoted to the subject in the final chapter of his study. I could not fail, however, to add some considerations showing how unjustified is the cheap outrage of those who rend their garments at the idea of performing Scarlatti on the piano. To be on the safe side, it is well to repeat that the harpsichord remains a certainty, the

pianoforte an hypothesis; and to offer pianists an ancient counsel imbued with eternal wisdom: *Nisi caste, saltem caute!* ("If you can't be
good, be careful!").

Salve Regina

Perhaps, while he was supervising the copying of the sonatas, Domenico
allowed himself some pauses for meditation. Having expressed his opinion of "modern composers for the theater,"he might have regretted giving up church music. Composing sacred music no longer meant obey-
ing his father's restrictions or duties connected with a post as *maestro di
cappella*. Now it was an opportunity to follow up his words with deeds,
to display his own magisterial capacities in those dominions of severe
counterpoint from which his letter of 1752 to the Duke of Huescar had
excluded modern composers.

In this somewhat vengeful spirit, Scarlatti perhaps composed
the two psalms copied by Soler and a *Missa quattor Vocum* transmitted
in an elegant manuscript. Its date (1754) might remind us of the letter of
two years earlier, with the mass as a demonstration "of the real manner
and of the true law of writing in counterpoint."

A *Salve Regina* in A major apparently dates from 1756. It is a
work that Kirkpatrick[45] interpreted as the pathetic self-commiseration
of the aged musician. I would be inclined to interpret instead as a last,
chaste homage to Maria Barbara, saluted as a generous helper of poor
sinners, on the basis of the verbal coincidences permitted by the text of
the prayer to the Virgin Mary.

Almost all of the manuscripts which transmit this piece bear
annotations like "The last Work of Dom.co Scarlatti written in Madrid
shortly before dying," but such pathetic manuscript glosses are not always historically based. Although I agree that the dating of the *Salve
Regina* is correct, the annotation seems to reflect the many legends inspired by similar swan songs. (Especially the *Stabat* of Pergolesi, detested by Padre Martini but relaunched throughout Europe—see Bach's
paraphrase—even before the *querelle des buffons* in Paris fed the
Pergolesi myth). Even leaving aside the *Salve Regina*, we would soon
come upon other manuscript annotations referring to the deaths of
Domenico and others. As a good Christian and a real man of the South,
Scarlatti did not turn away from the idea of death. In 1735 he had drawn
up a mutual will with his wife Maria Caterina. It has not been traced but

---

[45]Kirkpatrick, *Scarlatti,* 129.

it is mentioned in the young bride's death-certificate. On 19 October 1749, only five months after the birth of his last child, Domenico drew up a new will. The date coincides with that of the second unnumbered Venetian volume, in which he concluded the balance-sheet of his production up to the *Essercizi*.

The testament was published in its entirety by Kirkpatrick,[46] together with the inventories of two shares of the division of the inheritance.[47] From these he drew a plausible denial of the legends that Domenico's heirs had been left in a painful state of financial embarassment owing to the hardened gambler's foolish habits. There are loans to collect, there are 30,000 *reales* in cash, there are valuables and precious objects. Among them stands out a *Venera,* an important painting valued at 36,207 *reales* that the heirs wisely waited to sell at a good price. It is surprising to read in one of the lists that Domenico Scarlatti left, among his other pictures, a portrait of Martin Luther—the last thing I would have expected to find in eighteenth-century Spain.

The will and the inventories tell us in any case that the situation had been painted in darker colors, perhaps to solicit the liberality of the sovereigns: yet another act of generosity on the part of Farinelli. Although she preferred the latter, Maria Barbara had not left Domenico out of her will, leaving a ring and two thousand doubloons "to my music master who has followed me with great diligence and devotion."[48]

Although she was so much younger than her mentor, Maria Barbara had foreseen that she might depart this life before him. She was mistaken, but not by much. After months of terrible suffering, she died little more than a year after Domenico, leaving Fernando in a black despair that soon resulted in frenzied insanity that neither his doctors nor Farinelli could restrain.

Kirkpatrick found that the consternation with which the news from Spain was received in the courts of Europe was reflected in Metastasio's correspondence. I turned to this fascinating source persuaded that I could find details there that had escaped my predecessors, but the results of my examination were disappointing. Metastasio's absolute silence about Domenico Scarlatti, a musician whom he must have known in his youth and who could have been the second of the many

---

[46] Ibid., 127-128; the original, 341-343.

[47] Ibid., 345-356.

[48] Ibid, 131. He extracts the item from Maria Barbara's testament, providing the collocation of the original document: Madrid, Library of the Royal Palace, VII E 4 305, fol. 20r.

composers ready to set his *Didone,* is an interesting fact in itself. I cannot decide whether to attribute this determination to ignore the existence of a musician who had aroused the curiosity of all Europe—and in Vienna Metastasio's friend L'Augier—to some personal fact, to an old rancor from their youthful years (Metastasio had been engaged to Gasparini's daughter) or to a punishment for Domenico's about-face on the subject of theatrical music.

Kirkpatrick recounts that when Charles III came from Naples to succeed his half-brother Fernando he announced to his courtiers that he appreciated capon only insofar as it was an ingredient of a good banquet. He dismissed Farinelli munificently but coldly, since he was guilty of having had too much influence, even if irreproachably, in the past management of the the government. The great singer's pathetic and melancholy twilight in Bologna would have no place in this story if he had not brought to Italy a collection of musical treasures he had wished to hand on to posterity, with a wisdom and a sensitivity far from the capricious "star" attitude of so many famous performers.

On 20 February 1782 Farinelli dictated to the notary Lorenzo Gambarini of Bologna a will[49] in which he set up a special entail "in order to perpetuate my gratitude toward the fountain from which there came to me from the Sovereign Princes. . . the innumerable bounties of the Shining and Magnanimous Throne of Spain with which I was heaped while my Most Clement August Royal Patrons lived."

Quoting Maria Barbara's will, in which she left to the singer "the ring with a large round yellow diamond, and all my music books and papers, and three harpsichords, one with register, one with hammers, and another with plectra, the best ones" (note the difference that the queen established between a harpsichord "with register," a harpsichord "with hammers"—the Florentine fortepiano—and a harpsichord simply "with plectra"), Farinelli ordered in these words:

> I wish and command that such a brilliant legacy be one of the principal items of this *fideicommisso* of mine to be preserved perpetually, and that they take the most vigilant and exact care of this distinguished monument, neither lending any book to anyone whosoever outside the house, nor music papers, nor harpsichords (which bear as the *papelliere* described the painted arms of Spain) and to confide them to a good and experienced harpsichord-tuner, keeping the whole collection of music jealously preserved and in good order to be employed familiarly for the amusement only of amateur

---

[49] See Kirkpatrick, *Scarlatti,* 362-363.

and professional friends always in the same room of the musical archive of which music an inventory in the Spanish language will be found among my papers, in which preservation I wish to have included my other books and music papers with the other three harpsichords with my own arms, the largest of which has the movable keyboard which lowers, or raises by a semitone for the convenience of the singer, moving according to the need of the voices by raising or moving the said keyboard toward the treble, and lowering toward the bass. Another harpsichord of smaller size that folds in three parts and reduces itself to a [single] body in its case. Another small one which also folds and is put in its case, charmingly worked in *cina intarziato* of ebony and mother-of-pearl in its entirety; and another spinettina in its square and painted case and in addition a long case covered with red leather edged with little nails [and] lined with turquoise cloth with two violins[,] that is[,] one *dell'autore Amati*. Another violin (d'amore) with five strings of *Granatino (a Spanish maker) to be used as violin, or as viola.* Another violin of *Strdvario* [sic] in another case in the shape of a violin and since all of the above items form an ensemble for private and domestic concerts I consider it praiseworthy that it be preserved as I have disposed above."[50]

Absolutely scrupulous in observing the law, Farinelli could never have believed that the monument he had erected to the memory of his protectors, a perfect reconstruction of the surroundings in which so many musical delights had been born, could be dispersed by the jackals who trod his wishes underfoot. In such criminal malice, the instruments must have been deprived of their distinguishing marks, which provided clear evidence of their theft by the seller. Fewer precautions were taken for the books, perhaps because only the printed ones could arouse the interest of bibliophiles. Lost are the opera libretti with their covers of gold, silver, and multicolored silks which "on the evenings of performances Their Majesties (may they be in Heaven) held before themselves in the Royal Box." Lost are the precious harpsichords which, as I have said, would have helped us to reconstruct with great exactitude the sound-world dear to Scarlatti. Fortunately the two series of volumes I have described were salvaged from the general disaster. The first one ended up in the Fondo Contarini of the Biblioteca Marciana in Venice in 1835. The second was acquired in 1899 (from an antique bookshop in Bologna no longer in existence, and shipped only in April of 1908)[51] by the Library of Parma, whose musical section is deposited in the Conservatory of Music "Arrigo Boito" in the same city.

[50] Cappelletto, *La voce perduta,* 203-204.
[51] Information funished by the Library of the Conservatory "Arrigo Boito" in Parma.

Last Sonatas for Harpsichord of D. Domenico Scarlatti, composed in the Years 1756 and 1757, in which he died

In July of 1757 the great procession of copying the volumes was drawing to its close. The "main scribe" had already transcribed the contents
of the thirteenth Venetian volume into the fifteenth volume of the Parma
series when he must have received a group of the customary sketches
along with discomfiting news about their author's health: the maestro
was worse, he was dying, he was dead.

Twelve sonatas were thus omitted from Maria Barbara's volumes: the fanatical necessity of conforming to the model of the *Essercizi*
excluded the sonatas exceeding the number of thirty, and they ended up
copied into the last volume of the series I connect with Farinelli. If this
was the case, once again the great singer had known how to choose.
Having eliminated the less significant sonatas from the first volumes, he
willingly sacrificed the criteria for assembling the materials rather than
give up those precious, ultimately distilled relics.

Together with the autograph, or with the first sketch of the sonatas (the mysterious source, now irrecoverable, from which the scribe
drew his splendid codices) the scribe must have received the sad news
later copied in a pathetic annotation on a manuscript once belonging to
the abate Santini (the formidable collector of Italian music who introduced the sonatas of Scarlatti to his house-guests in Rome: Rossini, Liszt,
Moscheles, Mendelssohn, among others): "Last Sonatas for Harpsichord
of D. Domenico Scarlatti, composed in the Years 1756 and 1757, in
which he died."[52]

The text of the fifteenth volume of the Farinelli series brings us
a novelty. Some new consideration—perhaps the entire volume was
compiled after Domenico's death—induced the scribe to emerge from
his anonymity. The long task was nearing its completion, and the amanuensis began to drop from his pen the initials which give new weight to
the identification of Soler that I have already proposed.

A capital "S" slides between the final strokes of the first four
sonatas and of those which in the manuscript bear the numbers 7, 10-22,

---

[52] The last portion (sonatas 51-90) of this large volume today in Münster (Bischo-
fliches Priesterseminar, Santini Ms. 3964) is separated from the first fifty sonatas by a
leaf on which appears the manuscript inscription of which there is no trace at the
beginning of volume "D" of the Viennese series, once the property of Brahms, which
contains the same sonatas in exactly the same order.

and 25-28; at the end of sonatas 8 and 9 the siglum is extended to "S. A." (see Fig. 15 below).

Sheveloff[53] pointed out all of this in detail and has gone so far as to note that the initials could correspond as well to S(ebastian) A(lbero) as to A(ntonio) S(oler). He ruins his argument by forgetting that Albero died in 1756 and by declaring, in an absolutely *Barbarian* spirit: "The idea that one of them might be the main scribe is an interesting speculation, but no more."[54]

The comparison I have been able to make with the handwriting of Soler autographs, some twenty years later than the Scarlatti manuscripts, does not give absolutely negative results. To be honest, neither has it furnished the conclusive details that will come only from the further investigation of Soler's Spanish manuscripts. As I have already noted, we find in Soler's favor not only the coincidence of the dates of

Fig. 15 Sonata K.521, Parma manuscript. (Used with permission.)

53 Sheveloff, 50.
54 Ibid., 93-94.

the double series of manuscripts (1752-1757) with the years his biographers say he spent under Domenico Scarlatti's guidance, but also his
explicit references already cited to "algunas Sonatas de Don Domingo
Scarlati" and to the "trece libros de clavicordio de Scarlatti."

Having proposed a possible identification of the "main scribe,"
I have another and more suggestive observation to make, one which
gives an extraordinary conclusion to the biographical hypothesis this
book has attempted to advance: the letters which slipped from the pen of
the amanuensis after Domenico's death are the initials of Alessandro
Scarlatti.

Do you remember the thesis which Plato puts in the mouth of
Aristophanes in the *Symposium?* The androgyne, the terrible and arrogant offspring of the moon, is punished by the gods with a physical
doubling that is at the same time a mutilation. Their trauma leaves the
two halves with a consuming need to reconstitute their unity: "Then,
once their primitive nature was divided in two, each half seeking the lost
half that was its own, found it."

In those meager initials which emerge magically from the past I
no longer read the distrustful attitude of an oppressor who, despite the
emancipation which he had conceded, considered *his* the marvelous products of the talent of an eagle who had achieved his final maturity. In
these initials I seem instead to find the resurrection of an illustrious ghost
who, having left human passions and resentments far behind, waits at
the edge of Parnassus for his other "half" in order to realize the union
that, platonically, achieves a completion like a synthetic culmination of
two troubled human experiences.

I realize that I have unconsciously repeated the outline adopted
by Couperin in the apotheosis of his *Goûts réunis.* Here the *réunion of*
Lulli and Corelli gives way to a more meaningful association, and only
at the summit of Parnassus do Alessandro and Domenico Scarlatti achieve
the knowledge of the complementary nature of their personalities.

In their whole story death had played a decisive role.

Without the *death* of Pietro Scarlata, Alessandro would have
been a different man; only the *death* of Alessandro had permitted his son
to achieve his own equilibrium as a man and as an artist.

There follows a long parenthesis dominated by the figure of
Maria Barbara, a young symbol of life. Here death had to content itself
with a secondary role, tearing the former *puella romana* from a husband
who immediately replaced her in his haste to even up the demographic
score with his father's ghost. Domenico's numerous offspring and the
achievement of a patriarchal dimension in his family were to be attained

in order to annul the burden of bitterness accumulated in his relations with Alessandro. When these rites of exorcism had been completed, his reward was a state of artistic communion with sharing and sensitive patrons. The prideful Alessandro's most ambitious dream was realized in Domenico, but the latter's happiness was of brief duration. It was compromised by the mental decline of Fernando VI and by the vice of gambling brought on by Domenico's need to perpetuate the state of uncertainty, of unease, to which his relationship with his father had accustomed him.

When death returns to its leading role it is the seventy-two-year-old Domenico who succumbs, but only in order that the initials of the "main scribe" should raise Alessandro from Hades ...

It is easy also to establish speculative relationships among certain secondary personages in our story as well. To Sportonio, the singer who during Alessandro's adolescence had paradoxically assumed the paternal functions of the deceased Pietro Scarlata, there succeeds another castrato-father: Farinelli, a tutelary divinity who does not limit himself to hovering over Domenico's maturity and old age but who even charges himself with transmitting his masterpieces to posterity.

And it is not only Scarlatti, father and son, who melt into a single ideal personage: in classical mythology there exist confused figures of demigods and heroes on whom oral tradition bestows more or less appropriately the reflection of the deeds of the absolute masters of Olympus. This also occurs in our story, when another Santini manuscript attempts to call Don Emanuello Rincon de Astorga back from the not entirely clear epilogue of his human experience, only to send him off to the other world in probable confusion with Domenico Scarlatti: "The Baron d'Astorga died in Madrid in the year 1757."

Even after their deaths our actors do not succeed in freeing themselves from the spiderweb of sometimes unclear relationships which has given life to this account.

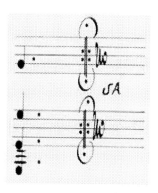

APPENDIX

Archivio Notarile of Naples, Prot. Notary Giovanni Tuffarelli,
Rep.45, 1717, fols. 45-46.

Emancipatio pro Dominico Scarlatti

Die vigesimo octavo mensis Januarii X.e Inditionis 1717. Neapoli — In nostra presentia personaliter constitutus Dominus Alexander Scarlatti filius q[uondam] ... mihi optime cognitus asserens et affirmans, Dominum Dominicum Scarlatti eius filium pluries penes ipsum, etiam per Epistolas transmissas debita cum instantia instetisse, et petisse, ut vellet, ipsum emancipare, et a Patria potestate, et paternis nexibus liberare, quas postulationes, et instantias iustas, et rationabiles agnoscendo illi annuere, et satisfacere non [?][1] dignetur, et cum non valeat de presenti se personaliter conferre ad almam Urbem Romae, ubi dictus eius filius moram trahit, decrecisse[2] constituere infrascriptum eius Procuratorem cum facultatibus inferius exprimendis, in quorum esequtione sponte coram nobis omni meliori via etc. fecit, et constituit eius Procuratorem etc.[3] Dominum Raimundum Scarlatti alium eius filium in dicta Civitate Romae degentem absentem uti praesentem ad ipsius Domini Constituentis nominem,[4] et pro eo coram quibusvis Dominis Iudicibus ordinarijs et competentibus toties quoties opus fuerit personaliter comparendum et coram eisdem supra-dictum Dominum Dominicum eius filium de more emancipandum, et a manu, et patria potestate, et paternis nexibus ipsius Domini Constituentis liberandum penitus, et absolvendum, adeosit post secutum dictum Contractum emancipationis dicti Domini Dominici eius

---

[1] A contradiction justifiable only as a scribal lapse that escaped not only the notary but also witnesses familiar with Latin.

[2] Typographical error ("cedrecisse") in Prota Giurleo.

[3] Prota Giurleo's "per" arises from an incorrect interpretation of an abbreviation that should be read as "etc."

[4] The ending in "e" in the mnuscript would properly give "nomine," but "ad" takes the accusative.

350

filij evadat, et fiat homo ejus juris, omniaque jura et bona consequatur, et ea quae nunc habet, et in futurum habebit in ipsum, eiusque haeredum et successorum quorumcumque potestate, administratione, usufructu, et dominio sit, habeatque liberam, plenam et omnimodam facultatem, authoritatem, et potestatem, et omnia, et singula faciendum, quae quidem homo sui Iuris facere potest, et valeat in futurum, negotia contrahere, et distrahere, testamenta condere, inter vivos, et causa mortis donare, emere, vendere, alienare, concordare et transigere, et ad favorem quarumvis Personarum se ipsum, eiusque haeredes, bona, etc. Iura etc. obbligare, nec non eum fidejubere, Caeterosque alios actus, contractus, et distractus licitos et honestos ubique locorum exercere, aliaque gerere, et adimplere, quae quidem homo sui Iuris facere, et disponere potest, et vale[a]t in Iudicio, et extra, ac in quibusvis Causis, et negotiationibus omni meliori modo etc. dictasque omnes expressas facultates, et authoritates dicto Dominio Dominico eius filio emancipando, cum omnibus alijs desuper necessarijs, et opportunis tradendum, et concedendum etc. et super praemissis omnibus, et singulis a dicto Domino Iudice vel Judicibus eorum decretum et Iudiciariam authoritatem in forma interponi petendum, instandum, et obtinendum, et super praemissis, unum, vel plura Instrumentum et Instrumenta, per quosvis notarios publicos fieri recipi rogari, et stipulari petendum et obtinendum, et pro praemissorum et per dictum Dominum Procuratorem promictendorum observantia et inviolabili adimplemento ipsum Dominum Constituentem eiusque haeredes, et Iura quaecumque in ampliori, et de Iure strictiori, et R. C. A. forma obligandum aliaque faciendum, quae in praemissis necessaria, et opportuna fuerint, et quae Ipse Dominus Constituens faceret, et facere posset si praesens et personaliter adesset etiam si talia forent, quae magis speciale procurationis mandatum exigerent, quam praesentibus est expressum. Dans, et concedens etc. promictens etc. habere ratum, et proinde iuravit etc. in cuius rei Testimonium etc.

Praesentibus Iudice Notario Iacobo Gerace de Neapoli regio ad contractus, Magnifico Utriusque Iuris Doctore Alexandro Binni, et Philippo Genovese de Napoli Testibus etc.

BIBLIOGRAPHY

MANUSCRIPT AND EARLY PRINTED SOURCES

I-Bu. *Gli equivoci nel sembiante. Drama per musica rappresentato nel real palazzo a 21 decembre 1681 giorno del Compleaños della Regina Madre nostra Signora.* (Naples:C. Porsile,1681).

I-Fr. *Storia della nobile e reale Casa dei Medici,* attributed to Avv. Luca Ombrosi (see below under Ombrosi).

I-MOs. *Relazioni d'alcuni musici* (quoted in Prunières, *L'Opéra*).

I-PLa. *Ceremoniale de' Signori Vicerè.* Palermo, Archivio di Stato, Protonotaro del Regno, vols. 1060-1067.

I-PLa. Notai defunti: Crisostomo Barresi, vol. 1565.

———— Antonio Fazio.

———— Gioacchino Miraglia.

———— Giovanni Luigi Panitteri, vol. 2780.

I-Plcom. *CXXXVI A 60:* libretto of *La moglie nemica* (1698).

I-Plcom. Ms. Qq. E. 9: Mongitore, Antonino. *Chiese ed Unioni di Confraternite.*

I-Plcom. CXXXVI D 33. *Argomento dell'Elena.* Palermo: P. Dell'Isola (CXXXVI D 33).

I-Plcom. Villabianca, Francesco Maria Emanuele e Gaetani, marchese di. *De' Teatri Antichi e moderni della Città di Palermo; Diario palermitano; Opuscoli palermitani.*

———— *Diario palermitano.*

I-Rc. Misc. dramm. A 28, no. 10: *Contezza del Giasone ... da Rappresentarsi nel Teatro di questa Città di Palermo, dà Musici Accademici Sconcertati.* (Palermo: Nicolò Bua, 1665).

I-Rvat: Archivio Segreto Vaticano, Segreteria di Stato—Portugallo.

I-Vicariato di Roma, Parish of Sant'Andrea delle Fratte, matrimoni.

PRINTED SOURCES

[Accademia Musicale Chigiana.] *Gli Scarlatti (Alessandro-Francesco-Pietro-Domenico-Giuseppe)*. (Siena: Ticci, 1940).

Acton, Harold. *The Last Medici*. (London, 1932).

Ademollo, Alessandro. "Le avventure di una cantante al tempo d'Innocenzo XI." *L'Opinione* XXXIII (1880), no. 206.

———— *"La Giorgina." Fanfulla della Domenica* III (1881), no. 49.

———— *I teatri di Roma nel secolo decimosettimo*. (Rome: Pasqualucci, 1888).

Alaleona, Domenico. *Storia dell'Oratorio musicale in Italia*. (Turin: Bocca, 1908).

d'Alvarenga, João Pedro. "Domenico Scarlatti, 1719-1729: o período português." *Revista Portuguesa de Musicologia* 7-8 (1997-1998), 95-132.

Badura-Skoda, Eva. "Ein Aufenthalt Alessandro Scarlattis in Wien im Oktober 1681." *Die Musikforschung* XXVII (1974),204-208.

Baini, Giuseppe. *Memorie storico-critiche della vita e delle opere di Giovanni Pierluigi da Palestrina*. (Rome, 1828).

Bernis, François-Joachim de Pierre, Cardinal de. *Mémoires*. Italian translation by Laura Guarino. (Milan: Feltrinelli, 1984).

Bianconi, Lorenzo. "Funktionen des Operntheaters in Neapel bis 1700 und die Rolle Alessandro Scarlattis." *Colloquium Alessandro Scarlatti*, ed. Osthoff, I, 13-111.

Bignami Odier, Jeanne, and Giorgio Morelli, eds. *Istoria degli Intrighi galanti della regina Cristina di Svezia e della sua corte durante il di lei soggiorno a Roma*. (Rome: Palombi, n. d. [1979]).

Bontempelli, Massimo. *Passione incompiuta. Scritti sulla musica 1910-1950*. (Milan: Mondadori, 1958).

Boyd, Malcolm. "Domenico Scarlatti's Cantate da Camera and their Connection with Rome." Paper read at the conference "Handel and the Scarlattis in Rome," June 1985, Accademia Nazionale di Santa Cecilia.

———— *Domenico Scarlatti: Master of Music*. (London: Macmillan, 1986).

——— Review of Pagano, *Alessandro Scarlatti. Music &
Letters* IV (1983), 474-5.

Brosses, Charles de. *Lettres familières écrites d'Italie en 1739 et
1740.* Paris, 1931.

Bulifon, Antonio. *Giornale del viaggio d'Italia dell'Invittissimo e
gloriosissimo Monarca Filippo V Re delle Spagne, & di
Napoli, &c.* (Naples: Nicolò Bulifon, 1705).

Burney, Charles. *A General History of Music from the Earliest Ages to
the Present Period,* ed. Frank Mercer. (New York: Dover, 1957).

——— *Memoirs of the Life and Writings of the Abate
Metastasio.* London, 1796.

——— *The Present State of Music in France and Italy.*
(London: Becket and Co. 1771).

——— *The Present State of Music in Germany, the Nether
lands and United Provinces.* (London: Becket and Co.,
Rosson, and Robinson, 1773).

Cabanés, Docteur. *Le Mal Héréditaire* (Deuxième série)(Paris: Les
Bourbons d'Espagne, n. d. [1927]).

Cametti, Alberto. "Carlo Sigismondo Capeci (1652-1728), Alessandro
e Domenico Scarlatti e la Regina di Polonia in Roma."
Musica d'Oggi XIII (1931), 55-64.

Cappelletto, Sandro. *La voce perduta: Vita di Farinelli evirato
cantore.* (Turin: EDT, 1995).

Carandente, Giovanni. *Giacomo Serpotta.* (Turin: ERI, n. d. [1966]).

Cetrangolo, Annibale. *Esordi del melodramma in Spagna, Portogallo
e America.* (Florence: Olschki, 1992).

Clark, Jane. "His own worst enemy." *Early Music* IV (1976), 19-21.

Clarke, Edward. *Letters Concerning the Spanish Nation, Written at
Madrid during the Years 1760 and 1761.* London, 1763.

Confuorto, Domenico. *Giornali di Napoli dal MDCLXIX al MDCIC,*
ed. Nicola Nicolini. (Naples: Lubrano, 1930).

Corti, Gino. "Il Teatro La Pergola di Firenze e la stagione d'Opera per
il carnevale 1726-1727." *Rivista Italiana di Musicologia* XV
(1980), 82-188.

Corticelli, Francesco, and Paologiovanni Maione. *Musica e istituzioni
musicali a Napoli durante il viceregno austriaco (1707-1734).*
(Naples: Luciano, 1993).

Coxe, William *Memoirs of the Kings of Spain of the House of Bourbon.* 2nd ed., London, 1815.

Croce, Benedetto. *I Teatri di Napoli. Secolo XV-XVIII.* (Naples: Arturo Berisio, 1968).

Culley, Thomas D. *The Jesuits and Music: A Study of the Musicians Connected with the German College in Rome during the 17th Century and of their Activities in Norther Europe.* (Rome/St. Louis: Jesuit Historical Institute, 1970).

D'Accone, Frank A. "Confronting a Problem of Attribution ossia Which of the two is Scarlatti's first opera." The Journal of Musicology XXVII (1999), 168-192.

————*The History of a Baroque Opera: Alessandro Scarlatti's* Gli equivoci nel sembiante. (New York: Pendragon, 1985).

D'Afflitto, Eustachio. *Memorie degli scrittori del Regno di Napoli, raccolte e distese da ..., domenicano.* (Naples: Stamperia Simoniana, 1794).

D'Arpa, Umberto. "La famiglia Scarlatti: nuovi documenti biografici." *Recercare* 2 (1990), 243-247.

Degrada, Francesco, ed. *Francesco Durante: Sonate per Cembalo divise in Studii e Divertimenti.* (Milan: Ricordi, n. d. [1978]).

Della Corte, Andrea. *Satire e grotteschi di musiche e di musicisti d'ogni tempo.* (Turin: UTET, 1946).

Della Seta, Fabrizio. "La Musica in Arcadia al tempo di Corelli." *Nuovissimi Studi Corelliani: Proceedings of the III Interna tional Conference.* (Florence: Olschki, 1982), 123-150.

Dent, Edward J. *Alessandro Scarlatti.*(London: Arnold, 1905, repr. 1960).

Di Blasi, Giovanni Evangelista. *Storia civile del regno di Sicilia.* Palermo, 1818.

———— *Storia Cronologica de' Viceré, Luogotenenti e Presi-denti del Regno di Sicilia.* (Palermo: Edizioni della Regione Siciliana, n. d. [1975]).

Di Giacomo, Salvatore. *Il Conservatorio dei Poveri di Gesù Cristo e quello di S. Maria di Loreto.* (Palermo: Remo Sandron,1928).

Di Marzo, Gioacchino. *Biblioteca Storica e letteraria di Sicilia,* XI: Paolo Mongitore, *Diario palermitano.* Palermo, 1871.

Di Stefano, Guido. "Omaggio alla Viceregina." *Sicilia Turistica.* (Palermo, November-December 1954), 17-20.

Doederer, Gerhard. "Aspectos novos em torno da estadia de Domenico Scarlatti na corte de D. João V (1719-1727)." Preface to *Libro di Tocate per Cembalo di Domenico Scarlatti.* (Lisbon: Istituto Nacional de Investigacio Cientifica, 1991).

———— and Cremilde Rosado Fernandes. "A Música da Sociedade Joanina nos relatórios da nunciatúra apostólica em Lisboa (1706-1750)." *Revista Portuguesa de Musicologia* III (1993), 69-146.

Dotto, Paolo. "Dov'è nato Alessandro Scarlatti." *Giornale di Sicilia,* 3-4 September 1926.

Drechsler, Otto, ed. Alessandro Scarlatti: *Correa nel seno amato,* Cantata for soprano, two violins, and continuo. (Kassel: Bärenreiter, 1974).

Duclos, C. P. *Morceaux Historiques.* (Paris: Belin, 1882).

Fabbri, Mario. *Alessandro Scarlatti e il Principe Ferdinando de' Medici.* (Florence: Olschki, 1961).

———— "Nuova luce sull'attività fiorentina di Giacomo Antonio Perti, Bartolomeo Cristofori e Giorgio F. Haendel." *Chigiana* XXI (1963),143-190.

Fienga, Pasquale. "La véritable patrie et la famille d'Alessandro Scarlatti." *Revue Musicale* 10 (1929), 227-236.

Florimo, Francesco. *La Scuola Musicale di Napoli e i suoi Conservatori.* Naples, 1882.

Fogaccia, Piero. *Giovanni Legrenzi.* (Bergamo: Edizioni Orobiche, n. d. [1954]).

Frati, Ludovico. "Un'Impresario teatrale del Settecento e la sua biblioteca." *Rivista Musicale Italiana* XVIII (1911), 65-84.

Fuidoro, Innocenzo. *Giornali di Napoli dal MDCLX al MDCLXXX,* ed. Vittoria Omodeo. (Naples: Società di Storia Patria, 1934-1939).

Furnari, Antonello. "I rapporti tra Händel e i duchi d'Alvito," *Händel e gli Scarlatti a Roma.* (Florence: Olschki, 1987), 73-78.

Gabrielli, A. "Un duca di Mantova a Roma." *Archivio Storico Lombardo,* 1889, 25-41.

Gallo, Caio Domenico. *Gli Annali della Città di Messina.* (Messina: Filomena, 1882).

Garstang, Donald. *Giacomo Serpotta and the Stuccatori of Palermo 1560-1790.* (London: Zwemmer, 1984).

Giazotto, Remo. *Antonio Vivaldi.* (Turin: ERI, 1973).

Gleichen, Charles-Henri baron de. *Souvenirs.* (Paris: Téohener, 1868).

Gosse, Edmund. *Father and Son.* (Boston: Houghton Miflin, 1965).

Griffin, Thomas. "Nuove fonti per la storia della musica a Napoli durante il regno del Marchese del Carpio (1683-1687)." *Rivista Italiana di Musicologia* XVI (1981), 207-228.

Hair, Christopher. "Scarlatti, Francesco *Antonio Nicola.*" *The New Grove Dictionary* 2,XXII, 397-398.

Hammond, Frederick. "Domenico Scarlatti." Eighteenth-Century Keyboard Music, ed. Robert L. Marshall. (New York: Schirmer Books, 1994), 154-190.

———— "Domenico Scarlatti: A la recherche des autographes perdus." *Fiori musicologici: Studi in onore di Luigi Ferdinando Tagliavini nella ricorrenza del suo LXX compleanno.* (Bologna: Pàtron, 2001), 275-295.

_____ Review of Boyd, *Domenico Scarlatti. Notes* 43 (1988), 476-477.

Hawkins, Sir John. *General History of the Science and Practice of Music.* London, 1776.

Heimes, Klaus F. "Seixas (José Antonio) Carlos de." *The New Grove Dictionary* 2, XXIII, 52.

Holmes, William C. "Lettere inedite su Alessandro Scarlatti." *La musica a Napoli durante il Seicento: Atti del Convegno Internazionale di Studi, Napoli,* 11-14 aprile 1985 (Rome: Torre d'Orfeo, 1987), 369-378.

Hopkinson, Cecil. "Eighteenth-Century Editions of the Keyboard Compositions of Domenico Scarlatti (1685-1757)." Edinburgh Philosophical Society, *Transactions,* III/1 (1948- 1949), 44-71.

Jackman, J. L., and P. Maione. "Mauro, Tomasso de." *The New Grove Dictionary* 2, XVI, 162.

Kastner, Macario Santiago. "Algunas cartas del P. Antonio Soler dirigidas al P. Giambattista Martini. *Annuario Musical* 12 (1957), 235-241.

Kenyon de Pascual, Beryl. "Domenico Scarlatti and his Son Alexandro's Inheritance." *Music & Letters* 69 (1988), 23-29.

———— "Harpsichords, Clavichords and Similar Instruments in Madrid in the second half of the Eighteenth Century." *Royal Musical Association, London, Research Chronicle* 18 (1982), 66-84.

Kirkendale, Ursula. "The Ruspoli Documents on Handel." *Journal of the American Musicological Society* XX (1967), 222-273.

Kirkpatrick, Ralph. *Domenico Scarlatti.* (Princeton, N.J.: Princeton University Press, 1953).

———— German trans. by Horst Leuchtmann, *Domenico Scarlatti: Leben und Werk.* (Munich: Verlag Heinrich Ellerman, 1972).

———— Italian translation by Mariacarla Martino. (Turin: ERI, 1984).

———— "Who Wrote the Scarlatti Sonatas: A Study in Reverse Scholarship." *Notes* XXVI (1971), 5-15.

*La Mara (Marie Lipsius). "Briefe alter wiener Hofmeister." *Musikbuch aus Österreich* VII (1910).

Lionnet, Jean. "A Newly Found Opera by Alessandro Scarlatti." *Musical Times* CXXVIII (1987), 80-81.

Litta, Pompeo. *Famiglie celebri italiane*, series II, I, XXI. (Milan: Giusti, 1819-1883).

Maccavino, Nicolò. "Una sconosciuta composizione sacra di Emanuel Rincon barone d'Astorga: *Ave maris stella*." *Studi Musicali* XXVI (1998), 89-122.

Mainwaring, John. *Memoirs of the Life of the Late George Frederic Handel.* London, 1760.

*Malinowsky, Wladislaw. "O teatrze Krolowej Marii Kazimiery Domenico Scarlattim u kilku innych sprawach Michalem Bristigerem." *Ruch Muzycyny* XX (1976).

Mariani, Valerio. *Gian Lorenzo Bernini.* (Naples: Società Editrice Napoletana, 1974).

Marpurg, Friedrich Wilhelm. *Historisch-kritische Beyträge.* Berlin, 1754-1778.

Martini, Giambattista. *Essemplare o sia Saggio fondamentale pratico di contrappunto sopra il canto fermo.* (Bologna: Della Volpe, n. d. (1774-1775)).

———— *Storia della Musica.* (Bologna: Dalla Volpe, 1757).

Marx, Hans-Joachim. "Die Musik am Hofe Pietro Kardinal Ottobonis unter Arcangelo Corelli." *Analecta Musicologica* V (1968), 104-177.

Mazza, José. *Diccionario biografico de músicos portugueses.* Ocidente XXIV (1944-1945), 32.

Mellers, Wilfred. *François Couperin and the French classical Tradi tion.* (London: Dobson, n. d. [1950]).

Méreaux, Amédé. *Les clavecinistes 1637-1790.* Paris, 1867.

Metastasio, Pietro. *Raccolta di lettere scientifiche, familiari, e giocose dell'abate Pietro Metastasio Romano.* (Rome: Gioacchino Puccinelli, n. d.)

Mira, Giuseppe. *Bibliografia Siciliana.* (Palermo: Gaudiano, 1881).

Mongitore, Antonio. *Biblioteca Sicula.* (Palermo: Diego Bua, 1708/ Felicella, 1714).

———— *Palermo divoto di Maria Vergine e Maria Vergine protettrice di Palermo.* (Palermo: Bayona, 1719-1720).

Morelli, Arnaldo. "Alessandro Scarlatti maestro di Cappella in Roma ed alcuni suoi oratori." *Note d'archivio per la storia musicale, nuova serie* II (1984),117-144.

Morelli, Giorgio. "Una celebre 'canterina' romana del Seicento: la Giorgina." *Studi Secenteschi,* XV (1975), 157-180.

Muratori, Ludovico Antonio. *Annali d'Italia dal principio dell'Era volgare sino all'anno MDCCLXIX.* (Naples: Alfano, 1758).

Napoli-Signorelli, Pietro. *Vicende della coltura nelle due Sicilie.* Naples, 1786.

Newton, Richard. "The English Cult of Domenico Scarlatti." *Music & Letters,* XX (1939), 138-156.

Ombrosi, Luca [?]. *Vita dei Medici sodomiti.* (Rome: Canesi, n. d. [1965].

Osthoff, Wolfgang, and Jutta Ruile-Dronke, eds. *Colloquium Alessandro Scarlatti.* Würzburg 1975 (Würzburger Musikhistorische Beiträge, 7). (Tutzing: Hans Schneider Verlag, 1979).

Pagano, Roberto. "Le Origini ed il primo statuto dell'Unione dei Musici intitolata a Santa Cecilia in Palermo." *Rivista Italiana di Musicologia,* X (1975), 545-563.

———— "Piena utilizzazione delle dieci dita: una singolare applicazione della parabola dei talenti." Domenico Scarlatti e il suo tempo. Siena, 1985, pp. 81-107.

———— and Lino Bianchi. *Alessandro Scarlatti,* with a General Catalogue of his works edited by Giancarlo Rostirolla. (Turin: ERI, 1972).

Petrone, Bonifacio. *Memorie dell'Abate Bonifacio Pecorone della Città di Saponara.* Naples, 1729.

Pincherle, Marc. *Corelli et son temps.* (Paris: Plon, n. d. [1954]).

——— *Vivaldi.* (Paris: Plon, n. d. [1955]).

Piovano, Francesco. "Baldassare Galuppi: Note bio-bibliografiche." *Rivista Musicale Italiana* XIII (1906), 676-726; XIV (1907), 333-365; XV (1908), 233-274..

Poensgen, Benedikt. *Die monodischen Lamentationen Alessandro Scarlattis: Wissenschaftliche Hausarbeit zur Erlangung des akademischen Grades eines Magister Artium der Universität Hamburg.* Hamburg, 1994.

Policastro, Guglielmo. *Catania nel Settecento.* (Turin: SEI, 1950).

Powell, Linton. "Albero [Alvero], Sebastián." *The New Grove Dictionary* 2, I, 297-298.

Prota Giurleo, Ulisse. "Alessandro Scarlatti 'il Palermitano' (La patria & la Famiglia)." Naples, 1926.

——— "Breve Storia del Teatro di Corte e della Musica a Napoli nei sec. XVII-XVIII." *Il Teatro di Corte del Palazzo Reale di Napoli,* 19-146. Naples, 1952.

——— "I Congiunti di Alessandro Scarlatti." *Celebrazione del Terzo Centenario della Nascita di Alessandro Scarlatti.* (Naples: RAI, 1960), 57-68.

——— "Francesco Provenzale." *Archivi,* XXV (1958), fasc. 1, 53ff.

——— "Giuseppe Porsile e la Real Cappella di Barcellona." *Gazzetta Musicale di Napoli,* 1956.

——— "Matteo Sassano detto 'Matteuccio' (Documenti napoletani)." *Rivista Italiana di Musicologia* I (1966), 97-119.

——— "Notizie intorno ad Anna Maria Scarlatti (1661-1703). *Archivi* XXVII (1960), nos. 3-4, 351-371.

——— *Pittori napoletani del Seicento.* (Naples: Fiorentino, n. d. [1953]).

——— "Un po' d'indulgenza per Ciulla ..." *Nostro Tempo,* IV, nos. 6-7.

Prunières, Henry. *L'Opéra italien en France avant Lulli.* (Paris: Champion, 1913, repr. 1975).

Puig Subira, Joseph. *Historia de la Música Española e Hispano americana.* (Barcelona: Salvt, 1953).

Raeli, Vito. *Da C. Cecchelli a R. Lorenzini nella Cappella della Basilica Liberiana.* (Rome: Tipografia Artigianelli, 1920).

Riccobene, Luigi. *Sicilia ed Europa dal 1700 al 1735.* (Palermo: Sellerio, n. d. [1976]).

Riepe, Julien, Carlo Vitali, Antonello Furnari. "Il Pianto di Maria (HWV 234): Rezeption, Ueberlieferung und musikalische Fiktion. Mit ein Anhang von Benedikt Poensgen." *Goettinger Haendel-Beiträge* V (1993),270-307.

RIME/DI DIVERSI AUTORI/PER LO NOBILISSIMO DRAMMA DEL TOLOMEO, E ALESSANDRO ...(Rome: Antonio de' Rossi, 1711).

Rostirolla, Giancarlo. "Il periodo veneziano di Francesco Gasparini (con particolare riguardo alla sua attività presso l'Ospedale della Pietà." *Francesco Gasparini (1661-1727), Atti del primo Convegno Internazionale,* ed. Fabrizio della Seta and Franco Piperno. (Florence: Olschki, 1981), 85-118.

Rousseau, Jean-Jacques. *Les Confessions.* (Paris: Garnier, 1947).

——— *Dictionnaire de Musique.* (Paris: Veuve Duchesne, 1768).

Saint-Simon, Louis De Rouvroy de. *Mémoires.* (Paris: Editions Ramsay, n. d. [1977-1979]).

Sacchi, Giovenale. *Vita del cavaliere Carlo Broschi scritta da Giovenale Sacchi* ... (Venice: Coleti, 1784).

Sartori, Claudio (ed.). *Alessandro Scarlatti, Primo e secondo libro di Toccate. I Classici Musicali Italiani,* Appendix. (Milan: Ricordi, 1943).

——— *I Libretti italiani a stampa dalle origini al 1800.* (Cuneo: Bertola e Locatelli, 1993-1995).

——— "Gli Scarlatti a Napoli: Nuovi contributi." *Rivista Musicale Italiana* XLVI (1942), 374-390.

Scherillo, Michele. *L'Opera buffa napoletana.* (Palermo: Sandron, 1914).

Seixas, Carlos. *25 Sonatas para instrumentos de tecla,* ed. Macario Santiago Kastner. (Lisbon: Gulbenkian Foundation, 1980).

Sheveloff, Joel Leonard. "Domenico Scarlatti: Tercentenary Frustrations." *The Musical Quarterly* 71 (1985), 399-436; 72 (1986), 90-118.

———"The Keyboard Music of Domenico Scarlatti: A Re-Evaluation of the Present State of Knowledge in the Light of the Sources." Ph. D. Diss., Brandeis University, 1970.

Simi Bonini, Eleanora. "L'attività degli Scarlatti nella Cappella della Basilica Liberiana." *Händel e gli Scarlatti a Roma*. (Florence: Olschki, 1987), 152-172.

Sitwell, Sacheverell. *A Background for Domenico Scarlatti*. (London: Faber and Faber, 1935).

Soler, Antonio. *Llave de la Modulacion*. Madrid, 1762.

———— *Sis Quintets*, ed. Higini Anglès. (Barcelona: Institut d'Éstudis catalans, 1933).

Sommer-Mathis, Andrea. "Nuevos documentos sobre la circulación de músicos a principios del siglo XVIII." *Artigrama (Revista del Departamento de historia del Arte de la Universidad de Zaragoza) Monográfico dedicado a la Música*, no. 12 (1996-1997), 45-77.

Sorge, Giuseppe. *I Teatri di Palermo nei secoli XVI, XVII, XVIII*. (Palermo: IRES, 1926).

Stevenson, Robert. "Some Portuguese Sources for early Brazilian Music History." *Inter-American Institute for Musical Research, Yearbook* IV (1968), 1-437.

Strohm, Reinhard. "Il viaggio italiano di Händel come esperienza europea." *Händel in Italia*, ed. Giovanni Morelli. Third Venice Festival, Venice, 1981, 60-71.

Sutherland, David. "Domenico Scarlatti and the Florentine piano. *Early Music* XXIII (1995), 243-256.

Tedesco, Anna, *Il teatro Santa Cecilia e il Seicento musicale palermitano*. (Palermo: Flaccovio, 1992).

Tiby, Ottavio. "Emanuele d'Astorga: Aggiunte e correzioni da apportare alle ricerche del Prof. Hans Volkmann." *International Musicological Society Congress Report* V. Utrecht, 1952, 398-403.

———— "La famiglia Scarlatti: Nuove Ricerche e Documenti." *Journal of Renaissance and Baroque Music* I (1947), 275-290.

Valesio, Francesco. *Diario di Roma*, ed. Gaetano Scano. (Milan: Longanesi, 1977-1979).

Viale Ferrero, Mercedes. *Filippo Juvarra scenografo e architetto teatrale*. (Turin: Fratelli Pozzo, n. d. [1970]).

Vidali, Carole E. *Alessandro and Domenico Scarlatti: A Guide to Research*. (New York: Garland Publishing, 1993).

Villabianca, Francesco Maria Emanuele e Gaetani, marchese di. *Della Sicilia Nobile*. Palermo, 1754-1759.

Villarosa, Carlantonio de Rosa, marchese di. *Memorie dei compositori di musica nel regno di Napoli*. (Naples, Stamperia Reale, 1840).

Voltaire (François-Marie Arouet). *Histoire de Charles XII*. (Paris: Bry Aîné, n. d. [1856]).

Voltes, Pedro. *La vida y la Época de Fernando VI*. (Madrid: Planeta, 1996).

Waliszewski, Kazimierz. *Marysienka, Marie de la Grange d'Arquien Reine de Pologne femme de Sobieski 1641-1676*. (Paris: Plon, 1896).

Walker, Frank. "A Libel on Anna Maria. Additional Notes." Dent, *Alessandro Scarlatti*, 239-241.

———— "Astorga and a Neapolitan Librettist." *Monthly Musical Record*, May, 1951.

Walther, Johann Gottfried. *Musikalisches Lexikon oder musikalische Bibliothek*. (Leipzig: Deer, 1732).

Wotquenne, Alfred. *Catalogue de la Bibliothèque du Conservatoire Royal de Musique de Bruxelles ... Annexe I. Libretti d'Opéras et d'oratorios italiens du XVIII siècle*. (Brussels: Schepens and Katto, 1901).

Zanetti, Emilia. "Händel in Italia." *L'Approdo musicale* 12 (1960), 3-46.

Zipoli, Domenico. *Sonate d'Intavolatura per Organo e Cimbalo*, ed. Luigi Ferdinando Tagliavini. Heidelberg, 1957.

INDEX

Abrantes, Marchese d' (D. Rodrigo Annes de Sà, Almeida, and Menenzes, Marchese de Fontes), 248-249
Acciarelli, Giuseppe, 174
Acquaviva d'Aragona, Francesco, Cardinal, 263
Acton, Harold, 47 and n
Adami da Bolsena, Andrea, 166, 227-228
    Osservazioni per ben regolare il coro dei cantori della Cappella Pontificia, 227
Ademollo, Alessandro, 10 and n, 38
Aglaura Cidonia, see Maratti-Zappi, Faustina
Agostini, Pier Simone, 11
    Works: Il Ratto delle Sabine, 11, 58
Ajrola, Duke of, see Caracciolo, Carlo
Alari, Paola, 226
Alba, Duke of, see de Silva y Alvarez de Toledo, Fernando
Albanese, Bernardo, 236
Albani, Annibale, Cardinal, 70
Albani, Carlo (nephew of Clement XI), 148, 220
Albani, Giovanni Francesco, see Clement XI, pope
Albani, Orazio (brother of Clement XI), 148
Albani, Princess Teresa, 244-245
Albano, Rosalina (wife of Francesco Scarlatti), 74
Albero, Sebastian, 324-326, 347
Alberoni, Giulio, Cardinal, 240, 282-284
Alberti, Domenico: and DS, 296-297, 331-332
    Works: Endimione, 296-297; Galatea, 296
Albinoni, Tommaso, 184

Albizzi (or Albizi), Luca Casimiro, 50, 52-53
Alexander VIII (Pietro Ottoboni), pope, 38, 42
Alfonso V, King of Aragon (IV of Catalonia, I of Naples) the Magnanimous, 14
d'Alibert, Count Giacomo, 4, 13, 140, 144, 150
Alliata e Bonanno, Giovanna, Princess of Villafranca, 102-104
Alliata and Colonna, Giuseppe, Prince of Villafranca, 102-103
Almeida, Francesco Antonio de, 286
Althann, Marianna, see Pignatelli, Marianna
Althann, Michele, Cardinal, Austrian viceroy of Naples, 268
Altieri, Gasparo, Prince, 187
D'Alvarenga, João Pedro, xix, 265, 273, 275, 286, 298, 299, 301
Alvero, Sebastian, see Albero, Sebastian
Alvini, Laura, xiv
Alvito, see Gallio, Tolomeo Saverio
Amadori, Giuseppe, 204
Amati (unidentified member of the family of violin-makers), 345
d'Amato, Eleonora: see Scarlatti, Leonora
Amato, Paolo, xxiv-xxv
Amato, Vincenzo, xxiv-xxv, 1
Ambrosio, Giacomo, 254
Amiconi (Amigoni), Jacopo, 307, 308, 320
Anna (niece of Maddalena Magistri), see Anzalone, Anna
Anne of Austria (wife of Louis XIII of France), xxi
Antoni (viola in the Portuguese Royal Chapel), 274

Antoni, Giuseppe (José Antonio Carlos de Seixas: vice maestro and organist of the Portuguese Royal Chapel), 274-275
Antonio di Braganza (brother of João V), 247, 250, 276-280, 306, 339
Antonio, Giuseppe (organist of the Royal Chapel in Lisbon), see de Seixas, José Antonio Carlos
Anzalone, Anna, 2
Anzalone, Antonia Maria Vittoria (wife of AS, mother of DS): 2-4
  petition quoted, 272
Arbuthnot, Dr. John, 76
Ardore, Prince of, see Milano, Francesco
Arquien, see de la Grange d'Arquien
Ascalona, Duke of, see Pacheco de Acuña, Francesco
Astorga, see Rincon d'Astorga
Astrolusco, Paolo Massonio, see Massonio, Paolo
Asturias, Princes of the, see Fernando VI, king of Spain, and Maria Barbara of Braganza
Augustus II, King of Poland, 132, 147, 152, 154-155
Aureli, Aurelio, 19
  Works: *La Fiordispina*, 19; *L'Orfeo*, 19
Avellino, Prince of, see Caracciolo, Marino
Azzolino, Decio, Cardinal, 135, 150

Bach, Johann Sebastian, 93, 115
  Capriccio sopra la lontananza del fratello dilettissimo, 227
Bacon, Francis, 297
Badia, Giacomo Antonio, 222
Badura-Skoda, Eva, xiv, 70 and n, 150
Baghetti, Alessandro, 274
Baghetti, Antonio, 274
Bai, Tommaso, 226
Balbases, Marchese de Loa, viceroy of Sicily, 175
Baldi, Antonio, 254
"La Bambagia," see Tarquini, Vittoria
Barbapiccola, Carlo, 62, 65
Barbapiccola, Giuseppina, 62, 65

Barbapiccola, Nicola, 57 67, 116, 118
Baretti, Giuseppe, 160
Battaglioli, Francesco, 315
Beethoven, Ludwig van, 227
Bellucci, Simone, 253-254, 256
Benavides, Francesco, Count, Duke of Santo Stefano, 38, 40, 47, 90, 255
Bencini, Pietro Paolo, 204
Berna, Roberto, 236
Bernini, Gian Lorenzo, 2, 3, 4, 48
Bernini, Pietro Filippo, 2, 7, 24
de Bernis, Cardinal (François-Joachim de Pierre), 313
Bertini, Argia, 149 and n
Besci, Paolo Pompeo ("Paoluccio"), 20, 21
Béthune, Countess (sister of the Duke of Saint-Aignan), 124
Béthune, Marquise (sister of Maria Casimira de la Grange d'Arquien), see de la Grange d'Arquien, Marie-Louise
Bette, Giovan Francesco, Marquis of Lede, 241-242
Biancardi, Sebastiano, 255
  early years and wanderings with Emanuello Rincon, 169-191
  Works:*L'Amor tirannico*, 172; *Dafni*, 173, 176-177; *Rime*, 170-172, 176
Bianciardi, Anna, 255
Bianconi, Lorenzo, xiii, xxiii, 78 and n
Bibbiena (Ferdinando Galli), 100, 101
Bicilli, Giovanni, 149
Biffi, Antonio, 296
Bignami Odier, Jeanne, 150
Binda, Alessandro, 76
Binda, Andrea, 64, 66, 67
Binni, Alessandro, 234
Bisagni (Catanian printer), 174
Bisignano, Prince of, see Sanseverino, Carlo Maria
Blancardi, Luis, 255
Bocca di Leone, Vittoria ("Tolla"), 135, 137-141
Boivin (Parisian publisher), 307
Bolsena, see Adami da Bolsena, Andrea

Bonanni e Marini, Filippo, Prince of Roccafiorita, 102
Bonavera, Giacomo, 315
Bongiovanni, Baroness Giovanna, see Rincon d'Astorga, Baroness
Boni, Antonio, 3
Bonlini, Carlo, 211
Bononcini, Giovanni, 166
Bontempelli, Massimo, xi and n
Borrini, Maria Rosa (wife of Francesco Gasparini), 79
Borromeo, Carlo, Count, viceroy of Naples, 216
Boschi, bass, 300
lo Bosco, Giuseppe, Prince of la Cattolica, 106
de Bottis, Giuseppe, 266
Boyd, Malcolm, xiii and n, xiv, 56, 109-110, 244, 248, 267
Branciforte, Geronimo, Count of Cammarata, 80
Brancifore e Barresi, Francesco, Prince of Pietraperzia, 71, 80
Breglia, Orsola, 62, 66
Brisacier, Jean, 129
Bristiger, Michele, 102-103
Broschi, Carlo, see Farinelli
de Brosses, Charles (Président), 42-43 and n
"Brunswick," see Costantino, Giuseppe von
Bruynings, Hamel, 222
Bukofzer, Manfred, xxiii
Bulifon, Antonio, 100
Buranello, see Galuppi, Baldassare
Burney, Charles, 80, 97-98, 163, 227, 264, 267, 295, 297, 300
   on Roseingrave's account of DS's playing, 192-194
   on DS and gambling, 320
   on M. L'Augier, 330-332
Buscaroli, Piero, xv

Cabanès, Dr., 284 and n
Caldara, Antonio, 70, 220, 222
Caldara, Sophia Jacobina Maria, 222
Calderón de la Barca, Pedro, 214
Calvière, Guillaume-Antoine, 120
Cammarata, Count, see Branciforte, Geronimo

Cannicciari (Scannaciari, Camicciari), Pompeo, 204, 230
Capeci, Carlo Sigismondo ("Metisto Olbiano" in Arcadia), 151, 160, 196, 207, 226
Cappelletto, Sandro, xvii and n, 258, 336
Cappelli, Giuseppe, 100
Caracciolo, Carlo, Duke of Ajrola, 30
Caracciolo, Francesco Maria, Prince of Avellino, 218
Caracciolo, Marino, Prince of Avellino, 30
Carafa, Carlo, Prince of Butera, 71-72
Carafa, Diomede, 14
Carafa, Domenico ("called Prince of Colobrano because of his wife"), 29-30
Carafa, Domenico Marzio, Duke of Maddaloni, 12-15, 29, 37, 39
Carafa, Emilia, Duchess of Maddaloni, 12-16, 23, 30, 95
Carafa, Fabrizio, Prince of Chiusano, 214
Carafa, Marino (brother of the Duke of Maddaloni), 15
Carafa, Tiberio, 214
Carandente, Giorgio, 242
Caravaggio (Michelangelo Merisi or Merighi), 61, 63
Carbognano, see Colonna, Francesco
Carbone, Antonia (wife of Tommaso Scarlatti), 66
Cardines, Eleonore, Princess of Colubrano, 29-30
Caresana, Cristoforo, 113, 118
Carissimi, Giacomo, xxiii, 1, 68
del Carpio, Eleonora (non-existent), see Cardines, Eleonora
del Carpio, Marchese, see de Haro y Gusman, Gasparo
Carano, Agata ("la Reginella"), 57
Cardines, Eleonora, 29
Carreras, Juan José, 259 and n
Carrese, Carlo, 2, 3
Casanova, Giacomo, 194, 299
   Works: *Mémoires*, 185
Casini, Giovanni Maria, xvii
Castelli, Anna, 74
de Castris, Cecchino ("de' Massimi"), 11, 53, 110

"Cat's Fugue," see Scarlatti, Domenico, Sonata K. 30
Cavalletti, Giulio, 100
Cavalli (Pier Francesco Caletti Bruni), xxiii
    Works: *Il Giasone*, xxiii
Cavana, Giovan Battista, 100
Ceccarelli, Giuseppe ("l'Orsino"), 166
"Cecchino" or "Checchino," see de Castris, Cecchino
Cenci, Baldassare, Cardinal, 148
de la Cerda, Laurentia (wife of Filippo Colonna), 38
de la Cerda, Luigi, Marchese of Cogolludo, later Duke of Medina Coeli, 37, 41
della Cerra, Angelo Antonio, 224
Cesarini, Carlo Francesco, 70, 204, 220
Cesarini, Dukes, see Sforza Cesarini
Chandos, Duke of (James Brydges),76
Charles I, King of Spain (V as Holy Roman Emperor), 221, 284
Charles II, King of Spain, 38, 91-92
Charles III (Bourbon), King of Naples, later King of Spain, 252, 313, 327, 344
Charles III (Habsburg), King of Spain (later VI as Emperor of Austria), 29, 92, 172, 174-175, 214, 221-222, 242
Charles XII, King of Sweden, 132, 147, 154
Checchini, Antonio, 179
de Chierichelli, Luigi, 205
"Chinese Rites," 251-252
Chiusano, Prince of, see Carafa, Fabrizio
Choi, Seunghyun, xiv
Chopin, Fréderic, 332
Christina, Queen of Sweden: 4-12, 24, 30, 31, 35, 41, 133-135, 150
    relations with the papacy, 5, 10, 145-146
    and opera, 20
    and AS, 35, 46-47, 111, 148
    and Arcadia, 158, 160, 168
    death, 10
Cicero, Marcus Tullius, 227
    Works: *Tusculanae disputationes*, 227

La Cilla (comic opera, 1707), 214
Cimarosa, Domenico, 32
Clark, Jane, xvii, 244
Clement XI (Giovan Francesca Albani), pope, 133, 137-138, 141, 145-147, 159
Cluter, Colonel, 153
Cogolludo, Marquis of, see de la Cerda, Luigi
Colantuono, Francesco, see Tullio, Francesco Antonio
Colignani, Francesco (puntator of the Cappella Giulia), 243, 246
Collinelli, Filippo Maria, 91-92
    Works: *I rivali generosi*, 91-92
Colon, Pietro, Duke of Veraguas, 82, 92
Colonna, Filippo (father of Lorenzo Onofrio), 38
Colonna, Filippo, Duke of Tagliacozzo (son of Lorenzo Onofrio), 37, 38
Colonna, Francesco, Duke of Carbognano, 205
Colonna, Lorenzo Onofrio, Grand Constable of Naples, 38-40, 61
Confuorto, Domenico, 15, 17, 23, 39, 54, 57, 131, 133
Contarini, impresario, 213
Conti, Prince of, see François-Louis de Conti, elected King of Poland
Convò, Giulio, 117
Cooke, Benjamin, 307
Corp, Edward, 244-245, 249
Corelli, Arcangelo, 36, 40, 43, 46, 68, 74, 97- 100, 109, 139, 163, 201, 348
    and Arcadia, 165-168
Corti, Gino, 52 and n
Corticelli, Francesco, 209-210 and n
Costantino, Giuseppe ("Brunswick"), 20, 21
Costanzi, Giovan Battista, 121
Cotumacci, Carlo, 265
Couperin, François, 98-99, 114-115, 194, 339
    Works: *L'Art de toucher le clavecin*, 339; *Les Goûts réunis*, 348
Crescimbeni, Giovan Mario, 158, 160, 167

Works: *Arcadia*, 165
Crimaldi, Placido, 3
Cristofori, Bartolomeo, xvi, 115, 336, 337, 339
Croce, Benedetto, 140, 157
Culley, Thomas, xxiii and n
Cunha, Luis de (Portuguese ambassador to France), xvii, 300-301
Cupis Ornani, Marchese, 228

D'Accone, Frank, xiv, 7 and n
D'Afflitto, Eustachio, 173
Daquin, Louis-Claude, 120
D'Arpa, Umberto, xxvi-xxvii and n
Daun, Wirrico, Count, 177
De Caro, Ciulla, 20, 140
Degrada, Francesco, 121
Del Chiaro, Giuseppe, see Rincon d'Astorga, Emanuello
Della Seta, Fabrizio, 159-160 and n, 165
Della Torre, Francesco, 24
Delle Chiavi, Gennaro, 18, 19
Dent, Edward, xiii, 73, 76, 263
De Santis, Belardino, 20
Descartes, René, 7
Diamantina, see Scarabelli, Diamante
Di Blasi, Giovanni Evangelista, 77
Di Dominici, Domenico, 79
Doederer, Gerhard, xvii, 246, 257, 281, 298, 299
Dominici, Bernardo de, q. on Flaminia Scarlatti and Solimena, 267 and n
Donizetti, Gaetano, 52
Dotti, Bartolomeo, "Contro lo Scarlatti," xiii, 68, 188-191
Dotto, Paolo, xxvi and n
Dumas, Alexandre (père), xxi
Durante, Francesco, 120-122, 163
Works: *Concerti per archi*, 121; *Sonate per cembalo*, 121-122
Durastanti, female singer, 300

Egitij, Domenico, see Gizzi, Domenico
Elías, José, 326
Elisabetta Farnese (wife of Philip V of Spain): 259, 312
marriage, 282-287
and Farinelli, 290-296

Emanuele, Benedetto, Marchese of Villabianca, 224-225
Emanuele e Vanni, Francesco Maria, Marchese of Villabianca, 80, 105-107, 224-225
Ercolani, Count (Austrian ambassador in Venice), 172

Fabbri, Mario, xv, xvii, xviii, 51, 53, 109, 178, 202, 220
Fabri, Annibale Pio, 268
Fadini, Emilia, xiv
Falchetti, Gregorio, 3
Farinelli (Carlo Broschi): 268, 330; and Spanish court, 290-294, 296, 314-316, 349; character, 292; collection of music and instruments, 258-259, 336-337, 344-345; harpsichord for Maria Barbara, 335-336; and DS, 306, 320
"Faustina," see Perugini, Faustina
Faxardo, Giovanni, Marchese of Los Velez, 17
Felipe, Kings of Spain: see under Philip
Fernandes, Cremilde Rosado, 299 and n
Fernandez, Diego, 335-337
Fernando VI, King of Spain: 285-286 character, 313-314; marriage, 286-289, 313-314; impotence of, 287-289; death, 344; and DS, 319-310
Ferrandini, Giovanni, *Pianto della Madonna*, xviii, 220
Ferrazzano, Francesco, 105
Ferrera, Filippo, 67
Ferrera, Giuseppa (wife of Filippo), 67
Ferri, Carlo Antonio, 3
Ferrini, Giovan Battista, xvi, 335, 339
da Filicaja, Vincenzo, 160
Fioré, Andrea, 224
Fitzwilliam, Richard, Lord, 331

Floriani (Roman castrato discantist
in the Portuguese Royal Chapel),
248, 249, 275
Florimo, Francesco, 122 and n
Floro, Domenico, contralto, 266
Flower, Newman, 208
Foggia, Antonio, 20, 202
Fontana, Carlo, 217
de Fontes, Marques (Portuguese
ambassador in Rome), 277
Fornari, Matteo, 97, 99, 166
Fortier, B., 307
Fortuna, Giuseppe, 3
Foscarini, Pietro, 172-173
Francesco I d'Este, Duke of Modena, xxi
Franchi, Giovan Pietro, 204
François-Louis de Conti, elected
King of Poland, 132
Frati, Ludovico, 214
Frederick II, King of Prussia, "the
Great," 274
Frederick IV, King of Denmark, 218
Frescobaldi, Girolamo, 114, 163
Freud, Sigmund, 182
Furnari, Antonello, xviii, 220 and n
Fux, Johann Joseph, 75

Gabriel, Don, Infante of Spain, 327
Gabrielli, Domenico, 184
Gallio, Tolomeo Saverio, Duke of
Alvito, 208
Galuppi, Baldassare ("il Buranello"),
179-180, 332
Gambacorta, Gaetano, Prince of
Macchia, 92
Gambalonga, Count, 222
Gambarini, Lorenzo, 344
La Gara concorde dell'Universo
(serenata), 92
Garstang, Donald, 243 and n
Gasbarri, Carlo, 149 and n
Gasparini, Francesco: 36, 57, 166-
167, 178, 193, 205, 229, 269;
activity in Palermo, 79-80;
in Venice, 183, 193;
and DS, 80, 161-163, 281
Works: L'Alarico overo
L'Ingratitudine gastigata,
79; L'Amor tirannico, 172;

L'Armonico pratico al cim
balo, 161; Tiberio Impera-
tore d'Oriente, 100, 183;
Totila in Roma, 79
Gasparini, Giovanna, 184
Gasparini, Maria Rosa, see Borrini,
Maria Rosa
Geminiani, Francesco Saverio, 97
Genovese, Filippo, 234
Gentili, Margarita Rossetti (mother-
in-law of DS), 309
Gentili Rossetti, Maria Caterina (first
wife of DS): 302, 304; death, 309,
342-343
Gerace, Giacomo, 234-235
Gerusalemme liberata (opera per-
formed at the Theater of Santa
Cecilia in Palermo in 1695), 79
Gessingerin, Maria Susanna, 222
Gesualdo, Carlo, Prince of Venosa, 111
Ghiringhelli, Giovanni, 254-256
Giaconia, Anna, 86
Giattini (or Giattino), Vincenzo, 78
Works: L'Innocenza peni-
tente, 78
Giazotto, Remo, 183 and n, 186
Gigli, Girolamo, 229
Gilbert, Kenneth, xiv
Gioeni, family, 84
Giordano, Luca, 24
"Giorgina," see Voglia, Angela
Giovanna of Austria, daughter of
Don Juan of Austria (wife of
Francesco Branciforte e Barresi),
71, 80
Giovanni Pietro (second violin in the
Royal Chapel of Lisbon), 274
Giron Pacheco, Isabella, Duchess of
Uzeda, 78
del Giudice, Antonio, Prince of
Cellamare, 101
del Giudice, Francesco, Monsignor,
later Cardinal, 38, 96, 100-103,
105, 107, 284
Giulietta, see Zuffi, Giulietta
Giunio Bruto o vero La Caduta dei
Tarquini (opera composed by Carlo
Francesco Cesarini, Antonio Cal-
dara, and AS), 70, 220

Giuseppe Antoni, see Antoni, Giuseppe
Giusti, Maria, 226
Giustini, Ludovico, sonatas, 276-277
Gizzi (or Gizzio or Egitij), Domeni-
  co, 254
Gleichen, Charles-Henri, Baron de,
  313 and n
Goethe, Johann Wolfgang von, xv
de Gondi, Jean François-Paul,
  Cardinal de Retz, xxiii
Gonzaga, Ferdinando Carlo, Duke of
  Mantua, 10, 54-55, 57, 141
Gonzaga, Maria, see Maria Luisa
  Gonzaga
Gonzales, Baldassare (impresario),
  73, 77
Gosse, Edmund, 93-94 and n
Granatino (Spanish luthier), 345
de la Grange d'Arquien, Henri,
  Marquis, later Cardinal, 123-131,
  133, 137-138, 140-144, 153, 155
  death, 156
de la Grange d'Arquien, Marie-Louise,
  Marquise de Béthune, 124, 130
Gratiani, Neapolitan impresarios, 213
Griffin, Thomas, xiv, 12, 23, 41
Grimaldi, Nicola, 100
Grimaldi (Prince of Monaco in
  1714), 283
Grimani, family, 178, 186
Grimani, Vincenzo, Cardinal, 151,
  155-156, 178, 205-206, 208-212,
  216, 245
Grossi, Francesco ("Siface"), 11, 20, 21
Grout, Donald Jay, xiv
Guadagni, Cardinal, 277
Guzzardi, Giuseppe, Baron of San
  Giorgio, 238
Guzzardi e Nicalaci, Emanuela (wife
  of Emanuello Rincon d'Astorga),
  238, 257, 260

Hair, Christopher, 76 and n
Hammond, Frederick, xiv and n,
  328-329 and n
Handel, George Frederic: 32, 76,
  156, 221, 243-244, 281, 307-308;
  encounter with DS in
  Venice, 195-199

in Rome, 196;
  contest with DS, 197, 281;
  Works: *Aci, Galatea, e Poli-
  femo,* 208; *L'Agrippina,* 211;
  Il Pianto di Maria Vergine
  (false attribution),xviii, 220
Hanley, Edwin, xiv
de Haro y Gusman, Caterina,
  Marchesina del Carpio, 29
de Haro y Gusman, Gasparo,
  Marchese del Carpio, 11-13, 19,
  21, 24, 37, 38, 41
Hasse, Johann Adolph, 121, 263-264
  Works: *Pallido il sole* (aria),
  292; *Per questo dolce
  amplesso* (aria), 292
Hawkins, Sir John, 231
Holmes, William C., xiv, 52 and n,
  210, 213
Hopkinson, Cecil, 307 and n
Huescar, Duke of, see de Silva y
  Alvarez de Toledo, Fernando

d'India, Sigismondo, 81
Infidi lumi (madrigal collection
  printed in Palermo in 1613), 80
Innocent XI (Benedetto Odescalchi,
  nicknamed "Papa-minga"), pope,
  5, 9-11, 38, 40, 41, 134
Innocent XII (Antonio Pignatelli),
  pope, 39, 126, 133, 134-135
Isotta, Paolo, xv

Jablonoski (candidate for the throne
  of Poland on the death of John
  Sobieski), 131
João IV, King of Portugal, 279
João V, King of Portugal
  character and religiosity,
  245, 274-275, 301;
  and DS and musicians, 246-
  252;
  and Arcadia, 159
John III Sobieski, King of Poland,
  124-131, 134
John Casimir Vasa, King of Poland,
  124, 126, 128
Jomelli, Nicola, 121, 263
José Emanuel, King of Portugal, 286

Joseph I, Holy Roman Emperor, 70, 219-221
Juan (Catalan, violoncello in the Royal Chapel of Lisbon), 275
Jürgens, Jürgen, 230
Juvarra, Filippo, 70, 217-220, 227, 299

Keene, Sir Benjamin
    on Fernando and Maria Barbara, 287;
    on Maria Barbara, 322
Kenyon de Pascual, Beryl, 115 and n, 320-322 and n
Kirkendale, Ursula, 208
Kirkpatrick, Ralph, xi and n, xii, xiv, xx, 93, 123, 161, 185, 193, 196, 225, 227, 229, 236-237, 243, 274, 278-279, 297-298, 299, 302, 304-305, 320, 330, 333, 340-345
Komarek, Giovanni, 176

La Barbera, Giuseppe, 72
La Cerda di Cogolludo, Luigi, Duke of Medina Coeli, 37-38, 90-92, 94, 96
Ladislao IV Vasa, King of Poland, 124
Lalli, Domenico, see Sebastiano Biancardi
Landolina, Francesco Maria, 174
Landowska, Wanda, 336
Latour (French, fourth violin and second oboe in the Royal Chapel of Lisbon), 274
de la Trémoille, Anne-Marie (widow of Prince Orsini, called "Madame des Oursins" or "Ursins"), 38, 282
    and Carlos II, 282
    and Elisabetta Farnese, 283
L'Augier, M., 330-333, 335
Laurenti (Florentine, violoncello in the Royal Chapel of Lisbon), 275
Lauri (or Lauro), Antonio, 100, 105-107, 269
Le Cene, 308
Le Clerc, Charles Nicholas, 307-308
Lede, Marchese of, see de Bette, Giovan Francesco
Legrenzi, Giovanni, 113
    Works: Il Giustino (re-

worked by DS), 117;
    L'Odoacre (reworked by AS), 33-34, 113
Leo, Leonardo, 120
di Leone, Don Giovanni, 22
Leopardi, Venanzio, xxi
Leopold I, Emperor of Austria, 247, 279
Leszczynski, Stanislaus, King of Poland, 154-155
Licari, Antonio, xxvii
Lionnet, Jean, 5, 7 and n
"Liparitan Controversy," 238-240
Lippmann, Friedrich, xiv
Liszt, Franz, 332
Lo Faso e Gaudioso, Francesco, Duke of Serradifalco, 106
Lolli, Antonio, 224-225
Lorenzani, Paolo, 139, 226
Lorraine, Christine of, 47
de Los Velez, Marquis of see Faxardo, Giovanni
Lotti, Antonio, 184, 296
Louis XIV, King of France, 127-130, 135, 138, 226, 284
Louis XV, King of France, 284, 285
Louise-Elisabeth d'Orléans (wife of Luis I of Spain), 284-285
Lo Vecchio, Matteo, 239
Lucchese, Don Antonio, 81-83
    Works: La moglie nemica, 81-83
Ludewig (Bohemian, bassoon in the Royal Chapel of Lisbon), 275
Luis I, King of Spain (first son of Felipe V), 284-285
Lulier, Giovanni Lorenzo, 36, 99, 166
Lulli, Giovan Battista, xxiii, 348
Luther, Martin, 343

Maccavino, Nicolò, 174 and n
Macchia, Prince of, see Gambacorta, Gaetano
Madalena, see Magistri, Maddalena, Maddaloni, Dukes of, see Carafa, Domenico Marzio; Carafa, Emilia
Maffei, Annibale, 240
Maffei, Count 224
Magistri, Maddalena, 2, 3

Maidalchini, Francesco, Cardinal, 4
"Main Scribe" of the Venice and Parma mss. of DS, 329-330, 347-348
Mainwaring, John: 51, 273
    on Handel and DS, 197-198
Malvasia, Carlo Cesare, 28
Mancini, Francesco, 107, 118-119, 205, 209-210
Mancini, Maria, 61
Manfré, see Manfredi, Maria Maddalena
Manfredi, Maria Maddalena, 100, 105, 107
Mann, Thomas, 55
Manna, Antonio, 268
Mannucci, Francesco Maria, false memoriale, xviii, 220
Mantua, Duke of, see Gonzaga, Ferdinando Carlo
Maratta, Carlo, 61
Maratti-Zappi, Faustina, 151, 167
Marcello, Alessandro, 166
Marcello, Benedetto, 166
Marchitelli, Pietro ("Petrillo"), 7, 98
    Works: La Donna sempre s'appiglia al peggio, 95
Marescotti, Galeazzo, cardinal, 149
Marguérite-Louise d'Orléans (wife of Cosimo III de' Medici), 47, 52, 61, 156, 201
Maria Anna Victoria, infanta of Spain, 259, 286
Maria Anna (wife of João V of Portugal), 249, 259
Maria Antonia, infanta of Spain (wife of Vittorio Amedeo III of Savoy), 315
Maria Barbara of Braganza (wife of the Prince of the Asturias, the future Fernando VI of Spain): 279-280, 302-303, 348
    and knighthood of DS, 305
    death and testament, 343-345
    character and abilities, 322
    her keyboard instruments, 335-336;
    and DS, 322-324, 335
    "Barbarian" hypothesis, 252, 297-298;
    and Essercizi, 306

Maria Casimira de la Grange d'Arquien (widow of John Sobieski, King of Poland): 2, 113
    early history and as queen of Poland, 123-131, 145-149;
    palaces and life in Rome, 141-156;
    relations with papacy, 205-206;
    and Arcadia, 159, 165;
    and AS, 150;
    and DS, 217-219, 225;
    last years, and death, 226
Maria Luisa Gonzaga (wife of Ladislao IV of Poland, then of John Casimir of Poland), 124-126, 133
Maria Luisa of Savoy (first wife of Philip V of Spain), 282
Maria Theresa of Habsburg (daughter of Philip IV of Spain, wife of Louis XIV of France), 123
Marini, Giovanni Battista, 161
Marpurg, Friedrich Wilhelm, 264
della Marra, Geronimo, 17-18, 21-22, 31, 33, 40, 111
Martini, Padre Giovanni Battista, 25, 80, 162-163, 289, 322, 327, 330
    Works: Esemplare, o sia Saggio ... di contrappunto, 327; Storia della Musica, 322, 327
Martinitz, Count Giorgio, 156
Marx, Hans Joachim, 201 and n
"Marysienka," see Maria Casimira de la Grange d'Arquien
de Massimi, Checchino, see de Castris, Cecchino
Massonio Astrolusco, Paolo, 58-60
Mattei, Duke of Paganica, 4
Matteo (Corelli's second violin in Naples), see Fornari, Matteo
Matteuccio, see Sassano, Matteo
Mattia (Comare of Anna Maria Scarlatti), 66
di Mauro, Tommaso, 95-96
    Works: La Donna sempre s'appiglia al peggio (libretto by Carlo de Petris), 95-96
Maxarti Ximenes, Anastasia (second wife of DS), 309

Mayone, Paologiovanni, 209-210 and n
Mazarino, Giulio (Jules Mazarin),
    Cardinal, xxi-xxiii
Mazarino, Giulio, Jesuit (great-uncle
    of the cardinal), xxii
Mazzarino, Pietro (nephew of the
    cardinal), xxii
Mazza, Carlo (or Luccio), 140
Mazza, José, 278-279 and n
"la Mazzarini," see Mancini, Maria
Mazzucchelli, 173
de' Medici, Anna Maria Luisa
    (daughter of Cosimo III), 48
de' Medici, Cosimo III, 47-54, 156,
    161, 173, 176
de' Medici, Ferdinando I, 47
de' Medici, Ferdinando, Grand
    Prince of Tuscany: 5, 11, 34, 46-
    56, 69, 168, 195, 196, 228, 338;
    musical abilities, 50;
    and AS, 111, 114, 163-164,
    180-181, 199-201, 202;
    reply to letters of AS, 180-
    181, 199-201;
    letter to Morosini, 181;
    death, 220-221
de' Medici, Francesco Maria,
    Cardinal, 196, 228
de' Medici, Gian Gastone, 48, 51,
    179-180
Medici, Giuseppe, Prince of
    Ottaiano, 16
Medina Coeli, Duke of, see La
    Cerda, Luigi
Meli, Filippo, 243 and n
Mellers, Wilfred, 194
Mello de Castro, D. Andrea, 249
Metastasio, Pietro (pseudonym of
    Pietro Trapassi), 268-269, 294-295,
    312, 330-331, 343-344
    Works: Didone abbandonata,
    344
"Metisto Olbiano," Arcadian name
    of Carlo Sigismondo Capeci, 151
Migazzi, Monsignore (later Cardinal),
    314
Mignard, Pierre, 284
"Mignatti" (or "la Mignatta"), see
    Musi, Maria Maddalena

Milano, Francesco, Prince of Ardore,
    120-121
Mira, Giuseppe, 240
Miraglia, Gioacchino, 256
Modena, Duke of, see Francesco I
    d'Este
Molitor, Simon, 80
Monaco, Prince of, see Grimaldi
Monaldeschi, Giovanni Rinaldo, 135
de Moncajo, Maria Francesca,
    Princess Pignatelli, 254
Mongitore, Antonino, 19, 77, 85-86,
    90, 141, 239-240, 243
Montalto, Lina, 36
Monteleone, Duke of, see Pignatelli
    and Aragon, Nicolò
Monti, Marianna, 254
Montpensier, Mademoiselle Louise-
    Elisabeth, see Louise-Elisabeth
    d'Orléans
de Moratilla, Gabriel, 326
Morellati, Paolo, 335-336
Morelli, Arnaldo, 2, 19, 149
Morelli, Giorgio, 10 and n, 150
Morelli, Giovanni, 156
Morosini, Alvise, 180-182
Mossi (Roman tenor in the Portu-
    guese Royal Chapel), 248-249, 275
Mozart, Wolfgang Amadeus, 32, 33
    Works: Die Zauberflöte, 5
Muscettola, 140
Musi, Maria Maddalena ("la Mignat-
    ta"), 100

Nairne, David, 244
Nannini, Livia ("la Polacchina"), 100
Napoli-Signorelli, Pietro, 261
de Nebra, José, 326
Neri, St. Philip, 160
"Nicolino," see Grimaldi, Nicola
Noris, Matteo, 78
    Works: Penelope la casta, 78

Odescalchi, Benedetto, see Innocent
    XI, pope
Odescalchi, Don Livio, 133-134,
    141-142, 218
Ogliastro, Baron of, see Rincon
    d'Astorga, Emanuello

Orléans, Gaston d', 48
Osorio de Astorga, Baron Emanuel, 260
Osthoff, Wolfgang, xiii and n
Ottaino, Prince of, see Medici, Giuseppe
Ottoboni, Prince Antonio, 42
Ottoboni, Pietro, see Alexander VIII, pope
Ottoboni, Pietro, Cardinal: 42-46, 97, 135-136, 138, 148-150, 152, 154, 176, 178, 205, 227-228, 244
    and Arcadia, 159-160, 166-168
    and AS, 56, 154, 201-205, 208, 27
    and DS, 113, 197
    and Maria Casimira, 206, 217-218
    Works: La Statira, 154
Oursins, Madame des, see de la Trémoille, Anne-Marie

Pacheco de Acuña, Francesco, Duke of Ascalona and Marchese of Villena, 73-74, 96-97, 108, 118, 119-120, 178, 209
Pacheco, Giovan Francesco, Duke of Uzeda, 73-74, 76-78, 81, 97, 155, 169-170, 176, 218
Pacini, Andrea, 268
Paganelli, Giuseppe Antonio, 332
Paganica, Duke of, see Mattei, Duke of Paganica
Pagano, Nicola, 58, 62, 65, 95, 215
Pagano, Tommaso, 40
Paisiello, Giovanni, 32
Paita, Giovanni, 172
Pallavicino, Carlo, 78, 184
Palliano, Prince of, see Colonna, Filippo
Pamphilj, Benedetto, Cardinal, 4, 36, 40, 42-43, 113, 152, 159, 196, 244
Pamphilj Pallavicini, Flaminia, 4
Paolo (Roman, contra-violino of the Royal Chapel of Lisbon), 275
"Paoluccio," see Besci, Paolo Pompeo
"Papa-minga," see Innocent XI, pope
Pariati, Pietro, 214, 228-229

Paris, Nicola, 100
de Pasquale, Giuseppe, 240
    Works: La Pazienza in cimento, 240; Il Totila in Roma, 240; Il Sebeucio,240; La Perfidia punita, 240
Pasquini, Bernardo, 36, 121-122, 163;
    and Arcadia, 165-168
"Pasquino," Roman statue and feigned author of satirical verse, 137
Passerini, Luigi, 52
Pazini, Barbara, 173
Pecorone, abate, see Petrone, Bonifacio
Pellizzari, Antonia (singer active at the Teatro della Pergola in Florence around 1722), 179
Perez, Gio: Gaetano, 242-243
    Works: Le Meraviglie in prospetto, 242
Perez, Maria del Pilar (wife of Alexandro Scarlatti, son of DS), 237, 320-322
Pergolesi, Giovanni Battista, 327
    Works: La Serva Padrona, 327; Stabat Mater, 18, 327, 342
Perretti, Felice, see Sixtus V, pope
Perrucci, Andrea, 19, 74
Perti, Giacomo Antonio, 110, 121, 184
Perugini, Faustina, 151
Peter the Great, Tsar of Russia, 132
"Petrillo" (musician in the service of the Medici), 50-51, 179-180
"Petrillo" (Neapolitan violinist), see Marchitelli, Pietro de Petris, Carlo
Petrone, Bonifacio ("l'Abate Pecorone"), 265-266
Philip V, King of Spain, 36, 92, 282-294
    visit to Naples, 97-98, 157, 174
    death, 312
Piave, Francesco Maria, 10
Piccinni, Nicolò, 32
de Piedz, Anna Maria, 107
de Piedz, Isabella, 100
Pierantonio, Tommaso, 205
Pietro, Giovanni, 274
Pignatelli, Antonio, Cardinal, see Innocent XII, pope

Pignatelli, Marianna, Countess of
    Althann, 222, 256, 268
Pignatelli, Princess, see de Moncajo,
    Maria Francesca
Pignatelli ed Aragone, Niccolò, Duke
    of Monteleone, 253-254, 256
Pincherle, Marc, 99 and n
Piovano, Francesco, 214
Pistocchi, Francesco Antonio, 110
Pitoni, Ottavio, 121, 204, 243
Pla, José (oboist), 197
Pla, Juan Baptist (oboist), 197
Plato, 348
"la Polacchina," see Nannini, Livia
Poensgen, Benedikt, xvii and n
Pollaroli (or Pollarolo), Antonio, 184
Pollaroli (or Pollarolo), Carlo
    Francesco, 184
        Works: Il Costantino Pio,
        219; Irene (reworked by
        DS), 117; Il
Porpora, Niccolò, 32, 52, 264
        Works: Berenice,regina
        d'Egitto (with DS), 236
Porsile, Giuseppe, 177
        Works: Il Ritorno d'Ulisse
        alla Patria, 177
Poussin, Nicholas, 46
Predieri, Luca Antonio, 214
        Works: Astarte, 214
Prinings, see von Bruynings, Hamel
Prota Giurleo, Ulisse, 12, 18-22, 24,
    41, 57, 58, 140, 177, 214, 234, 271
"Protico," see Pasquini, Bernardo
Provenzale, Francesco, 18, 21, 31
Pùlici, Ignazio, 78
Pullaroli, Giovan Battista, see
    Pollaroli, Carlo Francesco,
Puzzi, Giovanna, 254

Quantz, Johann Joachim, xvii, 264-
    265
Quondam, Amedeo, 159

Radziwill, Jacob, see Zamoyski,
    Prince
Raeli, Vito, 201 and n, 204
Raguenet, Abbé François, 97
Ranieri, Antonio, 255

Rapaccioli, Giovanni, 269
Redi, Francesco, 50-51, 53, 54, 160
Retz, see Gondi, Jean François-Paul,
    Cardinal de Retz
Ricci, Pietro, 254
Riccio, Pietro, 103-105
        Works: Il Concilio degli Dei,
        104; L'Oreto festivo, 104
Riccoboni, 290
Riepe, Juliane, xviii, 220 and n
Rinaldo, see da Capua, Rinaldo,
Rincon d'Astorga, Diego, 83
Rincon d'Astorga, Emanuello, Baron
    of Ogliastro: 75, 79-80, 82-83, 157,
    169-191, 231, 349
        performance in La moglie
        nemica, 81-83;
        family, 83-88;
        Roman period and travels,
        169-177;
        flight from Sicily, 175;
        in Vienna, 221-22, 256;
        in Palermo, 223-225, 232,
        238-240, 252, 254-257;
        marriage to Emanuela Guz-
        zardi, 238, 257;
        in Portugal, 257-259;
        in Spain, 259-260;
        cantatas and performance,
        259, 267;
        last years and death, 259-260
        Works: Aci e Galatea, 257;
        Cantatas, 257, 259; Il Dafni,
        173, 176-177; La Moglie
        nemica, 81-83; Il Sacrifizio
        di Diana, 257-258; Serenate,
        258; Stabat Mater, 230
Rincon d'Astorga, Francesco junior,
    82, 87-88
Rincon d'Astorga, Francesco senior,
    baron, 85-88, 169, 174
Rincon d'Astorga, Giovanna,
    baroness (wife of Francesco Rin-
    con d'Astorga senior), 85-87, 223
Rincon d'Astorga, Tommasa
    (daughter of Francesco Rincon
    d'As-torga senior), 85-87, 223
Riviera, Domenico, abate, 165, 167
Robinson, female singer, 300

Roccafiorita, Prince of, see Bonanni
e Marini, Filippo
Rodino, Pietro, xxvii
Roel del Rio, Antonio, 330
Rolli, Paolo, 227
    Works: *Le Tudertine*, 227
de Rosa, Carlantonio, Marchese of
Villarosa, 122 and n
Rosa, Salvator, 63
Roseingrave, Thomas: 199, 243, 301,
307-308
    account of DS playing,193-194
Ross, Scott, xiv
de Rossi, Giuseppe, 205
de Rossi, Mattia, 3, 4
Rossi, Laura, 20
Rousseau, Jean-Jacques, 120
    Works: *Les Confessions,* 185;
Dictionnaire de Musique, 120
Rouvroy de Saint-Simon, Louis, see
Saint-Simon
Ruspoli, Francesco Maria, Marchese
(later prince), 110, 149, 167, 196,
206
Ruspoli, Isabella, Marchesa, 338

Sacchi, Giovenale, 290-293 and n,
295, 314-316, 320, 335-336
Sacripante, Giuseppe, Cardinal, 139
Saint-Simon, Duke of (Louis de
Rouvroy), 37 and n, 43, 123-124,
126, 129-131, 133-134, 138, 153,
168, 283, 284
Salamone, Antonino, 19
    Works: *La Fiordispina,* 19
Salina, Giuseppe, 205
Salvador, Fra Vincenzo, O. P., 64-65
Salvagnini, Margherita, 254
Salvai, female singer, 300
San Giorgio, Baron of, see Guzzardi,
Giuseppe
San Martino, Carlo E., Count, 135
Sanseverino, Aurora (widow of the
Count of Conversano, remarried
with Carlo Gaetano di Laurenzano),
30
Sanseverino, Carlo Maria, Prince of
Branciforte, 30
Santini, Fortunato, 346

de Santis, Anna, 66
Santo Stefano, Count of, see
Benavides, Francesco
Santurini, Francesco, 183
Sarro, Domenico, 102, 113, 254,
266, 268
    Works: *Didone abbandon-
ata,* 268; *Ginevra Princi-
pessa di Scozia* (perhaps
reworked by DS), 269
Sartori, Claudio, 117-118 and n, 214-
215, 258
Sassano, Matteo ("Matteuccio"),
110, 186, 266
"Sassoferrato, il" (Giovanni Battista
Salvi), 63, 64
Scalfi, Giovanna, 254
Scannicciari, Pompeo, see Cannic-
ciari, Pompeo
Scarabelli, Diamante ("la Diaman-
tina"), 190
Scarano, Catherina (or Nina), 54, 57
Scarlata, Andrea (father of Pietro,
grandfather of AS): xxvi-xxvii; and
patria potestas, xxvi
Scarlata (later Scarlatti), Anna Maria
(later Scarlatti, Anna Maria): xxv,
3, 4, 9-11, 57
    illness, death, testament of,
62-67
Scarlata, Anna Maria Antonia Diana,
xxv
Scarlata, Antonio Giuseppe (later
Scarlatti, Giuseppe, brother of
AS), xxv, 3, 4, 63, 66, 117
Scarlata, Francesco Antonio Nicola
(later Scarlatti, Francesco, brother
of AS): xxv, 22, 23, 66, 215;
    career, later years, 73-77,
80, 83, 157, 243, 300
    Works: *Dixit,* 74; *Messa,*
74; *Lo Petracchio screm-
metore,* 215; *La Profetessa
guerriera,* 74
Scarlata, Melchiorra Brigida (later
Scarlatti Pagano, Melchiorra), xxv,
3, 19, 23, 57-58, 62, 66, 67
Scarlata, Pietro (father of AS): xxiv-
xxvii, 1, 348-349

Scarlata, Pietro Alessandro Gaspare (later Scarlatti, Alessandro: referred to as AS): birth, xxv
early life, and marriage, 2-10;
and Christina of Sweden, 111;
establishment in Naples, 34;
employment: Rome, service at S.Girolamo della Carità, 3;
S.Giacomo degli Incurabili,20;
S. M. in Vallicella, 149-150;
S. Maria Maggiore (Basilica Liberiana), 118, 178, 199, 202-205;
Naples, 40, 74;
court of Tuscany, 108-111;
Venice, 186-188;
knighthood, 304-305;
children, 3-4;
emancipation of DS, 233-236;
and Anna Maria S, 60-63, 66-68;
as teacher, 41;
in Arcadia, 158-161, 165-168;
playing, 264;
portraits by Vaccaro and Solimena, 24-28;
letter to Ferdinando de' Medici, 69, 199-201
letter presenting DS to Ferdinando de' Medici, 89, 163-164;
petition to viceroy of Naples, 270;
possible visit to Munich and Vienna, 70;
service in the Royal Chapel of Naples, 14-23;
reinstatement, 208-210;
and opera buffa, 214-215, 260-262;
workshop activities, 94-96;
last years, death, and epitaph, 260-272
Works: *L'Abramo* (*Agar et Ismaele esiliati*), 72;
L'Aldimiro, 20;
"Ammore brutto figlio di pottana" (cantata), 215-216;
Gl'Amori fortunati negl'

Equivoci (Venetian title of *Gli Equivoci nel sembiante*), 187; *L'Ariovisto o vero L'Amor fra l'Armi*, 107; *L'Arminio*, 69; *Bassiano o vero il Maggiore impossibile*, 101; *La Caduta dei Decemviri*, 91; cantatas, 227; *Clori, Dorina, e Amore*, 100; *Concerti*, 262-263; *Didone abbandonata* (doubtful), 344; *Gli Equivoci nel sembiante*, 4, 13, 71-72; *L'Erminia*, 268; *Il Figlio delle Selve*, 208, 219; *Giunio Bruto o vero La Caduta dei Tarquini* (in collaboration with C. F. Cesarini and A. Caldara), 70, 220; *L'Honestà negli amori*, 7; *Gli Inganni felici*, 91-92, 215; *Il Lisimaco*, 20; *Madrigale a tavolino*, 111; *Messa dedicata a S. Cecilia*, 263; *Il Mitridate Eupatore*,186-190;motet for Florence, 110; *L'Odoacre* (reworking of an original by Legrenzi), 33-34, 113; *L'Onestà negli amori*, 31-32; *Il Pastor di Corinto*, 101; *Penelope la casta*, 78; *Il Pompeo*, 20, 38, 73; *Il Prigioniero fortunato*, 101; *Il Primo Omicidio*, 188; *La Principessa fedele*, 97; *La Psiche*, 20; *La Rosmene*, 40; *Scipione nelle Spagne*, 253; *Serenata*. 300; 12 Sinfonie di Concerto Grosso, 262-263; 7 Sonate for flute and strings, 262; *Stabat mater*, 230; *Statira*, 154; *Il Telemaco*, 236; *La Teodora Augusta*, 79; *Il Teodosio*, 210 211; *Tiberio, Imperatore d'Oriente*, 97, 100; *Il Tigrane*, 262; *Tito Sempronio Gracco*, 101; *Toccate* for harpsichord or organ, 262-263; *Il Trionfo della Libertà,* 186-188; *Il Trionfo dell' Onore,* 261-262; *Il Trionfo delle Stagioni,* 91; *La Vittoria della Fede,* 207, 217

Scarlata (later Scarlatti), Tommaso, xxv, 3, 4, 63, 117-118, 215-216

Scarlata, Vincenzo Placido, xxv

"la Scarlati," 22, 57

Scarlatti, Alessandro (son of Pietro Scarlatti), 252

Scarlatti, Alexandro (son of DS), 237-238, 320-322

Scarlatti, Anna (daughter of Pietro Scarlatti), 252

Scarlatti, Antonia (wife of AS), see Anzalone, Antonia Maria Vittoria

Scarlatti, Antonio (son of Francesco), 74

Scarlatti, Benedetto, 3

Scarlatti, Carlo Francesco Giacomo (son of AS), 30

Scarlatti, Carlos, 237

Scarlatti, Cosimo (servant in the Bernini household), 2

Scarlatti, Cristina (daughter of AS), 66, 67

Scarlatti, Domenico (son of Pietro Scarlatti), 252

Scarlatti, Dorotea (daughter of Francesco), 74

Scarlatti, Eleonora (daughter of Francesco), 74, 76

Scarlatti, Ferdinando (son of DS), 304

Scarlatti, Flaminia (daughter of AS), 67, 267, 270

Scarlatti, Giovanni (son of Francesco), 74

Scarlatti, Giovanni Francesco Diodato (son of AS), 30

Scarlatti, (Giuseppe Nicola Roberto) Domenico (referred to as DS): birth and baptism, 29-30; sojourns, Naples, 63, 96, loses post as organist, 118; musical training, 80, with Gasparini, 161-163, 179-191; early operas, 117;

Florence, Pratolino, 108-111; Venice, 179-199; contest with Handel, 197; Rome, 197, 217-221, 226, 230; and Maria Casimira, 217-219: emancipation of, 233-236; reputed visit to England, 243-245, 252; possible presence in Palermo, xix-xx, 245-246, 251, 255; Portuguese embassy, 300-301; Portugal, xvii, xix, 246-251, 300-302; Spain, 273-349; character, 197-198; 96; visit to Paris, 300; mentioned as "abate," 301; knighthood, 304-305, 308; marriages, 302, 309; children, 252; portraits of, 333; reputed gambling, 244, 301, 318-319; possible corpulency, 331, 333; keyboard and compositional technique, 193-194, 332-333, 341; the fortepiano, 115-116, 338-342; letter to Duke of Huescar, 317-318; testament, 343; son Alexandro, 237-238, 320-322; death, 346

Works: *Ambleto,* 228-229; *Amor d'un'Ombra e Gelosia d'un Aura,* see *Narciso;* *Applauso genetliaco (= Triufos de Ulysses & Glorias de Portugal),* 248, 277; *Berenice, regina d'Egitto* (with Porpora), 236; *Care pupille belle* (cantata), 108; *Il Concilio degli Dei,* 102n, 103-104; *La Conversione di Clodoveo re di Francia,* 219; *Didone abbandonata* (probably a reworking of the first version by Sarro); *La*

Dirindina, 229, 277; *Dixit Dominus* (psalm), 328; *Dopo lungo servire* (cantata), 108, 110; *Essercizi,* 279-282, 305-309; *Festeggio armonico,* 286; *Ifigenia in Aulide,* 219; *Ifigenia in Tauride,* 219; *Lauda Jerusalem* (psalm), 328; *Il Maestro di Musica,* see *La Dirindina*; *Missa Quatuor Vocum,* 342; *Narciso* (reworking of *Amor d'un Ombra,* attributed by Burney to Roseingrave), 243; *Ninfe belle e voi pastori,* 108; *L'Ottavia ristituita al Trono,* 117; *Salve Regina,* 342; Sonatas for harpsichord: sources and copying: 309-311, 323-324, 346-348 (Venice and Parma mss.); pairwise arrangement, 310-311 K. 30, 281; K. 45, ; K. 119, 326; K. 120, 326; K. 140, 326; K. 141, 326; K. 145, 297; K. 146, 297; K. 148, 281; K. 149, 281; K. 150, 281; K. 155, 281; K. 158, 281; K. 426, 281; K. 427, ; K. 430, 281

Stabat Mater for 10 voices, 230; *Te Deum,* 275; *Tolomeo et Alessandro o vero La Corona disprezzata,* 225; *Tocata 10,* 280-281; *Libro di Tocate per cembalo,* 281
Scarlatti, Domenico, and Nicola Porpora,
Works: *Berenice regina d'Egitto,* 236
Scarlatti, Giuseppe, see Scarlata, Antonio Giuseppe
Scarlatti, Jane, 76
Scarlatti, Juan Antonio (son of DS), 304
Scarlatti (Scarlata), [E]Leonora (mother of AS), xxiv-xxv, 3, 4
Scarlatti, Pietro (eldest son of AS), 3, 118, 199, 245

Scarlatti, Pompeo, abate, 1 2, 139, 150, 237
Scarlatti, Raimondo (son of AS), 233, 235
Scarlatti, Rosalina, see Albano, Rosalina
Scherillo, Michele, 169 and n, 214
Schor, Cristoforo, 59-60, 64
Schor, Filippo, 24
Sciarp, Cavalier, 228
Scola, Adamo, 306-308
de Seixas, Giovanni, see Seyxas da Fonseca, João de, Bishop
de Seixas, José Antonio Carlos: 274-276, 278;
    Knight of Santiago, 305;
    sonatas, 278-279
Senato, Angela, 66
Senesino, castrato, 300
Serino, Nicola, 116, 213, 216
Serpotta Giacomo, 72, 242-243
Serradifalco, Duke of, see Lo Faso e Gaudioso, Francesco
Seyxas da Fonseca, João de, Bishop, 276-277
Sforza Cesarini, Duke Federico (father of Gaetano), 135-136
Sforza Cesarini, Gaetano, 135-136
Shakespeare, William, 106, 297
Sheveloff, Joel Leonard, xiv and n, 308, 310, 324, 347
"Siface," see Grossi, Francesco
Sigismund Augustus of Saxony, see Augustus II, King of Poland
Silbermann, Gottfried, 115
de Silva y Alvarez de Toledo, Fernando, Duke of Huescar and later Duke of Alba, 317-319
Silvani, Francesco, 81
Sitillo, Giancola, 157
Sitwell, Sacheverell, 275 and n
Sixtus V, pope, 142
Smith, William C., 306-307
Sobieski, Alexander, 138, 142, 138-139, 142, 152, 206, 226
Sobieski, Clementina, 245n
Sobieski, Constantine, 135-140, 138-139, 146, 152, 155
Sobieski, James, 131-132, 152, 155

Sobieski, John see John III Sobieski, King of Poland
Soler, Antonio, 326-330, 347-348
    Works: *Llave de la Modulación,* 326-327, 328, 329, 330
Solimena, Francesco, 25, 267
Somis Ardì, Lorenzo, 224
Sonneck, Oscar, 210
Sorge, Giuseppe, 102, 269-270
Spinelli, Giulia, Princess Tarsia, 30
Sportonio, Marcantonio, xxiii-xxiv, 1, 33, 349
    Works: *L'Elena,* xxiv; *La Fiordispina,* 19
Stampiglia, Silvio, 160
Stevenson, Robert, 276 and n
Stradivarius (probably Antonio), 345
Strohm, Reinhard, 51, 156 and n, 196, 210
Stuart, James ("Chevalier St. Georges," The Old Pretender), 244-245

Tagliacozzo, Duke of, see Colonna, Filippo
Tagliavini, Luigi Ferdinando, 162n
Tarquini, Vittoria ("la Bambagia"), 55, 90
Tarsia, Princess, see Spinelli, Giulia
Tassis (Tassi, Taxis), Michele, Prince and Postmaster of Spain in Rome and Milan, 143, 148
Teblonewschki, see Jablonowski
Tedesco, Anna, 73 and n
"Terpandro," see Scarlatti, Alessandro
Thiepoli, Pasqualino, 166
Tiby, Ottavio, 74 and n, 83 and n, 87, 88, 169, 173, 223, 232, 238, 257
Tiepolo, Giovanni Battista, 299
"Tirsi," see Zappi, Felice
"Tolla," see Bocca di Leone, Vittoria Tommaso (Florentine, third violin in the Royal Chapel of Lisbon), 274
Tornelle (Tournelles), Mademoiselle de, 144
della Torre, Francesco, 24
Trivisano (Trevisan), Bernardo, 172
Tullio, Francesco Antonio (Colantonio Feralentisco), 261

Works: *Le Fenziune abbentorate,* 261; *Gemini amore,* 261; *Il Trionfo dell'Onore,* 261
"Turcotta," see Turcotti, Giustina
Turcotti, Giustina, 105
"Twinkle Toes" (George Malcolm), 341

Ugolinucci, Massimo, 153
L'Ulisse in Faecia, 72
Union of Musicians (Santa Cecilia, Palermo), 76-78, 82, 242-243, 246, 255
d'Urfé, Honoré, 125
Ursins, Mme. des, see La Trémoille, Anne-Marie
Uzeda, Duke of, see Pacheco, Giovan Francesco
Uzeda, Duchess of, see Giron Pacheco, Isabella

Vaccaro, Andrea, 24-25
Vaccaro, Nicola, 24-28, 33
Valenti, Antonio, xxv, xxvii
Valesio, Francesco, 1, 134, 135-136, 139, 141-144, 145-149, 152-156, 196, 206, 211, 228, 237
Vangelisti, Vincenzo, 176
Vannucci, Fra Lavinio, 163
Varischino, Giovanni, 113
Vaz, Francisco (father of J. A. C. de Seixas), 276
Veith (Bohemian, fourth violin and first oboe in the Royal Chapel in Lisbon), 274
de Velasco, Domingo Antonio, 333
Velez, Antonio, 83
Velez, Marqués de los, 13, 17
Veneziano, Gaetano, 96, 113, 118
Venosa, Prince of, see Gesualdo, Carlo
Ventur (Catalan, viola in the Royal Chapel of Lisbon), 274
Veraguas, Duke of, see Colon, Pietro
Verdi, Giuseppe, 263
    Works: Quartet in E minor, 273; *Rigoletto,* 10
Viale Ferrero, Mercedes, 218

Victor Amadeus II of Savoy, King of Sicily, 221, 224, 240-241
Vieth (Bohemian, fourth violin and first oboe in the Portuguese Royal Chapel), 274
Vigliena, Marchese, viceroy, 97
Villabianca, Marchese of, see Emanuele e Vanni, Francesco Maria
Villafranca, Prince of, see Alliata e Colonna, Giuseppe
Villafranca, Princess of, see Alliata e Bonanno, Giovanna
de Villa Real y Gamboa, Sebastian, 47
Villarosa, Marchese of, see de Rosa, Carlantonio
Villena, Marchese, see Pacheco de Acuña, Francesco
Violante of Bavaria Neuberg (wife of Ferdinando de' Medici), 269
Vitali, Carlo, xviii, 220 and n
Vivaldi, Antonio, 52, 183
Voglia, Angela ("la Giorgina"), 10-11, 38, 54-55, 61, 90, 94
Volkmann, Hans, 176, 222
Volpe, Pietro Angelo (Neapolitan notary), 59
Voltaire (François-Marie Arouet), 127-128 and n
    Works: *Candide,* 152

Waliszewski, Kazimierz, 124-127, 134, 152
Walker, Frank, xvii, xxv, 57 and n, 76, 169 and n, 173, 300

Walther, Johann Gottfried, 274 275 and n, 298
Watteau, Antoine, 194
Wilde, Oscar, 24-28
Wisniowieski, Michael, King of Poland, 128
Worgan, Dr. John, 326

Ximenes, Anastasia Maxarti (second wife of DS), see Maxarti Ximenes, Anastasia

Zanoli, Gaudenz, 222
Zambeccari, Francesco Maria, 211-216, 318-321
Zamoyski, Prince (first husband of Maria Casimira de la Grange d'Arquien), 124, 125
Zanetti, Emilia, 196
Zappi, Felice, 160, 167
Zeno, Apostolo, 169, 171-172
Zeno, Apostolo, and Pietro Pariati
    Works: *Ambleto,* 228-229, *Astarte,* 214
Ziani, Marc'Antonio, 81
    Works: *La moglie nemica,* 81
Ziani, Pietro Andrea, 18, 20-21
Zimbelli, Agostino, 170
Zipoli, Domenico, 161
Zoccarelli, Camilla, 3
Zuccari, family, 142-143
Zuccari, Giacomo, 142-143
Zuffi, Giulietta, 15, 20, 23, 25, 33, 54, 57, 74
Zurbarán, Francisco, 284